"MOMMY! MOMMY! THERE'S BLOOD ALL OVER YOU!"

Yelling for help, Carol Christ felt her way out of the bedroom on her hands and knees. Her once beautiful face was badly disfigured and her left eye dangled from its socket. No longer able to see, she relied on memory to crawl toward the kitchen phone. She needed to get help or she would die.

"Mommy! Mommy! There's blood all over you!" Dani screamed and ran to her.

"Call 9-1-1! Call 9-1-1!"

"I can't, I can't!" the six-year-old sobbed. She held her mother's arm and led her to the phone.

Terrified that her husband might hurt her again, Carol somehow placed the call. "I need an ambulance," she told the 9-1-1 dispatcher. "I've been shot in the head."

UNDER THE KNIFE

Karen Roebuck

PINNACLE BOOKS
Kensington Publishing Corp.
http://www.kensingtonbooks.com

Some names have been changed to protect the privacy of individuals connected to this story.

PINNACLE BOOKS are published by

Kensington Publishing Corp.
850 Third Avenue
New York, NY 10022

All Kensington Titles, Imprints, and Distributed Lines are available at special quantity discounts for bulk purchases for sales promotions, premiums, fund-raising, and educational or institutional use. Special book excerpts or customized printings can also be created to fit specific needs. For details, write or phone the office of the Kensington special sales manager: Kensington Publishing Corp., 850 Third Avenue, New York, NY 10022, attn: Special Sales Department, Phone: 1-800-221-2647.

Pinnacle and the P logo Reg. U.S. Pat. & TM Off.

First Printing: February 2002
10 9 8 7 6 5 4 3 2 1

Printed in the United States of America

To Carol O'Keiff—
Eternal optimist

FOREWORD

Houston plastic surgeon John Christ (pronounced Krist) surgically remade his wife, then played with her mind and emotions. When she tried to leave him, he shot her in the head. Carol O'Keiff Christ didn't die right away, so he executed psychological warfare to try to finish her off, often using the legal system and other people, even his children, as his weapons.

The ordeal of Carol O'Keiff, a surprisingly strong survivor, is an example of the difficult journey many domestic-violence victims must make—one that doesn't end with a guilty verdict or fading headlines. It means coping with new wounds, both emotional and physical, and reopening long-hidden psychological scars.

O'Keiff wanted to share her story, even the humiliating parts, in the hopes that it would help others. Secrets she once sought to bury in shame, she openly revealed. Bravely, she detailed her story and the accompanying painful emotions, and encouraged her family, friends, children, doctors and even her psychiatrist to discuss her case and her problems freely and candidly. She granted permission for the author to review and use her confidential medical, psychiatric and legal records and offered her journals and other personal papers. She allowed scrutiny of her life and personality that few people, even those with the most blemish-free pasts, would find comfortable, let alone encourage. She is not proud of everything she's done. She is justifiably proud of all she has survived and overcome. Being shot by her husband cost O'Keiff much—physically, psychologically, emotionally—but she still has a surprising sense of humor, even when at times discussing traumas and injuries. Despite all the deplorable and egregious abuse John Christ had perpetrated on her, O'Keiff still can talk about the good she saw in him. She does not view him in black-and-white terms, as he seems to do with her and most everyone in his life.

John Christ also agreed to be interviewed for the book and his cooperation and comments were much appreciated, albeit limited, both by his choice and time. He was locked behind prison walls at the time of the face-to-face interviews; while Texas prison officials were generously accommodating, my time with him was limited. From the beginning, he made it clear that he thought Carol O'Keiff, his victim and former wife, was not important to his tale, merely the vehicle by which his life had been impacted. He refused to answer some questions and blamed other people for nearly every problem he had faced in life, portraying himself as Carol O'Keiff's victim.

While interviewing others for the book, I was struck by how many people John Christ had crossed paths with over the years who seemed to be everything from worried to genuinely frightened about what he might do to them once he is released from prison. These included a number of highly educated male doctors—none of whom seemed prone to overreaction. Some of these physicians had nothing to do with the case other than to treat his victim, and others hadn't even done that much. Christ has a widespread reputation as an exceptionally vindictive person, personally and professionally, who does not let go of a grudge or a perceived wrong.

Many of those who have angered him, however innocently or seemingly trivially, cannot let go of the fear of retaliation. Carol O'Keiff is one of them. She cannot escape the ongoing impact her former husband has inflicted upon her and her children's lives. Both a victim and a survivor—long before she met John Christ and long after because of him—neither word adequately describes her.

One

In August 1988, Carol O'Keiff returned to Houston, where she had grown up, determined to learn from her past mistakes, of which there were many, especially where men were concerned. On the rebound from another bad, unfulfilling relationship, her focus as she rejoined the nursing staff of the prestigious Methodist Hospital was on her career and her two children, nine-year-old Joe and daughter Dani, just three. These were her three true loves and the roles in which she felt most confident. An unquenchable flirt, she craved the attention of men and absolutely loved sex, for the physical release as well as the emotional connection. But unlike many women, O'Keiff easily could separate emotions from the physical act, compartmentalizing in a way more typical of men, and just relish sex. That hadn't always been the case for her; at one time, she had equated the two. So as she moved to Houston, it was an especially big deal for her to take a personal vow of celibacy and to swear off men.

She spent a lot of time at work and with her children, but eventually she longed for male companionship. An attractive, petite woman, about five feet three inches with shoulder-length light red hair, she was asked out regularly but accepted only occasionally, still resolving not to get wrapped up in a relationship. With only slight difficulty, she kept to her celibacy vow, which admittedly was made easier because she didn't go out with anyone to whom she felt any strong attraction. The dates she did accept were fine; the men were nice enough, but they did nothing to sway her intentions of remaining unattached. Secretly, she harbored crushes on a couple of surgeons she met at the hospital. They allowed her to keep her flirting skills honed, but she didn't expect anything to develop with either of them. She felt she couldn't measure up to the beautiful women the gorgeous neurosurgeon frequently escorted around town. And after being led to believe otherwise so many times, she had given up on ever finding a nice, decent man for herself.

In 1989, O'Keiff bought a small three-bedroom house in the Townwest section of Sugar Land, a growing suburb eighteen miles southwest of the Texas Medical Center. Bordering the Museum District and Rice University's tree-lined campus, the Medical Center was a city in itself, boasting forty-two nonprofit hospitals, medical schools and institutions. It was the world's largest health complex; it served more than 4.5 million patients a year, hosted more than 100,000 visitors each day and employed some 50,000 people. The one hundred-plus Medical Center buildings covered more than 675 acres south of Houston's colossal downtown and just north of the famed Astrodome. Methodist Hospital was among the largest and most elite institutions there.

After less than a year as a nurse educator, training colleagues on problems and skills specific to orthopedics patients, O'Keiff was transferred to the Plastics and Orthopedics Unit, where she was promoted to assistant head nurse, a highly demanding, pressure-filled position. She ran the day-to-day operation of the unit while head nurse Marcella Louis, her boss, tended to administrative duties. Part of O'Keiff's duties at the hospital known for pampering its patients included making rounds with the doctors and visiting every patient on the unit every day, making sure their needs were being met, listening to any complaints and generally seeing that they, their families and doctors were satisfied. O'Keiff was thrilled, and excelled at the job, winning the respect of her staff and the doctors with whom she worked. Although she was intelligent, pretty and outgoing, O'Keiff harbored a lot of personal insecurities, many inflicted by a difficult past. None of those, however, surfaced in her job. It was the part of her life where she felt most confident, secure and happy, despite the many responsibilities she had to juggle simultaneously and the demands—some of them less than polite—placed on her by doctors, patients and coworkers. She was happy and was achieving her goal of advancing into increasingly responsible positions. Methodist, a large, private, well-endowed hospital, offered plenty of advancement opportunities if she proved herself. Although she loved her previous job as a nursing supervisor at the Campbell Soup factory in Farmington, Arkansas, she saw no room for advancement there; that was the main reason why she had left that job and the region where her mother and stepfather now lived.

O'Keiff's colleagues and staff knew she had been married a few times—different people had different ideas of what the true tally was. No one suspected it was as high as it actually was. Many were aware she had had her colorful and adventurous past. She wasn't shy about talking about some of her exploits, like the time she spent with a traveling carnival. With a frequent, hardy laugh, she was personable, interesting and fun to be around.

On Dunn 8 West—another name for the Plastics and Orthopedics Unit, reflecting the building and floor it was on—O'Keiff met numerous surgeons, some of them attractive and a few of them available. Dr. John Christ was a plastic surgeon, but he wasn't particularly attractive nor was he exactly available. Still, he quickly expressed an interest in the new assistant head nurse when they met shortly after Christmas 1989. She had made rounds with him once, but he hadn't made much of an impression on her, positively or negatively. The next time he was on her unit, visiting his attorney, who had been in a car wreck, he stopped by the nurses' desk for a cup of coffee and spent a long time talking with her, quickly taking the conversation off business and into more personal matters. Christ confided that he was in the midst of a painful, protracted divorce. Nevertheless, he was flirtatious, commenting on O'Keiff's large blue eyes, which he told her were beautiful and suggestive. He said that he wanted her phone number in a way that was more like mentioning it in passing than out-and-out asking, so she let it slide, never answering. When he left nearly an hour later, O'Keiff was intrigued and somewhat attracted to the short, bespectacled doctor. Standing just five feet five inches, without the heeled Italian boots he generally wore, the surgeon was completely bald on top, his dark hair still somewhat thick around his head. He was a fairly good dresser, except for his trademark—rather large, brightly colored neckties with unusual, sometimes weird designs that his mother in Florida made for him. Many colleagues thought they were odd or even tasteless, but he wore them proudly. A dedicated marathoner, Christ had the sleek, fit physique of a runner and O'Keiff thought he exuded an electric sexuality. Later that week, he called her at work and asked again for her home number. This time, she gave it to him. Still determined to remain single, she thought he might be fun to go out with casually a couple of times.

He called a few days later and they made plans to meet at a local movie theater. He asked her to pick the movie. She chose *Driving Miss Daisy*, for its lack of sexual scenes. They arrived early and talked easily and openly; he held her hand during most of the movie. Afterward they got in his car, a 1987 Toyota Supra, and talked some more. Soon they were locked in a passionate embrace, necking like teenagers. It went far better than O'Keiff anticipated, and she fell hard for the diminutive doctor on their first date.

On their second date, she confronted him about the rumors that he had slugged his wife, breaking her nose and landing her in the hospital for days. In fact, Gay Christ, an operating-room nurse at Methodist, had spent a week recovering on Dunn 8 West, although that was before O'Keiff worked there. Christ cried as he told her a pained tale of how his wife had ruined his reputation with her spiteful vengefulness. Already separated, they had been arguing last summer when she swung at him. He grabbed her arm to protect himself and when she pulled away, she fell, slamming her face into the footrest of their son's high chair. So embittered and angry over the fact that he was divorcing her, she called 911 and told them that he had struck her, a story she repeated around the hospital, he said, crying harder. He had faced the humiliation of being arrested and hauled off to jail, booked and fingerprinted like a common criminal, when he only had tried to protect himself, he told her. Ultimately, he was sure he would prevail in court, he said, but he was sure his reputation had been scarred more than she was. Essentially, this was the same story Christ had told others about the altercation, but few—especially those who had seen Gay afterward, bruised in more places than just her nose—believed him. However, Christ, who failed to tell his new girlfriend he had pleaded no contest to assault months earlier, was so convincing that O'Keiff, who herself had been slapped around by more than one guy, did not think it possible that this sensitive man could have hit his wife. She knew firsthand how bitter divorces could turn. And with her own checkered past, she knew that some of her exes might say plenty of nasty things about her as well, regardless of their veracity. She was sure she would recognize the signs of abuse and told herself that she would get out if Christ proved himself undeserving of the benefit of the doubt.

That night, in his bed, they made love for the first time. She was captivated by his unexpected sexual prowess: "He was kind of a ladies' man disguised in a little Napoleon body." Their relationship progressed quickly, and they saw each other often. In the beginning, he was a gentle lover, spending a long time on foreplay and showing a lot of passion, sometimes turning rowdy but never rough. He cared about how she felt, if she was satisfied and what she wanted. He was adventurous and playful. Sex was a major part of their relationship and of their attraction for each other; they eagerly made time for it every day. Soon he had her convinced that he was the best lover she had ever had.

Christ, who always slept in the nude, made her feel sexy and loved. If she went to bed wearing a nightgown, he'd gently stroke the silky fabric or reach under and entice her to take it off, saying, "You don't need to wear this. I want to feel your skin." His flirtatious flattery won him his way.

But it wasn't just sex that bound the two together. In and out of the bedroom, they had a lot of fun. She was drawn to his personality, intellect, charm, seeming sensitivity and kooky nature, which he wasn't afraid to show her. While cooking dinner, they would initiate low-key water fights, playfully splashing each other with water, and he would pretend to operate on a fish they were serving. "Oops, cut his head off," the surgeon would say, laughing.

Both considered themselves intellectuals, and they enjoyed deep conversations, discussing philosophy, the afterlife, their childhoods and medicine, sometimes staying awake and talking until 4:00 A.M. Each was as good a listener as a conversationalist. He was a bit arrogant at times, but no more so than most doctors she knew. And arrogance in a surgeon isn't necessarily a bad thing. Who would want someone lacking self-confidence operating on them? O'Keiff was on Methodist's Standards Committee, helping establish detailed policies and procedures for how to care for certain types of patients, such as those in the cardiovascular unit. As part of this, she wrote articles for the hospital's newspaper as well as for procedural handbooks. Her new boyfriend, who took due pride in articles he had published in respected medical journals, took an interest in her work as well and they often worked on their papers in bed together, bouncing ideas off one another. They both took a lot of satisfaction from their intellectual exchanges. It was something that had been lacking in O'Keiff's past significant relationships.

Although he frequently made it a point of reminding her that he was intellectually superior to her, O'Keiff found this man to be nonjudgmental about the parts of her past that she shared with him. Embarrassed about the number of divorces, she told her new boyfriend that she had been married just twice, to the fathers of her children. She had led an exciting life and entertained him with detailed stories from her past, telling him about some of the significant men in her life, purposefully neglecting to tell him she had strolled down the aisle five times. As promiscuous as O'Keiff had been in her youth, Christ had been on the other extreme. But instead of judging each other or being turned off by their experiences—or lack of—they were in awe of each other.

Especially important to her was the fact that he was nice to her children and welcomed them into his home. Not just polite, he actually talked with them and did things with them. Joe and Dani liked him, too, and he obviously enjoyed fatherhood, boasting about his three children and doting on them when they were around, especially his daughter, Stephanie, six. That set well with O'Keiff as her daughter had never even met her biker father, who had abandoned them just weeks before she was born. Dani so longed to have a dad, she quickly attached herself to any man who entered their lives, even if he had shown up to take out O'Keiff for the first time. "I like this one," Dani had announced more than once, sometimes clinging to a man she had just met. And she plainly envied her older brother's weekend outings and close relationship with his father. So while O'Keiff hadn't been looking for a husband, she began missing having one, even if she wasn't quite ready to admit that to herself. Regardless, she wanted to be sure that any man, with whom she was going to be spending time, was kind, thoughtful and understanding with her children, especially with Dani. She was pleased that Christ wanted to fill that role and was easygoing with her daughter, a vivacious and cute pixie with short brown hair and an active imagination.

O'Keiff and her children spent a lot of time at Christ's apartment, especially when his kids were with him for the weekend. It didn't take her long to peg her boyfriend as an obsessive-compulsive. Everything in his apartment had to be put in its exact spot; the clothes in his drawers had to be folded a particular way and placed in a certain order. He took as many as four showers a day, even in his office in the middle of the day.

When he talked of his sometimes lonely childhood,

she again saw how sensitive he was. His mother and father were devoted, loving parents—and her boyfriend clearly loved them—but they were controlling, he told her. Christ was especially proud of his Greek heritage. He talked about his father, who ran a fishing-party boat in Miami, in what O'Keiff thought was a love-hate kind of way, talking about the stupid things he thought his father had done, like staying out on the ocean during storms and dressing only in brown. The elder Christ insisted that his sons learn to box, even though John had not wanted to. When his father tried to push him into it, John said he had run away crying. He believed that his father favored his brother, Bill, whom John seemed jealous of for a variety of reasons. He viewed his younger brother as more popular, better-looking and taller. Bill easily won over the girls in high school—a feat John couldn't accomplish, even though he thought that his muscle car should have caught him a few. Christ confided to O'Keiff that he had been so lonely at times during his teens that he often passed days sitting on a rock, looking at the Atlantic Ocean and contemplating suicide. He said he had never tried to kill himself but thought it was understandable that some people chose that route. They sometimes debated that topic. O'Keiff had a couple of firsthand experiences with it and thought it was a coward's way out. No matter how bad things might get, they always got better eventually, she firmly believed. That was another lesson life had taught her.

The couple often engaged in their discussions and debates at Marfreless, a cozy bistro near fashionable River Oaks, where they sat on overstuffed couches and chairs, listening to classical music, sipping wine, cuddling and getting to know one another in the dimly lit, intimate setting. It was a hard-to-find, intimate hangout off an alley and had no sign out front. O'Keiff had been introduced to the club during her freshman year of college by a professor she had been dating. The relationship with the anatomy and physiology professor—initiated during private tutoring sessions—had been short-lived, but the connection with the bistro continued through the years. Christ immediately fell in love with the place and it became one of their favorite haunts.

They dined out often; he treated her to nice places, frequenting The Doctor's Club, a private restaurant in the Medical Center that catered to the crowd for which it was named. Usually, they went out just the two of them. In social situations, O'Keiff found that it was usually she and not her boyfriend who carried the conversation. With her, he was charming, open and funny, but he seemed socially inept around others.

Occasionally, they ran into the attractive neurosurgeon she had once admired, usually with a different beautiful woman each time, prompting Christ's jealous nature to emerge. "Don't look now," Christ would tell her, "but your boyfriend's here." O'Keiff would stop by his table sometimes to say hello, but it was clear he didn't like Christ. "He thinks he's such a ladies' man," Christ said, "but he's really a piece of shit." O'Keiff ignored the insults, believing they stemmed from jealousy, but she was annoyed by the fact that he frequently called someone "a piece of shit."

O'Keiff and Christ didn't try to keep their romance a secret at work. The budding relationship was met with encouragement by some of the nurse's female coworkers while others, most of them doctors she respected, strongly urged her to back away. "Don't you know what he did?" they asked her, referring to Gay.

"Yeah, I know that they had a fight and she broke her nose, but how do you know she's not lying and broke her nose by falling?" she responded, repeating her lover's story. In dismay, they usually shook their heads and dropped the subject. The diminutive and abrasive plastic surgeon apparently possessed something they didn't see. He seemed to have no problems seducing attractive, intelligent women as evidenced by his nickname, "The Stairwell Stud."

That wasn't always the case. Eventually, he confided to O'Keiff that he had remained a virgin until after entering medical school. O'Keiff wasn't put off by his confessions, taking it as a sign of his profound loneliness. His relationship with Bill seemed strong now—he told her it had improved after both went to college—but O'Keiff occasionally detected some lingering spitefulness when he spoke of him. He spoke protectively of his younger sister, Marika Thiessen, but bad-mouthed her husband, Aaron. In conversations with O'Keiff, he worried that his brother-in-law would hurt his sister, although he could never explain why. She never saw or heard Christ say anything specific that, to her, even suggested Aaron had ever hurt her. "Nobody's going to hurt my sister. I don't care how big he is," Christ would tell O'Keiff. Thiessen had lived in Houston for a while, working at the Johnson Space Center, but by the time O'Keiff met her, she was living in Florida again. The couple visited Christ when he still lived in an apartment and O'Keiff thoroughly enjoyed getting to know both.

The story Christ told O'Keiff about his first wife, and the one she believed for years, was that he thought Ruth may have cheated on him with another resident while they were married, so he was not sure if the son, Phillip, she bore was really his. Ruth had never asked for child support and would not let him see the child. If Phillip were really his, this behavior was only hurting the son, Christ told her—although that wasn't quite the truth. He never told her that he had signed away his parental rights to that child eight years earlier. O'Keiff had no reason to doubt this story. The rumors that once had circulated among the plastic surgeons regarding his injuring Ruth had ceased long before she had any connection to him. Had she listened with her head and experience and not her heart, however, she might have added up the clues he gave. He admitted that Ruth was hiding from him, but he claimed to have no idea why. The Gilases, her family, were wealthy and served as vigilantes, keeping him from both her and the child, he told her. The Gilases had a "vindictive vendetta" against him, using a phrase that she would come to know as his aggravating mantra. He looked crestfallen as he told her that his first wife's family hated him and he had no idea why.

Christ had few good things to say to O'Keiff about his second wife, Gay. He told her she had been "funky-looking" but, transformed by his plastic surgeon's knife, she now was "really pretty." He told O'Keiff that Gay had been the baby-sitter for Phillip and claimed that they had slept together one evening when he drove her home. He had fallen in love with her while he was still married to Ruth. She was terrible in bed, though, Christ told her. Although O'Keiff hadn't heard his second wife's story, the one Gay told was quite different, claiming that she had not hooked up with her husband until after he had separated from his first wife. It also was well known that Christ had had an affair while still married to Gay, flaunting it openly around the Texas Medical Center, where they all worked, and in his humiliated wife's face. John and Gay had split and reconciled numerous times and people wondered why she kept taking him back.

Christ admitted to O'Keiff that he had had an affair while still living with his wife, and though he said he regretted it, he also seemed to try to justify it by blaming it on Gay's failures. Now he seemed to be afraid of Susan Novak, his former lover, telling O'Keiff that Novak was "a black belt, a dangerous maniac" he feared was going to kill him. O'Keiff thought his ex-girlfriend might be mad at him, but she thought it ridiculous that she would want to kill him. If the warnings of respected and concerned colleagues weren't enough to make O'Keiff drop Christ, the clues he revealed should have been enough. He admitted that he had cheated on both his wives before he had separated from either. As her past marriages had been drawing to an end, O'Keiff had been convinced that her husbands were cheating on her, although that had not always been the case. Still, she looked at her boyfriend's infidelities through his tainted lens, not her own.

The couple took a few trips to New Orleans, where they both enjoyed shopping among the trendy boutiques and pricey antique shops in the French Quarter and dining at some of the finer restaurants there. More than just patient, Christ seemed to actually enjoy shopping for clothes for O'Keiff. He had good taste and she thought he was just as good a shopping buddy as any of her girlfriends. O'Keiff had eclectic tastes in nearly everything—clothes, furniture, jewelry and men—and collected vintage clothing, favoring those from the 1930s era. Christ liked to peruse the shops for old surgical instruments, which he was beginning to collect but didn't display, instead keeping them tucked away in his closet. Among his other interests were things with an Egyptian motif and on one of these trips he bought an eight-inch gold tomb to sit on his desk to hold his pens.

They also perused the sex shops, looking through the toys and novelty items, sometimes buying a vibrator for O'Keiff. He purchased penis rings, which were supposed to give her extra stimulation when he wore them during sex, but it didn't work. O'Keiff enjoyed receiving the presents, though. "It was kind of an erotic thing to do with a lover," she said.

O'Keiff had been a fan of the blues ever since child-hood, and New Orleans was known as a hot spot for drawing the best of these musicians. She had greatly enjoyed these shows on past visits. Christ, however, would not indulge this passion of hers, refusing to go into any of the numerous clubs in the French Quarter, complaining the place was too crowded or the musicians no good. Later in their relationship, he told her he didn't like the blues. She could understand that but found it odd that he hadn't told her so at the time.

Although she believed they were growing closer on every level, there were things she would never learn about him until it was too late. Even then, she would never be able to understand it all. He would change her life forever and she would discover a lot about herself in the process.

Two

John Ernest Christ was born August 27, 1946, in Ipswich, Massachusetts, the first in his family to be born in the United States. Both his parents were of Greek heritage; his mother, W. Effie Christ, had emigrated from Palestine as a child, while his father, now known as Chris Christ after his father had shortened the family's long Greek name, came from Asia Minor, which is now Turkey.

Chris and Effie Christ met in Massachusetts, where Chris also was a commercial fisherman and restaurateur. Growing tired of the Boston winters, he moved his family south to Miami, Florida, when John was just four and the couple's second child, William "Bill," was still an infant. There, Chris Christ ran a fishing-party boat and his wife stayed home to raise their three children. John's sister, Marika, was born eleven years after John. John's mother was a housewife until after his sister had graduated from college and then Effie took a job as a secretary at a college.

John Christ later described his early years as trouble-free. Those who knew him well through the years gave a slightly different picture. Saying there was no dysfunction within his family, Christ said he never received a spanking or had a physical fight with either of his siblings, although they argued when they were kids. He came from a close family, he said. A therapist noted in public records that he was in counseling partly "to work on his family of origin." Another reported that he described his father as an alcoholic.

Growing up in Miami, Christ attended public schools and said he graduated sixteenth in his high school class of 1,052, with a 4.0 average. He didn't date in high school, having been told by his parents that girls would be a distraction and women were "the root of all evil." His mother repeatedly predicted that women would be the cause of his downfall. He seemed jealous of his brother, Bill, who in those days was more of a rebel and dated regularly. His parents always had been overprotective, especially of their oldest, whom they referred to by the nickname "Number One." Keeping with that moniker, they seemed to give him a disproportionate amount of their attention and affection; John relished being the center of attention.

He was raised being told by his parents and grandparents that he would be a doctor. He won a science fair scholarship but—at his parents' insistence—he stayed close to home and attended the University of Miami, graduating with honors with a degree in chemistry. At twenty-one, he, too, got a commercial-fishing license, working for his father's business during the summer and on weekends. He was accepted at several medical schools, but his parents again tried to make that decision for him, telling him to enroll locally. He wanted to move away from home, so he took a summer class at the Baylor College of Medicine in Houston and decided to stay to complete his doctorate degrees. His parents weren't pleased and refused to visit until his graduation. Once away, he found himself overwhelmed by feelings of loneliness. He said he would attach himself to a woman, believing it would fill that void. Later, he didn't tell his future wives, at least not all of them, that he had gotten engaged during that time to a previously married woman from his hometown. They applied for a marriage license in Houston but apparently did not get married. Dr. Ron Beberniss, his roommate for the first year and a half of medical school, described him as quiet, insecure and "the consummate overachiever." The two roommates, both already balding by then, looked like brothers except that Beberniss was blessed with height. The short Christ still drove a large, flashy muscle car, a 1969 Dodge Charger, seemingly part of his internal drive to compensate for what he physically lacked. Not comfortable around women, Christ didn't go out often, and whenever he had a date lined up, his medical school peers teased him mercilessly. "Hey, John Christ, you finally got a date, huh? I'll bet she's ugly," they chided. Beberniss, whose undergrad degree was from a small Baptist college in central Texas, admittedly entered medical school still a virgin and didn't think his Miami roommate was any more experienced. Books were Christ's frequent companions and he became an avid collector, habitually getting authors' autographs when they were in town, even from professors who had penned textbooks. Beberniss believed his roommate was obsessive-compulsive, insisting that all his *Playboy* magazines were lined up chronologically.

After finishing a six-year program, Christ had earned two degrees, a Doctorate of Medicine as well as a Ph.D. in cardiovascular physiology. Whether it was the impressive initials after his name—and the heady income assumed to be attached to the M.D.—Christ did better with women. "I always knew him as a cheerful, fun-loving fellow. He was popular with girls," said Dr. John Pinnella, a plastic surgeon who trained with Christ both in New York and Houston.

While doing his medical internship on Long Island,

Christ met and married Ruth Ann Gilas, a Greek woman from a well-to-do family, eight years his junior. They married on August 27, 1977, his thirty-first birthday. They moved to Houston, where he returned to Baylor to do his plastic surgery residency.

Christ's reputation as a plastic surgeon was pretty good but not outstanding by most accounts. He wasn't viewed as one of the bright stars, yet at times he executed ideas that made others think he was brilliant. Of particular note was his idea to use sonograms to diagnose cleft palates before birth; he wrote an original medical paper and worked on this about the time his own wife was pregnant. His colleagues were quite impressed and ultrasounds are now routinely used for that purpose. His personal reputation around the Medical Center was less stellar. While most doctors who knew him considered him anywhere from very smart to brilliant, his behavior and personality were thought by many to be bizarre, vindictive and sometimes unprofessional. "He gave me the creeps," a fellow plastic-surgery resident said. To some, he seemed charming and comfortable in social settings, while others saw just the opposite and thought he was socially inept. Regardless, he always seemed to think he was suave, interesting and not the least bit inappropriate in the things he said or did. In the early years, he was somewhat overweight and out of shape until he took up running and became a marathon runner.

Christ didn't socialize much with the others in his residency class. He wasn't the most dependable of the group, telling other doctors to call him if he was needed on a case but never being available when he was asked. Some suspected he was moonlighting at an emergency room somewhere else, but no one ever knew for sure.

Christ initially drew the favorable attention of Dr. Mel Spira, the chief of plastic surgery at Methodist Hospital and a great ally for an up-and-coming plastic surgeon.

More than just mentor and student at the hospital, he and Ruth even socialized with Spira and his wife. Any time another doctor said something unflattering about Christ or complained about something he had done, Spira jumped to his defense. For his part, Christ didn't take constructive criticism or even helpful suggestions well. Even at staff meetings in which cases were discussed and feedback and advice traded among peers, Christ got angry whenever he was told something he didn't want to hear. Where other surgeons were concerned if one of their patients complained of problems after surgery, Christ dismissed such complaints from his, either saying that the patients didn't have a problem or that they were crazy. "I guess you either loved John or you didn't like him. There was no in-between with him," said a plastic surgeon who did his residency with Christ. Regardless, Christ never accepted responsibility for any of the problems and seemed unconcerned about even trying to correct any, both he and others have said. He was unable or unwilling to empathize with any of his patients, they thought. Nor did he always practice the best judgment.

Dr. Robert Wiemer supervised Christ during his residency, seeing him on a daily basis at the Veterans Hospital. He said he was an average resident, but more arrogant than most. "He was sort of a volatile personality sometimes," he recalled. He once lost his temper and began yelling when the admissions office at the Veterans Hospital wanted to admit a patient to a service other than what the doctor-in-training wanted. The system was not set up to be a doctor's decision, and Wiemer advised him to suck it up. "He was sort of a person who tended to think his way was the only way," he said. He saw the resident as hotheaded, arrogant and single-minded, not attractive traits for a doctor-in-training—or a husband. He and others thought that Christ's excessive arrogance had developed as overcompensation for his small stature. "If John had been six foot five and had a full head of hair, he would have been a different person," agreed Dr. John Long, a University of Texas-trained plastic surgeon who considered Christ a friend.

Another Texas Medical Center plastic surgeon, who had observed more than 120 of his younger counterparts during their residencies, said Christ was well above average in developing new ideas and had a skilled pair of hands. From his perspective, Christ's residency went well and he saw no problems with him other than the strong feelings he seemed to provoke. He said, "There was no neutral feeling toward him." But, he added, "I have no doubt he could turn on people very quickly."

In 1980, Christ went into private practice, which he established in the Texas Medical Center with the generous financial backing of his wife's parents. He was accepted on the staff at the prestigious Methodist Hospital and retained privileges at a number of area hospitals over the years. Anthony Gilas, his wife's brother, managed his office. After Christ separated from Ruth, Anthony Gilas sued him for what he claimed was a bad nose-job. Christ also performed a rhinoplasty on his wife, a cytotechnologist in the Medical Center.

On June 2, 1980, Ruth gave birth to Phillip Stephen Christ, and John proudly showed off pictures of his son around the Medical Center. He and Ruth separated nine months later and she left town almost immediately, returning to her hometown of Lynbrook, New York. To those who knew them, it was one of the most sudden and strange splits they had ever witnessed. Soon rumors about what had happened began circulating among their colleagues. It was believed by some who knew them that he had physically abused her, which he denied. He did admit, though, that she was in hiding from him. John later said he had fallen in love with Gay Simons, a nurse who had baby-sat for Phillip, and Christ had an affair with her while he was still married.

Like Ruth, Simons was eight years younger than Christ. An operating-room nurse with a good reputation who now worked for plastic surgeon Robert Wiemer, Simons was pretty, friendly and generally thought of as a nice person. It was common knowledge that Simons had her sights on marrying a doctor. "She had one fault—she wanted to marry a doctor," one plastic surgeon said. Whenever a new male resident arrived, Simons always asked about him, one of her first questions being if he was married. Because of talk in the office, her boss said Gay certainly was aware of Christ's temper before they married. "She full well knew how everybody in the office felt about John," Wiemer said.

Ruth, then twenty-five, filed for divorce within a few weeks and Christ countersued, both citing the standard reason of conflicting personalities. Ruth received custody of Phillip; John was given visitation rights to his son, who now lived in New York. He was ordered to pay $800 a month in child support and $677.86 a month for two years of contractual alimony, meaning it was a court-approved agreement between the parties, not a court-imposed one. He also was to give her $5,000 on the day their divorce was signed and another $18,600 within two years. Ruth also got their dog, which she gave to the Spiras. Their divorce was finalized on August 14, 1981.

Exactly one month later, he and Simons applied for a marriage license, after the requisite thirty-day waiting period from his divorce had expired. That same day, a judge granted his motion to reopen the divorce case. In requesting a new trial, John claimed: "Ruth Ann Christ committed fraud on [John] and on this court in that she represented to all parties that Phillip Stephen Christ was a child fathered by [John] when in fact said child was not and Ruth Ann Christ first admitted this fact to [John] only after trial herein." However, he said in legal papers, if the court found that he was the father, then he was complaining that she had denied him visitation with the child and he wanted the visitation rights modified. He began telling others the same story about his ex-wife and had a handwritten letter, reportedly signed by her, which asserted that the child was not his. While he told his fiancée about those allegations, he didn't tell her that he had planned to relinquish his parental rights.

On September 19, 1981, John and Gay Simons were married. Three weeks after the wedding, Christ and his new bride were planning to go to New York for a plastic surgeon's meeting and to visit his son. The night before, he went home and matter-of-factly told Gay that he had dissolved his parental rights. Many years later, he admitted that he had been unfazed by giving up those parental rights at the time, but that it bothered him later that he had done that, never knowing for sure if Phillip was his son. He knew Phillip would be well provided for by his ex-wife's family, he said. Years later, when he was in New York City to run in the marathon, he went to his ex-wife's family's house to try to see Phillip, but her family called the police. Later admitting it had been quite a scene, he left without seeing the child.

At the time, Gay had been shocked when John told her he had given up his parental rights. She never doubted that the child was his and reportedly warned him, "One day, this is going to come back to haunt you." John's parents apparently stayed in touch with Ruth or someone in her family, so John occasionally heard updates about Phillip from them. John once paid a surprise visit to his parents in Miami and was upset to see pictures of Phillip displayed in their living room, but after that, photos of the child were sometimes sent to John as well, presumably by his parents.

Gay and John first lived in a stunningly decorated, three-floor town house on Barkdull, part of the Boulevard Oaks neighborhood near the Museum District and Medical Center. Yet all Gay talked about, according to one acquaintance, was her desire to move into adjacent West University Place. They were nearby, but that wasn't good enough. "That's when I realized how snooty she really was," the acquaintance said. Eventually, the Christs did move to a larger town house in West University Place. Although just barely over the border, it added to their financial problems, which numerous friends believed were self-inflicted by overspending by both of them. John always had seemed somewhat distant and hard to relate to, said one woman who had gone out with him once or twice during his medical-school days. Years later, when she and her husband had the Christs over for dinner, John was somewhat more relaxed but still more reserved than most. He seemed more interested in the hosts' three-year-old daughter than the adults' conversation, which was simultaneously rude and impressive. "My daughter was not the friendliest child around, but she just took to him," the hostess recalled. "I thought, 'God, he's going to make a good dad.' "

Gay worked for another plastic surgeon until their first child, Stephanie, was born on November 18, 1983. Christ had been hoping for a son but became so enamored with his little girl that when his wife got pregnant again six months later, he hoped for another girl. This time, he got his boy. Michael John Christ was born on March 26, 1985.

Gay had worked in a plastic surgeon's office for five years and had expected her husband's practice to mirror that thriving business. When he wasn't as successful as her onetime boss, Dr. Robert Wiemer, it created friction in their marriage. She tried to give him input, but he continually rebuffed her, especially frustrated if she proved to be right. Even though Gay didn't think he was doing well, he opened a second office on the north side of town.

Some of John Christ's colleagues also believed he wasn't working up to his potential, spending too much time on activities unrelated to his business. He had his own ideas for operating his practice. Christ was on the leading edge of marketing, advertising and offering free consultations, a rare practice when he started doing it. "He did some innovative things. He was a bright guy," Wiemer said. Much to the disdain of his colleagues and eventual embarrassment of at least some of his family, he began advertising on television and in print. His esteemed colleagues began looking down on him and other surgeons who advertised. At the time, it was viewed as sleazy and akin to ambulance-chasing lawyers. Some doctors took it as an affront, as if he was single-handedly lowering the profession, and weren't pleased when he seemed successful on account of it. Some refused to refer patients to a doctor who did so.

In this case, it turned out that Christ was ahead of his time. Other surgeons, even those who had once demeaned his efforts, eventually followed his lead and openly solicited patients through advertising, so much so that it became looked upon as a normal business practice in subsequent years. Christ formed another company in 1987, Plastic Surgery Information Center, Inc., advertised as an informational and referral agency that would help patients find the best plastic surgeon for their needs. Other surgeons paid him a monthly fee to receive referrals, but it seemed that few signed up.

Houston's plastic surgeons had trouble drawing business in the mid-1980s when prices of oil, then the basis of the city's economy, fell like a summer downpour. To Long, at least, it seemed that Christ was busier than his colleagues as a result, spending time working in the OR when others weren't. And his cases seemed to be high quality in terms of the procedures the doctors liked to perform. "It wasn't just removing warts from the butts of hogs," Long said.

His wife didn't think he was doing any better than his peers during this rough economic time and she suggested they move out of state so he could establish a more lucrative practice. He seemed to consider the idea, even interviewing at a couple of places, but nothing ever came of it.

Christ excelled at achieving "vertical growth" from clients, meaning if they went in for one procedure, he was able to talk them into another, according to Long. Such practices made him a "wonderful businessman," Long thought, but some doctors questioned if such practices were ethical. "John loved the sale. John could sell magazines from door to door," he said. There were times when Christ operated on patients two to four times and the procedure still did not look right, prompting the patients to find another surgeon to fix it, according to Long and other surgeons.

Several plastic surgeons said that Christ's nose jobs were better than average. But there were questions in the circle as to whether he exercised good judgment, giving a woman her first face-lift at too young an age and others bigger breast implants than they wanted, Wiemer said. Some thought he was doing exactly that with his wife, who had at least four cosmetic surgeries shortly after they were married, including breast implants and her nose, chin and eyes. "The guy doesn't want her as she is. He just married her and now he wants to redo her whole body," said one acquaintance. Many thought it was excessive, although most agreed that while Gay, not yet thirty, had always been attractive, she looked even better afterward. Christ said that Spira did two of the surgeries and Wiemer one.

Another plastic surgeon thought Christ took cases just for the money, regardless of whether or not the patient needed it. "Plastic surgery isn't just about surgery; it's about judgment," he said, adding not everyone who wants surgery needs it. Some doctors, like Christ, took those cases, he said, but he felt there were enough legitimate ones that they didn't need to.

As would happen throughout his life, Christ's judgment would be questioned outside the operating room as well. He had a bitter falling-out with the influential Spira, once his biggest supporter, and never let go of the grudge. Christ recalled the dispute this way: He had discovered a new operation when a male patient came to him with a profuse sweating in his armpits. Based on the previously developed fat-suctioning techniques, Christ said he experimented by taking the sweat glands out with the fat there. The surgery worked, so the surgeon went to Spira, the department chair at Baylor, with his idea, looking for more patients on whom to try the procedure so he could publish the results in an academic journal. Spira then got Dr. Sal Shenaq, another plastic surgeon who years later would replace him as department chair, involved in the study. Spira and Shenaq did the procedure on two other patients, but Christ claimed he did the research and wrote the paper. When he was finished, Shenaq insisted his name go first and Christ balked. "I said, 'No, it's my idea and I wrote the paper and if we're going to go by alphabetical order, I'm still C,'" he said.

Instead of someone giving in, Christ said, it was decided that they would do separate papers, Christ writing about his case history and the other two publishing the results of their patients. Christ claimed that his two highly respected and accomplished colleagues plagiarized his work, stealing credit for his idea. Neither Spira nor Shenaq would discuss the dispute or Christ, who admitted to making a lot of waves by complaining to national organizations of plastic surgeons and Baylor officials. He said he was vindicated two years later by a Baylor committee, but that could not be confirmed. Vindicated or not, Christ remained angry; even when other problems in his life far outweighed the importance of authorship of an academic paper, he would not stop discussing it or drawing hard-to-imagine conspiratorial links to that long-ago dispute.

Gay noticed a number of personality changes in her husband around his fortieth birthday. He seemed to hit a downward spiral and it never let up. They seldom fought during the early years of their relationship, but later, Christ never could admit he was wrong. He became more chauvinistic and arrogant. At first, it was okay if others called him by his first name, but he later demanded to be called Dr. Christ. Like many surgeons she knew, he thought highly of himself. His colleagues found it oddly pretentious that he insisted on using the initials for both his academic degrees after his name on everything, including his lab coat; John E. Christ, M.D., Ph.D. Such practices are common among professors or those in an academic setting but not among those in private practice, his colleagues said. One said that Christ boasted that he had more degrees than his peers, implying he was smarter. "Do you put H.S. for high school?" the colleagues quipped.

Gay reportedly had told her husband that if he wanted a divorce, do one of two things—have an affair or hit her. He would do both, but she repeatedly took him back even as he flaunted his affair in her face, around town and with their family. She seemed to make excuses for him, saying he was feeling pressured because his business wasn't doing well or he was going through a midlife crisis. She wouldn't leave him if he had a physical problem, she rationalized. So why should she leave him because he had an emotional one? The defining moment came when he hit her and broke her nose. She could no longer excuse his behavior. Until that time, she had continued to hope for a reconciliation. Gay, the oldest of four children of a nurse and optometrist, had witnessed at age twelve her own parents' divorce. Although her father had a drinking problem, she later described their divorce as amicable. She would not be able to say the same thing about hers. Years later, John had nothing good to say about the mother of his children other than she was a nice dresser.

An avid runner and marathoner, Christ was credited with planning a 1,700-mile run from Houston to New York City, dubbed the "Freedom to Liberty Relay Run," in June 1986. Two dozen medical professionals joined the eleven-day, round-the-clock relay as part of the celebrations for the rededication of the Statue of Liberty and the Texas Sesquicentennial. Each person was to run forty-five minutes every eighteen hours.

Gay complained in a lawsuit years later that she never knew where her husband was staying and had to wait for him to call her. During that time, she was trying to oversee his practice in his absence, train his new employee, take care of their two children, and, as their house had been foreclosed, find a new home. She later learned that it was on that trip that he began an affair with Susan Novak, just shy of his fortieth birthday.

In September, they moved to a new place. Gay had packed all their things, but after the movers unloaded their possessions, John announced he was leaving. Thinking it was just all the stress, Gay tried to talk him out of it and thought she had been successful. As she gave Michael a bath later that day, she realized her husband had left without another word. She didn't know where he went for three days.

John filed for divorce from Gay on September 3, 1986—two and one-half weeks shy of their fifth anniversary. He cited the standard legal phrase as his reason for seeking the divorce: "The marriage has become insupportable because of discord or conflict of personalities . . . that destroys the legitimate ends of the marriage relationship and prevents any reasonable expectation of reconciliation."

That same month, upsetting rumors reached Gay's ears for the first time. The hottest gossip circulating around Methodist was that her husband had been caught having sex in the stairwell of Scurlock Tower, her husband's office building, which was attached to the hospital. Novak, reportedly, was an exercise physiologist in the same building; she was also working toward her Ph.D. Consequently, Gay's husband had been dubbed "The Stairwell Stud" and made the butt of a few jokes. Albeit amused, his colleagues saw it as "a beacon of his judgment," and his professional reputation was tarnished as a result. Gay turned to Zen Camacho, her husband's best friend at the time and a Rice University administrator, with her suspicions. He told her that the affair had begun during the run to New York and that the two saw each other daily. Camacho said that John had told him that he was in love with Novak and was planning to divorce Gay. Her husband, however, returned home the following month. After just eleven days, he was out the door once again, telling his wife he needed to see what he had with Novak. The two rented a condo and moved in together. John continued to visit his children. Two months later, Gay let him move back in.

Five months later, Gay was pregnant with their third child. In August, when she was four months pregnant, Gay had an amniocentesis. Not feeling well, she went to bed early, only to get a disturbing call from Novak. She announced to Gay that she had been seeing John and was having a miscarriage. John was mad and went to bed, not to his mistress's. The next day, he took his wife to a travel agent, where he bought tickets for them to go to Boston the next month. They never went.

After he moved home following his affair, he seemed to feel overwhelmed. His recurring affair was well known around the Medical Center and people's opinions of him plunged further, though he didn't seem to notice. Trying to rebuild their marriage, Gay suggested they move to another state and start over, but he refused. Gay returned to work more as a way to rebuild her self-esteem than the couple's bank account.

In October, Gay received another upsetting call from Novak. According to court papers filed later by Gay, Novak told her that she was concerned for her [Gay's] safety, insinuating that John might try to poison her. She confided something that Gay already knew—John's brother was doing research on poisons in Massachusetts; unable to do animal testing where he was, he shipped some to John to test the poison on rats at Baylor. "What she was telling me was true, but what upset me was that I realized that John was continuing to see her and here I was six months pregnant," Gay said in court records. Apparently, she was unfazed by the poisoning allegation.

On January 16, 1988, Gay went into labor. When she woke her husband, who was planning to run in the Houston Tenneco Marathon the following morning, to tell him their third child was on his way, his response was less than enthusiastic. "What do you want me to do about it?" the doctor told his wife, according to court documents. He did take her to the hospital and stayed for the birth of their son, Jacob, but he left immediately after the newest member of his family entered the world in order to make it to the marathon.

Three weeks later, John took off alone to spend time with his parents and brother in the Caribbean, where the elder Christs had taken a cruise.

In April 1988, Christ gave Novak a blepharoplasty, plastic surgery of the eyelids and eyebrows, without charging her the usual $2,500 fee, according to Gay's allegations in court papers. She also said that he wrote prescriptions for Novak in Gay's name. The following month, John moved out again, this time to his own apartment.

Gay invited John to spend Thanksgiving with her, the kids and her family, but he didn't show up when expected, disappointing the children. As he had before, he told Gay how unhappy he was with Novak, complaining to his wife that his mistress wanted a commitment. He told her that he and Novak had argued and that it had led to "a physical brawl," according to Gay's court papers. That same month, John and Novak went to New York to run in the marathon.

He returned to Houston in December 1988, assuring her his affair with Novak was finished and that he was committed to their marriage. Gay had heard it all before but agreed to let him move back home yet again. He started seeing a therapist.

On January 17, Gay wanted to celebrate Jacob's first birthday, but her husband wasn't focused on that. He told her and his secretary that he was very depressed, even suicidal. Each of the women, unaware the other had the same idea, phoned his therapist for help. Gay spent much of the day taking care of her depressed husband and talking with his family, who called long distance and were concerned about him as well. Two days later, after six weeks at home, Christ moved out for the last time.

John planned to run in the Boston Marathon in April 1989, and the timing was good as his brother was getting married there two days earlier. Gay and the Christ children were not invited to the family event and she was humiliated when she learned that he had taken Novak to the wedding and rehearsal dinner. Even though they were separated, they still were married and she considered this an affront. After Christ returned to Houston, she confronted him about it. He admitted that he had done so but claimed to have broken up with Novak on the way home from the airport. A couple months later, Gay learned that he was seeing Novak again.

John spent the Fourth of July with his children at the home they shared with their mother. He planned to shoot off fireworks in the driveway and had the audacity to suggest to his wife that he bring his mistress and her child over to watch with them.

On July 21, John was at their large, luxury town house in West University Place, near the Medical Center, to visit his kids when he and Gay got into a violent argument. As she prepared dinner, John tried to show her a proposed divorce settlement and insisted that she agree to it. During the ensuing argument, she mockingly called him "The Stairwell Stud." Enraged, he rammed his fists into her face and head several times, then threw her on the table and bashed her head into it. He shoved her and she fell into the high chair, slamming her nose into the footrest. When he was done, she was left with a severely broken nose, requiring more surgery, and a lot of bruises. She called 911 and told rescuers what had happened. The surgeon had another story, one in which he merely had tried to defend himself: They had been arguing. When his wife raised a kitchen utensil to strike him, he grabbed her wrist to stop her. That's when she had slipped and injured herself, he claimed.

Her injuries made it clear that she had been struck more than once. After waiting for a friend to take care of the kids, paramedics took Gay to the hospital, where she spent many days recovering.

Officers in the upper-class community were not unaccustomed to such calls. What made it memorable to officers was the suspect's demeanor. When Officer Eddie Harrold arrived, the victim was crying but not hysterical. He asked Gay what had happened. "I called him a 'Stairwell Stud' and he punched me in the nose," she said.

The officer went into the house and saw Christ, now holding Stephanie in his arms, almost like a shield from police, the veteran officer thought. "This is a stud?" he recalled thinking. "He looks like a little Poindexter. He's a scumbag."

He asked the doctor to put his daughter down so he could talk to him out of the child's earshot. On such calls, he had no choice but to arrest the suspect, he explained, but told him he didn't want to do that in front of the children. "I'm not one who wants to arrest someone, even the worst scumbag, in front of their kids," he said later. He didn't want them to be left with the unsettling image of their father being led away in handcuffs.

Christ surprised the officer when instead of going quietly outside, "He starts yelling: 'Kids, your mommy's having your daddy arrested!' "

Harrold was pissed. "Shut the hell up!" he told him as he led him outside and arrested him. "Here I was trying to be compassionate, and after seeing the wife, it was hard to be compassionate." Now the kids were even more scared and confused than they had been before. "Even the worst of the worst scumbags doesn't want to be arrested in front of their kids," he said. "He was an asshole." The officer considered Gay's injuries serious and said in another jurisdiction Christ probably would have been charged with a felony instead of a misdemeanor. Even so, he was surprised Christ didn't draw any jail time for it. His standing in the medical community dropped significantly as a result, said one of his colleagues.

Someone working in the emergency room when Gay was brought in was shocked. "Her nose was over on the other side of her face," he said, adding he was astonished to learn that John had hit her. To those who saw her in the weeks that followed, she seemed more angry at her estranged husband than afraid of him. She asked more than one person: "Can you believe what he did?" Although they might not have told her, some people were actually not surprised. "Violence was there—the potential of him striking out was there," said one. Finally, after all the emotional abuse she had endured, she was ready for her marriage to be over.

John didn't visit Gay during her recovery in the hospital. One time he wrote a simple note—"I didn't do it"—on the back of his business card and slipped it under the door. It unnerved her that he wouldn't admit what he had done, even to her. Afterward, Gay complained in court papers that her husband repeatedly harassed her in numerous ways, including verbal abuse, going into her car, parking in her space at the hospital and telling their children lies about her.

John filed for divorce and Gay countersued. Instead of claiming "irreconcilable differences" as had become the routine in divorce cases, an angry Gay delineated her complaints against her husband, often in great detail, chronicling his affair with Novak, or what she knew of it. She hired a private investigator to record his activities. During court hearings in the divorce case, Christ always seemed to say something to irk the judge, such as implying that because he made it a point to attend one Little League game a year, he was a good parent. At one point, he opened his sport coat to show the judge the ripped lining in an effort to prove Gay was a bad wife. Gay also sought damages stemming from the assault, the result of which, she said, she now suffered from post-traumatic stress disorder, and claimed intentional infliction of bodily injury and emotional distress, breach of fiduciary relationship, mismanagement of the community estate and breach of the marriage contract. "John Christ also let his practice slide. He didn't strive to reach his full earning capabilities. Instead, he spent several hours daily working out in the gym and pursuing affairs with women in the gym and in the hospital. This began in 1985 or 1986 and continued until 1990. He also openly, knowing the effect it was having on me, dated and had affairs with other women," Gay complained in court papers.

On September 28, 1989, John pleaded no contest to assault in Harris County Criminal Court. He was given deferred adjudication of guilty, meaning the judge heard evidence of his guilt, and while he had to meet the conditions of probation, he would not have a conviction on his record. He was put on 180 days' probation and handed a $375 fine. He was released from probation three months early, just before Christmas, 1989, and just before he would meet O'Keiff for the first time.

Whenever Christ spoke of the assault, he continued to stick to his story that Gay had hurt herself when she fell and then blamed him. He claimed that, based on his attorney's explanation, he believed that "no contest" was tantamount to pleading "not guilty" rather than an admission. In Texas, defendants pleading no contest are routinely made aware that it means they are not disputing the charges and that they will be found guilty. Regardless of the evidence, guilty was a tag the plastic surgeon pinned on others, never himself.

Three

Carol Kristin O'Keiff was born December 3, 1956, the second child to a couple who didn't want any. Nevertheless, both babies were the result of intended pregnancies.

Financially speaking, Carol was born into a family of privilege, but she was emotionally deprived. Margaret O'Keiff never wanted children. Unlike many women, she wasn't drawn to them. Still, as a housewife in the 1950s, she felt it was expected of her, so she decided she should and would have them. Whenever she approached her young husband with the idea, she said he always had a reason to put it off, such as being in college. At the time, he never told her he didn't want them. That admission came only after they had been born.

Margaret Inman met Gustav Mason O'Keiff II, two years her senior, on a blind date. She was still a junior at San Jacinto High School in Houston while Gustav Mason, known as Mason, had just graduated and was preparing for college. "He had the best-looking black Buick convertible I ever saw in my life," she recalled. Shy but academically driven, he told Inman she was the first girl he had ever dated.

Margaret grew up in Houston and San Benito, Texas, a small community near Brownsville. Her fa-

ther, Clarence B., alternately worked as a traveling salesman and businessman, manufacturing first wooden
soda-bottle boxes and then, during World War II, ammunition crates. He lovingly dubbed his own daughter "Tinkerbell," eventually shortening her nickname
to Tink. Her mother, Erie, was a housewife, affectionate but manipulative and controlling. When Margaret
was four, an unwelcome intruder moved in with her
family—a baby brother, Jay. She was so jealous she
regularly tried to strangle him to death, she said, but
her tiny hands weren't strong enough. Their parents
never knew. She eventually stopped trying to kill him
and their youthful relationship evolved into a hostile,
taunting one. As adults, they grew closer, although
their personalities differed. He was as friendly and paternal as she wasn't, she said admiringly. While she
claimed Jay as her only sibling, her father had another
son, who lived in Louisiana, from a previous marriage.
Margaret had a difficult time in school initially as she
was dyslexic but didn't know it until many years later
when her son was diagnosed with it. At the time, she
thought she was stupid. She finally taught herself to
read in the fifth grade. She was good at memorizing
information and relied on that skill to get through
school, even managing to skip a grade along the way.
She believed her father, a college graduate, was dyslexic as well. During Margaret's senior year in high
school, O'Keiff drove to Houston every weekend from
Dallas, where he attended Southern Methodist University, to be with his girlfriend.

After Inman graduated from high school, her parents
wanted her to go to a finishing school to learn social
polish, but she wanted a career in commercial arts. She
headed to Sam Houston State University in Huntsville
instead. She had to take an IQ test when she entered
and, still believing she was stupid, worried about the

results. About six weeks later, she was called into a counselor's office where she was told she had registered in the top 10 percent. She accomplished this even though she had not finished most of the math questions. After her first semester, O'Keiff convinced her to transfer to SMU so they could be together. "I grew up in an era when going to college was simply to get your M.R.S.," Inman said. And that is exactly what she got, becoming Mrs. Gustav Mason O'Keiff a year later, in 1950, at the age of eighteen. Margaret was different and wanted a career as well.

The newlyweds continued going to college until Mason graduated the following year and was accepted into graduate school at the academically elite Rice University in Houston, known as "the Harvard of the South." Margaret hoped to finish her degree at the University of Houston, but she discovered that most of her credits would not transfer and never did graduate. Still, she took classes at UH that interested her, such as art history, and audited others at Rice. Mason continued to collect degrees, earning a Ph.D. in engineering from Rice, where he later taught thermodynamics.

By then the O'Keiffs were rich. Mason was to inherit millions but he would get it only after a protracted and exceptionally bitter fight over his grandparents' wills. At first, he watched his aunts and uncles trade lawsuits and nasty accusations before being drawn into the acrimony after his own mother died young, leaving him, her sole child, her heir.

Mason O'Keiff inherited about $3 million from his grandparents' separate estates. Even before getting the full amount, the interim payments generated from W. D. Haden's bequeathment had enabled the young married O'Keiffs to live richly. Now they readily jumped into a self-indulgent, jet-setting lifestyle that their new money allowed. Now they were counted among the beautiful people, in looks as well as affluence. Their crowd remained the academic elite rather than the upper echelons of Houston's high society in which some of the other Hadens circulated. They found a house they liked in River Oaks, which then and now is *the* address to claim in Houston, but bought instead in Braeswood, a fashionable but more southerly house in both location and prestige. They simply liked the view of the tree-lined bayou in front of the sprawling ranch. Mason O'Keiff further magnified their wealth through astute investments and no longer needed to work full-time. He became a Formula I race-car driver, racing at such tracks as Daytona and Riverside, a new passion that indirectly was the O'Keiffs' road to parenthood.

Four years after they had married, Margaret became pregnant—but only after making an unusual deal with her husband. She agreed to let him buy the car he wanted, a classic open-cockpit Jaguar racer, if he would impregnate her. When she went into labor with their first child on November 22, 1954, he dropped her off at the hospital and left. In those days, men were not allowed in the delivery rooms with their wives, so Mason didn't see the point of hanging around and waiting. He returned hours later to meet his namesake, Gustav Mason O'Keiff III, who they decided to call Gus. Carol followed two years later. Gus wasn't pleased with his new sister. "He really thought he came into the world with a guarantee that he was going to be an only child," Margaret said. He got over it and both were happy but active toddlers.

The O'Keiffs, both undemonstrative, were emotionally and often physically absent from their progenies' lives, substituting their attentions with those of the two women hired to do the housework and tend to their kids. "My motherhood gland is about as big as my little finger," Margaret admitted. While her own mother had read her stories and played checkers with her, she said, "I never wanted to play with my children. I had more interesting things going on. I got the maid to read to my kids."

Carol was an exceptionally sensitive young girl, easily injured by her father's solemn routine of ignoring her and her mother's hurtful remarks. Gus grew into a challenging adolescent for his standoffish parents, but both said that their daughter, during her prepubescent days, was easygoing and easy to take. "Carol was the sweetest little girl. I don't think we ever had to correct her," Margaret recalled. The only time Mason ever hit Carol was to slap her hand after she chipped a valuable jade plate, so thin it was see-through, after he repeatedly warned her not to go into the living room where it was displayed. When her father drove her to nursery school in his high-priced and highly coveted Jaguar XKE, its long nose extending far in front of its driver, Carol sat on the floor, hiding because she didn't want to be seen in the "weird car." To her, it was akin to the wiener mobile she had seen on television. She did the same in the Cadillac, "the square car." At age six, she was enrolled in St. John's, Houston's most exclusive private school, where her brother attended.

Carol was precocious and her devotion to wearing makeup began early. At just five years old, she began experimenting with her mother's palette of eye shadows, lipsticks, rouges and whatever else she could get her tiny hands on. She loved dressing up in her mother's cocktail dresses and shoes and parading around the house. Seeing her parents decked out, her father in a tux and her mother in sparkled glamour, preparing for a night on the town, Carol dreamed of such a lifestyle for herself when she grew up.

The family often spent weekends on Galveston Island, ninety minutes south of town, staying in a suite on the top floor of the historic Hotel Galvez, overlooking the Gulf of Mexico. Margaret spent the days on the beach with Carol and Gus. Lila Haden Brock, her father's eccentric aunt, whom Carol's entire family adored, lived on the island at another hotel and the family visited her a couple of times a year. Carol was enthralled by her look—flaming red hair with even more brightly colored lipstick, huge gold purse, rhinestone glasses and tier upon tier of beaded necklaces—with a personality to match. That is one of the few good memories Carol has of the time when her parents were still married. The O'Keiffs traveled frequently without their children, often leaving them with Margaret's mother, who was affectionate and doted on her two children as well as her grandchildren. A stern but caring woman with short bluish gray hair and diamond-studded glasses, she kept plenty of toys at her house for the grandkids. She read them religious stories and taught them to pray, which they didn't do at home. And if they were good when they visited, they left with candy. Their potbellied and mostly bald grandfather, who wore bolo ties and reminded Carol of Humpty-Dumpty, was less demonstrative with his affections, but they knew he loved them. He held Carol on his lap as they watched television or flipped through *National Geographic*. He drove a spacious Lincoln, slipping a piece of cardboard between the steering wheel and his stomach to keep it from rubbing his pants.

What time Carol's parents did spend at home, most often was with, or at least for, her brother, who frequently got in trouble in school and at home. He developed epileptic seizures as a child, which he outgrew as an adult. As Gus's medical and behavioral problems increased, more and more of his parents' attentions were focused on him. Gus got the attention; Carol got a piano and seven years of lessons, beginning at about age six, which she loved. She learned to play by ear. Although she had friends with whom she played, rode bikes and hung out, Carol spent a lot of time alone. Sometimes she just lay in the thick grass carpet of the family's backyard, staring for hours at the clouds. When she was seven, she waited in anticipation for the weekly garbage pickup. She would hop on her bike and follow it a couple of miles around the neighborhood until the garbagemen told her to go home. Sometimes she and her brother followed the "fog man," a city truck spraying chemicals to chase away the super-sized mosquitoes, which thrive in the humidity.

Mason O'Keiff has sometimes been perceived as emotionally distant with people, even with his wife and children. Carol's feelings were crushed when he returned from work and didn't even notice that she was on crutches, after severely cutting her foot on a sprinkler head. Devastated, Carol ran to her room and cried. Margaret followed and tried to offer comforting words. She stuck up for her daughter, but it caused another loud argument between Carol's parents.

Despite his standoffish nature, Carol loved being around her dad, sharing his enthusiasm for car racing, even going with him to the garage when one of his cars was being worked on. She loved to hear the rumbling engines being tuned and even the smell of oil, exhaust and rubber. Mostly, she was proud of her father, enjoying the respect he garnered and how his buddies treated her like she was special because she was his daughter. Whenever he raced close to home, she and Gus sat in the pits, close to all the action.

Carol not only adored her father, she idolized him. Although they had never been close, she convinced herself that they were. "No one could say anything bad about my dad," she said. Least of all, her mother. Whenever Carol heard them fighting, she decided it must be her mother's fault, even though she usually had no idea what it was about. Mostly, she recalled her mother screaming at her father, who would make some sarcastic remark and walk out. As a child, she viewed her mother as the aggressor and, therefore, a threat to the tenuous family bond. Even as an adult, Carol's memories sometimes exaggerated the nice things her father did and shortchanged those from her mother.

When their parents were home, Carol and Gus recalled a lot of loud arguments. Carol didn't remember the content, only the horrible sad feeling that scared her. Margaret doesn't remember it that way. She said that the marriage was strained but there weren't any problems she thought were insurmountable. She also insisted they never argued, so she was surprised when "Mason just walked in one day and said he wanted a divorce."

Like his sister, Gus recalled a lot of arguing between his parents; it was after one of those fights that the kids were summoned to the study for a family meeting. Mason told them he was leaving for a while.

"How long is a while?" Gus asked.

"I don't know," Mason responded. Gus blamed himself. A few years earlier, he had brought up some no-longer-memorable topic at the dinner table and it had led to a heated argument between his parents. Whenever they argued after that, he thought it was his fault.

Margaret blamed her son and her daughter, too, saying having kids resulted in the downfall of her marriage. Her husband hadn't wanted the responsibility. Years later, as their marriage was falling apart, she recalled: "He said, 'I've never forgiven you for having the children.' It wasn't the children themselves, he didn't want the responsibility." But she also believed his racing played a role. Then a wealthy and popular sportsman, O'Keiff, according to Margaret, saw himself as a playboy and had no problems attracting women. "He wanted the chance to be footloose and fancy-free," she said. Touted as a champion, Mason captured a celebrity endorsement ad for the very popular Vitalis men's hair tonic. After the couple separated, Mason O'Keiff spent less and less time with his children, sometimes going months without seeing or calling them, even though they lived in the same city. Countless times, Mason promised to pick up his children for a weekend visit but never showed up. He never called, and Gus and Carol spent hours waiting for him. Mason complained that Margaret always dressed the children inappropriately for whatever he had planned, ensuring that their time together was not as fun as it might have been. Calling her first husband "an emotional cripple," Margaret said that Mason "just walks away from people." He and his best friend had gone into business together during their marriage, but during the separation, he walked out on his friend and business as well, she said.

After fifteen years of marriage, the O'Keiffs divorced so bitterly, the aftertaste was still palpable nearly thirty years later. Their divorce resolved some of their problems but amplified Gus's. "Gus had a nervous breakdown. He thought it was his fault," Margaret said. "In a way, it was." As a result of his breakdown, his parents sent him to a school in Richardson, a Dallas suburb, that specialized in treating children with emotional problems. Carol's emotional response to her parents' divorce was less severe but would regiment her reactions the rest of her life. Though just eight, she decided that crying made her vulnerable and weak and she stubbornly decided not to do it any longer.

As part of the O'Keiffs' divorce settlement, Margaret got a half-million dollars, and Gus and Carol each were given trust funds worth about $250,000 in cash and stocks, which they were supposed to get at age twenty-one. Margaret estimated that her husband was worth about $5 million when they split up but said she had to fight to get the children's trusts established. She invested her money and did well for herself. Throughout the rest of her childhood, Carol's mother regularly reminded her of the trust fund that awaited her, repeatedly telling her: "You are one rich little girl." Under the terms of the children's trusts, Margaret was allowed to spend that money on them, and some of each of their funds were spent on their medical and psychiatric bills, Gus said.

In the divorce, Mason got the Braeswood house, but Margaret rented it from him while her new town house was being built. She said her ex-husband agreed to extend the lease, then secretly filed to evict her, forcing her and Carol to move in with the Inmans temporarily. Margaret always wanted both her children to go to college. After her divorce—when she found herself without a career and unable to support herself had it not been for her share of her husband's inheritance—she especially felt her daughter should have a career.

Mason O'Keiff remarried two weeks after his divorce from Margaret was final, taking Judy Holt as his bride on October 29, 1965. Carol was not fond of her new stepmother, who was alternately nice and unpleasant.

Margaret O'Keiff and Carol moved into a large, beautiful town house in the posh Galleria area. An attractive, personable, wealthy woman, Margaret had no problems finding dates and went out often with plenty of successful, attractive, well-to-do men, including her divorce attorney. Soon her attention and time were devoted to one man: Francis C. "Pat" Johnson, forty-one, a former naval commander of an atomic submarine and a recent widower with four children. Johnson's wife reportedly committed suicide by swallowing a handful of prescription pills. She had left a note and when her husband awoke one morning, he found his wife dead in bed, according to Margaret. Johnson met Margaret in November 1966 at a supper club at Rice University, where he was an ROTC instructor. In the beginning, Johnson tried too hard for Carol's tastes, forcing her to sit on his lap when he visited. Not used to receiving affection or that kind of attention from her own father, Carol just felt uncomfortable, but he persisted.

O'Keiff, thirty-four, took on four more children when she married Johnson on February 16, 1967, just three months after they met. Margaret and Carol moved into the Johnsons' Barryknoll house in the prestigious Memorial section of town and Carol was enrolled in a public school closer to her new home. The following June, after nearly two years at the Richardson school, Gus's behavioral problems disappeared and he returned home to Houston and a significantly expanded family.

Gus seemed an engineer- or scientist-in-the-making, constantly taking things apart so he could put them back together, inventing things and playing with chemistry sets and robots. Like many young boys of the 1960s, he was fascinated by the space program. Gus was determined to solve the antigravity problem. When his father took him to Rice University and showed him the massive computer, which ran on transistors, Gus was intrigued. He asked a scientist what it did and typed in his name and address and then printed it out. "This is pretty lame," he recalled thinking. Little did he know that was where his future lay.

Pat and Margaret Johnson's relationship was good for about the first year, according to Margaret, until her husband became verbally abusive toward her. In anger, Pat Johnson once hit Carol with his fists, she said. It was only *once* because she learned how to get away from him and his temper when necessary, Carol said. As conflicts in the household grew, so did Carol's problems and her ways of acting out. She started drinking alcohol in the fifth grade and began running away from home shortly after that. Margaret considered divorcing Johnson but worried about her son, who had had such a hard time after her split from his father. She asked a thirteen-year-old Gus how he would feel if she got another divorce. "Mom, I don't think I could take it," he told her.

So Margaret reluctantly stayed married another two years. She later regretted how she handled that situation. "It was stupid of me to ask a child to make an adult decision," she said. "I was just really stupid. There were lots of things I should have known." She said she was naive but also did not want to see what was going on. Years later, Margaret referred to her marriage to Johnson as "the biggest mistake of my life, and he was terrible for my children."

Margaret first noticed her daughter having problems late in her twelfth year. She obviously was depressed and she began shoplifting, and, according to her mother, "doing everything under the sun." That was the age Carol had sex for the first time, losing her virginity in the woods near her home. "This isn't all it's cracked up to be," she remembered thinking. "It hurts." But she loved being that close to somebody, so she continued having sex regularly with her boyfriend, who was a couple of years older, generally on a bed of pine needles beneath the trees. As her experience grew, so did her enthusiasm; she began to realize she actually enjoyed sex. After the two broke up, Carol's budding sex life remained active. Using it as a way to fight her loneliness and pump up her fragile self-esteem, the petite girl, not yet a teenager, shared herself with one boy after another. She felt loved and accepted—sometimes. One afternoon at the bayou in Memorial, three boys, whom she had considered friends, grabbed her and forced her to perform oral sex on all of them. It was her first time giving oral sex. She was afraid, repulsed and humiliated but didn't tell anyone. Mostly, she felt betrayed. However this did not deter her from continuing an active sex life with boys, some of whom claimed at the time to love her and told her she was pretty. Most never called unless they wanted more sex. Their lines continued to be effective on Carol, who never heard these things from her parents or anyone else in her life. Her grandparents showed some affection, certainly more than either of her parents, but even they never actually said they loved her. The cost of hearing compliments and declarations of love was at the expense of her reputation. "Everybody called me a slut, and I didn't even care," she said. She just wanted the closeness. She often went to parties and left with older boys; for the next several years, she buried her problems beneath daily doses of illegal drugs.

To her mother, who was unaware her daughter had been orally raped, Carol just seemed depressed during this time. To help pull her out of it, she offered to buy her new clothes. Johnson, rich and materialistic, wanted to take her daughter to one of the upscale department stores, like Saks Fifth Avenue, Neiman Marcus or the locally owned and just as ritzy Sakowitz.

"Where would you like to go?" she asked, anticipating a fun mother-daughter outing.

"The Salvation Army," Carol answered, preferring fatigues and army boots to the finer things. A few guys at her school sported military jackets, but Carol took it all the way, wanting the entire camouflage ensemble. "Everything fashionwise, I took a little further," Carol said. She altered her bell-bottoms to make the flares wider and her hip-huggers to ride even lower. Disgusted, Johnson didn't take her shopping anywhere. Gus was the opposite of his sister, a stylish dresser always insisting on the best and most expensive clothes and cars that his mother could afford. His mother thought he had impeccable taste and his sister had none. Carol saw her brother as intelligent but "a computer nerd," carrying a briefcase to junior and senior high. Gus was as establishment as Carol was beatnik. Carol felt that her mother constantly compared her and her brother, asking why she couldn't be more like Gus.

A good example of why Carol felt she had been singled out in the Johnson household happened one Easter. When the six children went to the dining room where their candy awaited, everyone's was in a traditional basket, except for Carol's. Hers was unfestively dumped in a grocery bag. The store had only had five baskets; as it happened at the last minute, someone had to do without one, Margaret said later. Carol was the fourth in age, but her mother assumed she would be the one least likely to care. Still, instead of singling her out in a way that would make her feel special, such as putting her goodies in a crystal bowl or some sort of keepsake, she had done just the opposite and never understood why her daughter had been so deeply hurt by the slight.

Carol continued running away periodically and Margaret Johnson and O'Keiff agreed that maybe it would be best if she moved in with her father. Carol was thrilled, as she secretly had longed to live with her dad, who now had a baby daughter as well. Keira Elissa O'Keiff had been born on November 18, 1969. Carol never felt jealous toward her younger half sibling because she didn't seem to get any more attention from their father than she had when she was younger. She thought Keira was cute but didn't see her often enough to develop a relationship with her. Unlike his sister, Gus never wanted to live with his father nor tried to run away from his mother's, but his memories from that time would be largely nonexistent, having blocked most of it out. As an adult, however, he said he still dreamed about being in the Johnson household. It was as if his mind was still struggling to make a bad situation good.

During the brief period Carol lived with her father, his second wife and the baby, Carol believed she was really trying to fit in. She wanted a home and she thought this was a chance to develop a better relationship with her dad, and she believed she was on her way there. She tried her best, staying off drugs and away from her old friends; she tried to behave and help with chores around the house. The only violation she committed was to sneak out of the house at night and walk up and down the neighborhood streets, never really knowing why she was doing it. To Carol, Judy seemed jealous and sometimes hostile, as if Carol's stay there was an intrusion. According to Carol, one day her father took her out to breakfast at Kip's Big Boy and seemed to struggle as he told her that Judy was jealous and one of them had to leave. He had a hard time looking her in the eye, but said that since Judy was his wife, Carol could no longer live there. "It hurt so bad," Carol said. "I didn't know what I had done." Her former step-mother denied that Carol's exit from their home had happened like that or for those reasons, but she declined to say why Carol had to move out.

She wasn't home long when she ran away again. This time, the thirteen-year-old would not return home soon and planned to live on the streets, thinking it would be better than the coldness of her large Memorial area home. She thumbed a ride to Surfside Beach, about seventy miles south of Houston. She thought she was streetwise but believed she needed someone to look after her. Not long after arriving in Surfside, she met Jake Morgan, who already knew she was a runaway. He seemed willing to be the one who would take care of her and offered her a safe place to sleep—with him.

After living in fear on the streets, Carol found the offer acceptable. Although Morgan was about twice her age, Carol began thinking of him as her boyfriend and he was affectionate with her. Soon the pair hooked up with one of his friends, whom she knew only as Doug. The guys decided to head to central Texas, with Carol, of course.

On their way, she became afraid of her "protector" for the first time. While the three were walking across a long bridge, high above a river, Morgan turned to her without warning and said, "Carol, you're getting to be too much of a burden. How would you like to go swimming?" Looking at Doug, he added, "Let's throw her off the bridge!" The two men grabbed a terrified Carol and hoisted her near the rails. Now kicking, screaming and begging them not to, Carol knew she would be killed either by the long drop or the swift currents below. Having successfully scared her, they put her down and walked away. Having nowhere else to go, she followed. Their new home was a lonely trailer sitting on about ten acres of barren land just outside of Denton. Another of Morgan's friends, a man she only knew as Bill, lived there and the three moved in. But Carol was not going to be a guest. She was to be the housekeeper and cook, Morgan told her. He had other things planned as well, but he did not clue her in yet. She was fairly good at cleaning but didn't know much about cooking, which infuriated Morgan, who physically abused her for her shortcomings. He hit, kicked and threw her around daily. After a few days, he added another chore to her list. "Carol, take all your clothes off and go wait for Bill on his bed in his room," he told her. "Do whatever he wants." She was shocked, believing she was Morgan's girlfriend, even if he wasn't nice. Too afraid to disobey, she did what he said. Bill walked in minutes later.

"Well, this is a surprise!" he said, nonetheless pleased when he saw her in his bed, naked.

"Jake told me to come in here and do whatever you wanted," she said. He started unbuckling his belt and unfastening his jeans but had second thoughts.

"Forget it," he said, and refastened his clothes. "I thought you came in here on your own when I first saw you. I'm not going to fuck you just because that damn Jake wants me to!"

"Get dressed," he said, and walked out. She was relieved. That wasn't the end of it, however. A few days later, Morgan ordered her to do the same thing, only this time she was to wait for Doug. Again she did as she was told out of fear. Doug wasn't as nice, however, and eagerly took advantage of the situation. When he got on top of her, she began crying. She tried to fight back her own tears, but not Doug. He was pissed. "Shut up!" he told her, and fiercely slapped her face several times. Only when he was sexually satisfied, did he leave. Carol finally realized that she had to get out of this situation, too. The next night, after the men had fallen asleep, she sneaked out the door and ran across the field and out onto the road. Then she realized that this was not a well thought-out plan. Alone on a deserted rural road in the middle of the night, miles from anywhere safe, the not-too-distant howling reminded her the barren fields were inhabited by coyotes as well as poisonous snakes, scorpions and other dangers. She decided she needed to flee at a more opportune time. She feared Morgan would discover that she had left and would come looking for her. She decided to slip back into the trailer and wait for a better chance to leave, perhaps when they were in town. When she walked in, Morgan was awake and waiting. "Where have you been?" he snapped.

"I just needed to get some fresh air, so I went outside

walking," she said, trying not to appear too nervous. He told her to get back to bed; then he raped her. That wasn't the end of it, though. The next morning, he was angry. "You tried to run away, didn't you?" he yelled.

"No, Jake, no!" she said, crying. He grabbed her hair and arm, shoved her onto the carpet and dragged her around, inflicting rug burns on her back and arm so severe she would be scarred permanently. "Don't you ever try that again!" he warned. He would not let her bandage the burns and they became infected, sticking to her clothes. Despite the painful wounds, he insisted she lie on her back during sex, the friction caused by his roughness aggravating her already deep sores.

Several weeks after arriving at the trailer of torment, the three men announced that they were returning to Surfside. She didn't know why but thought it might give her an opportunity to get away. Sitting in the backseat, she paid little attention to what the three talked about, trying to plan her escape. "Do you know why we're going to Surfside?" Morgan asked. "We're going to pick up some heroin. Have you ever had heroin, Carol?"

"No," she said truthfully.

"You'll like it," he said, not asking if she wanted it. "It will make you feel really good. I'll just put a little needle in your arm every day, and you'll never want to leave me again."

Normally, Carol was ready to try new things, but the stories she had heard about what it was like to be addicted to heroin had scared her and she never wanted to get anywhere near that. Now she couldn't risk waiting for an ideal moment to run away from Morgan; she would have to do it at the first opportunity or suffer an ever worsening fate. She kept quiet the rest of the trip, arriving at a twenty-four-hour restaurant on the pier at about 2:00 A.M., where they were to meet the men's drug contacts. She sat quietly as the men talked about their deal. Morgan gave her a small pill and told her to take it. She obeyed. A few minutes later, strung out on LSD, she slipped out of the restaurant and headed down the beach, stumbling on the sand.

That night, she was picked up by police. Even though she knew she would be in trouble for having run away and for being high on drugs, she was relieved, knowing she would be safe at least from Morgan. She spent the rest of the night in the Angleton jail. A Houston police officer from the juvenile division took her to another detention center where she passed the next week in solitary confinement, a few books for company. Her meals were slid through a slot at the bottom of the cell door. She had been gone for more than a month and already in detention when Mason O'Keiff first learned his daughter had run away. He called to speak with his children, talked with Gus and then asked to speak to Carol. Gus gave him a vague answer before finally telling him what had happened. Carol was released from detention and was placed in a Houston mental hospital for another month; in the meantime, her family wrestled with how to deal with her.

In early September 1970, at a loss as to how to reel in her wayward daughter, Margaret Johnson enrolled her daughter at The Brown Schools in Austin, a residential treatment center for children with emotional problems. Margaret wasn't happy about sending her young daughter away but believed she was better off away from the tense living environment and her mean stepfather. "She was so angry and she had a right to be," Margaret said. "He never said a nice word to her." Both of Margaret's children did not confide in her the problems they had with their stepfather until years later, but she hadn't been one to encourage them, either.

Initially, Carol was withdrawn at The Brown Schools, but when she began opening up, her counselors praised her candidness and ability to face her problems. Described as lonely, empty and "hypersensitive," she expected rejection, and feared close relationships, felt ignored by her father and rejected by her mother, and had a fragile self-image and deep feelings of unworthiness. She used drugs only twice during that time, marijuana once while living there and LSD once during an upsetting visit home. While her teachers and counselors described her as exceptionally flirtatious and easily distracted by the boys, her behavior became more age appropriate while there. Her nervous giggle had quieted somewhat, but it would stay with her throughout her life. Although she was not yet fourteen, her counselor wrote a telling paragraph that seemed true throughout her life, saying: ". . . as if she expects to meet her magic rescuer or white knight . . . when she finds out that people are not all that she expected them to be, Carol suffers disappointment, disillusionment, and depression. She probably denies the significance of her failures to find the ideal people as soon as she is over her last disappointment and continues to hope that truly wonderful people are just around the corner."

The biggest problem the school's staff saw for Carol was her family, both her parents and Pat Johnson. Neither her father nor stepfather seemed as willing to cooperate as the staff thought they should be, not calling or writing to her as they had been urged to do. Pat and Margaret Johnson, Gus and three of the four Johnson children, however, did travel the 150 miles to Austin for periodic family-therapy sessions.

On October 9, 1971, she left The Brown Schools a changed girl. Counselors noted that her time there had gone very smoothly, without the problems that had led her to be there in the first place. Her treatment had gone perhaps too smoothly, indicating the problem was within the home, a counselor noted. The blended

Johnson family would be the biggest factor in how well she did, the counselors concluded. Carol had learned a lot about her family dynamics but seemed less insightful into her own personality, a counselor wrote, noting that "her mother remained the one person in her life that she could become actively hostile with." For the two months previous to her release, she had been attending one of Austin's public high schools away from the Brown campus.

After being released from The Brown Schools, Carol's behavior did improve quite a bit, and she was notably less self-destructive. Other than smoking marijuana occasionally, she stopped using drugs. Margaret Johnson watched for signs that Carol might return to her previous self-destructive and problematic ways, but saw none. Still, her husband made no effort to make things any better for Carol.

As a child and an adult, Carol O'Keiff never felt secure in the strained relationships she had with her family, and she didn't think that they had any close ones with other people. Unconditional love? Carol didn't know what that felt like, but she kept looking.

Four

Shortly after leaving The Brown Schools, Carol met and casually dated Mark Olson. She soon developed a crush on his cute, older brother and often hung around the grocery store where Tommy Olson worked. After Mark and Carol broke up, Tommy asked his brother if he minded if he asked her out. He didn't, so Tommy, then nineteen, asked out the fifteen-year-old Carol in May 1972. Olson was trim and had sandy blond hair and a mustache; he also had a pointed nose and at six feet tall towered over the petite Carol. Soon they were exclusive and in love.

Carol lied to her mother, claiming Olson, who shared an apartment with a brother in Montrose, was a couple years younger than he actually was. That ruse ended when Margaret Johnson saw Olson bagging groceries in the middle of the day at Lewis and Coker Grocery Store. She asked him why he wasn't in school and he told her the truth. Margaret Johnson, who liked Olson, allowed the teenagers to continue dating. Unlike some of her daughter's previous boyfriends, Olson followed the Johnsons' rules, had Carol home by her curfew and did not try sneaking her out of the house at night. Olson found the rules set by the Johnsons, however, more lenient than those that other girls he dated had to abide by. A few times, though, he sneaked into the house and spent the night with Carol in her bed, leaving at about 4:30 A.M., before anyone else got up. One time, they overslept and when they awoke, the house was busy as the large Johnson family was getting ready for the day. Olson escaped out the bathroom window, across the roof and dropped to the ground, only to find the maid coming to work. She didn't rat on the young lovers.

Olson knew about his young girlfriend's unusually wild past, but it didn't bother him. He felt protective of her, like her rescuer, and she did not seem wild or promiscuous by the time they met. "She was pretty and I guess since I was older, she looked up to me. She was a lot of fun and easy to get along with," he recalled. And perhaps because she was younger, he said, "she pretty much agreed with everything I wanted to do."

Olson had every Tuesday off from work, and Carol often skipped classes to spend the day with him. "The next day, I'd write myself an excuse. Every Tuesday I was sick. They didn't give me any trouble about it," she recalled.

In the summer, Carol became pregnant. The young couple thought she should have an abortion and Olson took her to Planned Parenthood on his motorcycle. On the way there, the bike slipped on some oil on the street, tipping them over. Neither one was hurt, but the accident added to the anxiety. Abortions weren't legal in Texas at the time but were available under certain conditions in other states, and the counselor at Planned Parenthood said the organization could help arrange it. After she got home, Carol turned to her stepfather for advice on how to tell her mother. "I went to Pat first because I knew he didn't care about me," she said. She didn't want her boyfriend with her, because she feared her stepfather might hit him. Johnson was calm, telling Carol, "You just have to get yourself together and do it."

With Olson at her side, she told Margaret that she was pregnant. Margaret cried a little but agreed that an abortion would be best. Olson said he would pay for it.

"You can't afford it," Johnson told him. "Don't worry about it." Within a week, Margaret and Carol flew to Los Angeles for an abortion. Olson felt terrible that his girlfriend had to go through so much. Margaret insisted that Carol take birth-control pills but allowed the two to continue dating. Pat Johnson, though, had had enough of his stepdaughter's problems and angrily told his wife and Carol that—one way or another—she could not live in his house anymore. She either had to go to a foster home or get married.

Carol felt rejected again, even though she was confident that her boyfriend would marry her. She was in love with him and they already had talked about getting married in the future. Many years later, Olson was not sure how the idea for him and Carol to marry at that time first came up. "Seems like the idea was put in my head by her mom," he recalled. Olson could not afford to support a wife and said so.

"Don't worry about that, Carol has a big trust fund," Margaret Johnson told him, assuring him that they could live off that. She told him that as part of her divorce settlement with Mason, she had gotten a quarter of a million dollars for each of her children, which was in a trust fund. By then, the fund had gained another $100,000 in interest, meaning Carol had $350,000, he recalled Margaret telling him.

Olson didn't care about the trust fund and did want to marry Carol—but in the future when *they* felt they were ready. He thought it was strange that Carol's mother was pushing her into marriage at such a young age—and using her money as a potential motivator—

but he knew how bad her home life was. He did not care much for Pat Johnson, although the two always were congenial with one another. "He tried to run his family like a submarine. He was pretty weird," Olson said. Although he thought Margaret seemed to look at Carol's presence in her home as a burden, she made him feel special. "Her mom almost romanced me into the marriage—she took to me that well," he reflected later. His own father never encouraged him much and his mother just went along with whatever her husband said, so he liked the admiring attention he got from Margaret. He was pleased that his girlfriend's mother was so enamored with him. He felt the same about her. "I thought she was a pretty cool mom," he said. Olson, twenty, knew his young girlfriend needed him, so he eventually agreed to marry her. And once he had decided, he felt completely committed to the idea, believing their marriage would last a lifetime, like his grandparents' sixty-five-year union. His parents worried about whether he could support a wife and did not expect that it would last, but they did not tell him their fears until later. On November 17, the two got their required medical exams and four days later, their marriage license. Margaret gave consent for her minor daughter to marry but told her intended son-in-law, "If y'all ever get a divorce, I'm keeping you." Although he didn't have much money, Olson paid for the rehearsal dinner.

On December 1, 1972, at 7:30 P.M., Carol, two days shy of her sixteenth birthday, took what would be her first of many trips down the aisle. Clutching a small nosegay of pink azaleas, she looked beautiful in the high-collared, long-sleeved ivory wedding gown and fingertip length lace veil as she vowed to love Thomas David Olson for life. Her mother had chosen a Methodist church for the ceremony, even though Margaret attended a Catholic church with her husband and Olson was Episcopalian. The elegant, catered reception for more than one hundred people was held at the Johnsons' large, ritzy home. Pat Johnson invited numerous influential people, many of whom handed Olson cash—sometimes as much as $100—even though they also gave wedding gifts.

After spending their wedding night at the Hyatt Regency in downtown Houston, the couple flew to Acapulco for a seven-day honeymoon at the Hyatt there, all compliments of Mason O'Keiff, who included $700 cash when he handed the newlyweds their plane tickets. He also presented his daughter with her first string of pearls.

When they returned, the bride moved into her groom's small one-bedroom apartment. Carol was happy; her life was much better than it had been under her stepfather's roof. To Olson, it seemed that both Mason O'Keiff and Margaret Johnson had the attitude: "You're raising my daughter—good." Because he saw Carol off to high school each day, Olson sometimes felt like he was raising his wife. Neither ever considered, however, that she would drop out. Her husband often picked her up from school in his black Valiant station wagon, which her friends dubbed "the roach." Although her friends were busy dating, Carol was happy to be settling down.

Their young marriage started off happy, but when they argued, Olson thought Carol too often took it to the extreme. She became excessively argumentative, screaming and throwing stuff, like kitchen plates. At those times, he felt it was impossible to reason with her. Soon he began to wonder if she had a hormonal problem.

Although Olson knew otherwise, his wife did not seem to have a lot of sexual experience or seem very comfortable with sex. After they had made love, Carol sometimes jumped up and exclaimed, "This is gross," referring to the bodily fluids, and ran into the bathroom to clean up. "This isn't very romantic," Olson thought, but knew she had enjoyed their lovemaking in the past. At that time, Carol was not particularly adventurous and did not suggest anything kinky, Olson recalled, but he admitted, "I wasn't that creative back then."

One evening, though, he did propose a new sexual adventure. One of his best friends, Mike Langley, had been urging him to swap wives. Langley had had few sexual experiences before he married and later tried to make up for some of that, hitting on women when he was out with his buddies and doing what he could to get women other than his wife into bed, according to Olson. Eventually, Olson approached his young wife with the idea. Swearing he didn't care anything about Marie Langley, he suggested they should try it. Carol was reluctant when the subject was raised and was hurt that her husband even considered such an idea. She felt betrayed that he wanted to do it, and it also seemed to her that Marie had mixed emotions about the proposal, even though she said she wanted to do it. *Bob & Carol & Ted & Alice,* a movie about swapping wives, was popular at the time and the others referred to it when trying to talk Carol into it. "The movie was OK, but I didn't like the idea of doing it. I was jealous. I didn't want to think of my husband in the next bedroom with another woman," Carol said. Nor did she feel the least bit of attraction for Langley, who was slightly built and even shorter than the petite Carol. After the three pitched the idea on several different occasions, Carol relented and agreed to try it one night in the Olsons' apartment.

The couples swapped mates. Carol and Mike headed

to the bedroom while Tommy and Marie stayed in the living room. "It was like going to bed with Napoleon, except he wasn't as well built and he had no charm whatsoever," Carol recalled later. "It wasn't like they brought Tom Selleck in. Mike was a little weasel."

Hours later, the couples met back in the living room and the Langleys went home. The Olsons didn't talk about their experiences afterward—or ever. Had they, their relationship might have been spared some serious trouble. Years later, they both admitted that they had not had intercourse with their evening partners but assumed that their spouse had. Carol said she and Langley had not had intercourse because he had failed to get an erection. She thought it was because he had had too much to drink, but Mike blamed her for his problem, calling her "a cold fish." Carol had been so upset about the situation that, when she got in the bedroom with Mike, she stripped off her own clothes, got into bed "and just laid there, like, hurry up and get it over with."

Out in the living room, Olson said he and Marie agreed that: "this is stupid." They decided it was not something either of them really wanted to do, so they sat and talked instead. He regretted getting himself and Carol into the situation, feeling his friend had manipulated him. As for what he thought Carol was doing, Olson said, "It bothered me, but it bothered me more that I let it happen. I shouldn't have let it get that far." The awkward situation ended the friendship between the two couples and spawned tensions between Tommy and Carol, who continued to feel betrayed and began withdrawing from her husband. She was incredibly hurt by the episode and blamed it for the downfall of her young marriage. Afterward, Carol became paranoid that her husband was cheating on her behind her back and accused him of being with other women. Olson swore he had never cheated on her, either when they were married or dating.

The newlyweds soon moved to another apartment in Memorial so Carol could be closer to school. Right away, Olson thought the move had been a mistake because her friends ended up hanging out there after classes. Olson got a job with the Houston Fire Department in January 1974, graduating from fire school three months later. Like most firefighters, his work schedule was unusual: he worked three ten-hour days followed by three fourteen-hour night shifts and then had three days off. Carol planned on going to college but did not care that her husband's interests lay elsewhere. She was pleased with his career choice and tried to be supportive. Sometimes she baked a large lasagna and took it to the station house for her husband and his coworkers. In order to spend time with him, she joined him in his favorite activities, camping and fishing. Olson, a hunter and gun collector, also taught his wife to target shoot.

The Olsons bought a 2,054-square-foot three-bedroom house near Memorial, using Carol's trust fund, which Olson was against. He said he wanted to use it as collateral or some of her money as a down payment, but he was working and wanted to make the monthly payments on his own. The bank turned down that arrangement but allowed it to be purchased out of her trust fund, he said. Olson used his money and muscle to remodel the house, including replacing the roof and driveway. He had never done carpentry before but found he enjoyed it a great deal.

Carol often talked in her sleep, sometimes with her eyes open. Olson had fun with it, asking her questions, which she would answer even if they were nonsense.

"Did you feed the horses tonight?" he would ask her, even though they didn't have any. Nevertheless, Carol promised that she had. One time, though, she scared him. Sitting up in bed, she practically yelled, "Who are you? Get out of here!" Olson immediately lurched for his nightstand and grabbed his pistol from the drawer. Carol lay back down, still asleep. Even so, he got up and, clutching his gun, checked the house to be sure his wife had just imagined it. She had, but it took Olson the rest of the night to calm down and go back to sleep. The next morning, she remembered nothing about it.

Despite a bigger and better house, the couple's discord thrived. Carol threatened Olson with divorce several times during arguments. She didn't follow through on those threats, but her husband tired of them.

Margaret and Pat Johnson divorced in November 1975, and she changed her name back to Margaret O'Keiff.

Mason and Judy O'Keiff had separated on February 23, 1974, and he filed for divorce on March 8. In divorce papers, Judy said she hoped for a reconciliation but that her husband had abandoned her. The judge ordered Mason to pay his wife $3,250 a month during the separation, a hefty sum in 1974.

The Olsons only saw Mason O'Keiff a few times a year, even though he lived nearby. He wasn't someone they could drop by and visit or even call on the phone for a chat. Their visits were more reserved, and to Olson, it seemed more like they were visiting older friends or an aunt and uncle than his wife's father. Everything about the visits was impersonal, and O'Keiff didn't ask his daughter much about her life. He was generous, however. From her trust, Carol got a new 1974 Volkswagen Beetle. Olson bought himself a 1974 Chevy.

Things at home did not grow happier, though. One day, Olson returned from work and Carol greeted him by saying that she wanted a divorce. There was no argument. Weary, he simply said, "Fine." He thought that by agreeing to it, he would keep her from throwing it up every few months. That time, she did follow through. She filed for divorce on February 11, 1975, and Olson was served with divorce papers a short time later. Deep down, he believed that once his wife saw the finality of divorce, she would change her mind.

He moved out of the house and they spoke very little. Despite the work and money he had put into the house—remodeling the inside, laying a new driveway and putting on a new roof—it had been bought with Carol's money and she got the house. His mother-in-law gave him a check for $5,000, which he used to buy a lot in Conroe, a wooded community thirty-nine miles north of Houston, on which he eventually built his own house. The $5,000 was far less than he had put into the house he had shared with Carol, but he appreciated Margaret's generosity. He had never cared about his wife's trust fund and never considered making a claim on it. In the retrospect of a difficult life, Carol and her family agreed that Olson was a good guy and the best of her many husbands, a choice she had made at age fifteen. Nice guys, however, bored Carol.

Their divorce was final April 14, 1975, and for a long time, Olson was in disbelief that his marriage ended. Unlike his ex's family, his was the first divorce for the Olson clan. When friends asked what happened, he answered honestly, "I don't know. You'll have to ask Carol." He was heartbroken for two years. Later, he realized their divorce had been inevitable; they were so young when they married and they had different goals.

Each would recall the final reasons that led to their breakup differently. Carol felt pressured to start a family and balked at the idea: "I didn't want to be barefoot in the kitchen yet; I was too young for that." Her aspirations were of college and partying and she did not see kids in her near future. She felt that her husband was less than supportive of her goals. "She just wanted to have a career and no kids," he recalled, but said he had not been ready to have a family that early, either, but believed she never wanted children.

Although Margaret had feared that her intelligent daughter would drop out after she got married, Carol O'Keiff graduated from Memorial High School in 1975. She had gone back to using her maiden name. Despite the lack of religion in her own life, Carol enrolled at the University of St. Thomas, a small Catholic college in an artsy section of Houston. Her father had established a small college fund for her, which, along with some of the original trust, enabled her to pay the private tuition and expenses without having to worry about working her way through school. She sold her house, just breaking even on the deal, and moved into a one-bedroom apartment closer to campus, optimistically looking forward to the rest of her life. She chose UST because she believed it offered the best nursing school in the Southwest, but theological and philosophical courses were a required part of the curriculum. It was the first time she ever opened a Bible, sparking a new interest for her. She began praying off and on for the first time in her life by her own choice.

Carol quickly made new friends at UST and was happy to run into Kathy Wells, who had been her best friend for many of Carol's wildest years in junior and senior high. It had been Wells who had taken Carol food when she had run away from home and slept in the woods, and now both were going into nursing school together. Wells had her own problems, though. She suffered from hyperthyroidism, was tall, overweight and didn't get asked out by guys—the opposite of Carol.

One night during their freshman year, Wells asked Carol to go out partying, but Carol was sick and declined. Carol called her the next day, but it was too late. Wells's brother told her that Kathy had killed herself with a rifle to the chest. Carol thought he was playing a sick joke, yelled "Bastard!" and slammed down the phone. He wasn't kidding, and Carol was not only devastated but shocked. "We saw each other every day, and I didn't pick up on this," Carol said. Wells had not left a letter and her friend watched the agony her best friend's family was forced to deal with. Carol had trouble understanding what her friend had done; she, too, had had a difficult life, but she had never considered that route. Carol always believed better times were ahead for her.

Mason O'Keiff obviously didn't give up, either, marrying his third wife, Ann Gardner Farris, that spring. She was thirty-three; he was forty-six. Unlike her former stepmother, Ann seemed to appreciate everything her father did for her. And she seemed to have a genuine interest in Carol. She would ask Carol about her latest boyfriend and the two sometimes hung out together without Mason O'Keiff, going shopping and just generally having a good time as girlfriends. And her second stepmother was generous, offering Carol her designer hand-me-downs. She thought her father seemed happier.

Carol was happy, too, in college. She dated her anatomy professor, about ten years her senior. Recently divorced, he was a nice guy but not much of a partyer, as Carol was becoming once again. She was looking for a little more excitement but found more than even she wanted with her next boyfriend, Steve Peters, whom she met through a mutual friend. He soon turned angry and violent but, starting a pattern that would haunt her the rest of her life, she forgave him. After one argument, he spat in her face. They made up and she continued seeing him until she really got hurt. When she returned from visiting her father in Santa Fe, New Mexico, carrying a gift for Peters, her boyfriend became convinced she had been seeing another man while away. He became extremely irrational and, while standing at the top of a fire escape, kicked her, breaking a couple of her ribs, which, in turn, led to a bout of pneumonia. That was it—finally, she broke up with him.

Her father's marriage also was rough. After moving to Santa Fe, New Mexico, Ann told Carol that Mason was changing, becoming reclusive, being mean and generally acting like he no longer even liked her. She had no idea why. Carol confided to Ann, "I think he had done that with my mother, too." She had always believed that her mother's nagging and yelling contributed to the deterioration of the marriage, but Ann was mild and Carol was sad for all of them when that marriage ended. She loved Ann and didn't want her father to lose someone who had been so good for him. Carol never talked to her father about that breakup. "I always felt like my relationship with my father has barely been there, and I was always afraid to do anything to hurt it," she said. Eventually, Mason once again became more distant from her; sometimes Carol didn't hear from her father for years at a time. Neither was angry; that's just the way it was.

Carol began hanging out with another friend from her junior and senior high, one she had left behind with the drugs they had done together before Carol had gone to The Brown Schools. Sharon Jennings wasn't an especially close friend, but she was fun. Some of her friends urged Carol to try cocaine for the first time. Carol had heard it was popular for the good feelings it produced, and since it was a nonhallucinogenic, she figured, "Why not?" She snorted it and loved it. One of the men there, Ed Hankes, flirted with her. He said he was thirty-six—twice her age—but she later believed he was really forty-two. According to Carol, a few days later, Jennings called: "Come back over, we have more coke." Carol was ready for more but was surprised to find that the others already there were injecting it this time. More accurately, Hankes was shooting up everybody. Carol watched for a while and everyone seemed to be fine, enjoying their highs, so she again decided to go along and allowed him to shoot her up as well. She began dating Hankes, who she believed was an electrician and drug dealer who claimed to have done some amateur boxing. When Carol told him what her last boyfriend had done to her, he offered to teach him a lesson. "Go for it," Carol told him. Carol remembers Hankes later told her he had beaten Peters unconscious with a chain.

Carol quickly got hooked on cocaine and was going to classes and taking tests while high. She thought she was doing well until she got her grades. She failed four of her six classes and dropped out of college.

That summer, she and Hankes headed north. He had a large cocaine deal arranged at a dockside warehouse in Hampton Beach, New Hampshire. One of the men Hankes regularly did business with owned a traveling carnival and offered the couple jobs. They thought it would be a fun change of pace, so they signed on. Just before they left Houston, Carol got a tattoo of a heart with a rose through it like an arrow and Hankes's initials on her abdomen, just above her right hip. In the carnival, Carol ran the high striker, a contraption where people tested their strength by slamming a sledge hammer onto a platform, causing a large puck to rise up a pole and, hopefully, ring the bell at the top. Hankes watched over the gambling machines, trying to make sure no one was trying to cheat. In their months with the carnival, they traveled around the northeastern states and into Canada. Carol said she tired of it after the summer, although her mother said she had stayed much longer.

Back in Houston, Carol reenrolled at the University of St. Thomas, determined to do better and work her way toward a nursing career. On the weekends, she went to Houston Community College to make up some classes. In January 1977, Carol, still a sophomore in college, bought her second house. This one was smaller than the one she shared with Olson, having just two bedrooms and 1,534 square feet. Built in 1935, it needed some fixing up. The house, on Teetshorn in the Heights, one of the city's oldest neighborhoods, was affordable at less than $60,000. Paid for mostly with her trust fund, she had a monthly mortgage of only $114 a month.

It was here that Carol witnessed the painful effects of suicide for the second time, less than a year after Wells's death. Although she wasn't particularly close with them, she watched a neighbor couple, now in their sixties, struggle to deal with the aftermath of their only child's suicide. The couple seemed in constant emotional pain, fighting often. The husband ended his grief by compounding his wife's—putting a shotgun inside his mouth, pulling the trigger and killing himself. Carol saw his body from across the street and thought he had fallen. Rushing to help, she discovered the grisly scene. Although a nursing student, she wasn't prepared to see her neighbor's head blown apart, pieces of his brain stuck to the screen door.

That wasn't the only unnerving encounter around her house. Carol was keeping her promise to herself to focus more on studying and less on cocaine. She still used it, just less often. She frequently accompanied her boyfriend on drug deals, and Hankes spent a lot of time at her place. Sometimes men sat in cars near the house, seeming to watch their comings and goings, scaring her. Hankes would only say that he was having problems with customers or "workers." Planning a drug deal with the owner of one of Houston's totally nude clubs, Hankes wanted his girlfriend to dance there, believing she could help him get useful information for his dealings. Although she was reluctant, Carol eventually was convinced to do it. No alcohol was served in the club but plenty of sexual favors were doled out in adjacent rooms. Carol refused to do that kind of work. Still, she was humiliated by dancing nude in front of the customers and quit after a week.

Although she religiously used a diaphragm, she found herself pregnant again. Shocked, she held the rubber cap up to the light and saw tiny dots of light shining through. She suspected her boyfriend had poked it with a pin but couldn't be sure. She couldn't see a future with this man—at least not one she wanted any part of—so she had an abortion. Fed up with the life Hankes was drawing her into, she broke up with him—and the cocaine—a short time later. Hankes asked her to marry him and she considered it but ultimately refused, seeing that his lifestyle was causing too many problems for her. He cried but left that day.

She knew she could take care of herself and never stopped planning for her future. Once again using her trust fund, she invested in some rental property—a duplex, also in the Heights, that had a third apartment over the detached garage. She now owned two properties and two cars, her Volkswagen and a 1977 Volvo. Not bad for a twenty-one-year-old college student.

Five

Carol would not be single for long. An older friend, Joe Jackson, asked her to join him on a trip to New Orleans, where he was picking up his brother. Never having been to the Big Easy, she quickly agreed. As impressed as she was with the city, she was more taken with the good-looking brother, John Jackson, nearly ten years her senior. He had a well-built frame from his physically demanding job as a roughneck on an oil rig, and at six feet three inches, he was a full foot taller than the petite redhead, with whom he was equally taken. Brown-haired John Jackson, who had graduated from the University of St. Thomas years earlier, was moving back to Houston. He planned on staying with a mutual friend, but when that didn't work out, Carol offered to let him sleep on her couch for a few days. Things developed quickly and he moved into her bedroom a short time later and never looked for his own place.

Jackson was the youngest of four children of a wealthy and prominent Houston family, a clan that likely had a bank account to match Carol's father's. His mother was an operating-room nurse and the family lived in upscale Memorial. His uncle, John D. Jackson, for whom he was named, was a doctor and well-known philanthropist. A recreation center and numerous classrooms were named in his honor at the University of St. Thomas, where he also served on the board of directors. His family also was active with the popular Houston Livestock and Rodeo, the elder John Jackson serving as a lifetime vice president of the celebrated event, and Carol's boyfriend enjoyed working odd jobs there and riding a horse in the much-ballyhooed parade. One of the largest rodeos in the country, it roped in Houston's social elite and average Joes alike. Margaret O'Keiff, who had read about the Jacksons in the local papers, was duly impressed by the family's prominent standing. She liked John Jackson immediately; he was charming and seemed to care about her daughter.

A sergeant and a tank commander in the Vietnam War, Jackson, like so many of his comrades, had problems, many apparently spurred by the bad memories of the brutal war. "He would tell me about kids jumping on the tanks and he'd have to shoot them off the tank because sometimes the kids would throw grenades. He had a real hard time with it," Carol recalled. His tank ran over a mine, killing everyone else inside and making him deaf in one ear. Jackson did not want to talk about most of what had happened, just calling it "a bad war."

The two spent a lot of time camping and often enjoyed weekends alone at his family's rustic house, which was set on about 200 acres in rural Bonney, about forty-two miles south of town. One of Jackson's ancestors had built the house in the early 1900s, and although the family eventually added electricity, they still had not upgraded to indoor plumbing. Jackson took a bath in a claw-footed tub in the front yard. Carol did so, too, her loving boyfriend pulling buckets of water from the backyard well, heating it on the wood-burning stove and filling the tub for her. She enjoyed bathing beneath the sun, relaxing in the warm water and air. This practice irritated Carol's prim and proper mother, who always saw her daughter as "the perfect hippie." One afternoon as Carol bathed, she noticed prisoners from the adjacent Ramsey Unit, a minimum-security state prison, staring over the fence at her. That was her last front-yard bath.

After a while, their relationship soured and they broke up. He moved to Monroe, Louisiana, to work as a troubleshooter on offshore oil rigs in the Gulf of Mexico. Eventually, the two got back together and had a long-distance relationship for a short time, although Carol was aware he had another girlfriend as well. Jackson hated Louisiana and returned to Houston a few months later, this time living with his parents. The couple partied a lot and when Jackson proposed, Carol eagerly accepted. This time, her path to the altar would be more traditional and they planned a large celebration for the following August and lived apart until then. As they happily planned their nuptials, the Jackson family was hit by tragedy when his mother, to whom he was very close, died unexpectedly from a stroke.

Shortly before their big day, Jackson and Carol wanted to call off the wedding, fearing they weren't quite ready. No, her mother insisted, it was too late. The invitations were out. "Get married. If it doesn't work, get a divorce," her mother advised. The betrothed talked it over and decided they probably just had the typical jitters and so plunged ahead with their lavish wedding plans, funded primarily out of Carol's trust fund. They always had so much fun together and they truly did love one another. As scheduled, they got their medical exams and then their marriage license.

On August 13, 1978, a day drenched with the intense heat and inescapable humidity of a Houston summer, the two exchanged vows in an outdoor ceremony in a gazebo at Vargo's Restaurant, famed for its romantic parklike grounds lush with azalea bushes, winding walking paths, rolling stream, swan-decorated lake and strolling peacocks. Wearing a sundress-style white gown and floppy-rimmed hat touched with colored roses, Carol looked like a Southern belle as her father walked her down the lush garden path that served as her aisle. Jackson slipped a plain gold wedding band next to her small diamond solitaire engagement ring, and District Judge Henry G. Schuble pronounced them husband and wife.

As he had six years earlier, Mason O'Keiff gave his daughter and her groom a honeymoon trip to Mexico, this time to Cozumel. Ever the partyer, John Jackson had a few too many drinks on the three-hour flight and walked off the plane carrying a drink. Their first night in Cozumel began as it should but ended disastrously. They took a moonlit stroll on the beach, holding hands. They both had drunk too much at dinner, and after they returned to their room, Jackson spun into an angry depression. He ran naked onto the eighth-floor balcony of their hotel, screaming, "I want to die! I want to die!" Carol tried to pull her husband back into the room, but he pushed her away and then tore up their room in a rage, knocking over furniture, lamps and anything he could get his hands on. She barricaded herself behind a table, and even after Jackson had calmed down, she stayed there, sleeping alone beneath a blanket she had pulled off the bed, where he eventually had passed out.

When Jackson awoke the next morning, she said, he remembered none of it. She filled him in and he apologized. Although she tried to forgive him, she remained stung. How could the man she loved so deeply, and who had just a day earlier pledged to spend the rest of his life loving her, be so unhappy that he wanted to die?

The rest of the honeymoon went smoothly; while her husband did get drunk, he didn't lose control or do anything else to upset Carol, but it was an omen of heartache to come.

Gus O'Keiff married less than five months later, and he and his wife, Lynne, lived in the Heights, less than two blocks from the Jacksons, and the couples saw each other regularly. Lynne always felt that she could save, or at least help, Gus or Carol by loving them in a way that would make up for what they didn't get as children. For Gus, the marriage helped him even though it eventually ended in divorce. "The first marriage is probably what chilled me out more than anything," he said. Lynne thought her mother-in-law was classy and generous, buying the newlyweds things they needed but couldn't yet afford and sending money to a couple of relatives, who were not as well off as she. Every week, she cooked Sunday dinner for the young couple and made it a point to include Lynne's family in gatherings and dinners. And the newest member of the O'Keiff family really liked her fun and entertaining sister-in-law. "You could never be in a room with Carol without laughing. She laughed at life," she said. Gus had really liked Olson; he wasn't as crazy about Jackson. Where Gus was cerebral, Jackson was more macho and gruff and into partying.

Jackson's drinking continued, and he again flew into periodic rages and frequently had blackouts where he would remember nothing of what he had done. Carol estimated he drank as much as a fifth of gin—straight—a day. Sometimes Carol had to call brother-in-law Joe for help. He always came, often taking John back to his own house to sleep off his latest bout. Occasionally, one of them bailed John out of jail when he was arrested for drunk driving.

"His alcoholism took over everything. He was so disruptive," she said.

Margaret O'Keiff began to be troubled by other

things she saw going on in her daughter's marriage. Her son-in-law always seemed to have an excuse for why he did not have a job. When he did get a job, it usually did not last longer than six months.

But there were fun times for the couple, too, even with the drinking. They frequented dances and society balls, although Carol drank very little once she found out she was pregnant about two months after their wedding. Carol's pregnancy perplexed O'Keiff, who cringed at the thought of being called "Grandma" at such an early age. She joked the child would have to call her Mrs. O'Keiff but eventually settled on GrandMarg. (Her boyfriend and next husband, Dan Edwards, would be dubbed "GrandDan.") GrandMarg-to-be took Carol on a baby-supply shopping spree, treating her to all the necessities and frills—complete nursery, stroller and decorations.

The Jacksons' son was born on July 29, 1979, six days after John's thirty-second birthday, and named Joseph Roland after John's brother. His birth rated a mention in the newspaper's society gossip column, more because of his noted greatuncle than his parents. His paternal grandparents gave the baby $2,000 in stocks. Although O'Keiff wasn't any more of a hands-on grandmother than she had been a mother, she was a good, doting grandmother in her own way. She always seemed interested in what Joe was learning and doing and was amused by his childish ways. If her daughter was in another room, she'd always call her in to make sure she wouldn't miss a moment of her son's latest antics or expressions.

While fatherhood didn't sober up Jackson, motherhood forced Carol to do something about it. She got angry when her husband wanted to take the baby on a drive, even though he was clearly drunk, and they frequently argued. She and the baby often stayed at her mother's just to get away from her husband. When she returned home the next day, Carol sometimes found lamps and other things knocked over. Highly skilled, Jackson was then a troubleshooter who fixed problems on oil rigs; he didn't have to spend long stretches living on rigs like the roughnecks but had the opportunity of earning big bucks. Because of his drinking, Jackson went through a series of jobs, barely contributing to the family's financial support. She thought he was cheating on her and a couple of times feared that he was about to hit her, although he never did. "He came after me, but he was always so drunk he'd stumble or something," she said. He chased her up the stairs one day, and afraid of being hurt by her much bigger husband, Carol grabbed a metal ice chest sitting at the top and threw it at him, striking him in the head. He wasn't seriously hurt and he never went after her again. Worse, Carol was afraid he might accidentally hurt their son, although she knew he would never do so intentionally— no matter how drunk he got, he wasn't that kind of person. She fought to keep her son out of Jackson's car when he had been drinking, but she couldn't keep him from picking up Joe when he was stumbling around the house from too much alcohol.

Carol eventually grew tired of Jackson's problems and threw him out of her house on October 11, 1979, threatening to put his belongings on the lawn if he didn't get them out by the weekend. He did. She blamed his drinking for the death of their marriage. When Carol told her mother she was getting another divorce, O'Keiff was disappointed but realized how bad her son-in-law's drinking had become and tried to be supportive of her daughter.

On April 10, 1980, at the age of twenty-three, Carol was divorced for the second time. She kept the name Jackson to be in sync with her son. She was made managing conservator of Joe. Based on his income of just

$4,300 in the previous year, Jackson was ordered to pay $100 a month in child support, which he always paid. Jackson moved into a garage apartment near Meyerland, which he lovingly furnished with a baby bed and items for his infant son. He made a point of staying involved in Joe's life, not limiting their time to just the court-ordered every-other-weekend visits, and Carol was glad. Despite the divorce, which was congenial, the two stayed friends and Carol believed he made a real effort to stay sober when he was solely responsible for Joe.

Mason O'Keiff encouraged his daughter, who was doing well in nursing school, to go to medical school, offering her the money to do it. She had the grades to make it into medical school, but she knew she wouldn't have the support of her family that would allow her to raise a toddler, study and work long hours at the hospital. She desperately wanted to go, but after some serious consideration, she couldn't imagine making it through a grueling eight years as a single mother and regretfully refused her father's offer. She stuck with her original plans to become a nurse. "I didn't see any more husbands down the road—little did I know," she said.

Six

Sam Tilson always would remain a mystery to Carol.

Still saddened by her recent divorce, Carol met him shortly before Christmas, 1980, when she went to Royal Coins, one of Houston's many pawnshops, looking to buy a Krugerrand for her mother. She spent time looking at the coins and the other items for sale in the shop, casually talking with the handsome salesman with brown eyes and wavy dark hair, slightly graying at the temples. When she turned to leave, he asked for her phone number, and she gladly gave it to him. They talked a few times on the phone before he asked her to dinner—her first date since her divorce eight months earlier. She agreed but was surprised when he picked her up in a brand-new Mercedes Coupe limited edition.

They had a pleasant dinner at The Stables, a nice steakhouse but not one of the many exclusive restaurants found across the city—those came later. Charming and gentlemanly, he wasn't the least bit pushy. Eloquent and obviously well-read, he was intelligent and knew excellent wines, but she never knew if he went to college or where he learned about the finer things in life. Besides being good-looking, with a well-built five-foot-ten body obviously used to exercise, he was romantic, sending her cards and buying her gifts for no apparent reason. About a month into their relationship, they made love for the first time. They took weekend trips to Austin, staying at nice hotels overlooking the Colorado River. Soon the gifts became more and more lavish and expensive—a gold coin necklace was followed a short time later with a diamond encasement for it; an unset half-karat diamond and gold chains arrived as well. He liked Pouilly-Fuissé wine and brought Carol an entire case of it one evening. "He treated me like a queen. It was a new experience for me," she recalled. He enjoyed walking around the mall, especially the Galleria with its large collection of upscale shops. As they passed a jewelry store one evening in the Sharpstown Mall, he told her to wait outside for him. When he returned, he presented her with a lady's oyster-perpetual Rolex watch, the most extravagant gift he had given her yet.

"Oh, my God!" Carol exclaimed when she opened the velvet box. "It's gorgeous! But, Sam, I can't accept this," she said, tearing her eyes from the stunning watch to his deep dark eyes.

They argued back and forth about it for a few minutes, before Carol finally gave in, wearing the watch home. Still, she wondered how he could afford such lavish gifts, high-priced cars and expensive dinners on the salary of a pawnshop salesman. Although she would never receive a complete answer to that, he dealt her tantalizing clues. While running errands together one day, he stopped at a downtown Houston bank. As he was getting out of the car he turned to her and said, "Come on in, I want to show you something." More curious when the banker pulled one of the larger drawers from the vault and escorted them into a private viewing room, she was amazed with what she saw inside—a large amount of cash, some of it in obviously collectible coins. He said simply that he was a collector, but that didn't explain the bills that were locked away instead of earning interest. To explain his apparent wealth, Tilson claimed that he closely watched the stock market and traded often. After that first visit, Tilson regularly took Carol to the safety-deposit box, mostly to place more items inside. During another visit, he unrolled a dark jeweler's cloth, revealing a breathtaking collection of about thirty loose diamonds, which Carol quietly estimated were between a quarter and one karat, all of them clearly of exquisite cuts, clarity and color.

Carol told her mother about the safety-deposit box. "That sounds shady to me," her mother replied. She wasn't too thrilled with some of the other mysterious things she was hearing about her daughter's latest boyfriend, but she believed that "Carol enjoyed the dangerous element."

Tilson seemed to like little Joe and even was thoughtful enough to bring him little presents, a toy football or bubbles blower, nothing too extravagant, and would sit on the floor and play with him. Joe seemed happy to see Tilson, although he wouldn't run to him when he visited. They were friendly with each other but not affectionate.

Periodically, Tilson would go away for short periods of time, refusing to tell her where he was going or what he was doing. Invariably when he returned, they would make another trip to the safety-deposit box to store something else—she often didn't know what. "Just don't ask me," he would say.

Whenever Carol suggested going out with her friends or having him meet her mother, he always declined, saying he wanted them to be alone, so she stopped asking.

Eventually, he took her to his modern, expensively decorated town house, where everything was top of the line. He showed her his arsenal—.357's, .45's, .44's and a variety of rifles and attachments. Most of the guns were high-powered and he had several infrared scopes and an accompaniment of ammunition. Occasionally, he would playfully rest the red beam of a laser scope between her eyes. He never did this out of anger and Carol was not scared by these demonstrations. These were not the collection of a hunter, at least not of animals. He wasn't into hunting animals as many Texans are, but he did boast of being a sniper during the Vietnam War. Although Carol had no way of knowing whether or not it was true, he told her he wasn't the kind of wartime sniper who shot any one of the enemy indiscriminately. He was assigned to pick off specific people, he told her, and bragged again about how accurate he was.

During these conversations, Carol thought that Tilson was alluding to being a hit man. He would talk about how he could pick someone off without leaving any traces and how he would get his target each time. Carol was never sure if he was talking about the present or his past in the war. Perhaps to prove his keen precision, he sometimes took Carol target shooting, so she could watch what he was capable of. However, he never let her take a shot, saying, "The gun's too powerful. You might hurt yourself."

She was convinced that he could come and go without leaving any traces, as he eventually proved by repeatedly getting into her locked house. He also refused to ever let her take a picture of him. Despite the valuables he often returned with, Carol never believed he was robbing people or burglarizing businesses. She imagined the trinkets were payments for hits.

The arsenal and stash of jewelry didn't add up to someone who played the market. So Carol asked again what he did. This time, he snapped, "It's none of your business." And that remained his answer whenever she asked, despite how close they seemed to be getting.

Margaret O'Keiff advised her daughter: "Carol, you better find out what this man does." To her mother, Carol didn't seem alarmed, just intrigued.

The couple took frequent trips to Austin for fun nights out. Tilson usually drove his brown van, without any side windows, on trips and always put a gun between their seats, calling it "travel safety." He was once stopped by a cop for weaving on the freeway and, unbeknownst to the officer, kept his hand on the gun the entire time the officer stood at the driver's window. Why? She wasn't sure.

Often, after they made love at his place, he would grab a gun and work with it. Despite his obvious desire for privacy, he began trying to persuade Carol to move in with him in his town house. Carol resisted because she wanted to move to Austin after she graduated.

After graduating, Carol was ready for a change of scenery and saw it as a good excuse to break off with Tilson, hopefully without angering him. She landed a job in the cardiovascular unit at Seton Medical Center in Austin. She rented a house and she and her now nearly two-year-old son moved 165 miles west.

She was surprised when within the month, Tilson followed her, uninvited, quitting his job at the pawnshop (which she by now realized wasn't his main source of income) and rented a town house near her. He didn't get a job there but continued to take his mysterious trips out of town periodically. He became insanely jealous. Sometimes when she arrived home at night after a busy shift, she'd find Tilson waiting in her house, although he didn't have a key. He refused to tell her how he got in. At times, she spotted him following her in his van around the city, apparently making sure she was going where she had told him. Often he was angry and accused her of having sex with a doctor or resident at the hospital. When she denied it, he would cite his proof: he had called her earlier that day and no one could find her on the unit. More than once, he slammed her against the wall, saying, "Tell me the truth, you bitch. I know you were with someone." As is typical in abuse cases, the violence escalated. Tilson continued to profess his love for her and repeatedly asked her to marry him. She tried to put him off without angering him.

Despite the abuse and the "strange vibes" she got from him, she continued to date him, enjoying the attention, companionship and even the mystery.

Her family met him only once, at Dan Edwards and Margaret's June 3, 1981, wedding, held in Matamoros, Mexico, across the border from San Benito, where Margaret had spent some of her childhood. After dating for nearly eight years, the couple was ready to unite their lives.

A strikingly handsome, dark-haired geologist, originally from Arkansas, Edwards's work had taken him around the world. Sadly Edwards's two sons, the oldest of whom would become a fundamentalist minister, resented their father's second marriage, believing it was a sin. Carol and Gus O'Keiff, however, liked Edwards and were happy for their mother and were there to help celebrate.

Tilson managed to avoid being in any photos that day. O'Keiff thought his sister's latest boyfriend was weird, talking little except about himself. "He was not socially all there. He was in his own little world," he said. Even on this trip, he had what Gus called "some interesting toys"—guns and nightscopes. "I think he was playing up a fantasy," O'Keiff said. During the Edwardses' nuptial celebration, Carol announced that she, too, would soon be getting married. Her brother thought it was an inappropriate time to break her news, believing she was trying to be the center of attention.

"We were trying to ignore Carol. We didn't want to be part of another wedding [of hers]," he said.

Nine days later, Carol followed her mother down the aisle and wed her third husband as well. Tilson had become so insistent that they get married that she did out of fear, she claimed. On June 12, 1981, the two went alone to the Travis County Courthouse in downtown Austin and exchanged vows in front of a judge. He slipped a plain gold wedding band on her finger next to the expensive, emerald-cut diamond engagement ring. He refused to wear a ring, saying he didn't like them. Still, Carol refused to live with him, citing her fear of his job and living with all the guns around her toddler son. With his need for secrecy, he agreed to keep two places; more often than not, they ended up spending their nights together.

Just six weeks later, though, Carol realized she wouldn't be any safer married to this guy than not. As usual, though, Carol would have to have this proven to her in a way she couldn't excuse.

One night, Carol was sitting on the floor, eating dinner alone at a wooden Oriental coffee table, and Tilson stormed into her house in a jealous rage. He accused her of cheating on him with someone at the hospital. Calling her a bitch, Tilson hoisted the coffee table— which usually required two men to even move it because of its massive bulk—above his shoulders and slammed it down on both her legs, food and glass flying everywhere. As she cried in pain, he walked out. Fortunately, Joe was sleeping soundly down the hall and didn't witness any of it. She thought her legs were broken; luckily, they were only badly bruised. She was too embarrassed to go to a hospital, though she could barely walk. Instead, she stayed away from work for a week, claiming to have the flu, too ashamed to tell the truth. At the end of that week, Carol's roommate, Susan Robertson, a political science student at the University of Texas who lived there rent-free in exchange for baby-sitting Joe, abruptly said she was going on vacation with friends and couldn't baby-sit as promised. When Robertson returned days later, she was sporting a half-karat diamond ring. She admitted it was a gift from Tilson, who, she announced, had taken her to the Bahamas and made love to her.

Angry, Carol kicked Robertson out of the house and enrolled Joe in day care. She didn't hear from Tilson until two weeks later when he called, professing his love and claiming he wanted to stay together. When Carol resisted, he threatened to commit suicide. He just wanted to talk to her in person, he said. She continued to refuse to go to his side but felt guilty and eventually agreed to see him. When she got there, Tilson was calm and they sat on the couch talking about their relationship. Carol was up front, saying she didn't want to continue the marriage. He seemed to accept it, but when she got up to leave, he grabbed her by the forearms and dragged her into the bedroom. He just wanted to have sex with her one more time, he insisted. And in case she didn't hear the threat in his voice, a large gun, loaded with a clip, was lying on a pillow. She thought: "He's going to have sex with me and then kill me." He popped a porno tape into the VCR and moved her toward the bed. Carol promised to do anything he wanted, if he would just move the gun. He refused and ordered her to undress. She began slipping out of her clothes, trying to remain calm and think how she could escape. She began crying and told him she couldn't have sex with the gun right there and begged him to move it to another room. He agreed. She watched him walk across the floor and down the hall. She knew this would be her only chance. She grabbed her shirt—all she had removed so far—and her purse and ran down the stairs, taking two or three at a time. Somewhere behind her upstairs, she heard a gun go off. She didn't know if he was aiming at her or at himself but knew he wasn't one to miss. Digging into her purse, desperately searching for her keys, she kept running toward her car. She sped home and called the police; she was concerned that her husband may have shot himself or would follow her home. An hour later, an officer called to tell her that Tilson had fired his gun into the floor to scare her. He hadn't been arrested because, she was told, he had only shot a hole through the floor.

She never saw him again. Still, she feared that any day she would come home and find him sitting on her couch or turn a corner and spot him trailing her in the rearview mirror. She became so terrified of him and his ability to come and go without making a sound that each night before she went to sleep, she stacked cans and other booby traps around the doors and windows. She erected that makeshift alarm for many months. A week after the suicide threat, she drove by his place, wanting to see if her tormentor was still in town. She wasn't planning to talk to him, only to try to catch a glimpse of him. Peering in the windows, she was relieved to see that the town house was empty. He apparently had left with no plans of returning. She filed for divorce, which was granted on November 13, 1981, just five months and a day after they vowed to spend their lives together. Carol was in court, but Tilson was not. Only his attorney was present. Once again, she was to be known as Carol Jackson. For now.

Despite their value and beauty, Carol didn't want the gifts Tilson had given her; too many bad memories were attached. So, little by little, she pawned some and gave others to her mother for her birthday and Christmas. Once, when she was feeling particularly bothered by Tilson's memory, she drove down neighborhood streets and tossed jewelry, some of it with tiny diamonds, out the window of her car, a piece at a time. "Somebody's going to get lucky today!" she exclaimed, feeling freed by the symbolic gesture.

UNDER THE KNIFE   103

about a mile away. The next time they went out, she
was thrown onto the highway pavement when his motorcycle clipped a mirror of an oncoming car and
crumbled beneath them.

Seven

Les Connally and Jake Washington were at Lake
Travis, just outside Austin, on a lunch and beer break
from a nearby construction site. Connally, a twenty-
nine-year-old ironworker, noticed a beautiful, bikini-
clad redhead floating on an inner tube on the
glimmering lake. He instantly hatched a scheme in
which he would glide into her life, looking like a
hero. Connally, who was white, and Washington, who
was black, bet $100 on who could land a date with
her first. Washington swam out and got first crack,
but when Connally joined them he could tell his
buddy had struck out, as he had expected of his
somewhat obnoxious coworker. Connally asked the
woman if the other guy was bothering her. The sub-
terfuge worked; Carol O'Keiff Jackson believed he was
helping her. She and Connally were instantly attracted
to each other, and he thought her personality
matched her outward beauty. He thought the petite
and bubbly girl had a great body and a gorgeous face.
When he returned to work, he had her phone number.

Carol, dressed in a skirt, was surprised when he
picked her up for their first date on a motorcycle. Always adventurous, she rode sidesaddle to his house

about a mile away. The next time they went out, Carol picked him up in her car. They returned to Lake Travis for a picnic and ended up skinny-dipping, having a fabulous time together. He taught her how to ride his Harley. He sat behind her on her maiden drive, but she popped the clutch and revved the engine too hard, throwing Connally off the back. Surprised and unsure what to do, she went through some yards before laying it down while Connally watched, laughing. She was scared but ended up laughing, too. She eventually learned how to control the bike but preferred to ride in back.

Connally, himself married and divorced three times, wasn't the least bit intimidated by Carol's history. The son of a pilot instructor and a housewife, Connally was born in Sacramento when his father was based at Mather Air Force Base. The oldest of three children, he grew up in Arlington, a suburb of Dallas. Connally, who wanted to be an air force pilot but couldn't because he wore glasses, joined the army, where he became a medic attached to the Seventy-fifth Ranger Airborne. He had smoked pot since the age of thirteen and had tried most every street drug by the time he got to Vietnam. During his two years in that war-ravaged country, he got hooked on morphine and then heroin, a problem that he brought home with him in December 1971. He first killed a man, one of the enemy, at age eighteen and got physically sick. Later, he boasted of having forty-eight "confirmed kills" in 'Nam and none but the first had bothered him.

He told Carol about his past, admitting that he served time in the Texas penitentiary, proudly showing her one of his many tattoos—wrists with a broken chain and the date of his release on his back, typical of freed prisoners. He had been on probation for one trumped-up charge when he got busted on another, he told her. Sentenced to three years on a theft conviction, Connally served twenty months in the Ferguson Unit in Midway, Texas, before being paroled in July 1974. Fixated on heroin, he had gone to California where, with the help of a friend who was a former addict, he broke his addiction by being locked in a closet for eleven days without access to the drug. He returned to Texas and was staying with friends when they were busted for dealing heroin. His probation was revoked for being with known felons, according to his tale.

His first marriage lasted just two weeks, he said, because he found out that his wife had slept with her ex-husband the day before she married Connally. He stayed in his second marriage, to a registered nurse with an infant son, just six months before he said he called his wife's father and told him, "Dad, you're going to have to come pick up your daughter. I don't want her." Once they wed, her personality changed, becoming possessive and jealous, and she turned into a slob, he said. His third marriage had been his longest, lasting a year, although their relationship had spanned nine years. They married two years after their son, whom Connally adored, had been born. He claimed that he ended that marriage when he caught her in bed with his best friend. A short time later, he met Carol and the two quickly fell in love, fueled by their mutual sexual passions and adventurousness.

Connally regularly rode his Harley by Carol's house, revving the engine to grab her attention and then riding back and forth doing tricks. A friend of Connally's often lent him his small motorboat, and the couple would return to Lake Travis at night to make love while drifting on the still waters. Within a month, Connally moved in with the Jacksons, and he took three-year-old Joe to day care on his motorcycle. As far as Joe was concerned, Connally was the best stepfather he ever had.

The first year of Carol's relationship with Connally was intense, passionate and generally happy. Each had found his and her best sex partner—so far. Connally said Carol was the kinkiest woman he had ever been with, exciting and adventurous, and he loved it.

On a trip to Galveston, Carol had her tattoo altered, covering Hankes's initials with the words "property of Les" near the heart and rose on her abdomen. Connally got one, too—a serpent holding a crystal ball, in which he had Carol's name tattooed, on his upper right arm.

While Carol had developed an attraction to rowdy and stereotypical biker guys, she thought Connally sometimes played that role too often. He seemed eager to fight, even with the slightest provocation. When she tried to stop him, his friends held her back, allowing him to do what he wanted. He saw her as a "weekend warrior," only wanting to party on the weekends and only when Joe was with his dad or the babysitter and wouldn't see her.

Carol sold the rental houses she still had in Houston. A fire, caused by the tenant smoking in bed, destroyed the garage apartment, which Carol found out was not covered under the homeowner's insurance. She could not afford to repair the place, so she sold the property, losing money on the deal but receiving about $60,000 cash, the last of her trust fund money. Connally talked her into becoming business partners, opening L & C Custom Cycles, Inc. Carol was enthusiastic, believing her live-in boyfriend would be good at it. But before they jumped into that venture, Carol had another adventure planned. She loved to travel but hadn't gotten to go anywhere exciting in a while. On a whim, she bought airline tickets to Acapulco for her and her boyfriend and booked a room at the famed Las Brisas Hotel, where her father had taken her as a child. Connally was surprised and excited, but when he tried to get a passport, he realized he couldn't without a copy of his birth certificate. Neither he nor his parents had one and a phone call confirmed that one wouldn't arrive from California in time to leave the following weekend. Either they had to postpone the trip or he couldn't go, he informed Carol. But he would soon learn just how determined his girlfriend could be when her mind was set on something and just how badly she wanted to take this trip—now. She picked up the phone, dialed the airline but instead of postponing plans for Acapulco, she bought another ticket—this time one to Sacramento so Connally could fly there and get his birth certificate and passport in time to go to Mexico.

When they returned to Austin, they found a run-down shop just north of downtown, with an attached house that was just as run-down, and rented it. A tattoo parlor shared the building and short-term borders came and went in the second-story rooms. Connally ran the shop, hiring a couple of employees, while Carol continued working as a nurse. She spent her hours off helping out in the shop as well. He bought her a BSA motorcycle. With a tattoo parlor next door and a boyfriend who liked them, Carol added four more tattoos. The second was a vine with a rose wrapped around her ankle, followed by a shooting star at the nape of her neck in the back. She was careful to get them only in places that would be covered by her nurse's uniform. One evening after work, Connally, other bikers and a tattoo artist were hanging out and partying in her kitchen. Connally, who looked at her growing collection of tattoos as colorful artwork, suggested she finally get a Harley wings tattoo. She agreed, but the artist was so stoned, he tattooed a funky-looking bird on her right shoulder blade instead of the motorcycle logo, as well as a more accurately depicted lily on her left shoulder.

Margaret Edwards was annoyed that her daughter set

Connally up in business, believing he was milking her. When she visited them, she was aghast that her daughter would live in such conditions with her young son, Joe. While Dan Edwards was fond of Carol, he didn't approve of the way she led her life. "Carol was not his ideal of what a young lady should be like," Margaret said. She had long ago accepted that her daughter would not live as she had hoped but decided to accept her for who she was and try to be there for her whenever she was needed, as she often was.

It was obvious to Margaret that Connally adored her daughter, but she still didn't like the fact that he was a biker and the fact that her daughter was collecting tattoos because of him. The long-haired bikers who hung around the shop with Connally looked like trouble, too, she thought. For his part, Connally said he loved Margaret Edwards and appreciated the fact that she treated him respectfully and never talked down to him despite the fact he had not come from the upper-economic class. He disrespected and angered his girlfriend, though, by regularly telling her, "I bet your mother is a real tiger in bed. I know she hides it. I sure would like to get her behind closed doors."

Though she was pissed, Carol only answered, "No, she's not."

Otherwise, things went well between Carol and Connally for a short time after they went into business together. Here their stories differed. Carol said that Connally, meeting more and more bikers, got deeper into the rough side of that culture and into drugs. Soon, she said, he was giving away parts, wasting profits on drugs and spending less time trying to make a go of the business. They were unable to pay their employees, who naturally quit. Regardless of why, the business began failing and the tensions between the couple mounted. Connally allowed two-year-old Joe to wander around the motorcycle shop and sometimes failed to watch him closely enough. As Joe toddled around one afternoon, Connally and his friends were partying and one biker after another gave Joe a sip of his or her beer and soon the child was drunk. Carol was infuriated when she came home and saw her toddler stumbling around like a tiny bum. She grabbed her son, yelled at everyone there, took him to their house next door and put him to bed.

As Connally's partying increased, he became abusive, hitting and kicking her hard, she said. When she talked of leaving him, he sometimes threatened that he would find and kill her, she said. He denied most of the abuse, acknowledging only a couple of incidents.

Like Jackson, Connally also suffered from memories of the Vietnam War. He frequently had nightmares and occasionally had blackouts, although he was never violent with her during these episodes. One morning, she found him hiding behind the clothes in her closet, thinking they were bushes and he was hiding from the "gooks."

Carol was horrified when she learned she was pregnant. Connally had sworn to her that he had had a vasectomy. She was working hard and he was into partying and playing around. She had a lot to do taking care of Connally and Joe. Although Connally was a devoted father to both Joe and his own son, he didn't take the news of her pregnancy well, saying he didn't want the responsibility. She had an abortion and got back on birth control.

After L & C Custom Cycles folded, Connally wanted a fresh start. He suggested they move to Houston, saying he knew he could straighten out his life if they got out of Austin and away from the crowd he was hanging with. Carol agreed. Connally found a job as an ironworker at a construction project in Clear Lake, about twenty miles south of downtown Houston, and they rented an apartment nearby in the tiny town of Bacliff, on Galveston Bay. Carol landed a nursing position in the orthopedics unit at the prestigious Methodist Hospital in the city's renowned Medical Center.

She became pregnant, and Connally again didn't take it well. She recalled that he told her he didn't make enough money to support them and didn't want the responsibilities attached to a baby. Connally got on his Harley and rode off. This time, he didn't return. After just three months in Houston, he decided to settle once again in Austin—alone. Carol had another abortion. Years later, Connally claimed that he never knew Carol had had abortions on account of him, claiming he hadn't known she was pregnant.

Carol was once again alone with her son and determined to rebuild her life and live it the way she wanted. She and Joe moved closer to her job, renting an apartment off Braeswood, southwest of the Medical Center. John Jackson started comparing his ex-wife and son to gypsies because they moved so often. Margaret thought of her daughter that way, too, thinking she was moving too often instead of putting down roots as Margaret had been raised to expect. She hoped that would change once her grandson went to school. Carol was happy with her job, her son and her new friends. She dated some, but no one seriously.

About a year after he had walked out, Connally knocked on Carol's door, looking and acting much differently—better, as far as Carol was concerned. He had shaved his scraggly beard and mustache, cut his hair, which at one time nearly reached his waist and now was above his ears, and was wearing neat and clean clothes. He told her how much he loved and missed her and pressed for a reconciliation. Carol was hesitant but, admittedly, interested. She didn't open her house to him but agreed to date him, although he was still living in Austin. After spending more and more time with him, she was convinced that the changes were genuine. He moved to Houston and got a good construction job as a drywaller, earning decent money. And even when they had an argument or things weren't going smoothly, Connally never raised a hand to her.

On January 7, 1984, about three years after they met, Connally, thirty-two, and Carol, twenty-seven, were married by a reverend from the Houston Bible Church. It was a small ceremony attended by friends and held in the courtyard of her apartment complex. It was the fourth marriage for each. Dressed in a calf-length, off-white dress, Carol looked gorgeous while Connally opted for a more casual look: Harley shirt and jeans. Margaret and Dan Edwards were living in Yemen that year and could not attend, but Connally's parents were there. The wedding was put together on short notice and Carol did not tell her father about it until afterward. The ceremony was followed by a casual party in their apartment, for which Carol had prepared all the hors d'ouevres and even made her own wedding cake. They did not take a honeymoon—they couldn't afford it.

Connally transferred to a town house construction project in Clear Lake and soon tired of the forty-five-minute commute south, much of it over highways perpetually under construction. Carol agreed to move south and they rented a house in Kemah, a bohemian seaside community between Galveston Bay and Clear Lake. On her long drive to the Medical Center, she frequently was delayed by accidents and often was passed by screaming ambulances. "God, what a horrible way to start the day," she remembered thinking. Soon the commute wore on her, and she found a job at Humana Hospital, one of the two hospitals in Clear Lake, first as a nurse in intensive care and then in the orthopedics unit. The hospital was less than ten miles from their house, but the only opening was on the evening shift. She had less time to spend with her husband and the tensions between them increased once again. Connally and a cousin went into business together, installing flooring in homes and businesses. Carol and Connally's cousin never liked each other. Carol said Connally again got connected to the biker world. They shared one car—an old station wagon—but as Connally, who no longer had a bike, began to revert to his former ways, he sometimes forgot to pick up his wife from work. When he was straight, Connally was a wonderful father to Joe, but Carol didn't trust him to look after her child when he was not sober. Soon she was taking Joe to evening care, picking him up each night on her way home. Carol said Connally started missing work and the tension grew. With his wife at work, he started sleeping with other women, Carol said. He admitted it to her, saying, "I slipped. I'm sorry." Soon the downhill pattern was reminiscent of their time in Austin, and Carol said he started hitting her again and forcing her to have sex. Connally denied ever abusing Carol but admitted to pinning her against the wall and then chasing her down the road with his motorcycle helmet when they lived in Austin. He also denied cheating on her or raping her. He seriously asked, "How can you rape your wife?"

A year after they married, Carol became pregnant for the third time by Connally. This time, Connally was excited at the prospect of fatherhood and took an active interest in Carol's pregnancy, going to her obstetrician appointments with her. The pregnancy, however, was the only bright spot in their troubled marriage. Connally was heavily into gambling, and Carol found out when things around the house began to vanish. Connally was pawning their belongings to pay his debts. One afternoon, Carol took a call for Connally—the caller asked when "the stuff" was coming in. Carol was outraged, believing her husband was dealing drugs. When Connally arrived home, they had another huge argument. Nearly six months into her pregnancy, Connally's enthusiasm waned as he began feeling the weight of his pending responsibilities. He suggested she have another abortion. She told him it was simply too late to consider that option and refused to do it. He began hounding her about having an abortion, but she always resisted. Connally, who later denied ever asking her to have an abortion, still accompanied his wife to her doctor's appointments, giving her hope that he would get over not wanting another child. "I've always been someone who holds on to the very end," she said in retrospect.

Carol went through the newspaper, circling employment ads she thought might interest him. Instead, it got on his nerves. With her husband slipping away from her emotionally—and often physically as well—Carol sank into depression. They were living paycheck to paycheck, and Carol did not see how she could make it alone with two children, especially when she was facing an unpaid maternity leave. Seeing no way out, she often sat on the kitchen floor of their rented house and cried. She knew, though, she could not allow her situation to continue and she would have to leave eventually, so she began planning for that day. She secretly opened her own bank account and began depositing small amounts from her paycheck. But the day when Carol would once again strike out on her own came sooner than she expected—and it wasn't her choice.

Dan Edwards and his wife Margaret were building their dream home outside Springdale, Arkansas; it was a magnificent 3,700-square-foot main house with an ac-

companying 900-square-foot guest house, sitting atop a
grassy hill and 73 acres. They named their $340,000
estate "Tin Roof Farms." Carol begged them to hire
their son-in-law as he needed the work. They reluctantly
agreed and gave Connally close to $15,000 to do the
floors—installing the carpeting and laying the tile in a
number of the rooms. Connally arrived with three help-
ers and did part of the work they had agreed upon and
then spent a couple of days stoned in a hotel. The ma-
terials were to be included in the money they gave him,
according to the Edwardses, but they were hit with the
bill from the stores the following week. They called and
complained to Carol, who confronted her husband.
The two had a horrible fight over it.

Two days later, on August 14, 1985, she found Connally in the driveway, loading some things into a friend's
van, with the help of a couple of others. He told her
he was going to Florida where a better job was waiting
for him.

"What about the baby?" Carol asked, incredulously.

"Call me when it gets close," he said.

"What do you mean?" she shouted. "The baby's due
in three weeks!"

Connally insisted he would be back and gave her a
phone number where she could reach him in a few
days, promising to send money. When Carol called the
number her husband had given her, the people there
had never heard of Connally or his companions.

A few days later, her landlord evicted her. She was
shocked to learn he had not received any rent in four
months, even though Carol had given her husband the
rent money, which he assured her he had paid. Carol's
meager savings were not enough to make the payments
or put a deposit on another place. Even if she managed
to borrow that much, she still was going to be in trouble
with her unpaid maternity leave and the need for child

care when she went back to work. With nowhere else to turn, she and her mother decided that it was best for her and her children to move to Arkansas. She sold her cherished pool table, and with the money she had stashed away, she had just enough to pay for movers to load up the remainder of her and Joe's stuff and send it to her mother's. But with just a few days to go before the baby was due, Carol did not want to leave her obstetrician—he planned to induce labor the following week if the baby didn't make an appearance before then. For the next few days, she stayed with friends, and even spent one night sleeping in her car with Joe. Her brother, Gus, and his second wife, Helayne, invited the two to stay with them in their Houston house until the baby was born, and Carol thankfully accepted the offer. Saturday night, just two days before Labor Day, Carol went into labor in the middle of the night. She woke up Joe, got him dressed and then woke her brother to tell him she was in labor and was going to the hospital. O'Keiff wanted to drive his sister, but Carol insisted on going alone, even though the hospital where she was to have the baby was about thirty miles away in Clear Lake. With contractions coming at six-minute intervals, Carol sped down the Southwest Freeway at eighty miles an hour, breathing as instructed in Lamaze classes, timing her own contractions, trying to calm a crying Joe and hoping all the time that a cop would pull her over. She wanted an escort the rest of the way to the hospital. No such luck—she was on her own. Joe was terrified she would wreck the car, but she got him safely to Clear Lake, where she dropped him off with a girlfriend, and drove on to the Humana Hospital.

Once at the emergency room, Carol relaxed a little, knowing she would not have to deliver the baby herself as well. She checked into the maternity ward and lay there alone the rest of the night, with just periodic checks

from the nurses on duty. She didn't want to call her
mother until after the baby was born. Finally, at about
6:00 A.M., a friend showed up for her own nursing shift
and stayed with Carol, coaching her through the worst
of the labor, until Danielle Cara Connally was born at
7:00 A.M. on September 3, 1985. She named her daughter
after stepfather Dan Edwards, who, despite their differences, was the one stable adult male in Carol's life.

Despite being thrilled at having a daughter, Carol had
lots of reasons to be depressed—even without the hormonal changes provoking her. She watched the other
new mothers sharing their joys with the babies' proud
fathers and toasting their happiness with champagne
the nurses served to all new parents—all except Carol,
that is. They knew she was alone and giving her a cele-
bratory bottle of champagne seemed inappropriate,
and maybe even mean. Joe was taken to the hospital
and introduced to his new little sister, Dani, whom he
instantly adored.

On Labor Day, Gus picked Carol up from the hospital
and Joe from her friend's. The family of three stayed
with Gus for a couple of days until the Edwardses arrived to take them to Arkansas. Carol called Connally's
parents in Belton, Texas, to tell them about their new
granddaughter and asked them to pass on the message
to their son. The elder Connallys seemed happy to hear
about their new grandchild and sent a gift for Dani.
She told them they were moving to Arkansas. On the
nearly twelve-hour car trip to the Edwardses' large estate, the group had to stop often so Carol could hold
her new baby out in the sunshine. Dani's bilirubin
count was high, threatening her with jaundice. Carol
cried more than the baby, nearly all the way to her
mother's house in northwestern Arkansas. Although a
huge house with three bedrooms, a study and a library,
plus a small one-bedroom guest house, it still wasn't big

enough for two families used to living separately. Joe was happy there, and Dan Edwards tried to teach him how to behave like a man. He was strict, like Joe's father, but set and enforced some sensible rules. The youngster secretly respected these borders, even though he tested the limits and tried to resist.

Carol got a job as the factory nursing supervisor at the local Campbell Soup Company Poultry Research Farm. Margaret didn't want them to move out. She thought Carol should get her finances in better shape first, and it would be easier for her to help baby-sit her grandchildren. But Carol was determined to be independent and rebuild her life with her children. She rented a two-bedroom duplex just seven miles from her mother's and about ten miles from the plant. Overlooking a vineyard, their new home was especially small and Carol shared her bedroom with Dani.

After hearing nothing from Connally for five and one-half months, Carol filed for divorce. Since she didn't know where he was and couldn't serve him with divorce papers, Carol had to place an ad in a local newspaper, the *Springdale News*, notifying her husband that she had filed for divorce. A certified letter addressed to him was sent to his parents' Belton, Texas, home. Connally, through a Temple, Texas, attorney initially contested the divorce but later withdrew his objection. On March 26, 1986, Carol, just twenty-nine, was divorced for the fourth time. She was awarded $200 a month in child support, which she knew she had little chance of getting. Connally was awarded regular visitation with Danielle, which he didn't use. Carol continued to use his last name, though.

Despite the resentment she felt toward Connally for abandoning her when she was pregnant, Carol tried to avoid passing on those feelings to his daughter. But she didn't want to lie to her, either. As Dani grew up and asked about her dad, Carol Connally explained the relationship in a similar way she had to Joe about his father. She told her that her father had left because he was sick from taking drugs; it was an addiction and not his fault. She said he left because he didn't want to hurt Dani. As she got older, Dani envied the close relationship her brother had with his dad and always longed for a father. She asked her mother and brother lots of questions about Connally. Joe patiently answered, retelling the same stories and making her father sound the part of the big, tough biker.

Many years later, Les Connally said he had been elated when he learned from his parents about Dani's birth, just six days after she had been born. He was sure that any child of his and Carol's would be pretty, like her mother. He said his plan always had been to move his wife, child and Joe to Florida but that Carol had filed for divorce. Saying he truly loved her, he stated they never should have divorced. He was one husband who remembered Carol's personality as laid-back and fun. "For a redhead, she didn't fly off the handle all the time," he said, even describing her as "even-tempered."

In Arkansas, Carol made new friends, most of them fellow Campbell's employees, and she built an active social life. Her new baby and six-year-old son were often looked after by Margaret Edwards. Dani was a more rambunctious and more challenging child than her brother. She spilled drinks, ran around and irritated her grandmother's beloved dogs.

Carol and her mother frequently joked how opposite they were from one another. Carol always was a free spirit while her mother couldn't go anywhere without a plan. While her mother was materialistic and enjoyed having the finer things, Carol cared nothing about her possessions' value, other than their sentimental ones.

But despite all the mistakes and bad decisions Carol had made in her youth and in her relationships, she always seemed to make the best ones in her career. The two problems Margaret saw were that her daughter did not always seem emotionally stable, still prone to sharp mood swings and that she didn't seem to learn from her past mistakes where men were concerned. Carol attracted weak and/or abusive men, who leaned on her emotionally, especially when they did not have enough guts to do what was hard, like keeping a job, Edwards thought. In most of her relationships, Edwards thought, Carol was the responsible one, financially carrying too many of the men in her life.

Eight

Carol Connally met the next man in her life at work shortly after she started at the Campbell Soup Company Poultry Research Farm, a chicken-processing factory, one of the area's largest employers. James Lee Crow, a plant supervisor, would stop by the nurse's office with some regularity to check on injured or sick workers. Eventually, Crow, born on Christmas Eve and six years Carol's senior, asked her out and they soon were dating regularly. Although Crow had an ex-wife, Carol was embarrassed by her mistakes and didn't admit how many times she had been to divorce court. Their courtship was pretty routine for northwestern Arkansas, dining out, seeing movies, fishing and meeting each other's families and friends. Crow seemed as straight and dependable as Connally was wild and volatile.

As she got to know both Crow and their coworkers better, fellow employees began warning her about allegations and rumors concerning the bad way he had treated and tried to control his first wife, who also worked there. She asked Crow about the things she had heard and he told a different, more reasonable story. She didn't know who to believe, but he was nice to her, so she continued to see him. Some employees complained to her that Crow treated his workers badly, but she wrote those off to the fact that he was a supervisor and sometimes had to be tough. Dan and Margaret Edwards liked this boyfriend, though they thought of him as a bit of a redneck. Even Carol thought of him as "a good ol' boy," but that didn't bother her. He was nice to her and her kids and she thought this might be the one relationship that worked. So when he asked her to marry him, she didn't hesitate to accept. Carol especially wanted someone who would help parent her children, help her make decisions about them and share in the joys of every new thing they did or cute thing they said. Joe, just seven at the time, never liked Crow. "He didn't seem right," he said later, but he could not explain exactly why.

With her mother watching her children, Crow and Carol drove north to the tiny resort town of Eureka Springs. On September 6, 1986, they got married in a chapel designed to look like a small castle. "He's a nice guy; maybe it'll work," Margaret Edwards remembered thinking. "By this time, I had stopped hoping for happily ever after." For a honeymoon, the two drove through Tennessee and the picturesque Appalachian Mountains in her mother's van, camping along the way. It was low-key but nice.

On eight acres that he owned in the country on the south side of Fayetteville, Crow had built an A-frame house on Shafer Road. Carol and her children moved from their rental house into his home. Trying to please her, he agreed to add on to the house, but discussing what to do led to frequent arguments between them. They settled on adding a master bedroom and a den to the two-bedroom house. They bought a hot tub and plopped it down in the living room.

Now that they were married, Carol started noticing that he was more chauvinistic than the men she was accustomed to, but mostly in small ways, such as never letting her drive when they were together. Though fiercely independent, she dismissed such attitudes as coming with the part of the country in which they were living. She said he wasn't sexually adventurous, something which she had enjoyed in the past. For him, she said, "it was 'wham, bam, thank you, ma'am'; now, let's go to sleep." She was not happy about that.

They got separate bank accounts and were responsible for their own things, even food, according to Carol. She was surprised when he insisted that she pay two-thirds of the bills because the children were hers, even though she said he earned about twice as much money as she did. Their food was stored separately, and each was careful not to eat the other's. Occasionally, the two would be home for dinner together and Carol would cook enough for everyone, but she said her husband often refused to eat it.

Carol once excitedly returned from a trip to Houston—where she had gone to become certified in pulmonary-function tests—with live lobsters that she intended to be the centerpiece of a romantic dinner. Crow, who frequently dined on such rural fare as rabbit, was horrified, she recalled, and refused to eat the "big bugs." Carol was pissed and so enjoyed the lobsters and wine alone.

While Carol initially liked her latest mother-in-law, she soon thought the apron string was a little too tight, and she began thinking of her man as too much of a "mama's boy." It seemed that Crow was having trouble adjusting to living with two small children. Although she realized that, never having had kids of his own, it would take a while, she still thought he was rude and too critical of Joe. The fact that Carol worked days and he worked evenings didn't help their relationship—it had become more problematic now that they were sharing a house. Still, he didn't watch the kids while she worked; Joe was in first grade and Dani went to day care. Crow wouldn't help with the children in any way, even picking them up from school. "It's your problem; you take care of it," he told her.

Even at eighteen months, Dani was a handful and more active than other children her age. She showed little fear of things she should avoid and jumped—not climbed—out of her crib. She also had lots of allergies and Carol had to give her shots three times a week. Dani would run and hide, making the ordeal that much harder.

The growing signs of the strain in their marriage were not reserved for behind closed doors. They were openly hostile toward each other at work—when they bothered to acknowledge each other at all. Coworkers commented on the tension, and Carol even got them in on it. Several times, she noticed that her husband's zipper was down and instead of pointing it out to him, she told his employees. They, in turn, would look at Crow and laugh—making sure he was aware that he was being laughed at—but wouldn't tell him why.

Carol told her mother she was unhappy and thinking about getting another divorce. "You've messed up so many times before, give this one a try," she recalled Margaret telling her. Carol suggested marriage counseling, but her husband went once and refused to go back. After just nine months of marriage, Carol had had enough. Crow was basically an OK guy, she thought, but not someone she wanted to spend their first anniversary with, let alone the rest of her life. She had become bored by the little sex life they had left. She didn't feel connected to her husband, so it wasn't hard for her to walk away. "I was getting pretty good at trying to bail out," she admitted. She didn't even tell him—not in person or in a note. After he left for work one summer morning, a group of Campbells' employees in a half-dozen pickups pulled in, loaded her stuff and moved her into an apartment closer to town. She was careful not to take any of his stuff, but she couldn't resist one more prank—she hid his guns in the belly of the wood-burning stove, beneath the ashes. That evening, coworkers called Carol to report that Crow had been furious when he got home and found her gone. He had returned to the plant, demanding to know where she was. Eventually, he found out but never spoke to Carol again. He'd pass by her office in the plant without saying a word. In retrospect, though, Carol thought Crow was even more unhappy than she was by the time their marriage ended.

Within days, each independently sued the other for divorce. As part of the divorce, she received $1,000 from him and the pontoon she had bought during their marriage in exchange for releasing any claims on his property.

Their divorced was granted April 4, 1988. Carol Crow became Carol O'Keiff once again.

She and the children enjoyed passing days on the many beautiful lakes in the area on the pontoon. She really couldn't afford it, however, and reluctantly sold it. She also liked her job at the plant, but there was no room for advancement. She wanted a more challenging job with opportunities to move up. Since she missed Houston, she applied for work in the Texas Medical Center. She landed a job back at Methodist Hospital, this time as a clinical educator in orthopedics, teaching new nurses or ones becoming specialists. She was thrilled as she packed up her family and headed home once again, determined to do things a little differently. She did not realize John Christ would be in her future.

Nine

By early 1990, O'Keiff and Christ were in love. They were engaged in a romantic courtship, captivating sex and joint intellectual pursuits. Christ called her at work just to ask how her day was going, often ending their conversations on an amorous or erotic note, putting a smile on her face as she returned to her hectic job. Although he often didn't have any patients there, he stopped by her unit at some point each day, lavishing her with attention, stealing her away for lunch and generally making her feel important and loved. After so many abusive or boring relationships in recent years, O'Keiff was thrilled with the attention and felt like a teenager falling in love for the first time. To show his affection, he surprised her regularly with perfume, roses and other gifts.

With a coy, boyish smile, he gave her cards, sometimes slipping them to her at work. Always excited to receive them, she never knew if she would find a romantic verse or an erotic innuendo inside. He shared with her the beautiful poetry he had written over the years, much of it about loneliness penned during his younger years. She was touched by his vulnerability and moved by his passionate prose. Through it and the stories he told about his past and family, she thought she learned about his growth into the man she loved. It seemed to her that he had evolved from a once self-deprecating, insecure boy to a confident, even self-admiring man after becoming a physician and sculpting his body by working out fanatically and running daily. By the time he and Carol met, he had become so enamored of his own physique that he kept a photo of himself posing in a skimpy bikini on his refrigerator. She wrote it off as just one of his eccentricities, which she professed to having a few of herself. As always, he remained self-conscious about being short and wore heels to compensate.

The charming Dr. Christ seemed to be everything O'Keiff thought she wanted in a man—sensual, adventurous, interesting, intelligent and kooky—like she was. When she shared her feelings or opinions, he cared about what she had to say, empathizing when appropriate but always seeming to remain nonjudgmental about her and her chaotic life. She knew he could be a harsh critic of others. She saw him as a devoted father, respected professional and fun pal—all of it wrapped up in the best lover she had ever had.

As their relationship progressed and they became more comfortable with one another, O'Keiff learned about her boyfriend's sexual interests. Experimental herself, O'Keiff generally went along with what he wanted; she was willing to at least try almost anything.

"Sex was a major thing in our life, besides food," O'Keiff said.

Both voracious readers, he handed her a white paperback. The cover was simple, stating only *Story of O*, by Pauline Réage, and suggested she read it. She passed, saying she wasn't interested in porn. Still, he persisted, telling her it was erotic literature, not porn. Popular fiction and medical-themed books and journals were more her style but, at his repeated urgings, she agreed. Though considered a classic in its genre, O'Keiff was disgusted once she realized it was a tale of a young, beautiful French girl, desirous of nothing more than becoming a complete sexual slave to her lover, who put her through extreme, debasing sexual and psychological tests. Shocked by some of the explicit scenes, she revealed, "I had never heard of some of those things, even though I had been a carny and been with bikers." O'Keiff's own lover was enraptured with the book, and as she quickly thumbed through it, she read enough to realize: "That's where a lot of John's ideas came from." She soon discovered why he had been so insistent on her reading it. He had an ulterior motive. He wanted Carol, like the slave girl in the book, to have her labia pierced with an O-shaped ring. Of course, he intended to insert the band himself. She balked instantly; the idea was too painful to contemplate. "That was something I had never heard of back then, and I was pretty worldly," she said. As he usually did when he was determined to have his way, the surgeon persisted, telling her what a turn on it would be for him. Although *Story of O* had been made into a movie, he later showed her a porn film in which some of the women had labial rings. Like she had noticed with Tilson and Connally, she was finding that once Christ had learned she was adventurous and willing to experiment a little sexually, the more he pushed her to go outside her boundaries. Usually, she gave in. "They automatically take it further, whether you want to or not," she said. With other men, that had even gone to the point of rape.

Christ and O'Keiff's sex life was growing increasingly rowdy and rough, so much so that she literally walked differently sometimes, as if she had been horseback riding a little too long. That didn't go unnoticed or uncommented on by some of her more observant and forward coworkers. "I know what you've been doing," a couple of women on her staff told her more than a few times. She just smiled, a little embarrassed. O'Keiff obviously was happy and some of her female coworkers were excited for her, never having been convinced of the veracity of Gay Christ's allegations, even those who had seen her on the unit after the battering. They had known both Gay and John before, and many found Gay pushy and rude. They simply didn't like her and weren't willing to give her the benefit of the doubt about how she had been injured. Dr. Christ always had been pleasant and easygoing around them and his patients, and some of the staff on Dunn 8 West sided with him, choosing to dismiss Gay's allegations as those from an embittered soon-to-be ex-wife. Thinking O'Keiff and Christ were "the perfect match," they encouraged her to see him and were happy for her.

Many coworkers, however, had no doubt Christ had done exactly what Gay had alleged—and probably more—and openly worried about O'Keiff turning a blind eye to those things.

"Aren't you afraid of him?" some nurses asked.

No, she assured them. He was gentle and kind. She knew Gay, had seen what a rough time she was giving Christ in their divorce, plus she was lying, trying to get his money, O'Keiff said, repeating what her lover had told her.

"What do you see in that guy?" Dr. Spira, who was particularly fond of this nurse, asked sometimes.

"He's not what you think, Dr. Spira," O'Keiff said defensively.

"I don't want to see you get hurt," he said. She believed he meant emotionally because she believed her boyfriend had never physically hurt anyone intentionally.

"I'm a big girl; I'll get out," she assured him. She wasn't happy to have to be defending her lover from these false allegations, but still, she was touched that he was trying to look after her.

The ongoing gossip continued to make her uncomfortable around other plastic surgeons. As she had not been on the unit long, she first heard Christ referred to as "The Stairwell Stud" only after they had begun dating and she had fallen for him. She dismissed those stories instantly, believing he wouldn't be so reckless at the hospital, where his reputation was so important. She knew he was quite adventurous, but the guy had his own private office nearby, after all. Why would he risk that? She figured he probably had been caught in a passionate embrace in the stairwell and then the rumor mill stirred it into something more interesting. It wouldn't be long before she realized that, in this case, the grapevine was quite reliable.

Heading to the cafeteria for lunch one afternoon about a month after they had started dating, he grabbed her in the stairwell for a long, lustful kiss as he had in the past. This time, he pulled her against the wall and lifted her skirt, trying to entice her into having a quickie right there. She playfully slapped his hand away and told him, "No, there's going to be somebody coming." She was willing to indulge him in private, happy to try new things, but she valued her professional reputation far too much to risk having such rumors circulating about her. She thought she had convinced him, but it wouldn't be the last time he tried to get her to acquiesce to those desires. "Come on, come on," he pleaded. "It would be so erotic." She never would consider obliging him there and told him so. Still, he continued to persist and whenever she found herself needing to take the stairs with him, she began running down ahead of him, hoping to avoid the issue completely.

Although initially complimentary of her beauty and well-maintained figure, just five months after they started dating, he offered to do plastic surgery on her, wanting to surgically reduce a scar on O'Keiff's shoulder blade. Another plastic surgeon, using a laser, had removed the malformed bird tattoo, but Christ criticized that doctor's work, telling her he could make it look better. Even though no one but him would be seeing it, she agreed. On May 18, he performed the procedure in his office, billing her insurance company by falsely claiming it was a keloid, a raised pad of scar tissue that often requires surgical treatment. Though just a minor procedure, it was the first of many he would want to do on her in the near future.

O'Keiff's preoccupation with makeup had lessened over time, but only slightly. Before heading to bed, she removed her foundation, put on a series of lotions and let her skin breathe. Still, she applied a fresh coat of blush and lipstick, leaving the mascara and eye shadow to the daytime hours. One of the first things she did after waking up was freshen her makeup.

Excited to be dating someone new, she began spending more money on clothes, trying to satisfy her boyfriend's tastes. About the only good thing he ever said about Gay was that she had good taste in clothes and always dressed well. When he and O'Keiff went shopping, he pointed out things he liked. She took the hints and tried to present a more polished, tailored image than her large eclectic wardrobe of casual and vintage clothing reflected. Christ had more clothes than she did and seldom dressed down, except for running shorts and T-shirts. He owned just one pair of jeans, which he wore occasionally even though they looked too tight.

Carol O'Keiff warned her children not to discuss her past marriages, other than those to their fathers, and especially not to talk about Crow. Sometimes they slipped, saying a little more than they were supposed to, and their mother would raise an eyebrow or signal them to say no more, always maintaining their secret and invoking a few giggles. Joe thought it was his mother's business, and he never would have revealed how many men there had been or how many she really had married. But he was old enough now to worry about her. Even he could see that his mom was unusually flirtatious. Years later, Joe said the men her mother was interested in seemed to have a few things in common— none were "average Joes," each was involved in something exciting that he thought his mother wanted to be involved with, all had bad tempers and all wanted to control her. Even though his mother was strong-willed and quick-tempered, she always seemed to give in to the man in her life, apologizing even if she had been the one who was right. She would break off a relationship, only to take the guy back, and most of the men in her life ended up walking all over her, he thought.

But Joe also thought Christ was different than most of the others. Although he seemed a bit nerdy, Joe liked the doctor right away. He was nice and took time to talk with the adolescent and, unlike some other men, seemed to respect his mother, who appeared genuinely happy. As Christ and O'Keiff's relationship developed, her children began spending more time with them as well, sometimes at Christ's small two-bedroom apartment. Joe sometimes went running with his mother's boyfriend and the doctor helped nurture Joe's budding interest in track and cycling. The two often biked along Braes Bayou. Joe was so into it that his mother bought him a twenty-one-speed bike for his eleventh birthday in July.

Dani also liked Christ and felt comfortable around him. Never having met her own father, she thought it was cool to have a "dad" around. Sometimes he had a short temper or said something mean to someone, but the child thought that was normal. Unlike O'Keiff's last husband, Christ was used to being around children and willingly included them in their plans, talked easily with them and sometimes played games with them.

Even though Dani often clung to him or met him with an eager embrace, he wasn't overly affectionate toward Joe or Dani. That didn't bother O'Keiff, who thought Pat Johnson had been too eager to have her sit on his lap and try to get close to her when he had started dating her mother.

The one familial exception to Christ's endorsement came from O'Keiff's beloved Dalmatian, Nick, who clearly hated John and didn't want him around. The dog, friendly to nearly everyone else, regularly threatened Christ by slapping its long snout beneath the intruder's groin, looking him in the eye and growling. The normally congenial canine acted up whenever the doctor was around, peeing in the house, being ornery and even running across their backs as they made love. Carol didn't heed that warning any more than she did those from her coworkers.

Margaret Edwards, too, had heard a lot of good things about her daughter's new boyfriend. She liked the fact that her daughter finally was with a professional man. She was less impressed after she met him. When Margaret and Dan Edwards visited that summer, Christ treated them to dinner at his favorite restaurant, The Doctor's Club. It seemed to both Dan and Margaret that Christ had trouble maintaining a decent conversation, making stupid jokes instead, and while he obviously was intelligent, he did not seem to have the proper social skills. Margaret Edwards knew her daughter thought he was charming, but she had trouble understanding why. After hearing Christ ordering her daughter around for a while, Margaret saw a red flag and told Christ that O'Keiff was not going to change her ways.

She would after they were married, he answered arrogantly. He intended to "train" her, he added.

"This might be a real serious problem," Margaret remembered thinking, but she didn't express any reservations to her daughter, who wouldn't have listened to her anyway.

After six months, Christ told O'Keiff he wanted to marry her when his protracted divorce was finalized. O'Keiff recalled thinking, "Wow! I can't believe this is happening to me." After all of her nightmarish relationships, she thought life with her new boyfriend was a dream. In her usual attitude in which her optimism overwhelmed any warning signs, she could see nothing but a happy future ahead. She still missed having a husband around to help raise her children. Christ also told her he intended to fight for custody of his three children and, with the host of sins and shortcomings he attributed to his wife, he was convinced he would win. Although he was obviously bitter about his divorce and didn't respect his wife, calling her "stupid," O'Keiff believed the ugly tales he told about Gay and didn't blame him for fighting for his children. When Christ dropped off the children at the end of his weekends with them, Gay opened the door enough to let the children in and then closed it without talking to her husband. After hearing all the stories of the things she had done to him, O'Keiff could see why he wanted to be rid of her. They both knew blending a family with five young children could be challenging, but they felt they could manage. Dani and Stephanie played together during their first few visits, but that changed and they never got along too well after that. Each thought the other girl found a way to start trouble and get them both, if not all five kids, into trouble. Neither Dani nor Joe was particularly fond of Stephanie, who seemed to them a spoiled daddy's girl, but they really liked Michael, whom

Dani thought was bighearted and sensitive, and enjoyed playing with him. The youngest, Jacob, was just a toddler at the time and didn't evoke any strong feelings from them either way. They thought he was cute but too young to play with. While Christ and O'Keiff each loved their own children, neither wanted any more and she planned to have a tubal ligation.

Carol O'Keiff was always a harsh arbiter of her own looks, and Christ didn't help her self-esteem, judging her with the critical eye of a plastic surgeon bent on fixing her into his idea of the beautiful woman, as he had with Gay. His ideas for remaking O'Keiff emerged gradually, focusing on only one problem area at a time, or at least what he viewed as needing fixing. She knew he didn't like her tattoos, and she was ready to have a few but not all removed. He now badgered her about her breasts.

"We can fix those. They look like something out of *National Geographic*," he told her more than once, usually after they had just made love. Always proud of her once pert B-cup chest, she wasn't pleased to see them sagging from age and two pregnancies, but she thought she looked pretty good. "Have you ever heard the term 'socks with rocks in them'?" he asked.

"What?" Carol said, shocked that her lover actually would insult her like that.

"Your breasts look like socks with rocks in them," he repeated.

She heard it so many times over the ensuing months that she became self-conscious; she finally asked what could be done for the sagging. The easiest way to correct that problem would be to have breast implants, Christ advised, and offered to do them. Although she had once thought that only bimbos had boob jobs, working in the plastic surgery unit had shown her otherwise. He pressured her for months, and when she sched-

uled an appointment to have her tubes tied, he suggested that she get the implants at the same time. The
operating room and anesthesia costs already would be
covered, and he offered to do the cosmetic surgery for
free. After being made to feel so bad about her disap-
pearing youthful figure, she began to look forward to
it and thought having it done for free was a perk of
dating a plastic surgeon.

When she went to his office for a consultation, he
showed her two huge implants, about DD cups, which
he planned to use for her surgery. Primarily doing it
for the lift, O'Keiff had been thinking about going up
to just a C cup. A double D was definitely out of the
question, she told him, and they argued about the size.
During her last pregnancy, she had swelled to a DD cup
and hated having that much sagging weight on her
chest. He also suggested removing the tattoo on her
abdomen. She had had "property of Les" covered over
long ago, but the delicate heart and rose had been the
second of her six tattoos and remained her favorite. But
since she planned on marrying Christ, she gave in to
please him.

Once those issues were settled, he took the opportunity of her having surgery to again try to talk her into
his other desire, the labial ring. She always had refused
to have it done, citing the pain as an excuse. Now he
suggested that he could pierce her while she was under
anesthesia and unable to feel it. It would mean so much
to him and certainly would amplify his sexual pleasure,
he told her. Finally, she acquiesced under one critical
condition—absolutely no one could know about it. She
would be too humiliated, otherwise. No problem, he
assured her. He planned to wait until only he and the
anesthesiologist were in the operating room; then, as
he was working on her tattoo in that general area, he
would quietly pierce her. No one would know.

While Christ was busy planning to remake his girl-friend, he still was fighting bitterly with his wife, mostly about their three children, prompting the judge in the ongoing divorce case to look to others for recommendations. Juvenile probation officers with family court investigated the family, noting in a report filed with the court that it was "extremely concerned about his allegations of physical abuse to the children and his lack of involvement trying to prevent it." However, they found nothing to substantiate his allegations that she was "brutalizing" their children or that she was "stupid" and an alcoholic. The report noted that Gay had claimed her husband had spit in her face and that his sex life was bizarre. An investigator interviewed several of their friends, including Novak, all of whom said that both were good parents, although John always put his personal needs ahead of his children's. He would frequently leave them to go running or to go out on dates during weekend visitations. Some thought Gay wanted custody only to collect child support; others thought John wanted it only so he wouldn't have to pay it. The chief juvenile probation officer recommended that Gay be made managing conservator of the children but reported that the kids were confused about "splitting their loyalties between the parents. . . . The children are trying hard to love very complicated parents who keep accounts on each other."

A few months later, the judge appointed a Baylor psychiatrist to evaluate both parents and all the children and make a recommendation regarding custody. After meeting with each member of the family individually and each child alone with just the mother or father, interviewing their mutual friends or acquaintances, talking with the adults' individual therapists and reviewing records from the July 1989 assault on Gay, Dr. Richard B. Pesikoff wrote to the judge overseeing the divorce that he strongly recommended that Gay receive primary custody of the kids.

In the detailed, ten-page letter, dated June 17, 1990, which became part of their divorce records, Pesikoff reported that both Gay and John had said the case was a battle more about power than custody. Gay said her three children got along well with one another and she wanted them to stay together after the divorce. She told the psychiatrist that she did not believe that John truly cared about their children and that she always had been responsible for their care, education and other needs and had not abandoned them as her husband had. He resented having to pay child support, she claimed, and complained that while John always had supported the children's attendance at private schools, he now wanted them in public schools. She denied her husband's allegations that she had ever physically abused the kids.

In his interview with Pesikoff, John Christ verbally attacked Gay on several fronts, telling the examiner he had seen signs of physical abuse on the children, that he believed she was an alcoholic and that "she was never interested in the children." He claimed to have been "both mother and father" to their kids, even though Gay had wanted to have them. She had had others do much of the child care, he said. As proof of her alleged drinking problem, he said he had seen Gay drink one or two glasses of wine in the evenings and had seen bruises on her legs. Calling her a "cold person," he told the examiner that he was in "the wrong relationship." He complained that he had spent a lot of money on Gay, buying her cars and fur coats, but that she had refused to go back to work when his business slowed down. He said he had been seeing a therapist for most of the previous three years.

As he had with the family court investigator, he told the examiner that he currently was dating a few women but had no plans to remarry. He admitted taking the children with him when he visited his girlfriends. He told the examiner he had some friends but many of them proved to be "fair-weather friends" and had deserted him.

With the examiner, John stuck to his story that he had only grabbed Gay's arm during the July argument and that she had tripped and had broken her nose. He admitted having been arrested, fined and put on probation. To support his claims that his wife might have abused their kids, he showed the examiner a number of photos and described cuts and bruises he had seen on his sons. He admitted, however, that the children hadn't told him how they had gotten the bruises and that he didn't have any direct evidence that any abuse had occurred.

Pesikoff said in his letter to the judge that Hope Nordmeyer, John's therapist, reported that he initially went to see her "because of problems with his relationships with women and has worked on his family of origin. She felt he has made progress in sorting out his relationships with women," Pesikoff wrote. She thought he was a good parent.

Each of the three kids seemed comfortable and happy when left alone with either mother or father, the psychiatrist noted. Stephanie even sat in her father's lap during their meeting with the examiner, but John became sidetracked when talking about money and other issues in the divorce in front of the six-year-old. Both parents seemed to love their children, the examiner wrote, although John had not always been consistently available to his children. During his interview with just Stephanie, she was asked what her three wishes were: "I'd like to know when the divorce will be over"; "Mom and Dad to be good parents to me"; and "I want Mommy and Daddy to get back together." She believed both her parents loved her. Michael's three wishes were more childlike and less worrisome than his sister's. The five-year-old wanted all the Ninja Turtle toys, all the Lego castles and more toys than his sister. He, too, felt loved by both his parents.

In his summary, Pesikoff wrote that Gay had been "a very devoted and consistent parent," and he found no evidence of alcoholism or child abuse, as her husband alleged. "Dr. Christ has, while verbalizing a great deal of affection for his children, been less available to the children. . . . Dr. Christ appeared to have had problems with intimacy and has had difficulties consistently investing in a long-term relationship with a woman."

Christ, of course, never shared the report with the current woman in his life, the one he was operating on both physically and emotionally.

After O'Keiff's gynecologist performed a dilation and curettage and tubal ligation on July 6, 1990, Christ took control of the operating room, slicing an incision, one and three-quarter inches, beneath each breast and inserting the relatively large implants. After stitching her closed, he cut away the two-inch tattoo. Although he noted on the operating report that he was removing a scar and part of the tattoo, she said there had been no scar there until after he operated, taking the entire tattoo.

After Christ finished surgery, the operating staff prepared to leave.

"We're not finished yet," the surgeon said. He then shocked the others by piercing O'Keiff's labia.

The tale quickly made its way out of the OR and through the hospital corridors, sparing few ears. One story had it that an argument had ensued in the OR because the patient had not consented to the procedure. O'Keiff's signature, however, was on the consent forms, which listed the labial piercing among the pro-

cedures. Most found it kinky. "Eyebrows were raised,"
said one surgeon, adding that it wasn't something that
even needed to be done in an operating room. Still, it
was the juiciest, most salacious piece of gossip to surge
through the illustrious hospital in a long time and it
seemed everyone had heard. The patient's privacy
hadn't been spared. Everyone seemed to know that it
was O'Keiff who had been pierced and it had been
"The Stairwell Stud" who had done it. Christened "the
wedding ring in her vagina," the ridicule had it that "it
was being kept there until the divorce from Gay was
final." The only one who didn't know the latest gossip
seemed to be O'Keiff herself, who believed Christ had
pierced her in private and that no one knew.

As she slowly came out of the anesthesia, O'Keiff
glanced under her hospital gown and gasped, "Oh, my
God!" Her newly enhanced cleavage was bigger than
she expected and she thought he had put in implants
much bigger than she had wanted. The surgeon assured
her that her breasts were just swollen from the operation.

Following the outpatient surgery, Christ took her to
his apartment to recover. A friend was staying with Dani
and Joe, and O'Keiff assumed that her lover was going
to take care of her. She got her second shock of the
day when he told her he was going out with friends that
night and left without even telling her where he was
going.

Uncomfortable and in pain that evening, she went in
the closet looking for a more comfortable shirt to wear.
As she was thumbing through Christ's dress shirts on
the rack, she uncovered a box. Curious, she peeked inside and got her biggest shock of the day. She didn't
go through everything inside his "porn box," as she
would come to refer to it, but she saw several adult films,

pornographic magazines and a few dildos. "Oh, my God!" she said to herself.

Even after the post-op swelling subsided, O'Keiff's average B cups had expanded to head-turning Ds, a full cup size larger than she had wanted. She was surprised, though, at how much extra attention she now got from men—something she always had relished—and she rediscovered her fondness for low-cut blouses and dresses. Although initially reluctant, she was more than thrilled with her implants. Her labia still hurt like hell. Any friction made it worse, even that from wearing panties, and she couldn't walk in a normal fashion for a week, confirmation to those at the hospital who had heard the gossip. O'Keiff believed no one knew, so to cover her odd walk, she told everyone it was the pain of having the tubal ligation. Finally, three weeks later, Mildred Hall, one of the ward clerks whom O'Keiff was friends with, was brave enough to ask her supervisor if the rumor was true, though she couched it somewhat by saying: "You know what I heard? I heard Dr. Christ pierced somebody's you-know-what."

O'Keiff was mortified but hoped her face didn't reveal it. She tried to feign shock instead. "He did what?" she exclaimed. "You're kidding!" Inside, she was dying.

"Did you know anything about that?" Hall asked, scanning her boss's face for any telltale signs.

"No! That's awful!" O'Keiff said. Now she was paranoid everyone knew the truth but tried to act as though it weren't her.

That afternoon at home, she relayed the conversation and her embarrassment to Christ. Expecting a little sympathy and an explanation, she was disappointed when he laughed it off, saying, "Don't worry about it. Keep denying it and it will pass." For weeks, O'Keiff was furious, believing that her patient confidentiality had been breached by someone in the operating room other than her husband-to-be. She considered filing a lawsuit, but Christ, disturbingly unconcerned about her humiliation, talked her out of it. "You'll never be able to go back to work at Methodist," he said, knowing how much her job meant to her.

"I'm ruined there anyway," she concluded, but decided to drop the idea.

Two days after the piercing, they had sex for the first time, painfully for Carol. Even later, the labial ring never increased the sexual pleasure for O'Keiff, although it noticeably increased her boyfriend's enthusiasm. He told her it increased the sensations he felt, but she chalked it up to psychological effects. "Now, you're my sex slave," he told her. She laughed off his remark, not knowing if he meant it, but it made her feel a little degraded. She had done it to please him, as a sign of her commitment to their relationship.

Planning to marry once Christ was divorced, the couple decided not to wait to move in together. Although Christ lived in a small rented apartment, he didn't want to move into the house his girlfriend had bought only months earlier. He complained about the commute from Sugar Land to the Medical Center. Although it was just nineteen miles away, O'Keiff knew that the city's growing traffic problems could make it a forty-five-minute drive during rush hour, which, on her shift, wasn't a problem, but she knew it might be for him. Christ also didn't like her house, which she had purchased through the Housing and Urban Development (HUD) program for just $60,000, using $4,000 her mother gave her for a down payment. "I thought it was neat. I was proud to have a house," she said, and was in the process of slowly remodeling it. She agreed to move closer to the center of town, even though that meant they would have to find a house to rent and she, in turn, would have to become a landlord.

Christ also had new sexual plans for them. One night, she indulged his fantasies and she let him shave her pubic area. He returned the favors by making her sexual experience incredible that night. Afterward, as she lay in bed, he returned with a beautiful, albeit somewhat small, diamond ring and asked her to marry him. She immediately agreed. He popped open a bottle of champagne and they toasted their futures. A short while later, he admitted that he previously had given the ring to Novak. O'Keiff never knew whether or not Novak had worn it, but she told herself she didn't care. She knew Gay was giving Christ a hard time and costing him lots of money. It was a one-third-karat diamond solitaire, and O'Keiff wore it proudly. Naturally, she believed she was the only woman in his life. Had she gone to the courthouse and read her husband-to-be's divorce file, she would have found it far more interesting than the books he recommended.

The two found a large, airy three-bedroom ranch they both liked in Bellaire, a suburb with a more affordable but less prestigious address than the neighboring West University Place, where the surgeon once lived.

That summer, O'Keiff and her kids packed up their things and moved yet again, this time to Teas Street. She still had dreams of a better, more stable life. All three were disappointed when Christ insisted that she get rid of Nick, their beloved Dalmatian, who hated the surgeon. Though Carol loved animals, her intended would not let her have any other than fish. The four were basically happy, facing only minor adjustments to living together. However, when Christ's three children visited for the weekends, he insisted O'Keiff not spend the nights at home, claiming he did not want to set the wrong example for his children since the couple was not married. In truth, Gay still was giving him a hard time about having their children around his paramours, and they were under a restraining order that prohibited either from having someone of the opposite sex overnight, unless he or she was a relative, when their children were present. So, when he had his children overnight or on weekends, he dropped O'Keiff, and sometimes her children, at a local motel. She tried to be understanding but was not pleased with the cheap, somewhat sleazy places he took her. He insisted the motels were fine and claimed he couldn't afford better at the moment.

On October 3, Gay and John Christ finally were divorced, nearly twenty-one months after they had separated for the last time. Gay got custody of the children.

Following a hearing that day, the judge approved their fifty-three-page divorce decree, with the expressed stipulation that "it is a contract and judgment" agreed to by both Christs, as opposed to a judge's order. While it allowed each to later sue for revisions in issues that affected the children, including support payments, the rest of the contract could be changed only with their mutual consent. As part of that, at John's request, Judge Robert S. Webb III split the case in two—the injury claim would be decided later and separately from their divorce.

Both were named joint managing conservators of the children, meaning John had equal rights to make decisions regarding them and responsibilities toward them, all of which was spelled out in excessive detail, far more than the typical divorce case. But Gay had won what was most important to each of them—the children would live with her. Further, the estranged couple agreed to abide by the clause, which became part of the court order, prohibiting them from having an unrelated, overnight guest of the opposite sex with the children present. The decree also specifically ordered that they could not contact the other in any manner except for matters pertaining to the children. Christ was ordered to pay his ex-wife $2,550 a month in child support, in bimonthly payments. It would be reduced when each child graduated from high school or no longer was Gay's responsibility, but not by a third. Christ still would be expected to pay $1,700 a month when their youngest child was the only minor. He still owed his wife $1,100 from court-ordered temporary support he had not paid previously.

Eight pages of the decree were devoted to listing who got what of their material possessions, seemingly regardless of their value, from a can opener to eight Waterford cordial glasses to a bug light to bedsheets. Even what they listed as their separate property was spelled out, right down to Gay's makeup mirror, heating pad and iron. She also listed thirteen valuable pieces of jewelry and her full-length ranch-mink fur coat.

Although he had lost custody, Christ didn't see it that way. It was just a temporary setback, he told O'Keiff. He still intended to get custody. However, he happily told her that they could start making plans for their own future as husband and wife, neglecting to tell her that Gay's personal injury case against him had been split from the original divorce case and was still pending.

Ten

Christ and O'Keiff headed to Boston a couple of weeks later for a plastic surgeon's conference mixed with a romantic getaway. The historic city with its fine restaurants, beautiful architecture and splendid autumn colors invigorated them both. It was Christ's favorite city as well as neighbor to his birthplace, and while unpacking in the hotel room, he surprised O'Keiff by suggesting they get married during their trip. His ever-spontaneous fiancée excitedly agreed. The next morning, they headed to the Suffolk County offices at Pemberton Square and filled out the application for a marriage license so they could wed a couple of days later. The most special outfit she had packed—a Middle Eastern purple silk tunic and pant set her mother had bought her in Saudi Arabia—she had just worn to a surgeon's social. She loved it but her husband-to-be had not, although he lightened up once he heard the admiring compliments she received. But this was her wedding day and she wanted to look good for him, so she donned the next dressiest outfit she'd brought—a short black skirt, black blouse and a naval jacket. This time, he told her she looked good, and hand in hand, they boarded the subway and headed for Cambridge. On October 22, a justice of the peace pronounced them husband and wife after an unceremoni-

ous, one-minute rite. They didn't even have rings to exchange.

Afterward they took another vow—not to tell any of
their family or friends of their impromptu wedding. It
would remain their secret. They wanted their children
to feel a part of it, so they decided to have another ceremony and small reception back in Houston, settling on
November 3, 1990, for their second wedding, giving
them just a couple of weeks to pull it together.

When they returned home, though, they couldn't resist telling at least one person, so Carol shared their
secret with Kayla Falls, who had been staying at their
home with Joe and Dani. She was elated, jumping up
and down. Her children were less thrilled when told
about their plans to get married. Knowing this would
be his thirty-three-year-old mother's sixth marriage, Joe
was skeptical but kept his reservations to himself. Dani
was angry. Her mother wasn't asking what they thought
but telling her that she was going to do it—and in a
very short time.

Methodist's chapel was chosen for the locale because
they had met in the hospital. On October 30, just before
4:00 P.M., the couple received their second marriage license, this one from Harris County, Texas. Christ
checked the box that he had not been divorced within
the last thirty days, even though his one from Gay had
been finalized just twenty-seven days earlier. The wedding, however, would be a month to the day after his
latest divorce had been finalized. When he and Gay had
married nine years before, it had been forty-six days
after the doctor's divorce from his first wife.

For this ceremony, O'Keiff bought a new dress—also
black. It wasn't just the color that surprised the guests;
the top was a tight-fitting bustier with a satin bolero
trimmed with tiny red rosebuds. When her mother saw
her before the ceremony, she couldn't hold back her

surprise: "You're getting married in that! It's really pretty, but for God's sake, Carol!"

"I've been married so many times I want something I can wear afterward," she said, more practical than she had been in the past. Even her five-year-old daughter thought it was an odd choice for a wedding dress. Not only was it black but it was a bit too low-cut and sexy, some guests thought.

Before the ceremony, O'Keiff ran upstairs to her unit to show off her dress to those who were working and unable to attend. She got a better reaction—at least outwardly: "Oooooh, girl," one clerk gushed out loud, "that Carol sure do know how to dress." Everyone seemed pleased that she was marrying a doctor. Admittedly, O'Keiff was pleased about that, too. Having grown up with plenty of money and status, she wasn't impressed with the assumed wealth of doctors—which was a good thing, considering her husband-to-be wasn't as financially well off as many of his peers—but she liked the respect she thought accompanied the position of doctor and wife. Even there, she knew Christ wasn't on the top tier among those in the Medical Center, just average. What really made him attractive to her continued to be what bound them together at the beginning, the deep conversations they shared and his prowess in bed. Later, those both would become negatives as well.

O'Keiff insisted that the traditional promises of obeying one another be deleted from their vows. While reciting his, however, Christ, apparently thinking he was being funny, implied that Carol would be his slave, referring to his new bride as his "trusted servant." Carol held her tongue—at the altar anyway—and Reverend Joe K. Dunagan pronounced them husband and wife.

The surgeon's remark wasn't the only thing that upset Carol and raised eyebrows during the ceremony. Stephanie, then nearly seven, walked up to the altar after the ceremony had started, clutched her father's hand and remained there for the rest of the ritual. Her father neither told her to sit down nor invited the other four children to join them. It was an odd scene. The couple didn't host a reception, so after most of the guests had left the chapel, Carol Christ, not at all amused, turned to her new husband and snapped: "Servant, my ass!"

"I was just kidding. I was just kidding," he assured her. She let it drop.

Margaret Edwards had given up a lot of hope for her daughter's marriages, but she believed this one had the best chance of surviving. After all, both were mature, intelligent and gainfully employed. Her daughter at least wouldn't have to support this husband financially.

Her friends and coworkers were less impressed when they saw the small diamond-and-ruby band that the plastic surgeon had placed on his bride's finger, one Carol thought more fitting for a girl's sixteenth birthday present. She didn't tell him that but was even more embarrassed when another nurse married a urologist and sported a huge, beautiful yellow-and-white diamond ring. Some of their coworkers were blunt, asking Carol, "Why didn't Dr. Christ get you a nice ring?"

"He's tight on money because of the divorce," she said, believing it but being ashamed nonetheless.

Carol dreamed of taking a honeymoon, even a three-day getaway, but Christ always had an excuse why they couldn't go. Though making in excess of $135,000 a year, the plastic surgeon said they couldn't afford it, blaming that, of course, on his second wife and the huge amounts she collected in child support. Carol left enticing brochures of Jamaica's beautiful beaches on the refrigerator, hoping to lure her husband away. It didn't work, but it would be many months before she gave up trying, renewing her efforts as their one-year anniversary approached.

John decided on the couple's financial arrangements: they would not have joint accounts and would split expenses, even though Carol earned less than a third of what he made. Out of her income, Carol paid for everything for her two children—her own clothes, food for the entire family, her own car and the maid. John paid the rent, the utility bills and for his other expenses. Admittedly, Carol was not a good record-keeper, rarely balancing her checkbook and sometimes forgetting to note an expenditure. Invariably, she accidentally bounced checks, but only by small amounts, usually less than $100. She was getting better, but every now and then, she had to go to the bank, always embarrassed, and make good on the oversight. Her husband, however, kept perfect records as far as she could tell. John generally treated when the couple or the family went out to dinner, unless it was Carol's idea and then he sometimes insisted she cover the check. It always was his decision who would pay, and he didn't tell her whose treat it was until the bill was on the table.

Unbeknownst to Carol, the injury case brought by Gay continued well after their marriage. Gay's allegations of intentional infliction of bodily injury and emotional distress, breach of fiduciary relationship, mismanagement of the community estate and breach of the marriage contract were still part of the unresolved claims. There would be numerous delays in getting the severed case to trial, most of them sought by the doctor. In an apparent attempt to question his ex-wife's mental stability, Christ asked the court to order his ex-wife to undergo a psychological exam by a psychiatrist or psychologist he would select, a request Gay fought. The case was set to be heard December

3, 1990, Carol's thirty-fourth birthday, but Christ sought and received another postponement.

Carol's sixth marriage began happily enough but began deteriorating just a few months into it. For Dani, the problems began almost as soon as the guests left the chapel. Having been abandoned by her own father, whom she had never met, Dani ached to have a father, and both she and Carol had thought she had found one in John. Almost immediately after the wedding, Christ seemed to turn on his five-year-old stepdaughter, showing little patience and blaming her for nearly everything that went wrong in the house. He once yelled at her after he found cat-paw prints on his car, which he had left in the driveway. They didn't have a cat and no one ever understood how, in his mind, Dani had been responsible for what a neighbor's pet must have done.

Now when she ran to hug him, he often pushed her away, even when he opened his arms to everyone else there. He would show her affection just often enough so that the child continued to seek it, never knowing when she would be embraced or when she would be rebuked. He toyed with her emotions and played with her delicate mind and sensitive nature as he was beginning to do with her mother.

Still, the doctor now insisted that Dani respect him by calling him "Daddy John," yelling at her if she only called him John, with which she was more comfortable. Dani liked having a father figure but was not comfortable making that leap. Carol thought that forcing Dani to call him "Daddy" so soon into their marriage, before Dani felt ready, was pushing it. Still, she wanted them to be a family and decided to go along with it to make her husband happy, urging Dani to call him "Daddy John." Christ also wanted Joe to call him "Daddy John," but since his own father was such a big part of his life,

Joe adamantly refused. Christ eventually got over it. Carol urged Joe's friends to call her by her first name, but when she or Joe introduced his stepfather by his first name, John got irritated and told the kids, "I am not John to you. I am Dr. Christ."

As with many blended families, especially in the early stages, having their five children together was not always smooth. Christ, though, seemed to foster rather than neutralize the problems. He even squirreled away treats for when his children visited, not sharing them with Dani or Joe. He hid food for himself there, too, and arranged things in his closet in a precise way so he would know if anyone had been in there. When his three kids visited, he would call them to his closet where he would dole out Twinkies, cookies or whatever goodies he had hidden. Even if Dani and Joe were there standing next to his own children, he wouldn't give them any of the treats, crushing Dani's feelings.

"These are for my kids. You get stuff all week long," he would tell her. Carol felt caught in the middle, seeing the hurt look on her children's faces and knowing she would feel her husband's wrath if she tried to stand up to him. Instead, she winked at her kids, signaling them that she had a plan they would enjoy. As soon as Christ left the house, she would call her kids, and she would raid his stash, sometimes giving her kids triple what he had given his.

On weekends when Stephanie, Michael and Jacob Christ were there, the newly blended family often split into its two original factions—Christ with his three children and Carol with her two. Even when everyone was at home, they did things separately, each group often keeping to its own room. Joe and Dani thought it was strange, but both enjoyed having time alone with their mother. They and Carol thought that Christ acted differently when his children were around—more standoffish and testy toward his new family, almost to the point of being a bully. Joe felt as if his stepfather was backstabbing him when he acted that way. Sometimes Michael would join his stepfamily watching a movie or playing a game in another room instead of staying with his dad. He admittedly was the favorite of his stepfamily, and they were happy to have him around. Carol thought that being the middle child, he got the least of his father's attention. Joe spent every other weekend with his father, and since Carol frequently worked weekends, Dani too often was left alone with her stepfamily. Usually, she felt left out and ended up calling her mom at work, crying and complaining that the other kids were getting something she was not allowed to have. Carol did her best to try to comfort her, promising that when she got home, the two of them would sneak away for ice cream or to do something fun. That usually would be enough to soothe the child's feelings for a while. She knew Dani was especially sensitive and she wanted her to feel special, not shunned. When she got home, she would tell the rest they were going to the grocery store or on some other mundane errand that the others likely wouldn't want to go on, and mother and daughter would slip out for their secret treat and talk.

Still, Dani longed for a father-daughter relationship and Christ was the obvious candidate. Even as he insisted that she call him "Daddy John," he refused to treat her like a daughter. One time, Jacob, still making the most of his terrible twos, chased Dani around the grocery store, trying to bite her. Dani, who was a couple years older than the child, tried to get away rather than risk hurting either of them. As she ran past, John stuck out his foot and tripped her, causing her to slam into a shopping cart, injuring her psyche more than anything else. "He didn't treat me very nice," Dani remembered. "He called me bad names. I didn't like him, but sometimes I did, sometimes I didn't." He cursed at her and threw increasingly nasty invectives at her; by the time she turned six, he routinely called her "a little slut" or a "bitch."

Perhaps the most painful wound he inflicted on his small stepdaughter, however, was refusing to allow her to join him and his own daughter in the Indian Princesses, a father-daughter club, even though she begged to go along. Stephanie loved being a part of the group and so did her dad, and they routinely went away on fun day and weekend trips without the rest of the family. Naturally, Dani wanted to be a princess, too, especially now that she finally had the father for whom she had so longed. No, he told her, spewing insults like: "You're not fit for it"; "You're not ladylike enough to be with the other princesses"; "You can't; it's a father-daughter thing." Years later, she was close to tears as she softly recalled the hurtful remarks.

In reality, Dani simply wasn't eligible to join the particular club to which John and Stephanie belonged. Although this clique was not affiliated with the popular YMCA organization, they used the same name and followed its principles. Christ's group, mostly made up of wealthy lawyers, doctors and businessmen and their nine daughters, had a strict rule limiting membership to girls in a certain grade. They wanted to ensure that the fathers shared quality time with one particular daughter, not all his daughters at once. For those with more than one daughter, other Indian Princesses organizations abounded, and fathers were encouraged to take the other daughter or daughters there. Since Stephanie was two years older than Dani, under the rules, Christ's stepdaughter wasn't the right age. The doctor never explained that to Dani, choosing to verbally and emotionally abuse her instead. Nor did he consider joining another Indian Princesses or father-daughter group with his stepdaughter.

By all accounts—even Joe's—Carol was too lenient with her children, but anyone who saw them together or heard her talk about them knew immediately how intensely she loved them. If Joe needed disciplining, it usually came from his dad. Christ treated both of Carol's kids much more harshly than he did his own. All of them still talk about the time the entire stepfamily was having dinner at home, and Joe burped at the table. John was furious, stood up and cussed at Joe. When his son Michael did it a few minutes later, John laughed, as if it were cute.

Christ had told Carol not to discipline his children. Once, though, she was so aggravated when Jacob would not obey her—and her husband was not there to help out—she swatted his butt. The shocked child cried a little; his pride was hurt more than his derriere. After that, though, the toddler seemed somewhat afraid of his stepmother, staring at her as if he needed to keep an eye on her.

Seeing the developing problems, Carol suggested that their new family, all seven of them, go to counseling to work on blending the two families. "We don't need it. We can do fine without that," Christ said, and wouldn't even consider it. Knowing how difficult it had been for her as a child, having first a stepfather and then a stepmother, she knew the kids undoubtedly would face conflicting emotions, especially as they regularly witnessed the tensions between John and Gay, who seemed barely to try to hide them. Now, Carol also was getting a feel for how hard it was to be a stepparent; feeling this was especially important, she continued to try to persuade him. While his persistence generally paid off in getting Carol to do what he wanted, her arguments did nothing to sway him. Once his mind was set on something, he was not going to change it.

Because of her own childhood experiences, Carol also tried to forge a better relationship with Gay Christ, at least initially, knowing they would be in each other's lives indefinitely. She had been put in the middle of her parents' bitterness, and she didn't want to do that to anyone else's children. She had experienced the other side as well. The friendly relationship she continued to enjoy with John Jackson and his second wife made things easier on all of them, especially Joe. Often when John Jackson picked up Joe for a weekend visit, he and Carol spent time chatting and not always about their son. That only seemed to aggravate her current husband, who, she quickly recognized, was jealous of her second husband. Christ started bad-mouthing her ex, but she never paid much attention, sure that the strikingly handsome, tall Jackson's appearance was at the root of it. "John Christ hated anybody that was taller than him, and that was just about everybody," she said.

But Carol and Gay didn't get along, although Carol claimed she tried initially, believing it would make all their lives easier. She felt she and all her efforts had been snubbed by her husband's ex.

The only good thing Christ ever said about Gay was to continue to compliment the way she dressed. That, of course, was a way to manipulate his current wife to dressing more in the style he wanted. Carol was still not conservative enough for his tastes, so he told her she needed to dress more like a doctor's wife, more like Gay. The couple enjoyed shopping together, outings that gradually emerged into situations in which Christ picked out his wife's clothes. More often than not, they weren't gifts. He told her what to buy, and she obediently did, even when it went against her better judgment. Carol tried to encourage her husband to update his wardrobe. He usually wore sports coats with patches on the elbows instead of suits. They looked OK but were getting a little tattered after years of wear. He certainly didn't look as stylish or as professional as some of the other doctors she noticed at the Medical Center, who clearly bought the latest styles. Christ refused to buy new suits for himself, insisting those he already had were perfectly fine, and, besides, he couldn't afford it anyway, he told her. That was his excuse for most things he didn't want to do and another chance to gripe about Gay. Outside the office, the doctor's wardrobe seemed a bit outside the norm to some, including his wife, especially the skimpy shorts he wore on his daily jogs through the Medical Center and oak-lined streets of the Rice University campus.

Carol, who had far more intimate knowledge, began to wonder about some of her husband's sexual interests. As the marriage progressed, John pressured Carol into sexual acts that he had not mentioned during their courtship, the idea of which made her increasingly uncomfortable. He wouldn't let the subject drop and he now shared with her some of the videos he kept in his "porn box."

The pressure wasn't reserved for the bedroom; he continued to tell her that she needed more cosmetic surgery. On January 3, their two-month wedding anniversary, she allowed him to slice off another of her tattoos, this time the lily on her left shoulder blade. Once again, he listed the procedure on hospital records as a scar revision. He harped on her nose, saying it was ugly and that he could easily make it look better. She liked her long, thin nose and told him so; that didn't seem to matter to him. It was during conversations such as these that he would remind her how he had transformed Gay through cosmetic surgery from what he called a dog into a pretty woman. After repeatedly hearing him complain about how ugly he said her nose was, she agreed to a nose job, too. On the day after Valentine's Day, he performed a rhinoplasty on his wife and noted on hospital records that she had a nasal airway obstruction, a procedure typically covered by medical insurance. Carol said she had no medical conditions and the procedure was purely cosmetic. This time, in order to better protect her patient confidentiality from gossipy coworkers, she was admitted under the alias of "Natalie Cohn," using the first name of her father's fourth wife and the last name of her paternal grandfather, although with a different spelling. After one night in the hospital, she went home. When she returned to work a couple of days later, her nose and eyes were still bruised, so there was no hiding that she had had this procedure. But unlike the labial piercing, it wasn't an intimate secret, so she didn't really care who knew she had had a nose job.

She had barely recovered from that operation when her husband had suggested another. Now he thought she needed a tummy tuck to flatten her stomach after twice giving birth. Aside from not believing she really needed this one, either, she knew how painful an abdominoplasty could be and she flatly refused. But the doctor knew her well enough by now to realize that if he kept pursuing the issue, she would give in eventually. Throughout the months that followed, he would periodically grab a small handful of flesh below her belly button and tell her he could tighten it up and make it look better.

"No, leave me alone," she told him repeatedly, pulling away from his insulting grasp.

Many plastic surgeons either perform some cosmetic surgery on their wives or have one of their colleagues do it, most in the field agreed. Notably, most of the surgeons don't seem to admit to having had any done on themselves. Even so, the number of surgeries Christ's second and third wives had at such relatively young ages seemed excessive. Methodist later initiated a policy prohibiting surgeons from operating on spouses.

The Christs' sex life grew even more adventurous. Some of their sessions got so rowdy that they awakened the kids. Every now and then, one would become concerned, knock on the door and ask if their mother was okay. Embarrassed, Carol assured them she was fine and that they were just "playing around" or "wrestling." A couple of times, though, she actually was glad for the interruption as John was hurting her. It likely was her pleas for him to "stop it" that caught her children's ears in the first place. Still, he didn't stop until the knock on the door. According to Carol, sometimes the sex was so rough that she, still sore the next day, got further chiding from coworkers. She had been with overly aggressive sexual partners before, so she told herself her husband was just overzealous. He seemed to always have another idea to try sexually.

Along with the sex, Christ's comments and attitudes were growing increasingly rough where his wife was concerned. Now, if she dared wear a nightgown to bed, instead of trying to entice her out of it with flattery, he merely grabbed a fistful of the fabric, saying, "What's this? Take it off." Even if he was mad at her and had no intention of having sex or even holding her, he insisted that she take it off, regardless of her desire or reasons for wanting to wear it, like warmth. But her life was easier when she did what he wanted, so she usually complied.

For his pleasure, she continued to wear the labial ring to bed, but it wasn't comfortable with panties, so she often slipped it out as she was getting ready for work. Whenever he found out, he became upset and intended to make sure she wore it all the time. He had her lay spread-eagle on their bed so he could reinsert it himself. Eventually, she tired of hassling with it and him, so she wore it most of the time as her husband wanted. With few exceptions, he demanded sex every day, no longer concerned if she felt like it or not. Although she had to be at the hospital by 5:00 A.M., he woke her in the middle of the night, commanding sex. Even when she agreed, he sometimes was overly aggressive and more so if she refused, sometimes raping her, she said.

Occasionally, she grew tired of his demands, and she argued vehemently and boisterously instead of giving in. That tended to just make things worse. He would say something insulting or punish her by completely ignoring her for extended periods of time. Although once understanding about her lengthy sexual history, he now began using her youthful promiscuity to attack her. If she told him that she was uncomfortable or un-interested in some sexual activity he proposed, he replied, "Come on, you can't tell me you haven't done stuff like this before." If he thought she had been flirting, he'd get mad and unload insults: "You used to screw everybody else in town"; "I'm surprised you don't have any diseases." Since her childhood, Carol had never been one to cry when she was hurt emotionally; she either kept it in or released it in anger. Always a little moody or irritable when under too much stress, she was succumbing to the mental pressures, growing more easily agitated, unable to sleep and even tearful. So as his emotional abuse escalated, so did their arguments. "Most of the time, when he was mad at me, it had to do with sex because he considered me his sex slave," she said. Even he realized when he had gone too far; the next day, he would extend some conciliatory gesture, sending her flowers—a single rose or a dozen, depending on how egregious he thought he had been—or a note inviting her to dinner. Still, he never directly apologized, but he definitely made an effort to romance her once again. Then in bed, she could look forward to the gentle and exciting lovemaking she most enjoyed, temporarily released from his coercion there. She so desperately wanted to be loved, wanted this marriage to be the one that lasted for herself as well as for her children, that she always fell under the weight of his charm again. Each time, she convinced herself that things were getting better.

John told Carol *she* was getting worse. He often told her that she and her daughter were crazy, declaring that Dani had a "baby borderline personality disorder." He used his doctorate as a weapon, telling his wife, "I'm a physician; I know something's wrong with you." Both she and Dani needed to go to counseling, he told them, drumming his diagnosis into her head and hammering away at her plunging self-esteem. She so loved this man and knew how brilliant he was, maybe he was right, she thought, the seeds of self-doubt growing rapidly with the mental fertilizer he spread over and around her. She called the hospital's Employee Assistance Program for psychological help and was referred to a counselor. He confirmed her husband's theory. There *was* something wrong with her—her marriage.

Warning that the abuse would only escalate, the therapist urged Carol to get into marriage counseling with her husband and prescribed Prozac to help her deal with the depression. So in late May, less than seven months after she had gotten married, Carol went to marriage counseling. Initially reluctant to go, John joined her for a few sessions. When the counselor confronted him about the abuse he had been wreaking on Carol, he quit going, claiming he could no longer afford it. Carol continued going on her own, sometimes sitting in on group therapy. However, between her surgeries, the move into their new house and their financial problems, she was able to go only sporadically.

Even with their mounting marital problems, the two dreamed of buying a nice house near good schools and the Texas Medical Center. They started looking around but Houston's economy had bounced back from the mid-1980s recession when the slump in oil prices hit the city especially hard. Now real estate prices and interest rates were rising steadily, seemingly putting their dream a little further from their grasp with each passing week. The nicer areas near the Medical Center—West U, Bellaire, Meyerland—were rising especially quickly as they were close to the heart of the city, downtown, the Galleria, the Museum district, Rice University, the Village and other popular places to work and play. Carol already had one house in her name and with her credit history and Christ's financial burdens, they first had difficulty finding something in their price range and then had trouble getting approved for a loan. While many of their colleagues lived in upscale West U, where even the tiny, tear-down houses were selling for hefty sums just so the lot could be used for a much grander, newly constructed house, the Christs knew they couldn't aim so high. They hoped to find something for around $160,000, which wouldn't have been a problem if Christ had been willing to move farther out.

After much searching, the couple finally found a house they wanted and thought they might be able to afford. The redbrick house on Timberside wasn't perfect, but it had what the couple really wanted—three bedrooms, a spacious family room and kitchen and a good address. The neighborhood, while not on par with those many of Christ's colleagues called home, was respectable and solidly upper-middle class. The house was built about twenty years before, and the inside had been updated since then. Hardwood floors predominated; it was stylish, albeit a little too pink in some rooms. Both John and Carol could see their family living happily there. Carol planned to decorate in an Art Deco style. A large oak tree shaded most of the front yard, and neatly trimmed azalea bushes lined most of the front of the house. The driveway had a security gate, protecting the detached garage, and a few of the windows and doors had security bars—not the best look but not an uncommon accessory in the increasingly crime-ridden city. Still, this neighborhood was family oriented and did not have a serious crime problem. In the past, Carol wanted to buy a gun for protection, but John immediately rejected the idea, saying they could not keep it safely away from the children.

The couple was dejected, though, when their loan was not approved. Much of their stuff was already packed, and they had scoured the better neighborhoods around the Medical Center and hadn't found anything else they liked that was even close to affordable. Tired of throwing money away on rent, John urged his wife to ask her parents for help with the down payment. Her mother always had loaned her money when she really needed it and her father had given her a little money the few times she had asked, but she never had asked him for this much money before and was embarrassed and reluctant to ask now. John said he was embarrassed, too, but they had no other choice if they wanted this house. He had financial problems, which he again blamed completely on Gay. Carol now finally understood just why he complained so much. He had always told her he paid a lot of child support, but until they filled out the financial paperwork, she never knew the exact amount. Like her husband, she was outraged at the $2,550 monthly checks he was obliged to pay her. At a later date, that figure would go even higher. After eleven years, Carol still got just $100 a month from Joe's dad. Although Connally had been ordered to pay child support, she had never collected any for Dani. Christ suggested going after Connally for it, but he seemed to understand why Carol didn't want the hassle of dealing with him if she could support Dani on her own. Connally could be trouble and she didn't want him back in her life, she told Christ. He understood and, for once, dropped the subject.

Reluctantly, Carol turned to each of her parents for help, hoping to spread out the burden. Her mother loaned her $5,000 and her father another $3,000. The Christs now had no problem getting a loan, purchasing the house for $164,900, leaving them with a mortgage of $147,000 and house payments of $1,755 per month.

Despite these dreams and financial concerns, Christ extended an offer in mid-May to settle the lawsuit with Gay, offering her $30,000. Carol knew nothing of these plans and it's unclear where the doctor intended to get the money. Gay, however, rejected the offer, demanding $85,000. So the case continued, as did Christ's complaints about his ex-wife. During their marriage and in divorce papers, Gay complained that her husband didn't devote enough time to his practice, especially after he had found a mistress, costing him money. John, of course, had not relayed those complaints to Carol, who started voicing somewhat similar concerns. Actually, they weren't the only ones who thought he neglected the career for which he had spent so many years training; many of his counterparts made the same observations. "John was a lost talent," said one. "I think he had a far better future and career than what he allowed for himself." Carol thought he should pursue a more productive and what she viewed as a more noble career. Instead of limiting his practice largely to cosmetic surgery, she told him, he should branch out and get into reconstructive surgery as well, helping patients maimed in accidents or deformed by disease. She had witnessed firsthand the impressive results of reconstructive surgery after other plastic surgeons, like Spira, had operated on them. Those patients had to be followed closely, and she soon learned that he didn't have an interest in those cases. They both knew he would have to go for more training to hone his skills, even if it just meant observing other plastic surgeons in the operating room. For the brilliant Dr. Christ, however, that would entail admitting he wasn't good at an area in his field and it was unlikely he ever would do that, Carol thought. Eventually, she gave up trying to persuade him. She began to think of her husband as professionally lazy and lacking in compassion for his patients. Her nagging and declining view of him only added to the tension in their marriage.

His wife also was not pleased with the pictures he hung throughout his office, mostly nude pictures of women, the type more often found hanging on men's calendars than in art galleries; most of these prominently displayed women's butts. She had hinted while they had been dating that he should take them down and hang more tasteful artwork. Now she was more blunt, telling him they were offensive and that his patients didn't want to see them.

"They're beautiful. It doesn't offend anyone," the surgeon insisted. Her persistent criticisms of the pictures only upset him and so she eventually dropped that issue, too. Christ had his own ideas about increasing business and, still to the chagrin of his peers and embarrassment of at least some of his family, he continued to advertise. "It's the wave of the future," he still insisted. It just was a little further off into the future than perhaps he had anticipated.

She continued to be one of his repeat clients. In July, she let her husband remove the tattoo of a shooting star from the nape of her neck. This time on the operative report, he called the tattoo a lesion, as excising that would be covered by medical insurance. Not long after that minor surgery, Carol was putting away clothes in his dresser drawer and was shocked to find the star tattoo now shooting through a jar of formaldehyde, her underlying skin still attached, of course. She asked her husband why he kept it. The doctor, who always complained that the tattoos on her body were ugly, now said that he thought this one was kind of neat and he wanted to keep it as a souvenir. She thought it was gross and a rather bizarre thing to do, but she didn't want to upset him by taking it away. Her psychiatrist would later tell her that was a clear indication of his narcissistic nature.

That summer, Carol did something she had promised herself she would never do. She got into a nasty argument with Gay in front of the children. During an extended summertime visit with the kids, Michael became sick while waiting for his mother to pick him up to take him to his soccer game. He told Carol he didn't want to go, that he thought he wasn't any good, felt bad when he missed a play and thought his teammates didn't like him. So anxious was he about going that he became sick to his stomach. That was enough for Carol, who thought the child shouldn't be forced to play when it upset him so, but when his mother came, she insisted he go. Gay saw that her son looked tired and drained from a day in the sweltering intensity of the August sun and drenching humidity and felt sure he would feel better once she fed him and got him around the other children. Carol was incensed, believing her husband's constant criticisms that his ex saw the children's soccer games as more a social activity for herself and the other West U parents than recreation for the kids. The two women got into a shouting match on the Christs' front lawn, which even Carol admitted starting.

"You goddamned bitch," Carol screamed. "Can't you see what this is doing to the kid?"

"Mind your business, you bitch," Gay yelled back. "He's *my* child. You don't have anything to do with this." Christ, already angry at his ex-wife about nearly everything, just watched, laughing. Michael, dressed in his uniform, was probably more anxiety-ridden now that his mother and stepmother were fighting over him in the front yard. As they passed one another, Carol told him, "Well, I tried, Mike," and he went with his mother to the game. With that notable exception, Carol said she never dissed her stepchildren's mother in their presence because she knew firsthand from her own childhood how much that hurt the kids. She never heard John do so, either, although he was convinced that his ex was bad-mouthing him to the children. Carol noticed that he regularly looked them over for bruises or any other signs of abuse, but he never found any as he certainly would have told her about it if he had. She didn't think it was odd, because, she said, "all the stories he told me about her, I had a pretty grim picture of her, too."

Christ still was intent on getting custody of his three children. Although Carol worried about having so many children, and knew her own life would be easier if Gay retained custody, she was supportive of his desire to have his kids with him and believed they could work out whatever problems might arise. She trusted that a judge would award custody to whomever he or she saw as the better parent, and so Carol did not worry about taking the children away from their mother.

As the newlyweds prepared to move, Carol had to take care of another problem. Her period had become so painful, heavy and protracted that it was interfering with her life and even her job. Progesterone treatments hadn't helped, so she opted for a hysterectomy. Christ seized this opportunity to induce her into having the tummy tuck, which he had been nagging her about for months. Since she was going to be under the knife, she relented once again. And she still had another tattoo he could cut off—the ivy that wrapped around her ankle, one of the ones she had planned on keeping before she met the plastic surgeon. On August 19, she reentered Methodist Hospital as a patient and underwent multiple surgeries. Again, he labeled the tattoo removal as an excision of a scar, although this time he described it as a tattoo as well in the report. After three days of agonizing pain of both her abdomen and her ankle, she was released from the hospital. Even when she had healed, she discovered a scar now wrapped around her ankle, far uglier than any tattoo. She knew her husband had done a poor job removing that one and she regretted it instantly.

She didn't have time to dwell on her scars or spend much time recuperating, however, as she and the rest of the family looked forward to moving into their new home the following month. Joe was impressed. It was the nicest house in which he had ever called home. To Carol, it was achieving another part of the dream she and her husband shared for the life they envisioned.

Eleven

The family enjoyed being in their new house—still, it wasn't the happiest of homes. Carol Christ sometimes dreaded going home, not knowing what problem awaited her. Both John and Carol thought the other was growing moodier and more emotionally volatile. They fought with increasing regularity, often about their children or money; these were boisterous arguments, which the children could not help but overhear.

Hardly a shy, shrinking flower, Carol tried to stand up for herself, arguing loudly with her husband, and she often was the first to lose her temper. As she always had, when someone hurt her feelings, she didn't cry; she got mad and let him know it. He knew how to push her buttons effectively, and when it worked, provoking an angry outburst, he blamed her for losing her temper. That became the issue, not whatever it was that she was angry or bothered about. When she argued a point, he frequently refused to address it, instead arrogantly replying, "That's a non sequitur." Then he waited silently for her to go to him to apologize, give in to his demands or try to win back his good graces. So skilled was he at manipulation and psychological games, she nearly always gave in. Never one to apologize or admit to having been wrong, he forced Carol to bear the sole burden of their problems.

When the fighting got loud, so did Joe's stereo. Dani was less fortunate as her bedroom was right next door to her parents' room; although shielded somewhat by the closets in each room, she could hear everything. When it got too loud or tense, she went to her older brother's room, at the opposite end of the hallway from their mother's, and slept on the floor, feeling more secure by the extra distance and Joe's protectfulness. When it was really bad, he wouldn't wait for her to come to him. Instead, knowing how upset his little sister would be, Joe picked her up out of bed and took her to his room. "Look how good my kids are and your kids are such little bitches," Dani remembered her stepfather yelling one night. It was hurtful, but no more so than when he called her "a little bitch" to her face.

Dani began seeing her mother in a dual light, as her brother had earlier. She seemed so powerful, except when she was around men, she thought, as she watched her mother give in time and again to John. She knew her mother did it to stop all the frequent arguments, but Dani didn't like it. John seemed to be angry a lot and Dani, more than anyone, was subjected to his seething wrath. "I would look up to Mom, and she wouldn't know what to do. She wouldn't say anything. You could tell she wanted to, but she wouldn't," she said.

John thought Dani was too old to suck her thumb; when he caught her doing it, he ripped her hand from her mouth. Carol knew her daughter wanted to, and when her husband wasn't around, she told her, "John's not here, it's okay to do it." Dani continued to wet her bed regularly. It was a problem she had never broken with toilet training; as the Christs' arguments increased, so did the regularity of her accidents. This was one area where John was understanding with his stepdaughter, knowing that it is a common childhood problem, although not one he experienced with any of his own children. Dani was very embarrassed by her problem, refusing to go to any slumber parties and often hiding her dirty clothes in her room instead of admitting what had happened. At times, the child's room began to smell and they bought her pull-up diapers to wear at night.

One day, Christ noticed a dent on his car in the driveway. He stormed in the house, dragged Dani off the couch by her arm and out into the driveway, cursing at her and accusing her of doing it.

Carol, who was in the kitchen, ran after him, yelling, "John, quit it! Let her go! Let her go!"

Pointing to the ding on his fender, he yelled, "Look what the bitch did!"

"She didn't do that." Carol defended her daughter, but let the insult slide.

"Yes, she did. I saw her out here playing," Christ shot back.

"I didn't do it, Mommy!" cried Dani, scared by her stepfather's rage and that she might be punished for something she hadn't done.

"How do you know somebody didn't do it in the parking lot?" Carol asked, still incredulous that this educated man would blame everything on a six-year-old.

Later that evening, Joe pulled his mother aside and warned her, "If I ever see him do that again, I'm going to get a baseball bat and beat the shit out of him!"

Christ was easier on Joe, but there were times when he wasn't spared, either. Christ was enraged when he found his stepson working on a large model ship in the formal living room, where his mother had told him he could, and irreparably tore the half-completed project to pieces. Joe was still in tears when Carol arrived home from work hours later.

Now Carol was furious. She found her husband and yelled at him: "That was a really shitty thing to do! I told Joe he could build that there. You owe him an apology."

"I told you and the kids," her husband replied, "I don't want any of their crap in the living room or dining room. That's our formal area."

She was expected to obey that as well. When he found her and Joe working on a puzzle in the dining room, which he wanted reserved for special occasions, he knocked all the pieces onto the floor with one sweep of his arm.

Things became more heated whenever all the children had been together. Although Christ accused Carol of being jealous of his children, it was he who seemed intent on keeping them divided. She found herself looking for ways to make up his repeated slights to her own kids. Unable to change her husband's ways, she tried to avoid confronting them. She changed her work hours, scheduling herself for weekend shifts when Christ's children were with him. Christ said that when Carol came home from work, she barely spoke to anyone, poured herself a glass of wine and then locked herself in the bedroom for the night. His wife saw that differently, too. She said she didn't lock herself in, but instead took her kids there to watch television or play games because they were feeling left out of whatever Christ and his children were doing. Often Michael would join her group for the evening.

Whenever she arrived home, Carol tried to assess the situation and diagnose her husband's moods, wondering how she would get through the evening without having a fight, especially if she didn't want to have sex if she didn't feel like it. For Carol, their sexual relationship was either agony or ecstasy, nothing in between. When it was good, Christ was a remarkable lover. Despite anything he did or may do, she still counts him as the best lover she ever had. But when it was bad, he could be mean and cruel. She enjoyed the rowdy sex as much as he did, but the rough, painful acts she could do without. After these rough sessions, she told him that the pain didn't go away, hoping he would agree to take it down a notch. Instead, he seemed to be pleased, as if her pain made him more masculine somehow, she said.

As her problems with her husband became more and more frequent and heated, Carol slowly looked to others for support. She turned to three friends and coworkers, telling them some of what was going on at home. They told her to get help and move out, but she didn't sense any urgency in their advice. She confided much of it to her mother, except for sexual scenarios, which she found too humiliating to share with her. Margaret Edwards encouraged her to try to work it out. "She basically gave me verbal support and said try to hang in there. She did not tell me to leave," Carol recalled. In retrospect, she believed that her thrice-married mother, who herself had been emotionally and verbally abused by husbands, questioned whether the problems were Carol's fault. "I think that being a victim herself, she still questions herself as to whether it was her fault or not," she speculated.

Her mother had a different perspective than most people in Carol's life, knowing so much about her past and that she was in her sixth marriage, not third. "I'm sure after six, they couldn't all be at fault," Margaret Edwards reasoned. "Carol's as strong as horseradish," she said. "Carol can be extremely hard to live with, mainly because of the mood swings." Yet, that didn't seem to be the entire problem, either. Margaret knew that many of the men obviously stayed in love with Carol for years after their relationships had ended. "Usually,

I would encourage Carol to stay married to these people, which was a mistake, but I didn't know what was going on," her mother said. "Carol usually didn't tell me what was wrong until things fell apart." That seems likely as Carol had a long habit of leaving out key details, even as she confided to those whom she trusted. So it was possible, even probable, that no one was fully aware of how treacherous a situation she was in.

Even David C. Kolberg, her marriage counselor, wasn't given the full picture. To keep her story straight with her husband, and because she was so ashamed of having been divorced so many times, she also told Kolberg that Christ was just her third husband. How many times she had been married and divorced, of course, did not excuse the abuse, but it would have certainly helped her counselor see the patterns in her life and better understand why she was so reluctant to have another failed marriage tainting her record. But Carol was one to look optimistically toward the future, still refusing to see the patterns or the heart of her problems. Each marriage she considered separately and each degradation by Christ a separate act, never connected to what he had done previously to her or to past wives. She wanted to believe that he would change, so she convinced herself that he would, at least for a while.

Speaking from firsthand experience, Dan Edwards said Carol could be a terribly difficult person to live with, but from his perspective, John seemed to be the one who started their fights and the couple sometimes engaged in nasty arguments in front of others. In those he had witnessed, he saw John as the aggressor, starting an argument, often by complaining about his wife's outfit, and ending it with stony silence. Calling him a "control freak," Edwards said, "John was a superego, never wrong, knew everything."

Carol complained to her marriage counselor that she

thought her husband had unrealistic expectations of marriage. He expected that they would never argue, and after they did, he punished her for her obstinacy by shutting her out emotionally for long periods of time. Instead of trying to work out their problems, he gave her the silent treatment, at which he was very skilled. He wouldn't talk at the dinner table and spent entire evenings alone reading in the bedroom, avoiding the kids as well as his wife. In the morning, he would leave without even saying good-bye. Eventually, Carol would tire of it and long to connect with her husband; admittedly, she would do almost anything to end the silent treatment. Her counselor told her that her husband was "withholding love" from her.

He wasn't withholding medication, however. Carol, too, eventually stopped seeing her therapists. When she did, her husband offered to continue writing her prescriptions for the antidepressant. Since the Prozac was helping her, she agreed. Along with the pain medication he was giving her, he also prescribed other drugs for his wife, including an antianxiety medication, an addictive narcotic, which she decided to take only now and then.

The one time she really needed medication, he didn't give her any, deciding instead that she could handle the pain. The silicone in one of her implants had constricted, creating an uncomfortable tightness and hardening in her left breast. Instead of treating her in his office under local anesthesia as he and other surgeons typically did, John tried to take care of his wife's problem at home. Severe cases required surgery in which doctors cut the scar tissue that sometimes grew around implants. Christ told his wife, without even the benefit of painkillers, to lie on their bed; he knelt over her and, using the weight of his body, squeezed her breast repeatedly, attempting to break the hardened substance, causing her excruciating pain. When she could take no more, he allowed her to rest for a few minutes before he tried again. After several attempts, she had had enough. The manipulations had done nothing but cause her pain. Her psychiatrist would later tell her it was just another example of her husband's apparent narcissism.

Carol's own financial problems added to her anxieties. The Sugar Land house that she had bought before meeting her husband needed a new roof. She couldn't afford the repair; her husband refused to help; the renters moved out. Next she couldn't afford the mortgage payments, but her husband refused to lend a hand, even though he had extended his hand out to her parents for help just months earlier. She lost the Sugar Land house to foreclosure. While their financial problems fueled their arguments, it didn't douse their spending. Even Joe thought they were going overboard, thinking both acted a bit greedy at times. He knew they both must have been pulling down decent paychecks, but they seemed to be enjoying a lifestyle beyond that, with their spur-of-the-moment purchases. They dined out frequently, with and without the children, often at pricey places. "How are they affording all this?" Joe recounted wondering at times. They were, of course, going into debt. For Carol's birthday, John bought her a $300 camera. He liked it so much he went back out and bought two more just like it, one for himself and one for his brother for Christmas. Yet when Carol came up short for her children's Christmas presents, John wouldn't lend her the money. To get money, Carol turned to one of Houston's numerous pawnshops with some of the finest jewelry she owned, including an $8,000 diamond bracelet her mother had gotten from her second husband and handed to her daughter when they had divorced. Carol had no intention of selling that or any of her other valuables, only leaving it at the shop so she could get some cash. When she got her next paycheck, she either withdrew the jewelry or paid interest to the shop so that it would continue holding it and not sell it. Besides, she thought, her best things were protected in a safe.

John Christ was still protecting his secret from his wife. As much as he complained about having to pay his ex-wife so much child support, Carol had remained totally unaware that Gay's lawsuit against John continued after their divorce. As Judge Robert Webb was prepared to finally try the civil lawsuit on December 12, 1991, stemming from the assault seventeen months earlier, Gay and John reached a settlement agreement. He agreed to pay her $600 a month in contractual alimony for the next ten years, to settle the suit. He now had to pay her $3,150 every month, and he wasn't happy about it. Even so, the judge's unusual ruling stated that the judgment was entered in favor of John, who, nonetheless, agreed to cover court costs, which are typically paid by the loser. It likely had to do with Gay's cash settlement from the insurance company under the homeowner's policy, which would not have been paid had John been found at fault in court. Legally, once he had served his probation after pleading no contest, his criminal record was clean. Sometimes John talked to Carol about having been arrested for assault almost proudly. Initially, he had been taken to the small jail at West University Place but was transferred to the huge Houston Central Jail. He told her the guys he was locked up with there were pretty scary. When the diminutive doctor told them that he had been arrested for assault, they then looked like they were afraid of him and backed off, he boasted to Carol, sometimes as if it were a joke. If he playfully threatened her while they were goofing around, he would joke, "Call 911."

During a rare open moment, Carol confessed to Christ that she had been married more than she had told him—but only once more. She had told her current husband about having dated the mysterious Tilson but now told him that she had married him as well. "I didn't count it because it only lasted two weeks," she said.

"That's OK, I understand," he told her. He would later use that against her as well.

Keeping the words of her therapist in mind, Carol still entertained thoughts of leaving Christ. She wasn't quite ready to make that move. He was tearing down her self-esteem, but contemplating a sixth divorce was doing that as well. Thinking about even the possibility depressed Carol. She didn't want another failure on her record, but she couldn't cope with this relationship, either. "I really didn't get real strong support to leave from anyone, but then I only confided in a few people," she said. "The only one that gave me really strong support to leave John was the person that understood him the most and that was the psychologist that we had seen together in marriage counseling and he knew exactly what was going on." Even without the historical perspective of her past, her therapist understood and advised her to get out; things would only get worse. She could not escape the urgency in his warning. They talked about the abuse, the relatively calm periods that were always shattered by some form of abuse—be it physical, verbal, emotional, psychological or sexual.

That Christmas, her husband gave her what could have been a good present—the motivation to move forward with a divorce. The subject had been mentioned between them, but they told one another they really did want to make this marriage work. Carol's mother invited the family to spend Christmas at her ranch in the Arkansas Ozarks. John claimed he could not afford the expense or the time away from work, but he repeatedly urged Carol to take her children. He told her he planned on working and spending time with his own children. Carol and her kids headed north for the holiday, but after a couple of days, she missed her husband and wanted to be with him on Christmas. Even though she knew the kids were disappointed, she told them to pack up their things on Christmas Eve; they were heading home a couple of days early. Before leaving, she phoned her husband to let him know her revised plans. She couldn't reach him at home, so she called his answering service. Dr. Christ was out of town, but the operator offered to give her the name of the doctor covering for him. Now Carol was pissed. She called her mother-in-law in Florida, who told her that John was at his brother's in Massachusetts. Now she wanted to go home and find out more. Instead of spending the holiday with her mother as planned, Carol and her kids drove a thousand miles toward an empty house. On the refrigerator door, she found her husband's airline itinerary, which apparently had been the way he had planned on telling her of his whereabouts. He had claimed to her that he could not afford to drive to Arkansas with her and her children, but he had flown to Boston, accompanied by all three of his. He had not even told her that he was going to have custody of his children for the holiday, only that he would be seeing them. She was fuming.

When she finally reached him, his excuse was simple: he hadn't told her the truth because he knew it would make her mad. He couldn't afford to take everybody and he wanted to be alone with his kids, he told her—although he was staying with his brother's family and so they weren't exactly alone anyway. Carol was as mad as she had been in a long time, but he completely missed the reason why. He used it as an example of her jealousy over his relationship with his children, ignoring the fact that he could have been with his children as well as her, Dani and Joe. The fact that he lied was a fact he chose to ignore. Once she calmed down, she had a nice holiday with Dani and Joe, who were glad their stepfather wasn't around to spoil their fun.

John, though, was still intent on getting permanent custody of his children. Gay Christ was at her office on January 15 when she was served notice by a deputy constable that her ex-husband was suing her to change the terms of their child custody. Just a month after they had settled the other case, he was going after her again.

That same month, Carol contacted a divorce attorney, but her husband talked her into dropping those plans. They entered another honeymoon phase before the arguments got more heated. During an argument a short time later, she harangued him about his odd sexual desires. According to Carol, he shoved her against the wall, put his hands around her neck and threatened that if she ever wanted a divorce, he would kill her. She didn't take that as a serious threat, only something said out of anger and a desire to protect his secrets.

Twelve

John and Carol Christ agreed that something was missing in their marriage. However, they still loved each other and wanted to be together. During an increasingly rare and open conversation, they couldn't quite finger what was wrong but thought it would help if they spent more time together and communicated better. Each missed the long, serious talks they had enjoyed in the early days of their relationship and they recommitted themselves to making this marriage the one that survived.

They always had so much in common and even now supported the other's career aspirations. Carol decided to pursue a master's degree, hoping to become an orthopedic specialist or nurse practitioner, who could prescribe some medications, do in-depth physicals and diagnose some conditions, kind of a frontline handler of the more straightforward cases, freeing doctors to see more patients. Carol called the numerous nursing schools in the Houston and Galveston areas that offered these programs. In December 1991, she had taken the prerequisite Graduate Record Examination and her scores were pretty good. The high-aiming Carol hoped to do better and planned to take the test again, this time studying first.

Christ also was excited about new developments in his career. He had been working with Dr. Gerald Johnson, a controversial Houston plastic surgeon, reputed for growing his business on the chests of topless dancers who worked at the city's numerous strip bars and more ritzy gentlemen's clubs. Johnson was famous for giving them enormous breasts, sometimes nearing the size of basketballs. Johnson, who reportedly had performed the implant surgery on Anna Nicole Smith, had a built-in backyard swimming pool in the shape of a breast, an expression of his gratitude for the money he made off them. What most interested Christ, though, was Johnson's surgical invention of inserting breast implants through the belly button, called the transumbilical insertion of saline-filled breast implants. In this procedure, the implants were implanted while still deflated, threaded into place and then filled with saline, leaving less scarring.

Johnson taught Christ the procedure and the two wrote a paper on the pioneering surgery, which they planned to publish in a medical journal. To go along with the article, Carol shot photos during some operations her husband performed. Despite the problems in their marriage, this project drew the couple closer together. They always had gotten along well intellectually and Carol was pleased to see that they still could. Christ showed his wife a thank-you he had written for her help as coauthor, telling her it would be published with the piece. She was touched by the gesture from her usually credit-hungry husband. Johnson wasn't pleased when he saw the proposed article; his name was listed second and he thought, as inventor, he should be listed first. Even in that relationship, Carol thought her husband was preparing to screw over his colleague, telling her—but not Johnson—that he planned to write a book about Johnson's controversies and legal problems. It was as if

Christ took every opportunity to gain the goodwill of his more established or respected peers, only to jeopardize that in the end. He never saw it that way, though.

Nothing could have knocked that point home for Carol more than when she accidentally came across what she came to call his "revenge jar." Waiting in his office for him after work one day, she went in search of candy, which he often had hidden somewhere. Eyeing a decorative Oriental jar on his desk, she hoped some M&M's were tucked inside. What she found when she opened the lid was something quite bitter. Inside, she saw just three slips of paper, each with a name on it: Spira, Shenaq and Gay. When he returned to his office, she asked what it was about. "Those are people that have done terrible things to me. Someday, I'll get them back," he said. Only then, when he felt he had exacted his revenge on each one, would he remove his or her name. When she started to comment on it, he warned: "Leave it alone. Just leave it alone." Having discussed divorcing this man recently, she let the subject drop, not wanting her name added to the mix. She knew he could be vengeful; she had seen it so often. He frequently saw it in the reverse, though, claiming one person or another had a "vindictive vendetta" against him. She had once seen him key a Jaguar in the hospital's garage, saying the doctor who owned it was "a piece of shit" and deserved it, not telling her who or why.

Unable to pay back the Edwardses' loan, Christ bartered with his mother-in-law, offering to give her a facelift as a partial repayment. Margaret said having been born during the Great Depression, she realized money was important to her; even when she had plenty of cash and didn't have to keep track of every penny, she still did. Although she had not planned on having cosmetic surgery, she agreed, feeling she would at least get something out of her investment. As a gift for her upcoming sixtieth birthday, he would throw in a nose job. She agreed to that, too, and her son-in-law now turned his scalpel on her, planning to make her nose smaller and her always attractive face more youthful. The nose turned out fine, but she said she didn't notice much of a difference after the painful face-lift.

Christ wasn't talking much to his wife these days, and she thought he no longer liked her as a person, let alone a companion. When he did talk, it often was about his problems. He worried a lot about the pending and ever-growing breast implant litigation that he, like all plastic surgeons, was facing. Women who had silicone implants were getting ill and there were allegations that the silicone, which had been found to leak into the bodies of many of these women, was at the root of their illnesses. The attorneys representing these women really were targeting the manufacturers of the prosthetics, but in the beginning of the lawsuits, everyone connected was named as a defendant. Eventually, the surgeons who performed the procedures usually were dropped from the lawsuits, but in the interim, they had to spend time and money defending themselves. Christ was facing a number of malpractice suits from dissatisfied patients.

Carol feared that her husband was no longer monogamous and suspected he had resumed his affair with Novak. Although he once had professed to be afraid of her, she now was calling him late at night, after the Christs already had gone to bed. If he wasn't seeing his former mistress, Carol felt he was trying to. Then her husband began getting unusual late-night calls that Carol just assumed were from Novak. Following such calls at 11:00 P.M. or midnight, she asked him who was on the phone and he'd say it was a patient freaking out about her implants. Knowing that patients never called their home directly, she knew he was lying but wasn't sure about what exactly, so she imagined he was having an affair. As each of her past marriages had been coming to an end, Carol had been convinced that every one of her husbands had been cheating on her. While that might have been true with some, it wasn't with all five. Of course, she had reason to worry about Christ, seeing he had admitted cheating on both his wives and didn't even try to hide it when he had been cheating on Gay with Novak.

In April, he got another call that disturbed Carol; only this time, it was her husband's reaction that bothered her. A general-surgery resident working in the Methodist ER called wanting a plastic surgeon's help on a severe laceration to a man's leg. The resident said he had felt uncomfortable suturing the man's leg and had been told to call Christ.

Complaining that the resident was cutting into his weekend with his children, Christ was rude to the caller. He asked the resident if the patient was black or white. Having overheard her husband's end of the conversation, Carol was mad. When he hung up, she let him know it, telling him a good doctor would treat the man and he had no excuse not to go to the hospital. She would watch the children.

Christ said he didn't care and complained that the attending physician, who had told the resident to call him, always dumped the crummy cases on him.

It wasn't the first time he had refused to go to the ER when doctors called for help, telling lies to get out of going. Why did he become a doctor if he didn't plan on helping people? she asked.

He said he didn't know. About ten minutes later, Christ called the ER and said he would go, but it would take a while to get there. He didn't leave for another forty minutes, first eating a leisurely dinner.

"There's someone waiting for you in the ER, John," his wife reminded him.

"Let 'em wait. They'll be fine," he said.

After he left, Joe, who had been raised to treat everyone the same and had friends of different races and religions, complained to his mother about his stepfather's prejudicial remark. This time, Carol couldn't defend her husband's remarks or attitude.

In March and April, Carol was spending some of her free time searching the area for possible rental houses for her and her children, emotionally preparing herself to move away. Sometimes Dani and Joe went with her, but they never let John know what they were doing. It was just a tentative step as she jotted down addresses and names of apartment buildings that she thought might work for them and peered in windows of obviously vacant houses, but she never even went inside any of the places. Still, Carol felt she was taking the first move toward breaking free of another troubled marriage, even though she hadn't decided to do it yet. There were times when their marriage was still good, although they were less and less often, and she knew she would be losing a lot if she walked out.

On the way to dinner at The Doctor's Club in the spring, Carol gave her husband a blow job while he drove, knowing her evening and night would be much happier for her if she satisfied him first. On the way home, Christ told Carol he found a good deal on life insurance through the American Medical Association, covering each of them for $500,000. The couple had been talking about their need for more life insurance for months, worrying about the high house payments and their children's futures should something happen to one of them. It sounded good to Carol, but he never brought home any paperwork, so she assumed he dropped that idea.

In April, Carol was hospitalized, but this time, her husband had nothing to do with it. An asthmatic, Carol developed pneumonia. She talked with her doctor, Ronald Sims, with obvious pride about her husband running in the upcoming Boston Marathon. On April 20, 1992, Christ finished the marathon in four hours and fifty minutes—well behind his own time of four hours and eleven and one-half minutes the previous year.

Back home later that month, she and Christ were watching a fact-based TV drama in which someone was using a gun fitted with a silencer.

"Carol, where do people get silencers?" Christ asked, knowing his wife was more streetwise than he.

"How the hell would I know?" she snapped.

"Considering your past, I thought you might have some idea."

Carol just huffed in disgust and the subject was dropped.

The first weekend in May, the blended family, all seven, headed west for a weekend at the Mayan Dude Ranch in Bandera with Stephanie's Indian Princesses group and their families. It was one of the few gatherings where anyone other than fathers and daughters were invited. Although this was a family outing, the Christs didn't act the part. Christ and his three children made the four-and-a-half-hour trip in his car while Carol, Joe and Dani drove separately in her Explorer. All seven could have fit in the Explorer, but Christ wanted to take both cars. Carol assumed he wanted time alone with his children, so she didn't protest much. They followed one another and the kids kept in contact with one another via walkie-talkies.

Carol met most of the other fathers on the outing as well as attorney Bob Sussman. Carol wanted to go tubing on the river, but her husband wouldn't join her, complaining that the water was too cold and dirty. Carol donned her bikini and went to the river with Joe. Floating along on an inner tube, soaking up the sun and enjoying the refreshing cool water, a handsome college coach, not with the same group, floated up beside Carol and the two engaged in some harmless flirting. Carol didn't know or care if he had a wife—she just basked in the attention that she hadn't gotten from her husband in a long time.

Back in the cabin, Joe and Michael argued over who got to sleep in the loft, dubbed "the cave." Carol suggested that each boy get it for one night, but her husband overrode her, deciding that his son would sleep there both nights. Stephanie slept there as well while the other three kids shared the second bedroom. Jacob kept his stepsiblings awake longer than they wanted. The parents got along for the most part and enjoyed their weekend together.

But the truce didn't last long. Carol's first cousin was getting married a couple of weeks later in San Antonio and she longed to go. It was the son of her favorite uncle, Jay Inman, Margaret Edwards's brother. That was the weekend, however, that Christ was supposed to have his children. Carol asked him to switch weekends and he refused, sparking a heated argument between the two. As he had the previous Christmas, he encouraged his wife to go without him. They had had his children the four previous weekends and Carol didn't understand why he wouldn't change in order to have a fun getaway with her. They rarely went out of town together. Besides, she wanted her extended family to finally meet her husband of nineteen months. They had a big argument about it, but Christ wouldn't even think about changing his mind. Carol told him he was selfish and had no conscience, stubbornly ignoring her feelings while she had made many concessions to him. He dismissed her, telling her she was being ridiculous. She took her husband's refusal to make any concessions to her desires as a betrayal. Nevertheless, she told her children they were going to San Antonio without him.

That Friday, Christ came home with a surprise for his wife. He had picked up the dress she had put on layaway at a boutique, paying off the $143 balance. Smiling, he handed her a hanger with the plastic wrapped dress and told her it was an early Mother's Day gift. Thrilled, she told him she would wear it out to dinner the next evening when they and Dani went out for an early celebration, and they talked about where to go.

The peace of the evening was pierced, though, when they got into another argument about going to San Antonio for the wedding the following weekend. Christ still refused to go. It was not a big fight, especially for them, but they were a little edgy when they got in bed that night, enough that neither wanted to have sex.

Thirteen

Carol Christ awoke the next morning, Saturday, May 9, 1992, looking forward to the Mother's Day weekend. She had rearranged her work schedule, taking a day of vacation, so she could have it off and spend time with her husband and daughter. Joe was with his father for the weekend, and since her stepchildren had been there for the past four weekends, she expected they would be spending the Mother's Day weekend with their own mom. Carol and Dani planned to spend Saturday afternoon at the neighborhood park for a fairlike benefit aimed at increasing awareness about crime and supporting the local police. Carol had volunteered to paint faces.

It was shortly after 8:00 A.M. when Carol walked out of the bathroom, still in her nightgown, after brushing her teeth and putting in her contacts. "What are we going to do today?" she asked her husband, hoping that he would go to the park with them. Apparently, he had other plans, as she was surprised to see him packing some clothes in a small blue duffel bag. "Where are you going?" she asked incredulously.

He snatched a flyer off his nightstand, thrust it toward her, hitting the tip of her nose with it, and snapped, "If you communicated better, you bitch, you'd know!"

"What are you talking about?" she asked, startled by his vehemence.

"I'm going to Lake Livingston boating with the Indian Princesses today," he said, referring to the state park seventy-two miles north of Houston.

This was the first Carol heard of this outing. She had rearranged her schedule and they had discussed going out that night for an early Mother's Day celebration. She was hurt that he had made other plans, ones that excluded her and her daughter. Fed up, she knocked his duffel bag off the bed and kicked it. She felt something hard against her ankle and yelled, "Ouch!" She bent over, saying, "What was that?"

"Hey, my camera is in that bag! If you hurt it, you're going to pay for it, you bitch!" he yelled back.

"I'm sorry!" Carol yelled, still rubbing her foot. "If your camera is hurt, I'll give you mine." They had identical cameras, but that was not her immediate concern. She walked quickly over to the closets where Christ was standing, grabbed both of his shoulders in her hands to keep him from turning away as he usually did, and shoved him against the closet, rattling the doors and his nerves.

"I'm tired of being treated like shit! I'm worth something! It's over! I want you to move out! It's over! No more!" she screamed.

Dani's peaceful slumber was interrupted by the explosive argument. Despite the early hour, neither of the Christs made any effort to keep their voices low. Dani sighed heavily, and realizing further sleep would be impossible, she got up and headed toward the kitchen. Glancing at her parents' closed bedroom door as she passed, she feared the entire weekend would be nonstop arguing and tension. She had been told by her stepfather repeatedly not to bother them when they were arguing. In the kitchen, she decided to get her own breakfast.

Standing on tiptoes, she pulled down the box of Trix, poured some into a bowl, covering it with just the right amount of milk. She was careful to put away the cereal box and jug of milk, not wanting to give her parents anything else to be upset about. Grabbing a spoon, she headed for a morning of cartoons in the family room. She settled on the couch and turned on the big-screen television. She flipped around until she found her favorite cartoon, *Popeye*, then cranked up the volume, hoping it would help drown out the arguing. It did help; she could still hear their loud voices, but not enough to understand what they were arguing about. *Popeye* helped ease her tension a little; it was funny, even though the characters were fighting, too.

Fed up and fighting back tears, Carol stopped trading loud barbs with her husband, turned and walked away. Standing next to the bed, she stared at her dresser on the opposite side of the bed, trying to remember which drawer her camera was in so she could give it to her husband. Christ grabbed his duffel off the floor and rustled through it. Carol assumed he was checking his camera, and heard him walking up behind her on the right, but she didn't want to argue any more at the moment. She just wanted to give him her camera so he would leave.

Suddenly she felt a sharp blow to the back of her head. She fell forward onto the bed, wondering what had hit her.

Dani heard a loud noise coming from her parents' room. Startled, she looked that way, but she saw only the closed door. She wondered what it was and guessed that maybe a dresser or shelf had fallen. She was tempted to go ask but quickly dismissed that idea, knowing she would only get in trouble with her stepdad.

He came out, closing the bedroom door behind him,

and walked into the den. Looking a little rattled after the argument, he paced the floor.

"Is Mommy OK?" Dani asked.

"Yes, we're both OK," Christ responded before heading back into the bedroom.

Carol, lying facedown on the bed, was semiconscious but could not move, speak or see. She had no idea how much time had passed, and a fierce pain unlike anything she had ever felt enveloped her head. She heard her husband's footsteps walking across the hardwood floor, near the windows and then at the foot of the bed. He was fumbling with something. She heard a loud gunshot and was startled by the blast. She was not hit.

"Ouch!" the surgeon screamed, and dropped the pistol to the floor. Carol heard the thud but was confused where the shot had come from because, as far as she knew, they did not have a gun in the house. Before she could figure it out, she blacked out again.

Christ again left the room, holding his left hand, the little finger dropping a trail of blood as he headed into the kitchen.

"Is Mommy OK?" Dani asked again.

"Yes," Christ answered.

"Are you OK?" she asked, concerned by the blood.

"No, I'm not OK! Does it look like I'm OK?" Christ said abrasively. He dropped a .45 clip into the trash compactor and washed his injured left finger under cold running water. Worried about potential swelling, he carefully slipped off his gold wedding band on the adjacent finger and placed it on the counter above the trash compactor.

When Carol regained consciousness, she slowly became aware of her surroundings. Although she still could not see, she could now move. Lying on her stomach, her head turned to the right, she felt around with her hands. The bed was soaked and sticky everywhere

she could reach and she knew she was lying in a pool
of her own blood. What felt like a pile of warm worms
were stringy blood clots, indicating she had been bleeding for a while as the blood was already coagulating.
She was not sure exactly what had happened.

In a strained, raspy voice, she called, "John! John!
Help me, John!" He didn't answer or go to her side,
so she yelled for him again, trying to make her voice
louder. He was pacing back and forth in the family
room, near an increasingly scared Dani, hearing but
not responding to her pleas. When he did not come,
Carol yelled for her six-year-old daughter. "Help, Dani!
Help, Dani!" she yelled as loud as she could. The terrified child heard her mother's anguished cries and got
up from the couch, intending to go to her mother and
find out what was wrong. Jamming both his hands into
the child's chest, her stepfather forced her back down,
assured her that her mother was fine and ordered her
to stay where she was. She started to cry, increasingly
scared about what was happening and frustrated that
she could not go to her mother.

Carol knew she needed help or she would die. But
because no one was coming to her aid and she didn't
hear anyone, she assumed that she now was alone in
the house. Phones sat on the nightstands on either side
of the bed, but she didn't think she could dial 911 without being able to see the numbers. A fear of being alone
in the room, where she might die alone, was welling
inside her and she knew she had to get out of there.
She thought she should get outside where someone
would see her and summon help.

She rolled over and off the bed, landing with a thud
on the floor. The trauma of the fall knocked her unconscious once more.

Christ decided he needed to make a few calls, and
though the order of those calls remained forever in dis-

pute, the most likely scenario was that he first called Gay. He was due to pick up his daughter in less than a half hour. He hit the speed dial and when his ex-wife answered, John blurted out, "I'm sorry I cannot come pick up Stephanie this morning for Indian Princesses." He was hysterical and crying, and Gay could hear a distraught Dani crying loudly in the background. "My wife and I, we have a gun and we shot each other," he told her. Despite the chaos and hysteria unfolding around him, the doctor thought to call his ex-wife so his little girl wouldn't be waiting for him.

He called his attorney, Thano Dameris, at home and left a message for him on the answering machine. He hung up and, finally, punched 911.

"Houston 911. Do you need Police, Fire, Ambulance?" the dispatcher asked.

"We need an ambulance. We've shot each other," said Christ, sounding frantic. Dani became more hysterical, learning that her mother had been shot.

"All right, sir, stay on the line for an ambulance then," she said, transferring the call.

"Houston Fire and Ambulance. What is your emergency?" a male operator asked.

"Oh, all right," the first dispatcher said, unaware that Christ had hung up and yanked the phone out of the den wall. "There's a man on the phone. He says he shot someone and they need an ambulance. I don't know whether he put the phone down or what. Are you receiving on Timberside?" she asked her counterpart, referring to the computerized system that automatically showed dispatchers the address from where the call came.

"Uh-huh," said the other one, sounding bored.

"Okay, they need an ambulance there."

The call was logged at 8:28 A.M. and an ambulance, fire truck and police were sent to the scene.

In the bedroom, Carol came to and tried to stand, but she could only get onto her hands and knees. Blinded, she felt her way across the rug, over the hardwood floor and toward the closed door, periodically yelling for John or Dani to help her. Still, no one came. She fumbled with the doorknob and opened the door. Relying on touch and memory, she crawled into the hall, turned left, heading toward the den and kitchen, aiming toward the back door.

Christ was shocked to see his wife had gotten off the bed and was making her way through the house. Seeing her mother's head soaked in blood, her once beautiful face badly disfigured, her left eye seemingly dangling out of its socket and her blood-drenched nightgown, Dani screamed in horror. She ran to her mother's side, sobbing, not knowing what to do. She tried to hug her but didn't want to hurt her more.

"Mommy! Mommy!" the child screamed. "There's blood all over you! Your head! Your eye!"

Carol reached out and felt for her child and Dani grabbed her.

"Call 911, Dani! Call 911!"

"Mommy, I can't! I can't!" Dani sobbed.

"You have to," Carol said. Unable to say much, she repeatedly told her daughter to call 911, hoping it would give her the unquestioned strength to go and do as she was told. Instead, the child cried and stayed by her mother's side, but she was leading her in the right direction and that comforted Carol, who was terrified that her husband might do something else to hurt one of them.

Dani held on to her mother's arm to keep her from falling over, trying to guide her to the kitchen phone, knowing the one in the den no longer worked.

When Carol got close to the kitchen phone, her husband told her coldly, "I've already called 911."

"I don't care. I'm calling them," Carol said, not knowing whether to believe him.

Sitting on the cold tile floor, still unable to see, she found that the phone receiver somehow was in her hand and someone had punched 911. She wasn't sure who but was relieved to hear the dispatcher say, "Houston 911. Do you need Police, Fire or an Ambulance?" The call was logged at 8:30 A.M., two minutes after Christ had called.

"I need an ambulance," Carol said weakly.

"Stay on the line for an ambulance, ma'am."

She heard the sounds of a phone ringing, and the dispatcher told her, "Ma'am, I'm transferring you to Ambulance. Stay on the line."

"Oh, hurry," Carol pleaded softly.

"Houston Fire and Ambulance. What is your emergency?" a male voice asked.

"I've been shot. I need an ambulance. I'm bleeding everywhere."

"OK, you've been shot where? Where are you shot at, ma'am?"

"I think I'm shot in the head, I'm not sure," she said.

"You think you're shot in the head?" he asked calmly.

"I think," she told him.

She lay on the tile and as she held the receiver loosely to her ear, she was afraid and anxious, but strangely, physically comfortable, no longer feeling any pain.

Then, emotionally and physically, she actually felt good. She knew she shouldn't, and she recollected thinking, "This is it—I'm dying."

Feeling herself slipping away, she whispered into the phone, "I'm leaving now."

"Hold on! Someone will be there soon!" the dispatcher said, nearly shouting. "The ambulance is almost there. You should be able to hear the sirens soon." The dispatcher told her to keep talking, encouraging her with questions: asking who had hurt her, who was with her now and seeking other answers that could be used as evidence later, although their call no longer was being recorded as the dispatch center took new ones.

The doctor was not helping his wife and was walking back and forth between the kitchen and the couple's bedroom, never saying a word to Carol or his stepdaughter. Dani was crouched down in front of her mother, one knee up, crying and repeating, "Mommy! Mommy!"

Although she couldn't really hear her daughter, Carol was thinking of her, of how she would be left alone in the world if she died. "I can't die; I can't die," she decided.

Snapping back into a more conscious state, Carol heard sirens in the distance. She mumbled into the phone, "I hear them. I think I hear them." The phone fell from her hand and John Christ hung it up. Carol silently thanked God that help had arrived.

"Dani, go outside and flag down the ambulance," Carol said, not wanting rescuers to take a second longer than necessary. The child was momentarily torn, wanting to stay with her mother but wanting someone to help her right away. She ran out the side door and onto the front lawn, waving her arms at the approaching ambulance and fire truck.

John Christ still had one more call to make. He punched the speed dial on the kitchen phone, and moments later said: "Swordfish." Carol knew it was her husband's family's secret code word, signaling there was serious trouble and he needed help. "Bill, Carol and I have a gun and we've shot each other," he said, and Carol knew that he was talking to his brother in Andover, Massachusetts. He hung up after just a moment and Carol again heard her husband's heavy footsteps on the kitchen floor. Christ went outside, leaving his wife dying on the cold tile floor and alone in the house.

Fourteen

At 8:34 A.M., the dispatch call was relayed to paramedic Roland Hobbs, a twenty-nine-year-old go-getter, with nine years' experience, based at Houston's Fire Station No. 33. The station's territory, which included the Third and Fourth Wards—some of the city's roughest neighborhoods—had been dubbed "Shooters' Alley" because of the common type of call to which paramedics responded. A couple of shooting calls per day was the norm, sometimes more on weekends. Hobbs and his partner, thirty-seven-year-old Darnell Evans, were among those eager to respond to shootings—calling in to dispatch as soon as they heard one drop—as it pumped their adrenaline and gave them another chance to practice their skills. This time, though, dispatch assigned them to the Timberside address; they didn't have to volunteer. This was the first time Hobbs, who had been a paramedic with the city for two years, responded to that neighborhood, known more for its family atmosphere than its crime.

At the Beechnut substation, Officers Charles K. Hutchinson and Jeff Hackett were getting ready to go on patrol in the volatile 17th District with their rookies, just two days out of the police academy, when the call of a shooting on Timberside went out as a general broadcast over their radios, meaning whoever was close should respond. With an ideal training opportunity, Hutchinson and Hackett jumped on the call, even though the address was just outside their district, in the adjacent 15th. Rookies John Siewert and Clemente Reyna were psyched to respond to their first shooting. Since they were assigned to patrol one of the most violent areas of the city, commonly known as "the Gulfton Ghetto," their training officers knew they'd get a shooting call during the three-week probationary period. A hotly disputed territory among rival gangs with heavy narcotics trading, the Gulfton Ghetto at the time was known to cops as a bloodbath. They didn't expect to be sent to a shooting in the Timberside neighborhood, however. As is customary in training, the rookies were behind the wheels as lights flashed, sirens blared and the adrenaline pumped.

Despite the 911 calls, the officers actually responding to the scene had no idea what happened—they didn't even know if the victim was male or female, let alone how the shooting reportedly occurred. The dispatchers generally gave little information over the radio but usually sent the responding officers a mobile call slip, written information sent over their vehicles' computers. In the race to get to a crime scene and safely navigate through Houston's busy streets, Hutchinson, thirty-five, who had been a training officer for eleven years and a cop for thirteen, said there usually wasn't time to read the call slip. The rookies had gotten lots of theory in the police academy. They were about to get the real thing and it would be memorable for reasons other than being their induction into what it's like to be at an unraveling crime scene. Being rookies, Reyna and Siewert were eager to take this call. Years later, that excitement would wear off as Reyna realized how much grief accompanied them.

Hackett, thirty-one, a training officer for the past year, considered a shooting to be the best training opportunity, especially if a suspect was still at the scene. It gave rookies the opportunities to observe or participate in all aspects of police work—crime scene protection, evidence gathering, arresting a suspect and filing charges, or, as Hackett described it: "The whole show all at once."

The ambulance and a pumper truck from the fire department arrived first, at 8:37 A.M., just three minutes after getting the call. The paramedics jumped out of the ambulance even before the driver had the vehicle in park. As Hobbs rushed toward the house, he heard a child in the front yard plead: "Somebody help my mommy!" She looked just a couple years older than his own three-year-old daughter, he thought.

Someone, he was not sure who, yelled, "She's in the house." As Hobbs rushed on, he noticed a balding man standing in the driveway with a wounded finger, but that was not his first concern. Hobbs and Evans rushed inside, where they found the victim lying on the floor. She and the area were covered with an enormous amount of blood. They set their equipment on the floor and set to work in the rhythm that came with working together for years. Hobbs put on a headset, which connected him to a doctor in the emergency room at Ben Taub Hospital, the city's bustling trauma center. He had no way of knowing that his patient was a nurse and understood everything they were saying, even their "codes."

"We have an entry wound in front of the right ear and an exit wound below the left eye," Hobbs said into his microphone. Carol realized for the first time that she had, in fact, been shot. Her forearm was wounded and bloody, but that wasn't a life-threatening injury. She felt her cold, bloodied nightgown being cut and pulled away from her body, the ballooning of the blood-pressure cuff and the stick of the IV needle. "BP seventy over thirty. Pulse one-forty," Hobbs reported. He noted the increasing swelling of her face but could not tell the extent of bruising because of all the blood. Despite her injury, Carol knew this blood pressure was dangerously low and her pulse rate too high, indicating she was ready to check out, confirmed when the paramedics reported this as a "Code 3," the most critical condition.

Christ interrupted the paramedics, who were furiously working on his dying wife, and asked, "What about my finger? I'm hurt, too."

"Sir, you will have to wait. We have a very, very serious injury here," one of the paramedics answered. When Christ took a step closer, the rescue worker said in a firmer voice, "Step back, sir!"

They hooked up Carol to an IV of saline and Hobbs noted that his patient, while talking, was bleeding badly, her mouth was filling quickly with blood and her airway was impacted. Paramedics suctioned it constantly to keep her from choking to death. Someone wiped the blood from Carol's right eye, enabling her to see a little bit for the first time since she felt that blow to her head. Hobbs believed that despite the efforts of him and his colleagues, this patient was too far gone and would soon die from the gunshot injuries. His experience had taught him that even mortal wounds did not always stop a victim from talking right up to the end.

Siewert screeched his police car to a stop in front of the house, with Reyna right behind him, eight minutes after the call came in—about an average police response time in the city at the time. Officer Richard Duillo, from the HPD, arrived about the same time. "You just stick with me," five-foot-eight Hutchinson told his six-foot-four rookie, Siewert, nicknamed "Big Bird," as they rushed toward the house. One of the officers asked Dani if she was hurt.

"No. Inside," she said, pointing toward the side of the house, where a gurney was waiting outside the door. Hutchinson and Siewert headed that way while Hackett and Reyna went through the front door.

Hutchinson was the first cop into the Christs' house, where a huge pool of blood sat as an unwelcome doormat. Paramedics were furiously working on someone lying to the right on the kitchen floor. He couldn't see the victim clearly but saw enough to know she had taken a gunshot wound to the head and was losing a large amount of blood. "We're working a delayed DOA," Hutchinson remembered saying to himself, meaning he expected the victim would be dead by the time she arrived at the hospital. "She's not going to make it."

The cop walked over to Christ and saw the injury to the man's finger but didn't ask about that. Christ, who apparently had wrapped his own hand with a dish towel, started complaining about his own injury, demanding help immediately, seemingly oblivious to what was happening with his wife dying several feet away on the kitchen floor.

Annoyingly persistent and insistent on getting his injuries attended to, he said, "I'm a surgeon; you're going to treat me right now."

"Hey, you're just going to have to wait. This ambulance is not going to work on you," Hutchinson told him, appalled at the surgeon's excessive self-centeredness and his lack of concern for his wife. Although a surgeon, Christ was not even attempting to help her.

Disgusted, Hutchinson told Siewert, "Cuff him and read him his rights." Stay with him, he added.

"I've already called my attorney," Christ said. Since he clearly informed the officers that he had called his attorney, legally they could not question him further about the shooting. Hutchinson said that once a suspect invoked his right to remain silent, he could not give that up. Even if a suspect were to make incriminating statements after he was arrested, the cops would effectively have to turn a deaf ear, unable to use it as evidence against him.

Christ did not shut up completely. The doctor repeatedly demanded that his injured little finger be attended to immediately—frequently reminding anyone who would listen that he was a surgeon and needed it for his job—and showing no regard for his wife's far more serious injuries.

"We heard of gall before, but this was a new level," Hutchinson said.

Coming into the kitchen from the opposite direction, Hackett, a cop for thirteen years, the last ten with HPD, went straight to the victim. He could tell she was bleeding pretty badly, even though her head had been bandaged. Her face was covered with blood and badly disfigured. She was talking, but he couldn't understand what she was saying; he knew that this was not the time to try to get a statement from her. Her injuries were life-threatening and obviously demanded immediate attention. Not knowing whether the patient's neck was broken, paramedics strapped a cervical collar around her neck, gently placed her on a backboard and covered her with a blanket. They carried her to the gurney waiting just outside the kitchen door, pausing briefly as Carol vomited blood.

Hearing the sirens outside, Stella York, seventy-four, still dressed in a nightgown and robe, poked her head out the side door of her house and saw the fire truck parked next door and Dani standing in the front yard, shaking in apparent fear. With the crime scene still unraveling, one of the cops escorted Dani to the friendly-looking neighbor and asked her to keep the child inside until an officer returned for her. York, petite with short reddish brown hair—similar to Carol's current color—looked like an elderly version of Dani's mother. "What's wrong?" she asked the child.

"My daddy shot my mommy!" she said.

"Oh, my!" The shocked neighbor gasped, and instinctively hugged her.

"I was watching TV and then I heard a loud bang!" Dani said.

As the EMTs carried Carol to the gurney, John Christ told them, "Take her to Methodist Hospital. I'm a doctor there and she's a nurse there."

No way, the paramedics told him. The gunshot wound was too serious and they were taking the victim to the city's trauma center, Ben Taub. Carol heard this and was relieved. She and her husband both knew that the best care for trauma victims, especially gunshot injuries, was at Ben Taub and that's where she wanted to go. A renowned hospital in many areas, Methodist did not have a trauma center and was not as well equipped to treat her injuries as Ben Taub. The officers also were sure that Christ had to know that Ben Taub was the best place for his wife in such a condition; it was common knowledge even among lay people. The fact that he wanted her taken elsewhere seemed just another demonstration of his disturbing coldness. "If you're dying, you want to go to Ben Taub. Once you're stabilized, you want to get the hell out," Hutchinson, the veteran officer, said later.

"We're going to the Tub," Hobbs told the cops as he rushed toward the ambulance, using the rescuer vernacular for Ben Taub Hospital. He added that this was a Code 3.

"What about my baby?" Carol asked as she was being taken down the driveway.

"Don't worry, we'll take good care of your little girl,"

she heard someone say, and out of her right eye, she got a brief glimpse of the cop who said it. It was the most relief she had felt all morning.

Hackett and Reyna escorted the gurney to the ambulance and watched as Carol was carefully loaded into the back. "It was pretty bad, pretty gruesome," Reyna said of the first shooting victim he had seen. Less than five minutes after it arrived, the ambulance sped away from the Christ house.

Already, a news cameraman, who must have heard the dispatch call on a police scanner, had arrived and filmed Christ, her head bloody and badly injured, being loaded into the ambulance. The news report, replayed throughout the day, was the way several of her friends and colleagues first learned that she had been shot.

Next door, Dani, still shaken by that morning's events, was rehashing them in her mind, volunteering a few details now and then to her neighbors. The six-year-old said, "It was not an accident, and I hope my mommy and daddy don't get a divorce." Privately, she was fighting her own fears that her mother would die and was wondering who would take care of her if that happened.

Everyone at the scene was convinced Carol would soon die.

In the ambulance, she was hooked up to a heart monitor. She heard the sirens blaring, clearing Houston's busy streets for her as they raced to Ben Taub. "So this is what it's like to be riding to Ben Taub dying in an ambulance" was her thought.

"What happened?" Hobbs asked his patient.

"My husband shot me," she said.

"Why?"

"We were fighting," she answered, her voice strained and barely comprehensible as her mouth filled with blood.

A couple times, she tried to recite her mother's phone number so they could reach someone who cared about her. Although she thought she was speaking clearly, her words no longer were intelligible and the paramedics had no idea what she was trying to tell them. Lifting her oxygen mask, the paramedics continued suctioning blood from her mouth, making further responses from her impossible.

"Take it easy, shhh," the paramedic said as Carol tried to repeat it.

Carol felt herself drifting in and out of consciousness during the seven-minute race to the hospital, but she heard much of the paramedics' conversation.

"We're losing her! We're losing her!" one of the men next to her yelled to the driver. "Run the light! Faster! Go!"

She tried to convince herself it was just a nightmare and urged herself to wake up. She wanted to snap out of it, open her eyes and find herself still wrapped beneath her warm comforter. When that didn't happen, she urged herself to do something even more important: "Don't die. Don't die. Don't die."

With the victim on her way to the hospital, a firefighter bandaged Christ's injured little finger. At 8:44 A.M., five minutes after the first officers arrived, Officer Duillo read him his Miranda rights and told Christ he was under arrest. The surgeon said he understood. Handcuffed, the doctor was escorted to the back of Hackett's patrol car under the curious stares of neighbors. Hutchinson called for a crime scene unit and then called the Homicide Division, advising them that the victim would likely die. It was up to each of those units to decide whether they would go to the scene to do the investigative work themselves or leave it to the patrol officers. In this case, both said they would be there as soon as possible. Part of the patrol officers' job now was to keep everyone out of the house until the investigative officers arrived and took control of the crime scene.

Across town in Channelview, Sergeants Glen Matthews and John Swaim were helping fellow officers execute a search warrant when Swaim's pager went off at 9:00 A.M.. He called Lieutenant I. O. Franks, who assigned the partners the follow-up investigation on Timberside. He gave Swaim a brief rundown on the situation, adding, "It looks like the victim isn't going to make it."

Walking around the house as they awaited the crime scene unit and detectives, the officers tried to piece together what had happened and told the rookies what would need to be done to preserve the crime scene. The bed was soaked with blood, and Hackett pointed out the bone chips he saw there as well. The patrol officers, who were not responsible for conducting a thorough search of the crime scene, spotted just one bullet casing, although two people were injured. The surgeon was claiming that two shots had been fired, so they looked for a second shell, but didn't find another. Hutchinson said they surmised that "He basically held her down . . . and in the process caught his finger with the bullet." The cops followed a trail of blood drops from the bedroom, down the hall, across the corner of the family room and into the kitchen, stopping right in front of the trash compactor, which was ajar. On top of the trash, in plain view, was a clip. Hutchinson smiled at the ease with which this case was coming together. In the midst of everything, he noticed an older firefighter from the pumper crew that remained after the ambulance raced away, beginning to mop up the blood in the kitchen.

"What the hell are you doing?" the officer yelled, flabbergasted that an official actually was about to destroy the crime scene. The firefighter told him he was supposed to clean up, but Hutchinson assured him that wasn't going to happen, and stopped him before very much had been wiped away.

The officers waited outside, near the patrol car where Christ sat alone in the backseat. He rolled over on his side and held up his handcuffed hands, yelling: "What about my finger? What about my finger." The officers couldn't believe his gall. "It wasn't really hurt that bad, to be honest," Hutchinson said. Still, their prisoner kept yelling. "He was red-faced angry," Hutchinson recalled later. "He kept screaming at us: 'I need medical attention.' It was so outrageous." This truly seemed to be a doctor with a God complex, he thought.

Meanwhile a van pulled up to this macabre scene, delivering a cheery, cut-flower arrangement for the victim. It was her Mother's Day gift from Joe and Dani, which Christ had ordered a couple of days earlier.

Speeding across town, siren blaring and lights flashing, the detectives arrived at the Christ home at 9:30 A.M. They saw the apparent suspect sitting in the back of a patrol car. They approached the car and exchanged a few words with the officers waiting outside the car, each detective mentally reviewing how he planned to question the doctor.

Hutchinson and Hackett gave the detectives a rundown on what they had learned. Swaim opened the back door of the patrol car and saw the doctor handcuffed in front, with a large bandage on his left hand. Swaim pulled a blue card from his pocket and again read the surgeon the Miranda warnings. Christ said he understood his rights and added that he had already tried to contact his attorney.

Swaim asked who the attorney was. Christ gave him Thano Dameris's name and phone number.

"OK," Swaim said, closing the door to both the car and any questioning. Hackett walked through the crime scene with the detectives, pointing out what the patrol officers had noticed and letting them know where the officers had gone.

Hackett and Reyna were responsible for the prisoner, who continued to insist he needed treatment and wanted to be taken to Methodist Hospital. Hackett called Methodist Hospital. "I talked to someone there who said she was well liked there, and he wasn't, and it was probably best if we took him somewhere else. The sympathy was definitely with her," the officer said.

Christ also told Swaim he wanted to be taken to Methodist, where he was on staff. Swaim told him that he was under arrest and would be taken where they took all prisoners—to Ben Taub. Christ was upset about it and complained to Hackett. "You're a prisoner; this is where prisoners go," Hackett told him as they drove to the county hospital. As the officers ferried their prisoner to Ben Taub, Christ said at least three times that the shooting had been an accident. Reyna recalled that Christ sobbed for a short time, although Hackett didn't remember that, but the surgeon soon returned to worrying out loud about his finger and career. Christ lied to the police officers, claiming to be the chief plastic surgeon at Methodist Hospital. The officers had no reason not to believe him.

Regardless of who Christ was—or who he pretended to be—he had made a lasting impression. Years later, all the cops on the scene remembered Christ as the most arrogant, callous and cold-blooded of all the suspected and successful killers they had ever encountered. It was a memorable case, one that incoming officers still hear about. "Rookies want to hear stories like that—the bad doctor that shot his wife," Hackett said.

Fifteen

Ben Taub's trauma team met the ambulance at the emergency room door, working in unison as the paramedics handed off their patient, running along side, giving doctors and nurses the relevant numbers—blood pressure, pulse and other vital statistics. It was 8:51 A.M., twenty-one minutes after Carol Christ first called for help, and she was rushed to the shock room. She was awake and alert but in critical condition. Asked several times by various nurses and doctors, she said that her husband had shot her. Afraid, she heard the urgent orders being barked around her, for various specialists and tests. The entry wound was about one centimeter by one centimeter, the size of a man's pinkie nail. Specialists in general surgery, laryngology and ophthalmology examined her; despite what looked to be a piercing, through-and-through wound of her left eyeball, she still was able to move both eyes. She said she could not see out of the left, though. An IV was put in her injured left arm, and as she saw a nurse preparing a Foley catheter to put into her urethra and drain her bladder, she felt sudden embarrassment, even humiliation. Even as she lay dying in the emergency room, she immediately thought of the labial ring Christ had pierced her with. She reached down under the sheet, unhooked it and tossed it onto the floor beneath the crash cart, out of sight of the hospital workers. Or so she thought.

She heard her vital signs being called out and knew her blood pressure had fallen too far and that she was close to death. She felt the groin sticks and knew they were going to push IV fluids through her—used in emergency situations to get fluids in at a much quicker pace than a drip—to try to raise her blood pressure. Called a femoral line, it also was another way to monitor her blood pressure, which had fallen too low to be picked up by simpler methods. Fearing that one of the main arteries that supplied blood to the face had been injured, doctors ordered a cerebral arteriogram (a series of X-rays taken after a radioactive dye is injected) of her carotid arteries, which branch out to those in the head and face. A facial angiogram also was prescribed to determine if the blood vessels had been blown apart as they suspected.

As doctors and nurses frantically tried to save her life, John Christ refused to provide authorities with the names or phone numbers of his wife's family, leaving Ben Taub's staff to try to find someone at Methodist who would know how to contact her family. Since it was a Saturday, personnel records weren't readily accessible and those working at Methodist were unable to provide the information immediately. Knowing an embolization, a procedure to repair damaged blood vessels, might be needed to save her life, three doctors gave consent for the urgent care in case it was needed—hospital policy when next of kin is not available.

Christ's pulse rebounded spontaneously. A large amount of blood was flowing into her throat, so a tube was inserted down her esophagus to ensure that she could breathe. After being intubated, she became combative and was paralyzed with the drug Pavulon, making her unable to respond. She was taken to have CT scans, which were crucial in enabling doctors to diagnose the full extent of her injuries, but she still was fighting their help, requiring more of the paralysis-inducing drug. That finally solved that problem and allowed the staff to get a series of CT scans.

Ken Mattox, the chief of staff at Ben Taub, the hospital's top administrator, was notified that Carol Christ was in the ER, as was policy whenever a VIP or a Texas Medical Center doctor or spouse was brought in, and that she was not expected to live. Mattox went immediately to the ER and summoned the department heads of whatever medical specialties the ER doctors thought might be needed, theoretically giving Carol the best care, instead of leaving it to whatever resident or doctor happened to be on call.

Among the first Mattox notified was Dr. M. Bowes Hamill, Ben Taub's deputy chief of the ophthalmology service; Hamill also was on staff at Methodist Hospital. At forty, Hamill was a respected and highly accomplished ophthalmologist; widely published, he was a frequent lecturer nationally and internationally and was active with numerous professional committees and organizations. A Baylor College of Medicine graduate and now an associate professor of clinical ophthalmology there, he specialized in ocular trauma as well as the cornea and external eye diseases at Baylor's renowned Cullen Eye Institute. He had never met either of the Christs and knew nothing about them. By the time he got to Ben Taub, Carol Christ already had undergone several tests that showed the substantial damage to her face, particularly the right side, and to her left eye. Looking at her, he could easily see the powder burns around the massive entrance wound, indicating she had been shot at close range, as well as the gaping hole where the bullet exited. She was bruised and swollen, but he had seen worse obvious injuries inflicted in beatings. That's not unusual with gunshot victims, however, where most of the damage lay beneath the surface. Her right eye looked pretty good, but Hamill quietly estimated that the chance she would ever again be able to see out of her left eye at 5 percent at best. When he looked at her CT scans, however, he was shocked with the extensive damage the bullet had done. It seemed that the bullet had traveled nearly straight through her face, pulverizing the bones in its devastating wake.

Throughout the morning, high-ranking physicians and Carol's friends gathered in Ben Taub's emergency room; some of them were summoned by Mattox, and others had heard about the shooting on the news or through the already spreading Medical Center grapevine. Carol Christ was undergoing extensive tests and most of the doctors, not directly involved in her care, stood by discussing the morning's unbelievable events and shaking their heads.

Betty Steinfeld, Carol's friend and fellow nurse, was at home ironing when a friend called and asked; "Did you know Carol got shot by John? I don't know if she's dead or what."

Until recently, Steinfeld, a nurse, had worked on Dunn 8 West with Carol but currently was taking courses for six months to transfer to the operating room. She knew that her friend didn't have any family in town other than her young children, so she and her boyfriend headed to Ben Taub, hoping to help Carol in whatever way she could, even if it were only to offer comfort. Having no information on her family, hospital personnel noted Steinfeld's name and number on Carol Christ's admissions records. After waiting for a long time, a doctor came and talked to Steinfeld, telling her Carol was still alive and responsive and about to undergo a series of CT scans. There was no way she could see her, she was told.

When Dr. James R. Patrinely's pager went off, he was in the maternity intensive-care unit across the street in Methodist Hospital. An ophthalmic plastic surgeon, he was with his wife, who had gone into premature labor with their first child. He went to the nurses' station and returned the page, getting a rundown of the very touchy situation unfolding at Ben Taub. His wife's condition had stabilized and, at the moment, the baby was no longer insisting on making an early appearance.

Patrinely returned to his wife's bedside and he repeated the grim story he had just heard. Having been a trauma nurse at Ben Taub's shock room, Vicky Patrinely understood. "Go help that poor woman," she told her husband.

The surgeon rushed to Ben Taub, arriving in the ER shortly before 10:00 A.M. Always a tense, busy place, this day was even more so. Many of the bigwigs associated with Ben Taub and Methodist seemed to be there, including those so high up they normally leave even the VIP cases to subordinates. Representatives of the neurology, neurosurgery, plastic surgery, ophthalmology, general surgery trauma and Ear, Nose and Throat services were there to consult on Carol Christ's case. Most of the esteemed doctors were just waiting around for her test results, trying to avoid any firsthand participation, Patrinely recalled. "Everyone was reluctant to get involved with it," he said. It was an uncomfortable situation. The prime suspect was not only a colleague but one with a reputation of being vindictive, litigious and somewhat bizarre. While many described him as "brilliant," some did not think he was mentally stable. Everyone knew that whoever treated the victim might be pulled into a legal drama—probably a murder case—on the opposite side of an unusually vengeful colleague, and many of the doctors seemed eager to avoid all of that, Patrinely said.

"It was kind of like a hot-potato game," he said. None of the doctors directly refused to work on the victim, he said, but their awkward reluctance was clear.

Patrinely was unfazed by such concerns and volunteered to take the case. He had seen John Christ around the Medical Center, jogging around Rice Campus, working out in the Scurlock Tower gym years earlier, and in the surgeons' locker room. He didn't know much about him—he soon would hear lots of disturbing rumors— but he had found him pleasant and soft-spoken. Whether or not Christ was guilty was irrelevant to him at the moment; his main concern was the victim. Because Carol Christ was undergoing the arteriogram, Patrinely was unable to examine the patient, so he, Hamill and the other doctors reviewed the CT scans and other test results and mapped out a treatment plan.

The CT images showed exceptional damage, including severe multiple fractures of her face, eye socket, nasal passages, sinuses and cheekbones. Neither her nervous system nor any of her major arteries or blood vessels appeared to have been damaged. The doctors had been worried that she had suffered permanent brain damage, but that didn't seem to be the case. The temporal and inferior frontal lobes clearly had been bruised, but the doctors didn't think she needed immediate brain surgery, if she would at all. They thought she had escaped the survivor's worst-case scenario, however narrowly. They would learn differently later.

She needed immediate surgery and specialized care, and the doctors decided that would be best accomplished at Methodist and arranged to have her transferred as soon as possible. She would go straight to the OR, they agreed.

John Christ walked into the Ben Taub ER under the escort of Officers Hackett and Reyna. No matter how minor the injury, Hackett knew that it normally took five or six hours for a suspect to be treated there, and he was prepared for a long wait. The surgeon, despite being under arrest, was treated well, at least initially. "I remember him really getting the royal treatment there because they recognized him," Hackett said. "He was playing it up big." Instead of having to wait in the public waiting room, Christ quickly was escorted to one of the nicer treatment rooms. The attitude toward him changed noticeably when news began circulating about what he had done to his wife, who was being frantically attended to elsewhere in the same emergency room. Christ, who asked to be seen by a plastic surgeon, worried aloud if he would be able to operate again. Christ said the shooting had been an accident but showed no concern for how his wife was doing. His focus continued to be on getting treatment for his wound, something that Hackett later described as "the cut on his hand." The officer had to stop some of those attending to Christ's injuries from asking too many questions about what had happened, so as not to interfere with the investigation. Christ wasn't telling them too much anyway, only giving them one- or two-word answers.

As things in the ER intensified with Carol Christ and other patients, John Christ was left to wait for treatment, too. Alone with the officers, he wondered if charges were going to be filed against him and why. Hackett gave him the standard, noncommittal answer and left Reyna with the suspect while he went to make phone calls, first reminding the rookie not to ask the suspect any questions about the case. Christ seemed unusually relaxed, laid-back and unemotional, especially given what was going on around him. The suspect talked about what doctors were going to treat him, what procedures would be needed on his little finger and even worried if there would be any visible scarring. "He was worried if anybody else could do as good a job as he could on it," the officer said, adding that seemed to have become the suspect's main concern. Christ talked about the respected position he held in the medical community and wondered if he would be able to do surgery again. Other surgeons said that even if Christ, a right-hander, had lost full use of his left pinkie or had it amputated, he would have been able to operate without a problem. For him to worry that he could not was absolutely ridiculous, they agreed. "You'd think being a plastic surgeon, he'd know it wasn't as bad as it looked," Reyna said later.

While Reyna wasn't allowed to ask his prisoner any questions, that didn't stop the doctor from voluntarily making comments about that morning's events now and then. At least once more, he repeated that the shooting had been accidental. "He didn't see any criminal aspect to it at all," Reyna said of his prisoner. "He would only say that they were arguing and the gun went off, and that he would never have purposely pulled the trigger and hurt his finger like that." Reyna didn't believe him and the doctor never said why he had been holding the gun if he hadn't intended to use it. None of these statements could ever be repeated in court, since Christ had earlier invoked his right to remain silent.

Christ asked to make a phone call, but the officer told him he couldn't. He persisted, saying he had to call work, but didn't say why. He was unaccustomed to not having his way, but his persistence didn't pay off with the cops. He wasn't going to get special privileges from them. Christ told Reyna about his medical career, again claiming to be the head of plastic surgery at Methodist. After a while, he even asked Reyna questions about his life and why he had joined the police department. After a couple of hours, Christ basically clammed up.

On Timberside, the Crime Scene Unit (CSU) was preparing to begin the meticulous evidence-gathering process. First Hutchinson and Siewert gave Officer D.S. "Dee" Wilker of the CSU a rundown of what was known about the case. Leading her through the front door and through the neatly kept house-turned-crime-scene, the patrol officers pointed out the evidence seen so far—the blood trail, the bloodied gold wedding band on the kitchen counter, the large blood pools in the kitchen, the blood-covered kitchen phone, the clip in the trash compactor, the .45 lying on the bedroom floor, the bloodied bed, the pillow with an apparent bullet hole and the bullet casing under the edge of the bed. Wilker, an eighteen-year veteran, the last fourteen spent investigating crime scenes, then walked back through the house, photographing the evidence on two rolls of 35mm film.

The two detectives divided up their duties in the investigation: this time, Matthews would be in charge of the crime scene and evidence collection while Swaim would interview witnesses. With a consent-to-search form signed by John Christ, Matthews and the CSU officers turned to bagging the evidence.

The king-sized bed, both the pillows and all the blankets and sheets were drenched with blood. Following the apparent path of the bullet through the pillow, sheets, mattress pad and into the mattress, Wilker made two small cuts in the blue floral mattress and dug down until she found the .45 bullet near the bottom and pulled it out. The bullet's path indicated that it had been fired in a downward direction, meaning the victim must have been lying on the bed, her head on the pillow, when she had been shot. The shell casing was found easily, a couple feet from the bed, lying on the floor between the bed and dresser. The gun, the hammer cocked all the way back indicating it was in position to fire again, was lying at the edge of the richly patterned rug at the foot of the bed, its barrel now pointed toward the dresser. The adjacent hardwood floor was stained with nearly dried blood. Wilker picked up the heavy weapon, a semiautomatic Colt .45 pistol, government model MK IV series 80. She noted its serial number so detectives later could trace its ownership history. The black steel weapon weighed more than two and one-quarter pounds. Swaim carried one like it. This one had three safety mechanisms on it and was designed to be fired by a right-handed person.

The investigators searched the room, looking for a second bullet or its empty hull that would support the suspect's claim that two shots had been fired. They found just one of each. Because the gun was designed to be fired with the right hand, the investigators concluded that the doctor must have supported the gun's weight with his left hand, accidentally putting his pinkie finger over the barrel when he fired it into his wife's head. Wilker returned to the kitchen, opened the trash compactor and pulled the gun clip out of the trash compactor. Three live shells were still in the casing, which could hold seven.

Outside, Swaim questioned Gay Christ about the phone call she had received from her ex-husband more than ninety minutes earlier, and her own tumultuous past with the suspect. After she had gotten the disturbing call from her ex-husband, she made a few calls herself, including to 911. She had made other arrangements for Stephanie to go on that day's Indian Princesses outing and had found someone to stay with her kids. Then she located a friend to go with her to Timberside to find out what was going on. By the time she arrived, Carol already had been taken to the hospital and Christ was in the back of the patrol car. Police wouldn't let her talk to their suspect, but they told her that they wanted to interview her. At 10:10 A.M., Swaim flipped on a tape recorder and asked her to repeat what she had just told him. Each time Gay told her story, she said that the first thing her ex-husband had said when he called that morning was "I'm sorry I cannot come pick up Stephanie this morning for Indian Princesses." He had been hysterical when he called, as was Dani, who was crying in the background. "My wife and I, we have a gun and we shot each other," he had told her before hanging up, she told the detective. Christ had received six months' probation after assaulting her in July 1989, she told him. Swaim asked if her ex had any mental problems or if he had ever been suicidal. Christ had told both her and his secretary one day that he felt suicidal and each of the women phoned his therapist, Gay said. After the two-minute, recorded interview with Gay Christ, Swaim spoke with neighbors, but no one had heard or seen anything until emergency crews screeched into their normally quiet neighborhood.

With the detectives and CSU now taking care of the evidence, Hutchinson went next door and got Dani. Asking her a few questions, being careful not to lead her story in any direction, it was immediately clear that she had not seen the shooting happen, only its gruesome aftermath. Still trembling noticeably, Dani asked, "Is my mommy going to die? Is my mommy going to die?"

The paramedics and doctors are doing everything they can to help your mommy, the officer assured her, adding: "We're going to take care of you."

Dani attached herself to the fatherly officer, who carried her around on his hip for a while. He took Dani back into her house—through the front door to avoid having her see as much of the blood pools as possible—so she could change out of her nightgown and into clothes. Hutchinson's daughter was eight and his son just five but he had learned long ago not to relate children at crime scenes with his own. "You don't ever let those things get in your way. You cannot visualize your children—it'll kill you. It'll rip your guts out," the veteran officer said. After slipping on purple pants and a white T-shirt, Dani joined him in the hall. At the officer's suggestion that she take along her favorite doll or stuffed animal for company, she grabbed her Raggedy Ann doll and went with him to his patrol car. She rode in front with Siewert while Hutchinson sat where the bad guys normally go. They distracted her by showing her the car's equipment and then, as they headed downtown, with jokes. One told her that the other officer sped so much, he wrote himself tickets. By the time Dani arrived at the police station on the outskirts of downtown, she had stopped shaking and was much calmer, outwardly at least. Inside, she was still scared.

While momentarily alone in the interview room, Dani began talking to herself about what she had seen. Her mom had been badly hurt and was at the hospital but, she said, "my dad is not that hurt. He just got his finger blown off." Her private narration was interrupted by Sergeant Wayne Wendel, who wanted to ask her about what she had seen. Sitting across the corner of a small table from the plainclothes officer, Dani said she heard a noise like a bomb or a gun and got scared; then she saw Christ. "My dad told me that he pulled out a gun and shot Mom," she said.

"Why did he do that?" Wendel asked.

"I don't know. They were in a big fight. He had no reason to shoot Mom," she said emphatically. She then described seeing her mother, covered with blood. "So my mom just took the gun away from Dad and just shot his finger off, and it was just bleeding a little bit," she added. Clearly, the child had heard her stepfather's phone calls that morning and repeated what he said the way she had imagined it. She had not been in the bedroom when either had been shot.

"I was so scared. I'm still scared," she said.

"Well, you're OK with us," the officer assured her. But in the midst of retelling the most frightening event of her young life, Dani looked for a diversion and popped her hand through a hole in the table and waved at the cop, who laughed. He asked her what her parents had been arguing about and her answer was nearly heartbreaking.

"Well, Daddy doesn't like us and Mom doesn't like his kids, so Dad just pulled out a gun," she said, pretending to draw a pistol from a holster as if to demonstrate, "and shot Mommy." He asked if she had seen the shooting and she said she had not.

"It popped two times," she said emphatically. This was not what police believed, having found just one shell casing, and Wendel asked if it had just been one time.

Although Dani had been correct, the question seemed to confuse her. "It was either two or four. Two or four. I think it was three," she said.

Wendel asked Dani the standard questions posed to children when they testify: Did she know what it meant to tell the truth and a lie? What happened to her when she didn't tell the truth? She answered his questions but seemed to think he was challenging her veracity. If he went to the hospital, she assured him, "and you saw my mommy and daddy, my mom will be bleeding a whole bunch. My dad won't be bleeding a whole lot. He said that he's not OK, just because, just because that bullet just went on his finger and it just got popped off, but my mom was screaming and yelling. She could barely talk." Even the six-year-old child had noticed how overly concerned her stepfather had been in comparison with her mother's far more serious injuries. The only one who seemed to miss that coldhearted fact seemed to be the suspect. After a ten-minute interview, Dani was taken to another room to watch television until police could locate a relative or friend to take care of her.

Just before 11:00 A.M. in Scottsdale, Arizona, about noon in Houston, Mason O'Keiff was outside cleaning his built-in swimming pool when his wife called him to the phone, saying it was someone with the Houston Police Department. After identifying himself, the officer gave Carol's father the distressing news. "Your daughter's been shot," he told him directly, adding police had a suspect.

"Is it John?" O'Keiff asked. He had no reason to think this would happen—he had only met his newest son-in-law once and hadn't seen Carol in about a year—but he couldn't think of anyone else. The officer told him that Carol was not expected to live and gave him a few details of what had happened nearly four hours earlier. He told her she was at Ben Taub but expected to be moved to Methodist soon; he assured him that his daughter had the best doctors in their fields treating her. Generally, Houston police officers don't notify victim's families, leaving that responsibility to hospital personnel or the coroner's office, so it was likely that an off-duty cop working an extra security job for the hospital called the victim's family.

Stunned, O'Keiff had to notify the rest of the family, including Margaret Edwards, to whom he had barely spoken, if at all, since their divorce nearly three decades earlier. This would not change that. Preferring to let their son break the brutal news to Margaret, he called Gus O'Keiff's Nashville home and learned from his stepgrandson that his parents were out for the day. Gus and Helayne O'Keiff were with friends at the Iroquois Steeplechase when they were paged over the loudspeaker and surprisingly asked to go to the police mobile unit. It was the first time Helayne's twelve-year-old son had been left alone at home for long and her first thought was that something was wrong with him. Nashville police broke the shocking news to the O'Keiffs, who then called Mason for what few details he knew. Gus called the Edwardses and matter-of-factly told his stepfather, who in turn told Margaret, that Christ had shot Carol in the head and she was in bad shape.

Within two hours, Gus and Helayne O'Keiff were on a plane headed to Houston, not knowing what to expect. The O'Keiffs and Christs spent the previous Thanksgiving at the Edwardses' and the group spent some time in the tiny resort town of Eureka Springs, about five hours north of Springdale. The Christs seemed to have a good time shopping at the many boutiques and art galleries, but both were a bit obnoxious, Gus thought. Even so, he said, "I thought for the first time maybe Carol had found a husband that she wouldn't divorce." Carol had seemed really happy, but Christ wasn't overly personable. Recently, he had heard that they had been having problems but didn't think they were severe or that his sister was in any physical danger.

After making calls to the hospital, Margaret Edwards learned a few more details, but not many. She believed she might have to decide whether to keep her daughter on life support and wasn't sure what her daughter would want or what would be best. Margaret decided to mull over the question on her long drive to Houston. Dan and Margaret Edwards had been planning to leave the next day on a trip, so they were prepared to leave town quickly, having lined up dog-sitters, withdrawn cash and taken care of other provisions.

Heading to Houston, the Edwardses stopped at the foot of their long, winding driveway to check the mail-

Carol O'Keiff, 35, with her children, Dani, 6, and Joe, 12, in late 1991. *(Photo courtesy Margaret Edwards)*

On December 1, 1972, two days before her sixteenth birthday, O'Keiff married the first of six husbands. *(Photo courtesy Margaret Edwards)*

O'Keiff with her brother Gus in 1981. *(Photo courtesy Margaret Edwards)*

O'Keiff posed for her sixth husband, Dr. John Christ,
a plastic surgeon. *(Photo courtesy Carol O'Keiff)*

Bloodied kitchen floor where police found O'Keiff
after she called 911.
(Photo courtesy Harris County, Texas District Clerk's Office)

The bed was soaked with O'Keiff's blood.
(Photo courtesy Harris County, Texas District Clerk's Office)

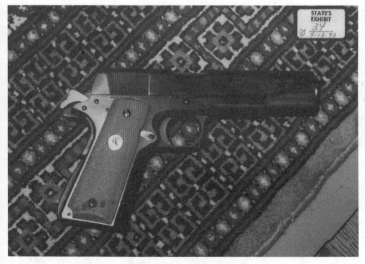

Cocked and ready to be fired, a bloody Colt .45 semiautomatic
pistol was found on the bedroom floor.
(Photo courtesy Harris County, Texas District Clerk's Office)

John Christ, 55, was arrested for the May 9, 1992, attempted murder of his wife. *(Photo courtesy Harris County, Texas Sheriff's Department)*

Dark spots on O'Keiff's CAT scan indicate areas in which bone and tissue were completely destroyed. *(Photo courtesy Carol O'Keiff)*

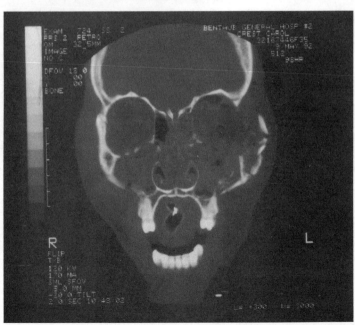

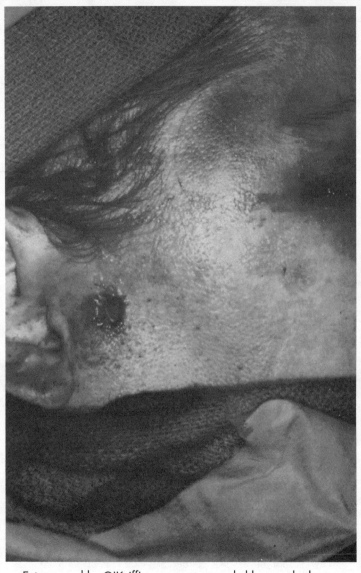

Entry wound by O'Keiff's ear was surrounded by powder burns.
(Photo courtesy Carol O'Keiff)

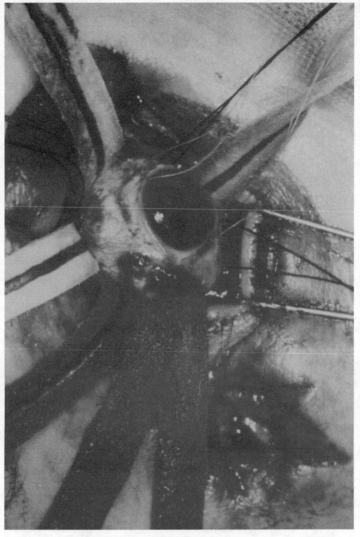

Doctors attempted to repair O'Keiff's ruptured left eye on the day she was shot. Bullet's star–shaped exit wound is at lower right.
(Photo courtesy Dr. M. Bowes Hamill)

Several days after O'Keiff was shot, the second bullet was found embedded in the floor under the bedroom rug. *(Photo courtesy Harris County, Texas District Clerk's Office)*

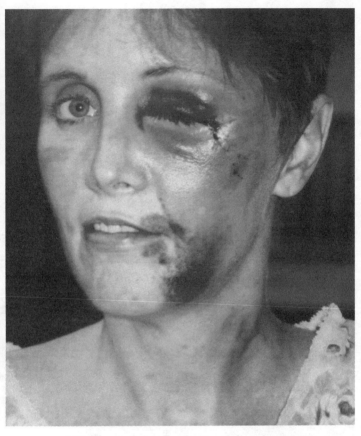

O'Keiff two weeks after the September 8, 1993,
reconstructive surgery. *(Photo courtesy Carol O'Keiff)*

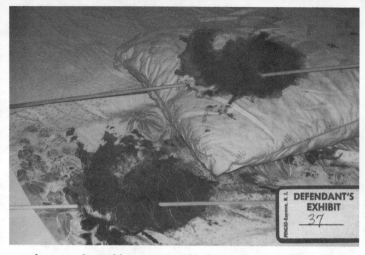

Defense used possible trajectory of bullet to show jury that O'Keiff had shot herself. *(Photo courtesy Harris County, Texas District Clerk's Office)*

Carol O'Keiff in November 1993. *(Photo courtesy Margaret Edwards)*

O'Keiff's mother Margaret and her husband Dan Edwards.

O'Keiff's father Mason and fourth wife, Natalie Kane O'Keiff.
(Photo courtesy Carol O'Keiff)

Dr. James Patrinely,
ophthalmic plastic surgeon.

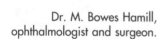

Dr. M. Bowes Hamill,
ophthalmologist and surgeon.

Dr. Chris Sermas,
psychiatrist.

Houston Police Detective John Swaim.

Houston Police Detective Glen Matthews.

Harris County Assistant District Attorney Kelly Siegler.

Defense Attorney Joe W. Bailey II.

Attorney Harry Herzog.

Carol O'Keiff with her dog Cathy in 1999.

box. Inside was a Mother's Day card for Margaret from her dying daughter. "I opened it, and it was terrible. It was one of the worst times in my life . . . totally beyond description," she said. As she usually did, Margaret did most of the driving on the long trip. Unsure what was going on with her daughter, she talked about nearly everything but that. During quiet moments, she thought about her daughter and couldn't decide if it would be best for Carol if she died or lived with whatever physical and mental impairments she would have. She couldn't help but think of Dan's son who had died of cancer not long after they had been married. Chris Edwards had moved in with them during his eight-month ordeal and been just nineteen when he died, but the couple had been together so long by the time they wed, Margaret felt like she had lost a child. Now she feared she might lose another. She was too numb to cry, which was a good thing as she needed to focus on the road. The torrents of tears would come later.

After finishing the witness interviews and evidence collection at the Christ house, the homicide detectives headed to Ben Taub to check on the victim and talk to doctors. Swaim was given a brief summary of Carol Christ's injuries but was not allowed to talk to her. He went in search of John Christ's doctor to inquire about his injury. He was pointed toward a treatment room and knocked on the door. Christ was the only doctor in the room but, as he had been all morning, was eager to talk about his injury.

In great detail, Christ droned on about the damage to the middle joint of his little finger, using a bunch of medical terms, which were lost completely on the detective. He then detailed a list of treatment options to repair the injury, again losing the sergeant in the medical terminology and excessive detail. He also complained about how the injury would negatively impact his practice. Christ then volunteered that he was unloading the gun so that no one else would get hurt. He didn't know what he was doing and the gun went off, injuring his finger, he said. Convinced that Christ was lying because the detective knew that only one bullet and one spent hull had been found at the crime scene, Swaim just listened. He was forced by the law to refrain from asking any questions about the shooting as the suspect had previously said he had contacted his attorney. When Christ clearly had nothing more to say, Swaim left, noting that the doctor never once asked about his wife's condition.

The detective then found an ER doctor who told him in simple terms what Christ's injuries were—a gunshot wound to the little finger on the left hand. The middle joint was damaged and would require surgery, but he would fully recover. Back at the station, Swaim and Matthews went over what happened. Despite Christ's stories—first that he and his wife shot each other and then that he was injured unloading the gun—the evidence suggested otherwise. They concluded what the patrol officers had earlier: Christ had his finger in front of the barrel when he shot his wife, accidentally injuring himself with the same bullet that devastated her head.

As doctors worked to ensure that Carol Christ was stable enough to be moved to Methodist, police were getting some disappointing news about their suspect.

Back in his office, Swaim dialed Kate Dolan, the assistant district attorney on duty, and summarized the case for her.

"I don't think we have enough to charge him," she said firmly.

Disappointed, Swaim hung up and called Hackett and told him to release the suspect because the DA would not accept charges. Hackett was shocked. A shot had been fired, and whether it had been an accident or not, it had hit someone and could now very well kill her. Hackett believed that generally was enough to at least hold a suspect. Swaim told him: "I think charges will be filed . . . but they are not filing them at this time." Incredulous, Hackett had no choice but to tell his prisoner that he was free to go. Christ didn't seem surprised. "He didn't bat an eye. He was just concerned about getting his treatment for his poor little finger," he recalled.

Reyna had spent nearly five hours with the suspect, more than anyone else that day, and didn't hear him voice concern about his dying wife even one time. Nor had he asked about what had happened to Dani. "Everything just revolved around how this was going to change his life," he said. It had been a strange second day on the police force and one that likely wouldn't be surpassed for many years, if ever. The doctor's unabashed and unmatched callousness and lack of concern for his wife left no doubt in any of the police officers' minds that Christ had shot his wife and that it had not been an accident.

Sixteen

The hubbub transferred from Ben Taub's emergency room to Methodist's with Carol and John Christ. About 3:30 P.M., nearly seven hours after being admitted to Ben Taub, Carol's vital signs improved enough to permit the five-block trip by high-tech ambulance, with two doctors accompanying her. As she was whisked through the corridors, she faded in and out of drug-induced unconsciousness and thought she saw her father. They clutched each other's wrists with one hand, giving each other emotional support. She was awash in the warm, sweet feelings of unconditional love, a feeling she needed now more than ever, and she settled into the warm, soothing feeling. When she got to Operating Room 3, Hamill and his resident, Dr. Jacklyn Wong, were waiting. She was responsive but terrified. She was given a large amount of morphine for the fierce, unwavering pain.

Another Ben Taub doctor drove John Christ, now free from arrest, to Methodist Hospital, where he checked himself into the ER for more treatment. Frightened more of her husband than her injuries or any surgeries that lay ahead of her, and unable to talk with the tube down her throat, Carol Christ managed through hand gestures and other means to ask where he was.

Hamill admitted that he was there in another room, but told her not to worry, she would be protected. She let her doctor and everyone around her know that she was convinced he was going to try again to kill her.

Dr. Raj K. Narayan, a widely respected neurosurgeon and one of the country's leading specialists in traumatic brain injuries, particularly gunshot wounds, arrived and examined the still blood-covered Carol Christ and her numerous films. It appeared to him that the bullet had skirted along the underside of the brain, but he could not be sure how much tissue was damaged. The brain damage could have been the result of direct contact with the bullet or from shock injury. "It's like an explosion inside your head. There are shock waves," he said. He concurred with his colleagues' surgical plans, feeling comfortable that she didn't need brain surgery now. He planned to follow her closely as he expected that she might develop some significant neurological problems. He saw how lucky she had been. It was hard to determine the precise path the bullet took as it seared through her head, Narayan said, but had it veered just a few millimeters in any direction, it could have easily hit a vein or artery and caused a fatal intracranial bleed. "That would be enough to bump you off. I guess her time had not come," he said.

Carol Christ, though, still feared that her time was about to come at the ruthless hands of her husband.

It all was overwhelming to Carol, but what was most wrenching was knowing that her husband had intentionally done this to her. They had their problems and it probably had been time to call it quits—that acknowledgment had been painful enough because she truly loved him—but accepting that he wanted her dead was horrifying beyond endurance. He had shot her in the head, and she knew she still might die, but the real irreparable damage had been to her heart.

For treatment reasons, Hamill and the other doctors needed to know if it had been an attempted suicide or homicide, although no one had suggested she had tried to kill herself. It was a standard question posed to gunshot victims. The path of the bullet—including the damage to her left arm—made it seem unlikely to the doctors that she had shot herself. It was unusual, they knew, for women to shoot themselves in the face—especially, as they would learn later, someone like Carol who cared so much about her appearance. They also were concerned because if her husband had tried to kill her, they knew he had access to the hospital and they needed to be able to protect their patient. Knowing the case likely would end up in court and that Carol Christ still might die before she would ever have another chance to tell her story, Hamill asked his questions into a tape recorder. Because of the tube down her throat, she could not talk, so she nodded her responses and Hamill verbalized them for the recorder, with Wong and Narayan as witnesses.

At 4:10 P.M., Hamill flipped on the recorder and began: "Ms. Christ, this is Dr. Hamill again. I want to ask you a couple more questions about how you got hurt. Did you shoot yourself?"

Christ shook her head no.

"Do you know who shot you?"

Yes, she nodded.

"Was it your husband?"

She nodded affirmatively.

"It was Dr. Christ? Is that correct?" She answered yes.

"Did Dr. Christ have the gun in his hand when he shot you?"

Christ shrugged her shoulders, as she had not seen him and did not know.

"How many times were you shot? Hold up your fingers," Hamill told her.

Christ raised only her index finger.

"I am going to ask you about how far away he was when he shot you. Was he farther away than five feet?"

The patient shook her head no.

"Was he closer than five feet?"

Yes, she nodded her head.

"Was he closer than three feet?" When she didn't immediately answer, he said, "Ms. Christ, were you shot from closer than three feet?"

She nodded yes.

"Near arm's length?" her doctor asked.

She signaled yes.

"What position were you in when he shot you? Were you lying down?"

Christ shook her head no.

"Were you sitting up?"

Yes, she nodded.

"Did you lose consciousness at the time you were shot?"

Christ indicated she had.

"Did you regain consciousness before the ambulance picked you up?"

Yes, she nodded.

"Are you absolutely sure that it was your husband that shot you?" Hamill asked again.

Christ nodded that she was certain.

"Was there anyone else in the room or near at the time you were shot?"

No, she shook her head.

"Was it intentional?"

Yes, she nodded.

"Were you threatened before he shot you?"

No, she shook her head.

By her answers and the look on her face, Hamill could see how afraid of her husband his patient still was.

At about 4:30 P.M. that afternoon, another emergency room doctor called hospital security and, following procedure, reported that a gunshot victim, John Christ, was there for treatment. Larry Lindquist, an HPD officer working an extra job at the hospital, immediately headed to the emergency room and was directed to Exam Room 2, where Christ was awaiting treatment, his finger again bleeding. Christ told him that he had accidentally shot himself while unloading a gun. When Lindquist asked if anyone else had been hurt, the surgeon answered by saying he wanted to talk to his attorney. He already had spoken with Sergeant Swaim, he added.

About five minutes later, Lindquist was again summoned to the ER, this time to speak with Carol Christ. The officer found the victim lying on her back, a tube in her throat, still very bloody but conscious. Narayan and Wong were at her side. Taking the victim's hand in his, Lindquist suggested she answer by squeezing his hand, once for yes and twice for no, or by nodding her head. The comfort of his warm grip around hers—and the knowledge that it was the protective hand of a police officer—as well as the much-needed human contact gave her unexpected but enormous relief.

"Did your husband shoot you?" Lindquist asked.

Carol nodded yes. A very definite yes, not just a slight nod, but a firm shake of her injured head.

"Do you want to file charges on your husband?"

She nodded affirmatively again and lifted her injured left arm, making writing motions in the air, indicating she wanted a pen. He gave her a pen, placing a sheet of paper, normally reserved for nurses' notes, underneath. Although her left arm had been shot slightly above the wrist, she took the pen in that hand and, with some difficulty, scrawled: "Id did not know he had g gu." The officer read it and knew she meant gun. At the bottom of the paper, she wrote: "The he just shot me."

"Inhaler," she also printed diagonally on the paper. "My purse asthma I need it." Having asthma, she always was concerned about having an attack and wanted her inhaler with her at all times just in case.

After a few more questions, to which she answered by nodding and squeezing his hand, Lindquist knew he had what he needed and that the victim needed medical treatment. She told him she wanted to file charges on her husband. Following procedure for handling evidence, he signed the paper, noting the time as 16:50 and the date, and had the two doctors sign it as well, indicating they witnessed the patient write it.

When he spoke with Swaim later that day, he told him about his conversation with the victim, exactly the news the detective wanted to hear. Swaim thought it would be enough to convince the assistant DA to file charges. He hung up and immediately picked up the receiver again, dialing Dolan. He told her of the victim's comments, the tapes and the witnesses. She readily agreed to file attempted murder and aggravated assault charges on Christ in the 230th District Court. The standard $5,000 bond was set.

Swaim called Lindquist and gave him the good news about the DA accepting the charges. He told him he was sending a patrol unit to arrest John Christ once again.

With the questioning out of the way, the doctors returned to preparing Carol Christ for surgery.

Dr. Patrinely now was there, too, and got his first look at his patient. Because she had been undergoing so many tests at Ben Taub, he had only looked at her films and test results earlier. She looked gruesome, even to the doctor accustomed to seeing traumatic injuries. He now recognized her as one of the nurses he had seen on Dunn 8 West, but he had not known before who she was or that she was Christ's wife. An ophthalmic plastic and reconstructive surgeon, he was drawn to his uncommon specialty because it combined his interests in the detailed precision of microsurgery and eye surgery along with the creativity of plastic surgery. Focusing primarily on the skeletal regions around and below the eyes, he treated patients requiring reconstruction due to trauma, tumors or congenital deformities as well as those who just desired it for cosmetic reasons. At thirty-nine, he was nationally renowned for his exacting skills. This year, Patrinely was listed in the first edition of the book *The Best Doctors in America*. An associate professor at Baylor College of Medicine, he also lectured nationally, and served on an exhaustive number of professional committees and organizations. He published extensively in his field, particularly on the topic of complex orbital surgery, which Christ certainly needed.

Patrinely examined her entry wound, a well-defined hole in front of her right ear, and the large, jagged, gaping exit wound, which had bone, muscle, clotted blood and tissue hanging out. She was alert but distraught. Carol indicated she could not see out of her left eye and wanted to know if she would be able to see again. It didn't look like it could be saved, but since he couldn't be sure yet, the surgeon told her they would do the best they could. Her eyeball, which had been split open like a grape, had to be closed within the first twenty-four hours of being ruptured to have any real hope of saving it, so that was a priority for the surgeons. This was a severe rupture and her eyeball was full of blood.

Beyond that, the surgeon's immediate plans were to clean out and close the gunshot wounds, determine the full extent of her injuries, get the patient on antibiotics to stave off infection, closely monitor her and wait for the swelling to subside. Once that happened, they could go back in later for the major work of reconstructing her face, which undoubtedly would entail a series of grueling operations.

Because of the massive injuries and potential for further extensive swelling, the doctors wanted to ensure she would be able to breathe easily. After she was under anesthesia, Dr. Robert B. Parke Jr., an ENT, assisted by Dr. John C. Moorhead, a resident surgeon, performed a tracheotomy, cutting a hole in her neck just below the larynx and inserting a tube, which was reattached to the ventilator. He then turned his attention to her severe facial injuries, noting that her sinuses had extensive damage. Parke cleaned all her wounds but decided it would be best not to operate on these areas now. The patient was turned over to the orthopedists.

Dr. Gerard T. Gabel, with the help of Dr. Omer Ilahi, turned to the lesser of her injuries, the gunshot wound to her left forearm. The bullet had gone straight through her arm, splitting it open about one and one-half inches above her wrist and a half-inch from the outer edge. The large-caliber bullet had cut a path through her flesh, but fortunately hadn't hit any bones or the artery. For the most part, the tendon was spared; only a slight portion was damaged and needed to be cut away. The worst damage had been to the main ulnar nerve, which had been bruised by the bullet and pushed into an unnatural position by a ballooning pocket of blood. It now wrapped around a bone, instead of lying straight over it. They drained the blood, helped the nerve to its normal position, repaired the damage to it and stitched her wound closed. The good news was that if she recovered from her other injuries, she could expect to regain the full use of her arm, although she would have a permanent indentation on the outside of her arm from where tissue had been ripped away.

When Gabel and Ilahi finished, Dr. Hamill took over the operating table for the delicate repair of her left eyeball. Originally planning to be a marine biologist, Hamill decided in his junior year at the University of North Carolina at Chapel Hill that he wanted a more secure career, not one subject to grant-funding or limiting in location, so he elected to go to medical school instead. At Baylor, he narrowed down his field of specialty to three choices—orthopedics, plastic surgery or ophthalmology. He decided on the latter because, unlike his patients, he thought the surgery was fun. Many surgeons who could cut open someone's chest, reach in and massage a human heart in their hands became squeamish just discussing the eyeball topic. Hamill enjoyed the high-tech tools of the trade and the intricacies of eye surgery with its demands for practiced steadiness and microscopic skills. Once he went into practice, he came to appreciate that ophthalmology provided him the added satisfaction of developing lifelong relationships with his patients. He loved the thrill of being able to restore a person's vision, but Carol Christ's injuries made that unlikely.

First he examined her right orb and found no damage. The left globe had been blown open by the powerful percussion of the bullet, a large S-shaped fissure winding nearly the length of the sphere.

Hamill inserted a speculum around the eyeball, its wires trimmed with cotton strips, pulling back the lids and surrounding muscles and tissues, giving the surgeon more room to work and giving the false appearance that the globe was slightly popping out of the socket. The surgeon removed the conjunctiva, a thin layer of tissue on top of the eyeball, by cutting a circle around the surface of the iris. He sutured the ripped muscles that attached the orb to the socket. The eyeball was ruptured just once, but it was severe, nearly twenty millimeters long on a globe measuring about twenty-five millimeters. Using silk and nylon sutures, the ophthalmic surgeon sewed the gash closed, placed a gelatin sheet between the muscle and globe to prevent scarring, stitched the conjunctiva back into place and hoped for the best. Several hours after he had begun the exacting operation, he wasn't any more optimistic about the likelihood that Carol Christ's eye would be functional ever again. Hamill was convinced that the eyeball had suffered significant internal damage, probably to the retina, but it still was filled with too much blood to fully assess or repair right now.

Next Dr. Patrinely, with the help of Dr. Charles S. Soparkar, who was completing a fellowship under his tutelage, attended to her facial skeletal injuries, specifically the left orbit, both cheekbones and areas above her temples. The exit and entrance wounds were so large, they went through those to repair the underlying injuries. Holding open the exit wound with retractors, the doctors rinsed Carol Christ's wounds with Bacitracin, an antibiotic solution. They found no bullet fragments. Where her bones should have been, they found a large hole, obscured on the outside because her skin was still largely intact. As the bullet had seared across her face, it crushed her bones as if they were potato chips, shattering them into pieces too numerous and small to count, Patrinely said. Before he had stepped into the OR, the surgeon consulted another colleague, Dr. Samuel Stal, a highly respected plastic surgeon who was considered by Patrinely and many other doctors to be the best craniofacial reconstructive surgeon in the region. Stal had been a year behind John Christ as a resident and knew him well professionally, although he neither liked nor respected him. Patrinely was pleased that Stal still didn't hesitate to get involved in Carol

Christ's treatment, which so many of their other colleagues seemed wary of doing.

Now as Patrinely looked directly at her horrific injuries, he found them far more extensive than the CT scans and other tests revealed. He phoned Stal from the operating room, telling him: "This is worse than we thought. Can you come take a look?"

Stal arrived quickly and the three surgeons formulated a strategy to reassemble what part of her face Patrinely and Soparkar could do that day. For now, their emphasis was to protect her sinus cavities, fend off infection and keep the damage from getting even worse. They would leave the most intricate reconstructive work until after the swelling diminished and her other injuries began healing somewhat. Stal later would become part of Christ's surgical team, but he was not a member this day.

Several large pieces of Christ's cheekbone still were attached to their muscles, and Patrinely stitched these together and placed them in a way that closed the exposed sinus cavity and blocked the large gap between her cheek and nose. Piecing together other shattered bones like a puzzle, he tried to rebuild her facial structure. Some, he knew, were just temporary fixes. He used the sutures to lift her cheek skin and reduce the pull downward on her eyelid. He tried to leave as much muscle as possible, even though it was damaged, to prevent her face from further caving in. Working meticulously but in somewhat piecemeal fashion, Patrinely joined the multiple skin flaps of the exit wound, which looked like flower petals, cutting off only the thinnest edges when necessary and painstakingly stitched them closed. He put a sterile dressing over that portion of her face and moved to the lower left eyelid, which was ripped and hanging away from the eyeball. But because of the severity of her other injuries, which the surgeon did not want to amplify, he opted to hold it in place temporarily with a single suture instead of the more intricate repair typically done. That might come later, depending on the other reconstructive surgeries she would have.

Working next on the entrance wound, adjacent to her right ear, he irrigated it with Bacitracin and carefully cut away the edges of the skin most damaged by powder burns, which peppered out in fine, dark dots about two centimeters all around the wound. He suture closed the muscle beneath the wound, then the skin and put another sterile dressing over that. Over her left eye, he put a thick dressing. After eight hours in the operating room, Carol Christ was taken to the recovery room in good condition. Doctors knew she would return to the operating room many times, but even they could not yet predict just how many procedures she would need.

"She was an attractive woman. We didn't want to leave her disfigured," Patrinely said. But before they could concentrate on restoring her beauty, they had to focus on keeping her alive. For now, they worried about an infection invading her severely damaged sinus area. When the surgeon later learned how his patient had crawled out of bed in search of help, he believed that by doing so, she had saved her life. Had she stayed in one place, she probably would have bled to death in her bed, he thought.

Carol Christ's family still were on their way into town but not yet there, leaving only hospital staff to comfort her.

John Christ's little finger was being operated on down the hall. Gay, the accused's ex-wife, along with his extremely worried mother and other relatives and his attorney, Thano Dameris, kept vigil in the waiting room to be sure he would be OK. None of them asked about Carol's condition and reportedly never spoke of John's critically injured wife. Like Christ himself, his mother worried excessively about his finger and how it might affect his career. What more likely would impact his practice, however, was the fact that as soon as he emerged from the recovery room, he was arrested once again, hospitalized or not. This time, John Christ chose to pass the interim time in a hospital bed rather than a jail cell. Other surgeons were dismayed that he was hospitalized overnight, saying he easily could have been released following treatment, even an operation. Christ later claimed to have been hospitalized for days.

Gus and Helayne O'Keiff had had trouble finding Carol once they had arrived at the hospital. Only after the hospital's security had authorities check their drivers' licenses and verified that O'Keiff was Carol's brother, they were told she was in the recovery room but they could wait for her in ICU. Despite all the precautions the hospital took before they could find out any information on her, the O'Keiffs were outraged to learn that John Christ was recovering in a room on the same floor. Helayne insisted that he be moved. Hospital staff insisted Carol was protected.

"I don't care. I want him moved," she persisted. Finally, they relented and moved John Christ elsewhere in the hospital. "I demanded that he be moved. I was pretty obnoxious about it," Helayne recalled.

After three hours in the recovery room, Carol Christ was fairly alert and cooperative. Under the protective accompaniment of a Houston officer, she was taken to the Neuro Intensive Care Unit on the eighth floor of Jones Tower, where her brother and sister-in-law now waited. Gus was shocked yet again; his sister looked even worse than he had expected. They let her know they were there for her. She was pale and still covered with dried blood over most of her body, including beneath the nails of her hands and feet and in her hair. Her face and head were badly swollen and bruised, especially on the left side. For her protection, an armed cop would stand guard at her door around the clock. Elsewhere in the hospital, another officer stood outside John Christ's room, not for his safety but because he was in custody until his attorney posted 10 percent of his $5,000 bond. For just $500, Christ would soon be free once again.

Despite the twenty-four-hour protection, Carol Christ was terrified her husband would find her and finish what he had attempted; fears that, despite being unable to speak because of the tracheotomy tube, she did her best to relay through notes. A ventilator was attached to the trach tube, as a temporary safeguard. She was able to breathe on her own, but the staff was unable to get an accurate respiratory count, indicating she might not be getting enough oxygen into her bloodstream. A metal patch covered her left eye; ice packs were placed over her face and tied around her head to reduce the swelling and bleeding. She asked for a pain shot, but because her blood pressure and heart rate were low, she was given only half of the usual dose. She was nauseous and still vomiting blood at times. Medication quieted that and her vital signs improved enough that she was given a full pain injection the next time she asked. Although Christ had been sure she had removed her gold labial ring in the ER, it was still there and noted on her chart. A few eyebrows had been raised when doctors and nurses first noticed it in the emergency and operating rooms, but they were more focused on her injuries. One of her nurses or other hospital workers removed it during the next few days, and it was many years later before she realized she had not removed it in the emergency room as she had imagined.

Her regular physician, Dr. Ronald Sims, was there, called in to consult on the case. He had been upset when he had received the alarming call earlier in the evening and told that Carol Christ, whom he respected and liked immensely, had been shot in the head and might not survive. It was only after he got to the hospital that he heard the nearly as disturbing news from one of the ICU nurses that John Christ had been the one who shot her. Sims had had no idea that there were problems in her marriage. He was given a summary of the severity of her injuries. When he reached her room, Christ was unconscious. A nurse was cleaning the skin of her incredibly swollen face. Given the extensive trauma to her face and the injury to the frontal lobe of the brain and her history of respiratory problems, Sims didn't think she would survive. The other doctors he spoke with didn't expect her to, either, but listed her prognosis as guarded. Sims was overcome by the atrocity and stood near her bed, watching, with tears running down his face. He liked Christ tremendously; he wanted to protect her but couldn't.

After a while, he approached her bed and, not believing it himself, tried to reassure and comfort her: "Things are going to be okay. You're going to get through it."

He choked back his personal feelings, and examined her. Because of her history of asthma, he kept her on bronchodilators and looked over her lab results for signs of developing internal problems. So far, she was doing OK.

Hamill came close to her bed, gently touched her upper arm, leaned over slightly and, as gently as possible, gave her the bad news. "Carol, your eye was badly damaged. You're going to be blind in the left eye. I'm sorry." Unable to talk because of the trach, Carol Christ nodded that she understood, but she was devastated.

On the other side of town, a somber Dani was brokenhearted and not saying much, waiting for news on her mother at Kayla Falls's apartment. Falls, a nursing assistant on Carol's unit as well as her children's sometimes baby-sitter, had been at home getting ready to go to Montgomery Ward for a family photo with her three sisters when she heard the distressing news about the shooting. The city was becoming increasingly violent and her first thought was that it had been a drive-by shooting. She was shocked when she heard John Christ had done it. She had always liked the plastic surgeon and had never seen him the least bit angry, even in situations that seemed to make other doctors mad. Her coworkers on Dunn 8 West on duty that day called a few more times with updates and then suggested that Falls take care of Dani. They couldn't think of anyone closer to Dani than her baby-sitter. After keeping her appointment, Falls and a ward clerk on the unit, Mildred Hall, picked up Dani from the police station. On the way there, they discussed how to talk to the child. Unsure, Falls drew on her pastor's frequent advice: "When you don't know what to say, don't say anything at all." They agreed to let Dani bring up whatever she wanted to discuss and not ask the many questions each was wondering about. When they walked into the station, Dani was playing a game with a female officer. Dani ran to Falls and wrapped her arms around her waist. The women were surprised that Dani wasn't crying as they had expected.

They went to a McDonald's and got Dani a late lunch, but she didn't eat it; then they stopped at Ben Taub to check on Carol. Hall ran in while Falls and Dani waited in the car, but she only learned that her friend had just been transferred to Methodist. They went there and Hall headed to their unit, hoping for answers. There wasn't any news, only sadness, shock and anger. She stopped by the ER and asked one of the plastic surgery residents on duty to tell Carol that they had Dani and that she was OK. As they drove back to Falls's apartment, no one said much.

The rest of the day and night, Dani was quiet, volunteering bits and pieces of what had happened and asking a few questions. She was bothered that her stepfather had kept her from going into the bedroom to help her mother, telling her Carol was OK when the child had heard her screaming and knew otherwise. She worried that her brother would go home from his weekend with his dad and be greeted by a house empty of its residents but full of bloody clues of the tragedy. She wondered how the doctors would put her mother's eye back into its socket and if she had to get a fake eye, whether she would get a blue one to match her other one or if she would get a brown one and look funny. Other times, Dani was hopeful, saying her mother was strong.

"Yes, your mother is young and strong and she's going to be okay," Hall assured her.

Sucking her thumb most of the day, Dani didn't cry. But Falls could tell the child was troubled. She always had been a vivacious girl, chatting happily with dolls or imaginary friends, but not today. She seemed deep in thought, staring into the distance. Always a cuddly child, Dani spent much of the time in Falls's lap or sitting next to her, resting her head on her shoulder. The women tried to distract her by playing games, but Dani's mind stayed on the tragedy.

She had some questions about Christ, but the women didn't know the answers to most of them.

"Who will keep me if my mommy dies?" she asked.

The women honestly didn't know, so they told her: "Somebody will take real good care of you." Privately, Falls wondered the same thing. Eventually, Dani drew her own conclusion: if her mother died, she would have to live with Daddy John.

Seventeen

The administration and staff of Methodist were greatly concerned for Carol Christ, her recovery and her security. Administrators checked with her doctors regularly for updates and wanted to limit those who had access to her. John Christ was charged with the shooting, but as he was on staff at the hospital and currently a patient there, hospital personnel wondered out loud if he might try again to hurt his wife or send someone else to finish what he had failed to complete. Not only was Carol Christ under twenty-four-hour guard, but it seemed to at least one doctor that security throughout the hospital had been increased.

The hospital corridors were rife with rumors about the shooting. Christ's past escapades—those proven and those only rumored—were trumpeted as examples of his weirdness and presumed capability for shooting his wife in the head. He was viewed as extremely clever but unnervingly vindictive. It was widely believed that he had assaulted his first two wives, although less was known about what really went on between him and Ruth. That didn't stop the gossip. The prevailing stories had Christ throwing her through a glass shower door or down the stairs, breaking her leg and prompting her to flee back to her family in New York. However, no police report apparently was filed in Harris County, but a prosecutor, while never officially verifying or refuting this story, said Christ had physically abused his first wife as well. Those who were acquainted with John and Ruth Christ during their brief marriage knew it ended strangely, with her suddenly fleeing out of town with the child.

Much more was known about what apparently had happened three years earlier between John and his second wife, Gay, as she had spent about a week recovering in Methodist, filed a police report, pressed charges, sued him in civil court and talked to some people about what had happened. But whatever sympathy those at Methodist may have once felt for Gay was now quickly evaporating. Once a terrified and battered victim of John Christ's, she now seemed to be standing by the man, and vicious rumors flew about her as well. Not all of them were true, but the prevailing opinion was that she was selling out for the alimony and child support payments. "People thought it was pretty mercenary," said one doctor.

Carol spent most of Sunday sleeping as doctors stopped by throughout the day to check her progress. She was stable, and although her prognosis still was uncertain, they hoped for the best.

Margaret and Dan Edwards arrived in Houston about 5:00 A.M. and headed directly to the Neuro ICU. Seeing an armed guard at her daughter's door was both a relieving and alarming sight. Margaret Edwards thought Carol's head looked as large as a watermelon.

Unable to speak yet with the trach, Christ scrawled notes with her injured left arm. "Dani saw me crawl out of the room saturated in blood," she wrote to her mother, who tried to reassure her that Dani would be fine.

"I didn't realize John had this potential!" she wrote.

It was one of the most difficult days of Margaret Edwards's life. She was too numb to cry. Weeks later, she wept daily, realizing the implications for her daughter's life. Somewhat reassured after seeing her alert and communicating, the Edwardses checked into the Marriott Hotel, part of the sprawling Medical Center complex. After calling to check on Dani, they went to Ben Taub to pick up the few items Carol had with her when she entered the ER the day before, including her wedding rings, now encased in blood.

That morning, Mason and fourth wife Natalie O'Keiff boarded a plane and flew to Houston. Since he had gotten the call, O'Keiff had been wondering what would cause something like this to happen. The only time he had met his latest son-in-law, O'Keiff had found the surgeon pleasant but a little withdrawn. Because his daughter asked for a loan to buy their house, he knew the surgeon had financial problems. His daughter was a grown woman who knew what she wanted and he didn't try to advise her on her love life. He had not even met Tilson or Crow, husbands three and five. "Sometimes you just have to keep shooting yourself in the foot until it hurts, I guess," he said years later, not noticing his ironic phrasing.

When he got to the ICU and finally saw his daughter, O'Keiff felt more relieved. He knew she had been close to death and still could die, but he was encouraged to see her responding to questions, writing some answers and moving her lips, even though no sound came out because of the tracheotomy. He also was pleased that she did not suffer any spinal damage. She scribbled: "You were there" and looked at him with gratefulness. He assumed that because of the trauma she was confused. Eventually, he understood that she thought he had been with her the previous day. No, he told her, he had just arrived. Carol was disappointed to learn it had not been her father and wondered who had been there comforting her. Years later, she concluded it probably had been Bob Margolis, a kind-hearted friend and a middle-aged plastic surgery resident who had been with her in Methodist's emergency room, although he had not been treating her. He always had been so gentle and good.

In the waiting room, it was an awkward family reunion as Carol's parents, separated by decades of divorce and bitterness, and their new spouses, Gus and his wife, Jackson, their son-in-law of long ago, a concerned grandson and a traumatized granddaughter hung out, worrying about Carol, waiting for their next chance for a limited visit with her in the ICU and trying to make conversation.

Having barely, if ever, spoken to Mason since their rancorous divorce nearly thirty years before, Margaret said, "Hello, Mason. Let's try to be civil to each other during this time."

He merely nodded his agreement, but the embittered ex-spouses found nothing else to say to each other during any of it. "We were feeling horrible for Carol, but we really wanted to nail the son of a bitch who did it," Gus said, referring to John Christ. They weren't talking about hurting Christ, only making sure he would be punished by the criminal justice system.

Dani had been dropped off by Falls earlier that day, and went from one relative to the next, searching for hugs and comfort from relatives she barely knew or from people unaccustomed to handing those out freely. Her grandparents and uncle always had been emotionally reserved. Her mother, the one person Dani always had been able to rely on, was badly hurt, and she was not allowed to even see her briefly. Dani worried out loud about her mother's status and repeatedly recalled details from the horrific morning before. The adults

had decided it would be too much for Dani to see her
mother as she looked now, so Dani was left with the last
image she had of her mother as she had lain bleeding
in the kitchen.

Joe finally heard the news Sunday night. He, his father, stepmother and five-year-old halfsister had been
in San Antonio for the weekend visiting relatives. After
John Jackson listened to the messages outlining some
of the grisly details, he called and spoke briefly with
Margaret; Joe heard none of it. Jackson then told Joe
to get in the truck. As they drove around, Jackson relayed the grim story to his son slowly, allowing him to
absorb one cruel detail at a time. "Your mom's been
in an accident. I don't know anything right now," he
said, other than she was still alive. Joe assumed she had
been in a car accident. Jackson gradually told him that
his mom had been shot by his stepfather. While she was
in bad shape, she was expected to live, he assured him.
Joe cried as he listened. He didn't know what to do but
told his father he wanted to go see his mother right
then. Jackson, visibly shaken, told him he could not see
her for a while, as she was unconscious and in bad
shape.

Joe and his dad ended up at the Christs' home on
Timberside. Margaret Edwards had suggested that Jackson take Joe there to get his things, as well as some of
his mother's valuables, reminding him not to forget his
mother's pearls hidden in a mock soup can in the pan-
try.

Jackson was visibly nervous to be there and told his
son not to go anywhere but his bedroom and the living
room. Joe didn't listen as he had things to gather from
other parts of the house as well. The kitchen floor was
awash in dried blood, including a five-foot pool near
the kitchen entrance. Needles, bandages and other debris left by the harried ambulance crew vividly illus-

trated where his mother had lain after being shot. He followed the blood trail from the kitchen door back to his mother's bedroom and saw the blood-drenched bed. Telling his father where to find his mother's photo albums and other valuables, Joe went to pack his own things.

The scene was worse than the teenager had anticipated and made him wonder about the seriousness of his mother's condition. Still, he refused to believe that she could die.

Monday morning, Joe and his father joined the rest of Carol's family in the ICU waiting area. It was a tense, trying time. Carol seemed to be doing better, they thought. She was more alert and seemed to them perfectly lucid. Those were hopeful signs, as they had feared she might be left in a vegetative state. While it was obvious that she still could die from her injuries, an infection or one of the surgeries, they began planning for her future, which would include a long, grueling recovery. It already had been decided that it would be best for everyone if Dani lived with Gus and Helayne and her son, and Joe was given the choice of living with his grandparents in Arkansas or with his father. He chose his dad, who lived in the Bunker Hill neighborhood on the west side, knowing he could finish the school year at Pershing Middle School and see his friends as well. His more immediate concern, though, was to go upstairs and see his mother, but the adults refused to let him.

Christ's arraignment was rescheduled but his attorney posted his bond, a court-ordered condition of which he was to have no contact with his wife. That was OK, he had other ways to get to her—one that would further destroy her and, he hoped, save himself.

John Christ summoned his second wife to his bedside, sending word through the hospital staff that he wanted

to see her. He told Gay that all was forgiven. He was
withdrawing his motion to reduce child support payments. A hearing on the matter had been scheduled
for the following week.

Christ also had a new story about how his wife had
been shot. Carol had shot herself, he now insisted. He
never presented an adequate excuse for why he had not
mentioned the scenario for more than two days. He
seemed to think that he had a reasonable excuse and
kept reminding anyone who asked that he had been
hurt, too. It was obvious she could breathe and there
was nothing he could do for her—he didn't have an
operating room at home, after all, he arrogantly proclaimed. This was his story and he was sticking to it, for
now. He had no other choice. He now had committed
himself to his legal defense. The next day, Susan Novak,
his one-time mistress, committed herself to someone
else in marriage.

Christ's allegations were enough to amplify the gossip
and speculation still whirling through the Medical Center like a Texas tornado. Those who knew Carol dismissed the allegations immediately, knowing she had
not been that depressed and that she would never
choose to leave her children. Most of those who knew
John Christ discounted the suicide theory even more
quickly. There was too much evidence that went against
it. The shot had been fired from slightly behind and
the angle she would have had to use was too awkward.
The right-handed .45 pistol was bulky and heavy, especially to be used with left-handed Carol's weaker right
hand. Additionally, those close to her all knew that
Carol had been depressed before in her life and had
overcome more than one bad marriage without getting
that depressed.

Doctors had no choice but to ask Carol about the
allegations, knowing it could be critical to her care.

Hearing that her husband actually was blaming her for his most heinous of crimes felt like yet another brutal blow. She was adamant. She had not tried to commit suicide. Her doctors and everyone who communicated with her about it had no doubt that she was telling the truth. Now the medical staff played detective, weighing the evidence and theorizing if each of their scenarios was even possible. Obviously, her story was possible, and those who knew Dr. Christ believed the most plausible. His story was filled with holes, most notably that he hadn't even raised that claim for two days and not until after he had been charged with trying to kill her. Further, he had told people "we shot each other," which was far different. Even though she was under armed guard, her husband still managed to psychologically torment her.

Later, when her mother visited, Carol angrily scrawled a note telling her what was going on: "John is trying to see I tried to commit suicide. <u>NO WAY</u>," twice underlining the last two words. Margaret Edwards thought the scenario was absurd. If there was one thing her daughter was, it was a survivor. She never would have killed herself over any man and her past proved that much. She always could be sure that another man would soon enter her life if she wanted one. She had loved and lost repeatedly but always moved forward with optimism and a renewed dedication to have learned from her experiences. If there's one thing an eternal optimist like Carol wouldn't do, it would be kill herself.

"No way; Carol's a survivor" was Mason O'Keiff's thought when he heard the allegation. There was too much evidence to suggest otherwise. She was left-handed but the bullet had been fired from the right side. She immediately had claimed John had shot her, but it took him two days to mention that she had tried to kill herself. It was absurd.

Carol Christ still was trying to piece together what had happened two days earlier. "After he shot me, I heard another shot. He shot himself in the hand," she wrote to her family. Gus O'Keiff asked if she was sure more than one shot had been fired. She had no doubt. Knowing the police believed otherwise, Christ's family began to wonder if the cops had overlooked something.

Gus O'Keiff called Swaim and told him what he thought might be important information: "Carol has been writing some notes about what happened. She says that there were at least two shots fired."

When he hung up, Swaim relayed the information to his partner.

"Do you think we might have missed something?" Matthews wondered out loud. Certain they and the CSU had searched the place thoroughly, they nonetheless decided to go out for a second look later that day.

Gus and Helayne O'Keiff and Dan and Margaret Edwards headed to the Christ house to collect Carol's and Dani's things. The house was locked, so they broke a window in Joe's bedroom. They then decided that hadn't been such a good idea, so they called police and waited until they arrived to go inside. Helayne was shocked to see the crime scene, so much more bloody and eerie than she had expected.

Seeing the blood-drenched bed where her only daughter had lain dying days earlier and the huge, dried pools of blood on the kitchen floor, Margaret grew more and more angry. Following the blood trails and recalling the stories they had heard from officials, doctors, Carol and Dani, the four tried to piece together what had happened. Dani's cereal bowl was sitting in the den, exactly where she said she was when she heard the gunshots. Gus emptied the remains into the disposal and put the dishes in the dishwasher.

Walking out of the master bedroom, Dan Edwards

spotted a spent casing lying next to the door, not the least bit hidden. He excitedly told the others and then telephoned his finding to Swaim.

"Shit," Swaim said to himself, but just asked, "Where?"

The detective told him to leave it where it was and that he would send a CSU over to retrieve it and look again for the other bullet.

The instant the receiver was back in its cradle, Swaim said aloud what he had been thinking: "Shit!" He told his partner, who was shocked. They wanted to have another look themselves; so after calling CSU, Matthews and Swaim headed back to Timberside. Dan Edwards pointed out the casing. Embarrassed, the detectives shook their heads in disbelief, amazed they and all the other officers could have missed it. The casing blended in with the golden hardwood floors but that didn't excuse their oversight. Leaving it to lie there until CSU arrived to properly tag and bag it and photograph it, the detectives went in search once again for the other bullet. The detectives tried to determine the possible path of the bullet. The casing likely had bounced once it hit the floor, so it could have been fired from almost anywhere in the room. If the doctor had been unloading it as he claimed when it went off, the barrel should have been pointing at a downward angle, but they could find no traces of it. If he had been aiming at his wife a second time, it should have struck higher up. They searched the walls and furniture but could find no trace of the bullet. On his hands and knees reexamining the floor and rug inch by inch, Swaim was growing frustrated as they failed to find it for the second time.

The detective pulled back half the rug to examine the floor underneath. Seeing nothing, he replaced it and pulled back the other half. He saw a nick in the hardwood floor underneath. "I think I found it," he exclaimed. Laying just the padding back on the floor, he saw a clear hole through it, but he could not see a bullet. Matching it to the corresponding place on the rug, the detective now saw a small hole, hidden mostly by the dark carpet fibers. At least he had an explanation for how they had missed the bullet hole—the percussion of the bullet had sucked the fibers back close to their original position, almost completely covering the hole.

The hole in the floor was elliptical, indicating to Officer L. L. Dawson that whatever had caused it struck the floor at an acute angle and had come from the direction of the doorway, where the casing had been found. Dawson asked Dan Edwards for permission to cut into the wood flooring to determine if there was a bullet burrowed into the floor. Dawson removed a strip of wood, revealing a bullet wedged in a floor joist that supported the slats. Before he removed the .45-caliber bullet, Dawson suggested spraying it first with leuco-malachite, generally known as Luminol, a chemical used to reveal the presence of blood that can't always be seen with the naked eye. The detectives agreed and Dawson mixed the solution, combining distilled water and liquid acetic acid with two powders—sodium perborate and leuco-malachite green. He sprayed the concoction onto the bullet and the police waited to see if it turned the telltale green, indicating blood was present. It did. The bullet was dug from the floor and evidence photos were snapped.

The doctor had been telling the truth about one thing—two shots had been fired but that didn't change the detectives' conviction that John Christ had been the only one who had fired the gun Saturday morning.

The house officially had ceased to be a crime scene two days earlier, and Gus and Dan cleaned up most of the blood on the floors as their wives packed Carol's and Dani's things. As they were leaving, Margaret noticed the fish Carol was so fond of, swimming in the large tank. Knowing no one would be there to care for them, they bagged them up to take to a pet store. As they were leaving, John's mother, sister and an attorney, who was a friend of his sister's, arrived. Christ's mother, Effie, told Carol's mother that she was sorry about everything.

"I can't believe John did this," Margaret Edwards responded, misinterpreting the sympathy.

"Oh, John didn't do this," the suspect's mother responded with conviction. She was convinced Carol had tried to kill herself as her son now claimed.

Edwards felt sorry for her. She had thought of her in-laws as nice people and knew how proud they had been that they had provided their three children with college educations, all of them seemingly in successful careers. "She was so proud of her doctor son," Edwards said. The attorney informed Carol's family that John Christ would get the house if the couple divorced. *If?* Did they actually believe that her daughter would stay married to him?

"I was so sure this would work. I thought John was so happy," Effie Christ told Margaret.

"I did, too," Margaret replied. She had known otherwise, but she thought it was time for sympathy, not recriminations. She didn't blame John's mother for what he had done and she couldn't fault her for believing in him.

When they returned to the hospital, Gus had Carol's hospital photo ID, which he had found on the kitchen counter. He gently pinned it to her hospital gown "to say this is what my sister really looks like," his wife recalled. "He was so upset to see her bandaged."

By Tuesday, Carol Christ was recovering well, although the most serious of the surgeries still lay ahead of her. She was communicating effectively with those around her through handwritten notes and hand motions. She seemed to be able to move all parts of her body, even her left injured forearm, indicating that her neurological functions remained intact. That day, the nurses got her to sit and stand for the first time. When she stood, though, her legs weakened beneath her and she fell, only to be caught by the nurses standing guard for such problems. Shaky, she soon stood on her own and, at the nurses' instructions, marched in place for three minutes without falling. The next day, the ventilator was disconnected. Carol Christ was sent to physical therapy, which her medical team planned to have her do until it was time for her next surgery. They didn't want to risk her growing weaker or suffering muscle atrophy.

That evening in the ICU, Carol felt like she was suffocating. Her head and neck were continuing to swell and she felt it tighten around her tracheotomy. It was a terrifying feeling; still unable to talk, she frantically waved her arms until she caught a nurse's attention through the glass windows of her small room. Using hand motions, she told the nurse she was choking. The nurse checked and assured her that the trach was fine. She was not suffocating; the swelling around the tube just made it feel that way, the nurse said. The explanation, though accurate, did nothing to soothe Carol's frantic fears. She was sure the nurse did not understand what she was saying, for the feeling persisted. She had taken care of innumerable patients with trachs and never heard anyone complain of what she was feeling. Of course, she had not worked with trauma cases, but that did not matter to her now. She knew what she felt. The respiratory therapist was called. He checked on her, verifying that it was still placed properly and clear of blood and mucus. Still, a short time later, her trach tube was replaced with a metal one, which couldn't compress as easily. Once the swelling subsided, Carol was taught how to use her fingers to control the intake and outflow of air so she could speak. Having worked with patients with trachs, it was more like a reminder than new information, so she caught on quickly.

A relieved Steinfeld was finally able to see her friend.

"Oh, Betty, can you believe he did this to me?" Carol cried over and over again.

"No," Steinfeld replied simply. She offered to do whatever she could to help, but right now, it seemed that was up to Carol's surgeons and the police.

Dani, still in shock, flew with Gus and Helayne to Nashville and an uncertain future. It was a big adjustment for everyone in the house. Dani barely knew her relatives but soon learned that they ran their house much differently from what she was accustomed to. Gus O'Keiff was a strong disciplinarian facing off with a child not used to many rules. Dani's mother had been permissive and her stepfather abusive; now she was learning what the middle ground was like. They gave her a large bedroom, decorated for and designated as Erin's, Gus's daughter who lived with her mother in Houston, with its own bathroom. They bought her lots of new toys and clothes.

Everyone expected Dani to have a breakdown as a result of the shooting, but she never did. After they returned to Nashville, Gus and Helayne sat down with her and asked her about what had happened, hoping to help her deal with her emotions. They were surprised when she recounted the horrific events without crying, seeming emotionally detached from what she had witnessed. She was upset about her mother's condition, though. "She missed her mommy and she was afraid she would not see her mommy again, and we were afraid that might be the case," Gus said. They reassured her that her mother would be fine.

Believing his daughter was on her way to recovery, Mason O'Keiff and Natalie returned home to Arizona. Dan and Margaret Edwards planned to stay until they could take Carol home with them.

When John Christ was released from the hospital, he went home and changed the locks on the house.

Dameris, still recovering from open-heart surgery several months before, only handled the initial proceedings for his longtime client. Christ quickly hired one of the city's top criminal defense firms, Hinton, Sussman & Bailey, to represent him on the criminal charges. While at the Mayan Dude Ranch the previous weekend, he had met Sussman, forty-five, who now was coming highly recommended by a fellow Indian Princess father, a successful businessman, whom Christ had called for advice after the shooting. Sussman and Bailey visited Christ while he was still in the hospital. Attorney June Cullom also signed on to Christ's expensive defense and generally met with their client en masse.

A graduate of the South Texas College of Law in Houston, Bailey, thirty-eight, a good-looking man with a heavy Southern accent and fondness for suspenders, hailed from the tiny town of Big Stone Gap, Virginia. It was a draw whether his wit or temper was quicker.

He wasn't one to ask if a client was guilty; he'd rather not know. He wasn't going to play hand holder, therapist or best friend to a client, regardless of their problems. The only kind of counselor he intended on being was the kind who dispensed legal advice. History convinced him that doctors generally were good clients; they knew what it was like to have their experienced advice ignored and the costly consequences patients could pay for disregarding it. As a group, doctors downed whatever advice their attorneys gave, however bitter the initial taste. Christ would prove an exception to that rule, shunning the very legal advice he was paying hugely for and opting to do things his way, as he had so often done in the past, even now when his future was on the line.

When he once announced to his attorneys that he was smarter than 90 percent of the people in the world, Bailey went ballistic. Slamming his fist onto the table, he boomed: "If I ever hear that again, if I ever hear that uttered again outside this office, you are going to suffer the consequences beyond anything you can imagine. . . . The wrath of God will come second to the wrath of Joe Bailey." He knew it would be a fatal mistake should Christ underestimate the prosecutor's immense talents, especially on cross-examination, or if he condescended to jurors, implying he were in a higher class. Another time, the plastic surgeon bluntly told Bailey that he wanted to fix his nose. The attorney wasn't interested in becoming his client's patient; he liked his nose, broken too many times to remember in football games. Sometimes Christ acted like he was playing a game and that the rules didn't apply to him. Even though he already had changed his story about what had happened on May 9, and then committed himself to a hard-to-support defense, John Christ eventually would tell friends and colleagues another scenario. He told a number of people that his wife, addicted to drugs, had first threatened to kill herself and when he struggled to stop her, he had been shot as well. His defense in court, however, would be that he had not been in the room when she had shot herself.

On Wednesday, Dr. Chris Sermas, a respected psychiatrist, well known in and out of the Medical Center, volunteered to see Carol Christ. He had known his new patient as a ready, energetic nurse from the plastic surgery unit. He also knew her husband. Although the two doctors never socialized, Sermas had felt a slight affinity toward his fellow Greek. Now he was sickened to think that one of his colleagues could commit such a heinous crime.

When he got to the Neuro ICU in the Jones Building, he immediately felt the tension. Rumors were swirling and an armed guard was posted outside Carol Christ's door. He had seen the news trucks gathered outside the hospital entrance earlier in the week. "It was really quite a hubbub," he said. He walked by the security and saw Carol, her head wrapped in bandages. No longer the pleasant, upbeat smiling nurse he once knew, she was overwhelmed by anxiety, tense and almost desperate. Her voice strained, she told him the awful story of the mounting marital problems culminating with her husband shooting her, and she recounted in vivid detail her crawl through the house in search of help, her frantic child clinging to her side. Carol's biggest fear, which dominated this and nearly every meeting after with her psychiatrist, was that her husband was coming back to finish his botched murder attempt. Clearly, she was suffering from post-traumatic stress disorder and was clinically depressed. Sermas, a soft-spoken man with a relaxed manner despite his hectic schedule of appointments with troubled patients, thought she was one of the most frightened people he had ever seen. She badly needed to vent her fears and feelings. His therapeutic approach varied depending on the patient and circumstances. For those with all their mental resources and a healthy ego, he said he tried to be more dynamic, listening, offering analysis and helping them link current and past behaviors. With someone going through a stressful situation, as Carol clearly was, his approach was to listen and offer support. He never hesitated to voice an opinion, such as "I don't think that's a good idea" or "I'd think twice about that." In these types of situations, the goal was to help the patient hold it together and offer her a place where she could feel secure. With Carol, it was an approach to which he would stick during their entire time together.

"The theme most often was her terror of John and what was going to happen next," he said of their sessions together.

Sermas had heard John Christ's allegations that she had tried to kill herself. But the sheer, unremitting terror she had of her husband, the psychiatrist said, "as much as anything convinced me that her story was absolutely genuine."

Whenever Sermas and Carol Christ's other doctors talked about their common patient, someone invariably prefaced their remarks with "John is such a bright guy." Everyone he spoke with was convinced that the plastic surgeon had tried to kill his wife but was stunned that he would act so irrationally and risk so much. As Sermas talked more with Carol about the problems she had faced in her marriage, the psychiatrist could see that John Christ apparently had carried a lot of unresolved anger for a long time. Carol had tried to be supportive, Sermas thought.

That day, Narayan again asked Carol about what had happened. She was adamant that her husband shot her and that it had not been a suicide attempt. He asked if she was left- or right-handed, a standard question for patients with gunshot wounds that might have been self-inflicted. Left, she assured him, pointing out that she had been shot from the right. She said she didn't even know her husband had a gun in the house. They had been arguing, she admitted, but she didn't think it was any worse than their usual fights and was shocked by what happened, she told him. She remembered being struck, but not necessarily shot, and falling forward, blacking out and awaking in a pool of blood. She heard a gunshot and Christ scream in pain.

She continued her physical therapy, but she was still weak from her injuries—most of which still hadn't been repaired—as well as from the surgeries. It was grueling, even though she did little more than walk on a padded surface between two rails. She wove back and forth as she tried, and she leaned on her arms a lot as her legs still were weak. The therapy upset Carol, as it was a vivid reminder of how much she had lost, and it increased her fears that she might be left with permanent disabilities, lacking even the most basic of skills. The therapists reassured her that she would get stronger with time and practice.

When Dr. Sims finally saw her awake, she was crying. "It was a sad, sad case," he said. "She would talk to me, but on the one hand, I think she felt embarrassed. On the other hand, she just couldn't believe what had happened. I think she wanted to die, too." She hadn't said so specifically, but she seemed at times to think she had nothing left to live for. He asked how it had happened. He had heard the reports and rumors, but he wanted to know what she recalled.

"Somebody said I tried to do this to myself—I didn't!" she said, and told him that Christ had shot her during an argument. Sims never doubted her story. He had seen her enough recently to know that she had not been that depressed. And the entry of the bullet clearly was from the back, at an angle on the right side, something she wouldn't have been able to do, he thought. "There was really in my mind never any other question who did it," he said, and no one he knew doubted her story.

Sims's office was just across the street, where John Christ's also was located, and the internist checked on Carol a couple of times a day out of concern for her medically and personally. When he found her awake, she always was crying. She was in disbelief that it could have happened, yet embarrassed that it did. He stayed and talked with her, sometimes trying to ease her concerns, sometimes commiserating with her. They even shed some tears together. A self-described "touchy, feely" kind of doctor, he often stroked her hair as they spoke. "Things are going to be OK. You'll get through it," he assured her, though he still quietly worried about the threat of an infection. He never left without hugging and kissing her first. He felt paternal toward her and still wanted to protect her. There was only so much he could do.

On Thursday, Christ had another CT scan, which showed the extensive bone and soft tissue damage she suffered. On what seemed like the upside at the time, it looked like no brain tissue was missing and that the brain injury was not as severe as it could have been. The truth, though, was that the CT could not reveal the most serious damage she had suffered, an injury that would not be discovered for quite some time. That afternoon, Christ was transferred out of ICU.

"I can't believe this is happening," she repeatedly told the nurses. Even though an HPD officer remained posted outside her door, and would be there twenty-four hours a day for the rest of her hospital stay, Carol was still terrified that her husband would find and kill her. It still was kind of surreal to Carol, accustomed to being the one giving emotional support to patients, not receiving it. She knew that each time the nurses reassured her, they jotted on her ever-expanding chart: "Emotional support given." Still, she appreciated and needed all the reassurances.

For that reason, she looked forward to her psychiatrist's daily visits. Like her husband, Sermas was proud of his Greek heritage, but at six feet with a full head of thick salt-and-pepper hair and dark mustache, he was much better-looking. His heavy, dark eyes and sympathetic nature comforted Carol and led her to trust him, although that didn't mean she would tell him everything right away. Still embarrassed about her past, she initially admitted to having been married only a few times.

If Carol was asleep when Sermas made his rounds, he simply sat beside her bed for a while, not wanting to disturb her but ready to help if she awoke. When Carol opened her eyes, she sometimes saw Sermas sitting quietly by her bed. "Hi, Carol," he'd say simply, and would study her face for whatever emotions might lie just beneath the surface. He usually waited for her to start the conversation. If she didn't, he started. "How are you feeling today? Are you able to get any decent sleep? Tell me how you are feeling," he said, still allowing the patient to open up with whatever she most wanted to talk about. Invariably, it was her unrelenting, ongoing fear of her husband.

Although Carol was able to eat and had no problems swallowing, drinking was much more difficult and frustrating. No longer able to close her lips completely due to nerve damage, drinking became a frustrating exercise. Trying to drink normally was tantamount to pouring half the drink down her chin and soaking her nightgown, and even a straw was no longer foolproof. After five days of physical therapy, she still was too weak to safely walk by herself and was told not to get out of bed without assistance because she might fall.

Parke, who coordinated Carol's team of physicians, was pleased with her steady progress and decreasing swelling. Her mental state seemed to be clearing as well, he noted. Carol Christ's medical team decided to hold off on the major facial reconstruction until her left eye had healed adequately. It was tested daily, finding that she had a little light perception, a hopeful sign. She was put on a high dose of steroids, but when her sight still did not improve, doctors discovered her left eye suffered from an extensively detached retina and scheduled her for surgery.

The worst thing about the trach was that the tube routinely got plugged with mucus, making it hard to breathe and requiring an uncomfortable and gross procedure to clear it. Periodically, nurses would use a saline jet, squirting salt water down the tube, which gave Christ the sensation that her lungs were filling with fluid. This forced her to cough out the mucus, which shot out of the tube and all over her and the bed. She had been on the other end of this unpleasant task as a nurse many times, but being on the receiving end was much worse than she ever anticipated.

As the days passed, Carol's pain increased—the headaches and eye pain were particularly excruciating, prompting her to ask for pain medication more frequently than prescribed. She generally got it.

On Sunday, eight days after the shooting, Joe finally saw his mother for the first time since his stepfather had tried to kill her. His grandparents and the nurses tried to prepare him for how bad she looked. She still was severely swollen, bruised and cut, and the black sutures and stitches were visible. Her head was bandaged, a trach tube revealed a hole in her throat, tubes sprouted from her body and she was weak and disfigured, they forewarned him. His grandmother told him that his mother might have some brain damage—it was still too soon to know—and that is what scared him the most. He equated brain damage with being brain dead, a vegetable.

When he saw her, he was relieved. He had imagined even worse. Mother and son's eyes met and they burst into tears, despite their attempts not to, and they gently hugged. He looked his mother over carefully, seeming to take in every tube, every bruise, every change in her features. Carol was sure her son thought it was gross and she tried to reassure him.

"I'll be OK. The swelling will go down and I'll get back to normal," she told him. Convinced she had the best doctors, Joe was optimistic about her recovery, but he also knew she was facing countless more operations and her life was more messed up than ever. He noticed she already was wearing makeup again. She now was wearing black mascara on her right eye only; her left was still too swollen. She slept in her mascara and lipstick, quickly removing the dark smudges beneath her eyes each morning and reapplying fresh coats before any doctors or nurses entered her room. "I felt like I looked so gross, I had to do anything I could to help," she said. This was a positive sign that she was feeling better and concerned about her looks—something about which deeply depressed people tend not to worry.

The other changes Joe noticed in his mother were more dramatic than he anticipated. Her once quick-paced, melodic voice was now measured and as deep and gruff as the menacing villain Darth Vader's. It pained him to watch her place her fingers over the hole in her throat, carefully controlling the intake and outflow of air just to say something to him. Just twelve years old and fascinated more than scared, Joe was inquisitive about all the tubes and the machines hooked up to her from all angles. His father, John Jackson, was with him, shaking his head at what his ex-wife's husband had done, saying that John Christ should be killed. Because Carol had survived, there was no chance of the surgeon getting the death penalty. The most he could get would be twenty years in prison, and few ever served even half their sentences, especially in Texas at that time where prison overcrowding was a huge problem and prisoners regularly were being freed en masse, even convicted murderers.

Later that afternoon, after Joe had left, Carol called her daughter for the first time. It was a tear-filled conversation for both of them. Now Carol's heart ached as well as her head. Mostly, Dani wanted to know if her mother was OK and if she was in any pain.

"Yes, but they're giving me medication," she told her. Many times throughout the ten-minute conversation, Christ had to reassure her child that she would be OK again, when, in fact, she was not sure herself if that was true. Carol worried whether she would live through her reconstructive surgery the next week, and, even if she did, what permanent disabilities she would be left with. She felt like she was lying to her daughter, but she knew that as the mother, she needed to comfort the child, not worry her. She wanted desperately to see and hold her.

Likewise, she needed some reassurances about her daughter's well-being, and Dani assured her that she was fine. "Are they taking good care of you?" Carol asked.

"Yes," Dani said, "but I want to see you. I want to be with you. I want to come home."

"No, you can't. I'm still in the hospital. There's no place for you to stay in here with me. Uncle Gus and Aunt Helayne will take good care of you."

How long before she could return home?

"I don't know, but it won't be too much longer," Carol lied to her daughter. She didn't know when she even would be able to see Dani again, let alone care for her.

They talked briefly about the shooting and Carol praised her daughter, as she would repeatedly in the months to come, for guiding her to the phone so she could get help. Mother and daughter talked a little longer; when it was time to hang up, neither wanted to go. Repeatedly, they told one another that they loved each other.

"OK, we've got to hang up," Carol said. Neither wanted to be the first, so they promised to hang up at the same time, on the count of three. Neither did. Finally, Carol had to be the one to place the receiver back in the cradle. She did, then lay back and cried.

Carol had done her best to console her daughter via long distance but ached to hold her and comfort her in her arms. She was a mother unable to mother completely. The day had been one of the most emotional for Carol so far; she hurt for what her children were going through, missed them terribly and worried what kind of mother she would be able to be again.

As she grew more comfortable with Dr. Sermas, her trust in him grew as did her determination to face everything about herself. She yearned to do better, to learn from her mistakes and to move forward to a better life. She now faced what had been so obvious to those around her—she repeatedly was drawn to the wrong type of men. Now she wanted to understand why.

Eighteen

Although the chances were slim, Dr. Hamill still had hope that Carol Christ's left eye could be saved, eliminating the need for a glass one and the numerous problems that would bring. She would never be able to fully see out of that eye again; a best-case scenario would be that she would be able to see light and dark, which would help with her depth perception. Hamill warned her he was not sure the surgery would work, but there was still some hope. This time, the ophthalmic surgeon would be assisting Dr. Michael W. Hines, a retina specialist, in the painstaking procedure. A B-scan echography, a specialized ultrasound, was done the day before surgery, confirming the surgeons' suspicions, the retina was completely detached, significant hemorrhaging had occurred and the ocular contents badly hurt. On the positive side, the globe didn't seem to be damaged beyond what already had been repaired the day of the shooting. But because the eye was still filled with blood, reflections and internal shadows could be obscuring true damage, Hamill knew.

Carol was ready to have this surgery because she was so afraid of being blind and was anxious to have fixed whatever could be. As she was prepped for surgery, she was calm, asked a few pertinent questions about what the doctors were going to do and looked forward to having this behind her. It was another step in moving forward, and before she could truly rebuild her life, her face would have to be rebuilt.

Once Christ was under anesthesia, a heavy wire speculum was inserted beneath the upper and lower lids, and the conjunctiva was again cut in a complete circle and removed. Three small incisions were made in the globe, enabling the surgeons to have their first comprehensive look at the extensive injuries to all the delicate structures. The most serious were a hole and tear in the retina, eviscerated so severely by the bullet, it was beyond functioning ever again. The optic nerve also had been destroyed. A small instrument was placed in each of the surgical openings: a light pipe to illuminate their working space, a small tube connected to a saline infusion to keep the pressure at a constant level, and a guillotine cutter, used to remove the large amounts of blood, clots and damaged tissue from inside the eyeball. Formally called a victrector, the guillotine cutter is a notched needle inside which is a tiny circular blade that removed the clots and vitreous, the large gel-filled area that sits behind the lens and occupies the bulk of the eye. As the blade nibbled away the once-clear vitreous, now inundated with blood and clots, the gel and debris were sucked through the needle and into an attached tube. The trick for the surgeons was to remove the vitreous gently enough so as not to tug on the retina or other structures and cause more harm. Once removed, the vitreous never grows back, being replaced instead by the aqueous fluid that circulates through the eyes. Until enough aqueous fluid was produced naturally, air that had been pumped into the eye would hold the detached retina against the inside wall of the globe, keeping the pressure steady and the eyeball intact. Hines next inserted a scleral buckle, a band that wraps around the orb like a belt, holding the white part of the eyeball against the retina with the hope that the retina would reattach itself as it healed. Hamill likened the procedure to putting "wallpaper on the inside of a basketball." Over several hours, Hines and Hamill carefully reconstructed as much of the eyeball as possible, but they realized that the chances that Carol Christ would be able to see anything out of her left eye, or even perceive light, were extremely slim. After spending several more hours in the recovery room, Carol was taken to a room in Jones Tower, where she would recover for a few days before having to undergo more extensive skeletal reconstruction. That night, the pain in her eye was excruciating and, again, her medication was increased.

The next day, Carol was handling her medical problems with a positive, even pleasant attitude, but her fear over what her husband might do was still growing. Nearly everyone who visited her, including the doctors and nurses, had to reassure her that he would not get to her, that a policeman always was outside her door. But, she thought, they did not know how devious John Christ could be. They did not appreciate how far her husband would go to silence her, she believed.

She had not believed what he was capable of until he shot her. Twice he had confided to her a plot to kill Gay. Each time, Carol had dismissed the scheme as the frustrated ramblings brought on by the ongoing, stressful, bitter custody battle and divorce. Now he seemed to be drawing on his blueprint for murdering his second wife to build his defense for trying to kill Carol Christ. John had told Carol that he wanted to kill Gay and make it look like self-defense or an accident. He planned to injure himself, not seriously but with scratches or something that would make it look like Gay had attacked him.

Carol, unaware that John's former mistress had

claimed that he had outlined a plot to poison his second wife, advised him to drive such thoughts completely from his mind. Most people get angry enough at some point to *want* to kill someone, but they don't do it, she told him. But, then again, John Christ wasn't most people.

Over the next few days, as Carol Christ spent more time awake and had more time to think, the full impact of what had really happened to her, that her husband had been capable of such extreme violence and all that lay ahead of her, set in—realizations that greatly increased her fears and anxieties. Mostly, she felt safe while in ICU under the watchful care of the staff, but whenever she left the unit for various tests or procedures, she was scared, almost paranoid. Her mother, nurses and doctors all stepped up their reassurances.

Along with these fears, she was facing serious operations in which a team of doctors would attempt to rebuild her badly mutilated facial structure. Dr. Spira came to see her. She wanted him to lead her surgical reconstruction team. He was the best plastic surgeon she knew and she trusted him completely as a surgeon and as a person. But he insisted that Stal was the best surgeon to do this intricate type of work, and he wanted her to have the best, he told her. Because she respected Spira so much, she reluctantly accepted his judgment, but because she did not know much about Dr. Stal or his work, she continued to worry about the results. Also, because the surgery was going to be so extensive and she would be under anesthesia for an expected ten hours, she was afraid she would die on the operating table.

When Carol arrived in preop this time, she was extremely anxious, in sharp contrast to her calm manner just three days earlier. She was nervous about the surgery and had some questions about what they would do, but she was terrified that her husband would somehow manage to get into the operating room and kill her. "Be sure that no one else comes in the operating room," she begged before being given anesthesia.

The doctors and operating staff smiled. "Don't worry, you're safe," Stal assured her in his quiet voice. "We're not going to let anyone in here except for us." Although her fears were irrational, they seemed very viable to her at the time.

Once she was under anesthesia, her metal tracheotomy tube was again replaced. Dr. W. Douglas Appling cut across the inside of her mouth between the upper lip and gums, from one molar to another, carefully following the shape of her mouth. He then cut the tissue under her nose allowing him to lift the skin off the face, exposing the structure of her entire midface, a gruesome sight even for one of the OR nurses there. He suctioned the hematomas, encapsulated pockets of blood, which he found inside her nose and sinuses. Injured tissues were growing together haphazardly. After cutting them apart, he inserted gel-filled sponges to prevent re-adhesions. Noting the multiple fractures, he began fitting the bones together, placing a titanium plate over the sinus cavity on the left side, from the middle of the face to the outer edge near her ear. Another plate was fitted on the outer edge of the right side of her face, also over the sinus cavity. Appling then placed the skin back over her face and stitched his incisions closed.

The ENT surgeon turned the patient over to Stal and Patrinely, who together would perform the most delicate of the reconstructive surgeries. Her hair was thin and instead of shaving it, Stal parted it, weighted it down with gel, in preparation for the surgical degloving. He sliced across the top of her head, from above one ear to the other. This time, her skin was gently peeled forward from the top down, exposing what lay beneath the surface. As he lifted the skin, he had to cut away the connective tissue and through the membrane covering the cranium, peeling down to the eyebrow. Here he cut deeper, then extended the incision over toward the left ear. After another deeper cut, he gently pulled the skin back toward her nose. With the left side of her face revealed, Stal searched for the facial nerve but couldn't find it, only a scarred mass of tissue where it should have been. Christ's cheekbone and orbit—both the rim and the walls around her eyeball—were shattered like dust, large pieces missing altogether. It was much worse than the surgeons had expected. The entire skeletal support was missing and had to be rebuilt, and the surgeons were concerned about possible damage to her muscles, nerves and soft tissues. Stal once again focused on the top of Christ's exposed skull, carefully harvesting four pieces of bone from her cranium as if using a cheese slicer, each piece about the size of his thumb. He worked his way across the top of her skull. The bone eventually would grow back but not necessarily uniformly. The reconstructive plastic surgeon—what the patient had once wished her husband would become—rounded off the edges around the areas from where he had taken the bone to prevent further deformity. Stal then meticulously shaped the pieces he had removed to fit where the surgeons needed them. He and Patrinely used these newly formed bones to begin the arduous process of rebuilding their patient's formerly beautiful face, painstakingly aligning pieces to rebuild her prominent cheekbones, upper jawbone and the orbital rim—everything she needed to support an eyeball. Even though she likely wouldn't be able to see out of it ever again, they needed to keep it from falling into her sinus cavity. Still, there were gaps in her facial structure, which had to be filled in with yet more plates and held together with screws and wires. Stal then tried to gently replace the skin, but with the extensive injuries to the skin, muscles, fat and connective tissue, this was unusually difficult even for the skilled surgeon. Patrinely repaired her two tear-drainage ducts, which now drained into her nose, by inserting silicon tubes and stitching each closed. Once the ducts healed, the tubes would be removed through her nose, a painless procedure that could be done in his office if she were out of the hospital by then. The ophthalmic plastic surgeon also tried to tighten up the corners of the eyelids, which were detached and drooping. They once again cleaned her wounds and implanted a drain to catch the accumulating fluids, which would be removed later, and sutured the incisions. This time, they did not wrap her face with a bandage.

After spending several hours in recovery, Carol Christ was taken back to the ICU in Jones Tower. It would be three to six months before the patient had healed enough to determine how well the reconstruction had gone. The surgeons had meticulously positioned her bone fragments and grafts, but Patrinely knew that some deformity always remained after the initial surgery. Once the swelling subsided, they would need to go back in and correct those problems. Carol looked as if she had been battered again, with sutures covering her hairline, eyelid and her forearm, her face bruised nearly everywhere, a splint covering the bridge of her nose and an IV, with a self-controlled morphine pump, stuck into her chest. Once again, ice packs were placed over much of her face.

When the surgeons stopped to check on Carol, Margaret Edwards was duly impressed. And not just with their surgical skills. "You are the best-looking surgeons," she flirted. "In order to get on Carol's surgical team, you must have to be really good-looking." The distinguished doctors, much younger than their admirer, giggled, but it wouldn't be the last time they heard it. Had they known Carol Christ before she was shot, they would have known that flirtatious talent ran in the family. The next time the surgeons stopped by, Margaret reminded them: "I just can't believe how good-looking y'all are." Despite her pain, Carol Christ found it amusing as she watched these esteemed doctors blush at a little flattery.

Three days after surgery, Carol was well enough to leave ICU and was given a wonderful surprise by the hospital administration. She was taken to a huge, private suitelike room usually reserved for VIPs; it was about three times as large as most hospital rooms. She was still very emotional and fearful, however. Her mother spent the first hour with her that morning but did little to relieve her anxieties this day. They talked about Joe and Dani. Carol missed her kids terribly and wanted to know how they were doing and how they were coping. Talking about them made her yearn even more for them. They also discussed the attorney Margaret Edwards had hired on her daughter's behalf. Using her power of attorney, Margaret withdrew all the money in her daughter's checking account, about $1,400, to pay the retainer for lawyer Harry Herzog.

Christ's anxiety continued to increase as did her pain and she became a trying, albeit knowledgeable, patient. She knew she needed to see Dr. Sermas, and she repeatedly asked to talk with him—at length, she said—but he was busy seeing other patients and not able to come right away. Complaining at every opportunity about the head and eye pain, she demanded another self-controlled morphine pump, after the first had been removed. Since a doctor would have to order that, Carol demanded that the nurses call one of them right then, even though she knew that was not the procedure. The

nurses, who were tolerant of her if not overly nice, did
not break protocol for her, knowing that the doctors
would be by on their rounds and that she did have pain
medication in the interim. Every time one of her doctors stopped by to check on her—about half a dozen
of them—she practically insisted that each one support
her request for the pump, which she did get later that
day. Then she worried that it would be taken away again
and pleaded with her doctors to promise that they
would continue it. She was well aware that the standard
time to have the pump was just three days because morphine was so addictive. Her pain was so intense and so
unrelenting, however, she feared that more than addiction. Her left eye was sore and she wanted it repeatedly
irrigated with saline and ointment applied. Having been
a nurse, she knew what was possible and was not going
to wait until someone else suggested such procedures.
One nurse, apparently feeling taxed by the assistant-
head-nurse-turned-patient, wrote on her chart: "Need
occasionally to remind patient, she is patient, and not
the nurse now."

Carol Christ was facing her own challenges. With the
help of a nursing assistant, she showered for the first
time and dressed in her own navy nightshirt, a satin
one that her mother had bought her. On the way back
to bed, she became dizzy and had to sit in a chair about
fifteen steps shy of the bed. The area around her eye
continued to swell. The saline irrigation helped as did
the ice packs, but not enough. She was given a gel-filled
sinus mask to quiet the pain and, hopefully, her as well.

Her mood swings took on a new meaning, from being
overly, almost inappropriately cheerful to crying without any seeming provocation. That evening, Sermas
talked with her for half an hour and noticeably calmed
her fears and anxiety. The nurses even noted that she
cried less afterward. Her mother and friends continued

to visit, but never long enough; when they left, her anxieties returned.

She awoke one morning in a cold, wet bed. She reached for her glasses on the nightstand and propped herself up on her elbows and looked around. Her bed was soaked with blood, a traumatic reminder of when she had awoken after having been shot. Her IV had become disconnected during the night; the tube now was working in reverse, drawing blood out of her arm, instead of pumping fluids into it. She was frantic and angry. Carol buzzed for the nurse on duty and let her have it.

When Dr. Appling stopped by that morning to check her progress, he said, "I hear we had a little incident this morning." She realized she must have become one of those demanding patients that the nursing staff gripes about. After examining her, he removed her trach, leaving the hole to heal shut without sutures. He stood beyond the foot of her bed as they talked, about eight feet from where she sat. Suddenly and without warning, he tossed a wadded piece of paper at Carol, saying, "Catch this!" Amazed, she instinctively reached both hands up in an attempt to catch the paper, which she did. Having just lost the vision in her eye, she still was adjusting to seeing the world through one lens and was understandably nervous about things flying her way—or things that appeared to be flying toward her.

"Just wanted to see if you'd catch it with your left hand. Are you sure you're left-handed?" he asked, not hiding his skepticism.

"Yes, I'm sure I'm left-handed!" Carol said loudly, but was too dumbstruck to say anything more. After that, she didn't care for that surgeon too much personally, although she remained grateful for his skilled efforts rebuilding her face.

Knowing she would be released from the hospital,

Carol had been worrying about where she would go. She knew she wasn't capable of living on her own yet and was terrified of leaving the security of the hospital and being left unprotected from her husband's deadly intentions. Her mother came to her rescue, announcing, "This is what we're going to do; you're going to come home with me." She could live upstairs until she felt well enough to move out to the guest house. They would find the appropriate specialists she needed in the Springdale area to follow her through her long recovery, but she would return to Houston for any major or reconstructive surgeries. It was a done deal. Carol was relieved to have a plan but horrified at having to live with her mother. Giving up her independence felt like another injury; every change in her unraveling life began to feel like another assault. She also was afraid to leave her doctors and the nearly unmatched Texas Medical Center, feeling she would be medically vulnerable too far away. She had no choice, however. There was nowhere else to go, but she and her mother had had problems trying to live together in the past and even on extended visits. Her mother, though, had been especially good to and supportive of her while she had been hospitalized, and she knew she would need a lot of help, at least initially. Still, she couldn't help but worry about how they would get along once they lived under the same roof. Margaret had the same concern, especially as she watched how emotional and edgy her daughter, who always had been prone to mood swings, had become. She knew this was not her fault, that it understandably stemmed from the brain injury, medications and psychological trauma, but that wouldn't necessarily make it much easier to endure.

Every time Carol Christ thought of her own daughter, whom she missed terribly, she cried. As her fears of dying from her injuries subsided, other issues emerged during therapy. One huge problem causing her a lot of distress was the severe facial disfigurement. She even wondered out loud to her psychiatrist if she would have been better off dying from her injuries. She never talked about finishing the job herself and remained terrorized that her husband would do it. Further, she had such an intense bond with her daughter, Dr. Sermas could not imagine Carol abandoning her in that way. Sermas explained to Carol that the loss of one's children could be as painful as all the other losses she was feeling. Despite the fact that John Christ generally treated her six-year-old badly, Sermas said Dani would be feeling the loss of yet another person in her life. After all, they had been living as a family for a couple of years. Emotions and relationships are complicated at any age, but a six-year-old doesn't even know how to put all her feelings into words. The psychiatrist tried to be supportive and help Carol figure out what she wanted to do.

Despite the restraining order that he was to have no contact with her, John Christ sent a letter to his wife in the hospital. Complaining that their separation was difficult on him, he made no direct mention of the shooting, which had created it. Calling her his "soul mate and best wife," he wrote: "No set of circumstances can change how I really feel." He told her to call if she needed him.

No one was pleased with the surgeon's audacity, and his tenacity to get to her scared many people, but no one more than his victim. No one was quite sure what his intention was—if he wanted to frighten her, letting her know he could reach her even with an armed guard at her door, or if he wanted to win her back so that she would drop the charges against him.

As her June first release date neared, she feared more and more for her safety, not wanting to leave the security of the hospital, where she had eventually felt safe. The armed police officer at her door, of course, had nearly everything to do with that. The nurses continued to try to ease her anxieties and encouraged her that she did have a life to look forward to and needed to get on with it. She remained terrified that John wanted to kill her or harm her children or family, and she was afraid that he might find them after she left the hospital. Nothing or no one could completely allay those fears, try as they did.

The day before her scheduled release, Carol Christ, riding in a wheelchair pushed by her mother and accompanied by an HPD officer, visited her coworkers and friends on Dunn 8 West, saying good-bye and not knowing when she would see them again. That evening, her son and his father visited. When Joe left, she did not know when she would see him again, and she got teary-eyed, although she tried to be strong for him. "Mom, everything's going to be okay. I'm going to be fine," he told her. Because Joe was always close with his father, the changes in his life were not as traumatic as they were for Dani. He assured her he was happy and they talked about school and the things he was doing.

The next day, just twenty-three days after being shot through the face, an extremely nervous Carol Christ was released from the hospital. "I'm afraid to leave," she told one of the nurses on duty that morning. "I really don't want to, but my mother wants me to." Before she left, she badly wanted to talk with Dr. Sermas. He had become like a drug for her, soothing her fears with his quiet, calming manner and insights. She had come to rely on his daily visits and worried about doing without those once she was in Arkansas.

The eye surgery had not restored Carol's vision, but the reconstruction had been successful, so she could keep her eyeball. Once the eye stopped functioning, the aqueous fluid production would cease and eventually cause the globe to shrink inside the socket to about half its original size. Doctors could not predict how long that would take as it varied greatly from one patient to another, as short as a couple weeks to as much as several years. While a dehydrating eyeball was an unattractive process, ultimately it aided in creating the most natural appearance. Eye surgeons and ocularists, those who make the prosthetics, prefer to place the glass eye over the real one, as then it would move in unison with the other, still-functioning eye.

Carol made it a point to go to the nurses' station and thank the nurses and staff for everything they had done for her. Four of her doctors stopped by to check on her, and Appling removed most of her sutures from on top of her head, in front of her ears and chest. The doctors and nurses asked if there were any signs of a cerebral spinal fluid (CSF) leak, especially the telltale clear fluid dripping from the nose. A not infrequent condition in severe head injuries, a CSF leak could be a serious problem. Carol said she had no symptoms. "But," she added honestly, "I cry so much, it's hard to tell, but I don't think so."

She was given prescriptions for ten different medications. Since she still had a lot of difficulty opening her mouth very far, Dr. Stal had prescribed a bite device for her to use at home. Placing the contraption between her teeth, she squeezed the upper and lower arms together, causing a reverse reaction, forcing her mouth to open farther. It was painful but she was told to use it several times a day and she complied begrudgingly.

Just before 4:00 P.M., a hospital staff member helped Carol into a wheelchair and, with Margaret walking by her side, pushed her down the hall, into the elevator, through the front lobby, and out the front doors into the fresh but humid air, Carol saw Dan Edwards waiting in her Explorer. Both she and her mother were extremely anxious about what lay ahead. For one of the first times in her troubled life, Carol was not optimistic. "I feel like I'm closing just the first chapter of a horrible experience," she told herself. That night, she and the Edwardses stayed in Houston with one of her parents' friends before making the eleven-hour drive to Springdale, Arkansas, the following morning.

With Carol slightly reclining in the front passenger seat, Margaret Edwards drove her daughter's Explorer back to Arkansas as Dan followed in theirs. Carol didn't look good at all and her mother, who had thought she was ready to go home, spent the entire trip terrified that her daughter, having survived all that she had, would die in her car, somewhere in rural Texas or Arkansas with no hospital nearby. She sped the whole way home. She was stopped by an officer somewhere along the way, but when the cop approached and saw Carol Christ, ailing, bruised and in obvious pain, he didn't write a ticket. "Go on, ma'am, just be careful," he told Margaret Edwards. He did not even tell her to stop speeding.

Nineteen

Because of the nerve damage, Carol Christ had lost some of the feeling in her face and, embarrassingly, could not even feel her nose running. At the dinner table, her stepfather often noticed before she did. Without saying a word, he reached over and gently wiped it for her, a gesture Carol appreciated greatly. Within a couple of days of arriving at her mother's, her fever spiked to 102 degrees. She felt increasingly lethargic and her headaches grew more intense. A local doctor suspected a cerebrospinal fluid leak and Carol called Dr. Narayan, who told her to return to Houston immediately. The neurosurgeon now suspected a CSF leak, a complication he had not seen evidence of earlier but had known could possibly develop over time, or, if it were a small leak, could have healed itself. Dan Edwards carried Carol down the stairs to the car and rushed her to the Tulsa Airport for the next flight to Houston. The Edwardses decided that Dan should go instead of Margaret because, he was eligible, at sixty-three, for a senior discount and she wasn't. She would drive down once again.

Although she had been afraid to leave the security of the hospital five days earlier, she now was terrified of going back, believing she would be more vulnerable to her husband, especially since she would no longer have a twenty-four-hour guard posted at her door. The letter John Christ had sent to her during her previous admission, in direct violation of the restraining order, highlighted his determination to reach her. Her stepfather suggested that she check in under an alias to make her more difficult to find, offering his sister's name, Juanita Toller.

So on Saturday, June 6, "Juanita Toller" was admitted to the emergency room of Methodist Hospital and put in Room 4. The ER doctor evaluated her condition and placed a four-inch square surgical sponge beneath her nose to catch some of the discharge. A brown halo formed, confirming it was CSF. As Carol thought back on her condition when she had left the hospital five days earlier, she realized she had probably had the leak even then. She mistook the telltale sign of nasal drip for just her usual allergy problems, she now believed, and was a little upset that the nurses, who were more familiar with CSF leaks than she was, did not test the discharge. A CSF leak, however, can be hard to confirm, especially if the fluid drains down the throat or in someone, like Carol, whose sinus problems could complicate detection. In addition, leaks may not become evident until the brain swelling subsides and blood clots begin to dissolve. The doctors, however, now classified it as "a delayed CSF leak."

She was taken by stretcher to the neurology ICU, Dan Edwards at her side. Listed under the alias Juanita Toller, she was also listed in hospital records as "a no-information patient," meaning no questions from callers would be answered. Hospital security was informed Carol Christ had been readmitted and reminded of the circumstances that had put her in this position and her need to be protected. None of this, however, provided her with the emotional security she so desperately needed.

Dr. John Thompkins, a neurosurgery resident, inserted the lumbar drain, a plastic catheter, into her lower back. The purpose of the drain was to redirect the cerebral spinal fluid from leaking inside her head and into the drain instead, reducing the built-up pressure inside her skull, the cause of her intense headaches. If the CSF was leaking through a hole in the covering of her brain, the dura—the suspected area because of her gunshot wound—then by diverting the fluid elsewhere, the hole should have a chance to heal naturally. Generally, the drains are effective at stopping such leaks in two to five days. The procedure wasn't as bad as she anticipated. She was left to rest on her left side, an IV with antibiotics hooked up to her right arm. The biggest worry now was that a CSF leak puts the patient at high risk of contracting the potentially fatal meningitis, an infection or inflammation of the membranes that cover the brain and spinal cord. So far, she showed no signs of that complication. The nurses and doctors regularly checked the draining fluid, noting both color and amount. If the usually clear liquid turned cloudy, that would signify an infection was setting in. A little blood mixed with the CSF, turning it a slight pinkish tint, was expected.

Carol's hospital stay proved torturous. Lying on her back most of the time, without so much as a television for company, she found herself alone with her thoughts, emotions and fears—and not enough outlets for them. She cried a lot and was terribly anxious, and sometimes was not even able to explain exactly why. "I don't know why God let me live," she cried to one of her nurses.

John Christ had been told by Dr. Spira in the days after the shooting that his privileges at Methodist were suspended. However, just weeks after the shooting, he was on Dunn 8 West asking to see one of the administrators. Falls believed he really was there to see how the staff, who had worked for Carol and with him, would react. Falls now was afraid of him but pretended otherwise. "Thank God I wasn't a Caucasian, because he would have seen it all over my face," she said later.

On June 15, as Carol Christ tried to escape from her overwhelming fears, John Christ once more sent a love letter to his wife saying he had been thinking of her and the good times they had together. He wrote that if he could relive the past eighteen months since they were married, he would take her on the honeymoon she had so wanted. Of course he wouldn't say anything in writing to implicate himself nor did he say anything about his avowed concerns over her alleged suicide attempt. This letter didn't reach her, as the hospital's staff redirected it to authorities, who were angered over the surgeon's continued insolence; the police threatened to jail him for violating the restraining order.

The CSF leak coupled with her brain damage, medications and the immensity of her problems were wreaking havoc with Carol's emotions. She had extreme mood swings, laughing one minute—sometimes at inappropriate times—and bawling the next. She bounced from the deepest depression she had ever known to irrational optimism to hostility, and she was straining the doctors, nurses, friends and family around her. Although her mother and a few friends visited, her numerous doctors stopped by regularly on their rounds and the nurses always were just a call button away, Carol felt like she was in solitary confinement most of the time. And that, too, can do strange things to one's mind.

It would be another month or so before Carol faced her fears and confided to her psychiatrist her fantasy of reuniting with her husband. They discussed it, but he wasn't overly concerned that she would actually act on it. He saw it as a reflection of her own self-doubts and insecurities, her need for financial support and worries that she would never feel whole again or have someone else love her. He saw it as emblematic of how helpless she was feeling at the time. He likened it to the Stockholm syndrome in which victims sometimes fall in love with their captors or abusers. "Sometimes the devil you know is better than the one that you don't," he said. Imagining that she could reunite with him was almost like pretending the whole traumatic ordeal had never happened so she wouldn't have to be afraid anymore or feel threatened, he said.

Exacerbating the torrents of emotional pain were her numerous physical problems. Nauseous almost always, she vomited only occasionally; her left eye, teeth, neck and face hurt and part of her face was numb, and she felt as if she was constantly drooling. Her speech was shrill and altered, and she knew people sometimes had trouble understanding her. She worried about the extent of brain damage and how permanent it was. Her short-term memory loss was maddening and she had trouble concentrating. The worst of her physical pain, though, was that her head hurt continually, often excruciatingly so, symptomatic of the CSF leak. Overcome with the enormity of her situation and her overwhelming emotions, she sought refuge in a continuous state of sleep. At times, she admitted as much to the nurses, although not always. One wrote on her chart: "States she 'wants to be kept asleep, this way I won't have to think about this mess.' Patient allowed to verbalize feelings."

During the next few weeks, whenever she awoke— either by nurses doing routine checks or by herself—she immediately demanded sleeping medication. Often a nurse would return with a pill or shot, only to find the patient, distraught just a moment earlier, now soundly back asleep. When Carol knew she was not due for sleeping medication, she would demand more pain medication, most of which had sleepiness as a now-welcomed side effect.

Carol who always had been overly concerned about her appearance and had put on whatever makeup she could during her initial hospitalization, now sometimes refused daily hygiene care, usually because her head hurt so fiercely that she did not want to move the slightest bit. Often she was given a cool washcloth to place on her forehead to soothe her headache and nauseousness. Generally, she unrolled it and used it to cover her entire face. It helped soothe her physical pain, but hiding beneath it was another way of escaping emotionally.

Carol's anger toward her husband swelled. With nothing to do but think of all he had put her and her children through, the emotional pain overwhelmed her. She kicked and slapped the bed rails in frustration. She didn't want to hurt herself—or even him necessarily—but she wanted to hurt something. As Dr. Sermas got up to leave after one emotional session in which they talked a lot about her understandable rage at her husband and how she had been beating up her bed, he stopped and told her, somewhat jokingly: "Just pick up your bedpan and throw it against the wall."

"Too bad it's not metal," Carol shot back.

"True," Sermas said. He thought for a moment, smiled and told her, "Just make sure it's empty." He left, leaving his patient in better spirits.

Although her psychiatrist visited daily, Carol also wanted to talk to a chaplain. While she had never asked to see one during her previous stay, she now wanted to see one nearly every day. Usually it was Chaplain Brian Gowen, a caring man she had known when he had visited patients on Dunn 8 West. There, when her staff was in the midst of a particularly hectic day, he always stopped to offer comfort to them as well, and Carol considered him a friend. After Gowen or Sermas visited, the nurses usually noticed that their patient was in better spirits, so much so that they noted it on her chart. She was a patient who needed a lot of emotional support and turned to wherever she could to find it. Just talking about everything helped a great deal, and the nurses tried to give her as much reassurances as possible. Every now and then, someone inadvertently made it worse, referring to the shooting as "an accident."

Carol would respond emphatically, "It's not an accident when someone tries to murder you." Then she would explain in detail what happened.

She remained fearful of her husband.

The following Saturday, after lying in bed for a week, Carol again began leaking CSF fluid from her nose, although none had been found in the drain for a while. Her problem had not been resolved; rather doctors discovered the drain was no longer working, not an uncommon problem with the finicky devices. To help pinpoint the location of the leak, doctors injected dye into her arm and put her back in the noisy CT scan machine. This time, they didn't see clear evidence of a leak but suspected that it was through her badly damaged right sinus. Another working lumbar drain was inserted, seemingly curing the problem. After a week, she had no further symptoms of a leak, so Narayan removed the lumbar drain. Within a couple of hours, however, a small amount of clear fluid was again dripping from her right nostril, although her headache was gone. That night, a nurse wanted to place a drip pad beneath her nose to catch the increasing nasal discharge but Carol refused this quick and harmless test. She also refused to elevate the head of her bed as they instructed, preferring to lie flat, saying her back hurt. Not thinking clearly because of the CSF leak, brain damage, medications and emotional turmoil, she was becoming increasingly difficult, slightly hindering her own care with her uncooperativeness. The nurses wanted to wean her off the IV-infused medication and onto ones she could take on her own, but she insisted on keeping the IV.

The next day was a particularly tormenting one for Carol and she rambled about her problems and fears to the nurses. She was convinced that her husband wanted to do her more harm and that he would try to get to her in the hospital. So distraught by the end of the day, she told one nurse: "I'm scared my husband and his ex-wife will come kill me." She had no evidence that Gay Christ wanted to do her harm or would help John in any way, but, rational or not, she now was afraid of her as well and knew she worked in the hospital. Unable to calm or reassure her, the nurse called the psychiatric resident on duty and hospital security, both of whom went to the ICU to talk with her. The security officer, an off-duty police officer, spent time listening and reassuring the patient and told her he would fill out a report regarding her concerns. She felt better after talking with him, although no one could quash her fears completely. Later, John Christ testified that Gay had volunteered to him where Carol was, an allegation Gay strongly denied.

Despite the difficulties she was having, the next day, Carol Christ was transferred out of the Neuro ICU and into a regular care room in the main building of the hospital. Still in a private room, she remained incredibly distressed and in severe pain, likening the headache, which wrapped around her entire head, to labor pain.

Back in physical therapy on June 23, it wasn't easy, but Carol was happy to go. "It feels good to work," she told the therapist. She tired easily but was driven to do the exercises and recover as soon as possible. Along with the strength and endurance training, she was guided through some occupational training, working on various kitchen tasks. After eleven days, the therapists were pleased with her physical therapy progress—she was gaining strength and better able to keep her balance while walking—but they were concerned about her working safely in the kitchen, noting that she had short-term memory problems.

Dr. Patrinely's wife, Vicky, who had been in premature labor when he was summoned to the ER to treat Christ, gave birth June 29 to a healthy boy, named after his proud father.

That same day, Carol Christ took another step toward her recovery by filing for her sixth divorce. She never had more justification, but the reason cited was the standard phrasing of "discord or conflict of personalities . . . that destroys the legitimate ends of the marriage relationship and prevents any reasonable expectation of reconciliation." The shooting was not mentioned as her attorney just wanted to get the clock running. Later, Herzog would file amended pleadings, adding as additional grounds for divorce: "John Christ is guilty of cruel treatment toward Carol Christ" and had intentionally shot her. Along with the divorce, Carol would seek civil damages, in an unspecified amount, for the injuries he had inflicted when he had tried to kill her. "Independent of any debate as to who fired the shot," the lawsuit said, the doctor's inaction as his wife was dying was a breach of duty of good faith and fair dealing toward his spouse. It was kind of an understatement.

As her discharge date neared, Carol grew more anxious and weepy again, worrying about her future and living with her mother. "I just want to get on with my life," she told her occupational therapist during a particularly tearful session.

The nurses suggested she use relaxation and self-hypnosis techniques to combat the pain, along with her medication, and they encouraged her to wean herself from the narcotics. She knew they could be addictive, but she had to have something for the pain, she responded, not yet ready. The drug, self-administered through a pump, did ease the pain enough that she was ready to focus again on other things. She now was ready to take Sermas's suggestion and start a journal of her experiences, another therapeutic way of releasing her emotions, which she clearly couldn't find enough ways to do.

By Wednesday, the headache and accompanying pressure were so profound, she told doctors it felt like she was "about to deliver a baby through her ears." On Friday, the pain again was so severe that even the pump was not helping.

She demanded that a doctor be called again, declaring, "These doctors need to work with me on pain control!" The nurses gave her what medication they could and did their best to console her. That night, she was an exceptionally difficult patient and spent nearly three hours alternately yelling and crying while the nurses did whatever they could to comfort her. Exhausted, she slept most of the next day. After getting out of bed, she discovered a few drops of yellowish discharge draining from her right nostril. The nurse put a drip pad beneath her nose and alerted Narayan. That night, Carol got a pleasant surprise when she stepped out of bed and, for the first time, that simple action did not give her a headache.

Carol was spending more time awake but no less time worrying about her problems, even though she now had more things to occupy her thoughts, such as physical therapy and television. She worried aloud to the nurses about living with her mother, where, she believed, she would be far from her friends, everything she was used to, and, especially, her two children.

The nasal drainage returned on Tuesday, although in just small amounts, but it scared Carol, who told the nurse that she felt like she might die. She also spoke anxiously about her medical and financial problems and the impending legal matters unfolding as a result of the shooting. The nurse calmed her down and the two spoke more rationally about her discharge that weekend. Carol took a shower and washed her hair, which made her feel better, more like herself.

By Wednesday, she was regaining her emotional composure. While she was still anxious, she felt more ready to face things again, no longer wanting to hide beneath a veil of sleep—at least not around the clock. She asked that the self-controlled medication pump be taken away as the dose had been reduced to such a small amount, it was no longer helping. Somewhat cheerfully, she discussed being discharged on Saturday and hoped to get her nails and hair professionally done on Friday by friends. She still had some nasal drainage, but she wrote it off as a cold, believing the CSF leak had been effectively stopped. She finally was becoming more confident and self-assured, more hopeful about her future.

Plastic surgeon Greg Smith, a friend of John's, dropped by for an unexpected visit. During her first hospitalization, Carol had called and asked him and his wife to visit. This time, he came alone. He wasn't as interested in talking about Carol's health as he was in discussing his buddy, although he did, perhaps out of politeness, ask about her medical progress. An interesting character with a controversial reputation, the tall, blond, good-looking Dr. Smith was one of the few friends John Christ had left in recent years. After John had turned on Gay and tarnished his reputation in other ways, few of his onetime friends seemed interested in maintaining a relationship with him. Carol had gotten to know Smith and his wife somewhat over dinners and other occasional outings. Known for his cowboy boots with clanging spurs, which he wore even with his surgical scrubs, his practice, like Johnson's, also was reputed to be built largely off topless dancers. Smith stood out on his own, dressing in a way that could only be called unusual even in the flamboyant, sometimes over-the-top Texas ways. He favored custom-made suits—often in flashy colors like pink, orange or lime green. He didn't see patients often at Methodist, but when he was there, he couldn't help but draw attention. "God, he's so good-looking, but he dresses so awful and he's so bizarre," Carol had heard nurses say about her husband's friend. They never complained about Smith's attitude the way they did with some of the more arrogant surgeons; he seemed friendlier than most to the nurses. Most of the other doctors ignored Smith, rolling their eyes when they saw him. His wife, though sweet, also drew attention wherever she went with her enormous implants and bizarre outfits, favoring stiletto heels and short skirts even in her husband's medical office where she worked.

Now Dr. Smith seemed to be in Carol Christ's hospital room as an emissary for John. Her husband loved her immensely and wanted to talk to her, Smith told her. Carol immediately dismissed the idea, telling him she was afraid of her husband, but Smith said they could meet at his house. He was sure his friend wouldn't hurt her, but to appease her fears, he promised he would be there to protect her if needed. He wouldn't allow anything to happen to her. Carol kept saying no, but she clearly was considering doing it. She admitted to herself that she was curious about what her husband was thinking.

"I just don't trust him," she told Smith.

"Carol, I'll be there. Look at my size," Smith assured her, spreading his arms as if to show off his muscular chest. "I'm a big guy. All he wants to do is talk to you." The two continued talking; Carol continued to resist, but just barely.

She could tell by the way Smith talked that he wasn't even convinced that John Christ had shot her—and that bothered her.

"If John did it," Smith said, "it was a crime-of-passion-type thing. He loves you so much, and if he did it, it was just out of passion, and he didn't mean to do it." It was something Christ had considered herself, but she knew now the stakes were higher for them both. What would prevent him from acting on the anger she knew he must feel over being indicted for attempted murder?

Although Smith had never been anything but nice to her, Carol was so afraid of John Christ, she worried that maybe Smith now was his accomplice in finishing her off. She wondered about it out loud.

"Carol, that is silly. That is just silly. I'm your friend just as much as I am John's friend," he told her.

After about fifteen minutes, Smith left, not having convinced Carol to meet her husband, although she wasn't as firm in her conviction not to as she should have been. That would change by the next day.

She was scheduled to be released on Friday. While she was nervous about returning to live with her mother, it had been an exceptionally rough hospital stay and she was ready to go.

On Thursday, Carol met with a social worker. She would need someplace to stay for about a week after she was discharged. Carol was extremely emotional, somewhat inappropriately so, the social worker thought, as she worried about her job, finances, children and helpless feelings. The social worker was concerned enough about her bizarre behavior to speak with one of Carol's nurses about it. The nurse, however, believed Carol's reactions may have been the residual effects of the frontal lobe injury. He told the social worker that a program for head-injury patients might be in Carol's future, but she currently had too much going on for that now. Margaret Edwards also was concerned about her daughter's cognitive functioning, memory problems, emotional instability and how she would deal with those once she took her daughter home from the hospital. In those areas, she seemed to be getting worse, not better, and mother and daughter had a difficult time getting along together for extended times even under the best of circumstances. Margaret knew she would have to hold her tongue even more now, but she wasn't sure how to get around her daughter's hypersensitivity, especially where she was concerned.

A patient down the hall from Carol began receiving repeated phone calls about noon on Thursday from a man asking for Carol by name, not her alias. The nurses, believing it was John Christ, were alarmed and told Carol immediately. Now the terror that had again begun to fade was back.

A single red rose was delivered to "Juanita Toller's" room about 12:30 P.M. The attached florist's card, preprinted with the words "I love you" at the top, carried a message in her husband's writing: "I miss you and need you. Juan." There was no mistaking the message: her husband knew where she was and wanted her to know it. He had found a way to reach her. Doing better emotionally just a couple hours earlier, she now was hysterical. Dr. Sermas was called and he rushed to her side. He spoke with her for a long time, trying to calm her fears, although the psychiatrist thought it sent a chilling message as well. Security was notified and it was decided that it would be safest to move Carol to another room immediately. The quickest change would be down the hall, to Room 430, where a security officer met her and tried to reassure her that she was safe. Still concerned about whether the lumbar drains had stopped the CSF leak, Dr. Narayan checked on her. He noticed only a slight bit of moisture draining from her nose, but he thought the problem had been resolved.

That same day, Carol Christ was moved once again. For security reasons, she was taken out of the main hospital building and taken to the second floor of Fondren Tower.

She got a much-needed boost from Dr. Jay Oates, an orthopedic surgeon with whom she had worked on Dunn 8 West. Passing by her room on rounds, he noticed Carol lying on her bed, green scrubs as her pajamas.

"What are you doing lying around?" Oates chided her. "Get your lazy butt up out of bed; let's make rounds."

Happily, she obeyed, not even pausing to put slippers over her bare feet or to worry about the sutures in her head. He wrapped his arm around her shoulders and acted as he always had whenever they had made rounds together, joking on the way to a patient's room, but he turned serious once inside. This evening, he was checking on a middle-aged woman recovering from a serious broken leg, which had required extensive orthopedic and plastic surgery. Oates explained to his patient that Christ was on staff at the hospital and currently a patient herself and that he wanted her opinion on the tissue graft. They discussed it as colleagues, reminding Carol Christ that she still had something to offer to others, that she still was a respected nurse, not just a pitied patient.

As he walked her back to her room, she told him, "Thank you, I needed that." It was the coolest thing anyone had done for her in a while and she talked about it for weeks.

On Friday, Carol's friend and usual hairdresser carried all his necessary beauty equipment to her hospital room and gave her a stylish, short haircut and a much-needed lift to her spirits. Unfortunately, it couldn't erase her husband's onerous behavior even as she lay in a hospital. She would never let herself forget how ruthlessly persistent and focused he was when he wanted something. And, she believed, what he wanted was her dead.

Twenty

On Saturday, the Fourth of July, 1992, Carol Christ was again discharged with little to celebrate. This time, wanting to avoid a repeat of their last scare, Margaret and Dan Edwards took her to a nearby Embassy Suites hotel, where they intended to stay for a couple of weeks. That way, Christ, who still was taking nine prescriptions, could be close to her doctors in case she needed further emergency treatment. Time was not healing her emotionally. She was still nervous and worrying about everything.

Kelly Siegler, who as chief prosecutor in the 230th District Court's felony division doled out case assignments, took this one for herself as soon as she got to work the Monday after the shooting. Siegler was an aggressive, take-nothing assistant prosecutor who was respected by defense attorneys, judges and police; John Christ would come to see her as another of many women in his life who set out to get him. Leaving the victim alone to recover, Siegler had not yet met Carol Christ; the attorney was busy preparing other aspects of her case. Although Carol still had conflicting emotions, she was anxious to have her husband locked safely behind bars so she could once again live her life without fear of him. The Edwardses thought Carol was ready to meet the prosecutor, and since she would be in Arkansas indefinitely, it seemed best to take care of this now.

Carol, suffering the bewildering effects of brain damage, medications and fear, paced the floor and recounted the events nonsensically. In her mind, she was proving that she would be OK, but in actuality, she was demonstrating just the opposite. It was a disastrous meeting.

"Is she like this all the time?" Siegler privately asked the victim's mother.

No, the embarrassed Edwards assured her, it was just the effects of the newest medication. She had behaved much more normally in the hospital and her story always had been consistent. Even now, the details she told weren't any different from what she had said before, she just seemed unable to tell the story clearly.

Unfortunately, if the victim didn't recover any more, Siegler bluntly told the Edwardses, Carol was too messed up to ever be able to testify. Everyone realized that would make a conviction much more difficult. The Edwardses remained hopeful that their daughter would calm down, at least to the level she had been during her first hospitalization. After nearly two weeks in the hotel and with clearances from Carol's doctors, the three again headed back to Arkansas.

They were there just a couple of days when Christ again had some troubling nasal discharge. Clear and dripping out of the right nostril, it was not as much as before she had received the lumbar drains. She felt a lot of drainage down the back of her throat, the vision in her eye was growing blurry and her headache again was steady, though not nearly as bad as before. This time, the nurse turned to one of her textbooks on lab tests, which she had saved from nursing school. Thankfully, her mother had thought to retrieve it from her house. Reading that CSF contained glucose, she went

to the drugstore and bought testing strips sold for dia-
betics to test their blood sugar levels at home. She held
the strip beneath her nose. It showed the highest level
of glucose the strip could measure.

Again, Dr. Narayan wanted to see her in Houston
right away. She really didn't want to be making this journey alone, but she knew her family had been through
hell with her and didn't ask her mother and stepfather
to go with her. By the next morning, Christ was even
sicker. Dan Edwards again drove her to the Tulsa Airport, but this time she would go to Houston alone.
Weaving when she tried to walk and feeling very weak,
she was in a wheelchair and her stepfather escorted her
to the gate, where he left her in the care of the airline's
personnel. Once in the air, inside the pressurized cabin,
she realized that less fluid seemed to be leaking out of
her nose and down her throat and she felt a little better.
Once she arrived at Houston Intercontinental Airport,
she had to rely on airline personnel for help. Inside the
sprawling airport's main terminal, she was escorted
partway through the Texas-sized terminal by wheelchair
and then left on her own to collect her bag and hail a
cab. Telling the driver not to hit any bumps but to get
her to Methodist Hospital as soon as possible, Carol
looked so bad the driver seemed nervous about the
forty-five-minute trip.

Entering through the emergency room, Carol
checked in under the name "Margaret McClane," her
mother's first name and the last name of a maternal
great-grandmother. Her fever was down, but she still
was showing other signs of a possible CSF leak, including her unsteady walk. The next evening, an extensive
CT scan was performed. Along with the dye, the doctors
injected her with saline to increase the pressure of the
CSF. If there was a leak, the increased amount of fluid
would flow out faster, making it easier to identify the

location of the seepage. Boots were strapped onto her feet to hold her in place when the table was inverted, sending the dye, which had been injected in the CSF sack in her lower back, into her skull. Lying on her back with her head inside the doughnut-shaped CT scan, Christ could see the doctors and radiologists on the other side of the window, reviewing the images. When she saw their jaws drop, she knew they were seeing confirmation of what she suspected—she had a severe CSF leak. What she didn't know was that they also saw a large cyst, caused by the persistent CSF leak, reaching from her temporal lobe into the sinus cavity. Due to Carol Christ's extensive injuries caused by the bullet, Dr. Narayan had a difficult time getting a handle on exactly what was happening inside her head. CSF fluid seemed to be leaking from several places along the front of her brain. Having tried unsuccessfully to stop the leak with the lumbar drain, the doctors felt that they had no choice but to try to fix it surgically. This required a major operation, even by the demanding standards of delicate brain surgery.

Narayan and the other doctors would decide the best surgical approach, either a transsphenoidal, in which they accessed her brain by going through her mouth and nose, or subtemporal, in which they entered through the side of her skull. Dr. Narayan and the nurses in the Neuro ICU warned Carol that the transspehnoidal approach would be the most grueling for her. Carol, who had returned to the hospital expecting just another lumbar drain, was scared, fearing she might die on the operating table, but by her husband's hands. She gave her family the grim news, hoping her parents would rush to her side. Neither did. She hadn't asked but understandably expected them to realize the gravity of the situation and that she needed them. "I just kind of had had it with all my family stuff," she said. Her doctors were incredulous that her family wasn't there and did their best to support the emotionally fragile patient, as did her friends. Her husband, of course, was still nearby, and she suspected if he didn't kill her, the brain surgery might.

John Christ called his mother-in-law in Arkansas, not only professing that he hadn't shot her daughter but having the exorbitant gall to suggest that he should be put in charge of her medical care. He was, after all, her husband and he truly loved her, he claimed. He put down the nationally renowned and highly accomplished neurosurgeon overseeing her case. He cried as he tried to explain to Margaret Edwards that Carol had tried to kill herself. Although Margaret had never considered that a true possibility, he was so convincing, she was beginning to wonder.

"If you really didn't do it, John, I wouldn't want to see you prosecuted for something you didn't do," she told him honestly. She would arrange to have her daughter hypnotized to see what she could recall. Several seconds of silence passed on the other end of the phone and Margaret never questioned her judgment or her daughter's recollection again. Now she could see firsthand the mind games Carol had been up against for so long.

After more tests and discussions among themselves, Carol Christ's doctors ultimately determined that they needed to approach her brain using both methods, the transsphenoidal and the subtemporal, as the damage was far more severe than anyone initially thought. She was about to undergo the most difficult and critical surgery of her ordeal.

She couldn't have been more confident in her surgeon. Dr. Raj K. Narayan, Chief of Neurosurgery at Ben Taub, a nationally renowned expert on head trauma and gunshot wounds, had through the years done a lot of research regarding such injuries. About fifty to one hundred victims with gunshot wounds to the head were treated at Ben Taub each year of the seven years that Narayan had been with the busy trauma center, and he worked on about half of those. He also was on the neurosurgery staffs at several institutions in the Texas Medical Center, including Methodist. Born and raised in India, Narayan decided to become a neurosurgeon at the age of eleven after reading *Death Be Not Proud* by John Gunther, a true story chronicling the author's son's treatment for a brain tumor, his subsequent deterioration and death in the 1950s. After completing medical school and a two-year internship in India, Narayan accomplished the unusual feat of landing a neurosurgery residency at the Medical College of Virginia in Richmond—a hard-to-get position for anyone, but especially difficult for a foreign-trained doctor. After completing what, at the time, was considered one of the best academic residencies, he joined the faculty at the National Institutes of Health in Bethesda, Maryland, for three years. He joined the staff of Ben Taub and the faculty of the Baylor College of Medicine in 1985, continuing to do research and collect honors along the way.

The day before Carol Christ's operation, Narayan explained the brain surgery to her and what he and Appling expected to do; then he ran down the required list of possible complications. These should have been no surprise to the nurse-turned-patient. "One: You could be paralyzed. Two: Your brain could be damaged more. Three: You could die. Four: You could lose your sense of taste and smell."

"If I can lose my taste and smell, I'm not going to do it," O'Keiff said, surprisingly serious. "That's all I've got left, and I enjoy eating. I finally learned how to do it again."

"That's ridiculous. You will go through with this surgery," Narayan insisted.

"No, I will not." She wasn't kidding. It seemed odd that after all she had endured and lost that this would dissuade her from life-saving surgery, but it was the last straw. After a short discussion with the frustrated neurosurgeon, she agreed. She knew she had no other viable options.

Brain injuries, especially ones to the frontal lobe, like Carol's, can cause numerous problems, including cognitive deficits, possible personality changes and impaired memory and perhaps even unpredictable consequences. The experienced trauma expert, however, thought Christ was more anxious than most other gunshot patients. He believed it was a combination of her trying circumstances and the stress of her injuries and medical treatments as well as just her basic personality. What she was most nervous about throughout her numerous hospital stays was her husband, and she often broke down crying when telling Dr. Narayan about it.

Appling also stopped by Carol's room and explained in detail the risks once again. During surgery, her carotid artery, sinuses, optic nerve or brain could be injured, he said. She could suffer bleeding, infection, nasal septal perforation, numbness in her upper teeth (which she already had), recurring CSF leaks, blindness, stroke or death, he told her. This time, Carol just acknowledged that she understood and accepted the risks and, without arguing, signed the consent form.

Carol Christs' veins collapsed often from having been stuck so many times in the ten weeks since she had been shot. Knowing that would continue for a long time to come, the nurse-turned-patient asked the doctors to insert a central line, a six-inch catheter that is surgically implanted in the subclavian vein, just below the collarbone. It allowed continuous access for intravenous fluids and medications and for withdrawing blood, essentially eliminating the need to stick her elsewhere. Although a local anesthetic was applied to the skin, it was a painful procedure as the catheter was pushed to the proper location, and Carol had seen grown men cry while having it done. Knowing she would be completely anesthetized for surgery, she figured this would be the best time for her to have it done. Her doctors agreed.

When he visited Carol the evening before the scheduled brain surgery, Dr. Sermas found her less anxious and emotional than she had been in the past, even less fearful of what her injuries meant for her life. Even before her injuries, Carol seemed more bothered by smaller problems or slights. The larger, more threatening ones, she seemed better able to cope with. She was afraid of the brain surgery, worrying that she might end up paralyzed or in a vegetative state, but she wasn't as anxious as those around her would have expected, given her erratic emotional state during the past month. For the first time since being shot, she prayed she would get through it, asking God: "How could you let this happen to me?"

On Thursday morning, July 23, the neurosurgeons would get their first direct look at Carol Christ's damage. They would be surprised by what they found. In preop, Carol's vital signs were checked, she was hooked up to the appropriate monitors and placed in a lawn-chair-type position on the operating table, a pillow beneath her knees, her left arm strapped to an armrest and her right arm secured across her chest. Her head was placed in a "crown of thorns," a three-pronged frame to hold her head perfectly still. The crown was rotated so that her face tilted toward the right.

At 10:30 A.M., Dr. Narayan began what would turn into an exhausting, twelve-hour operation. Narayan removed some abdominal fat to use later in a graft in her head, using the scar from her tummy tuck and hysterectomy incision to avoid scarring her any more than necessary. At the same time, Appling began the difficult transsphenoidal surgery to approach her brain, made unusually complicated by her previous reconstructive surgeries and extensive injuries. He cut through her mouth, between the lips and gums, and through her nose as he tunneled his way toward her frontal lobe. He then turned the patient over to the neurosurgeon.

Using an operating microscope with a 350 focal length, Narayan completely opened the right sphenoid sinus, located behind and just below the eyes; it is the deepest of the four pairs of sinus cavities. Part of the protective covering of the brain, known as the dura, was protruding into the sinus through a hole in the bone, and Narayan used a thin needle to drain a large amount of what looked like cerebrospinal fluid. He turned the microscope to the right and entered the sinus. Then he used fat and muscle as a graft to fill the hole where the dura had been protruding, sealing it with surgical glue. He took cartilage from her nose, laid it across the sinus to hold the fat in place, sutured the entrance, and after packing her nose with sponges, the transsphenoidal surgery was completed. The patient was turned onto her left side, and Narayan inserted a lumbar drain.

Now he focused on the second brain surgery he would perform on Carol Christ that day. Her right temple area was shaved. Narayan etched a reverse question-mark incision down toward her cheekbone. He then drilled four burr holes into her skull. Cutting through the bone, he connected the holes until he was able to raise a square piece of her skull like a flap, exposing her brain. Using a surgical ultrasound machine, he found the large cystic cavity in the right temporal lobe. Now he penetrated the brain's protective covering. While the temporal lobe looked normal on the surface, it clearly was sunken in, indicating a problem beneath the surface. An ultrasound once again showed that this was where the cyst had formed. Narayan made a small incision into her brain and was surprised to find that a large portion of her temporal lobe was encephalomalacic, meaning it was decaying and dying like an old piece of fruit. The neurosurgeon believed this had been caused by the shock effect of the bullet as it forcefully whisked perilously close to the underside of her brain, similar to a torpedo propelling through water. Using the microscope, he could see that the cyst, about the size of a plum, seemed to go deeper into the brain than he had detected during the transsphenoidal surgery.

Scar tissue had grown around the cyst, attaching the brain to its protective covering in an unhealthy way. He carefully cut away those sections and removed the cyst, which was like a balloon filled with water. Now he got his biggest surprise of the surgery. He could actually look through a hole in her brain, a tunnel about three millimeters wide, and see the fat that he had just grafted into her sinus. That should not have been possible and posed a unique challenge for the veteran neurosurgeon. This was an area where it was impossible to suture any tissue and was too large to close with fat, but the hole needed to be somehow filled. From the operating room, he phoned a colleague, Dr. Robert Grossman, Chief of Neurosurgery at Methodist, where Narayan now was operating. After much deliberation in which various options were discussed, they decided on an unusual procedure. Narayan had performed the operation a few times before, but the two neurosurgeons weren't sure it would work for Carol Christ. It was, however, her best chance for survival, they believed.

Narayan loosened a piece of the temporalis muscle, used for chewing, from the right side of Carol's head, leaving one side still attached to keep a healthy blood supply flowing to it and preventing the muscle from dying or atrophying. He surgically tunneled a path beneath her forehead and then cautiously threaded the strip of muscle through the burrow, through the dura and into the hole in the temporal lobe. He then closed the skull flap he had cut earlier and hoped for the best. At 10:30 P.M., twelve hours after the first brain surgery had begun, Narayan finished the second, and Carol once again went to the recovery room. Her surgeon phoned her mother in Arkansas and briefly told her about the operations.

Back in the Neuro ICU, Carol Christ was given a room not far from the nursing desk. As is common after patients have been under anesthesia for long periods of time, Carol was delirious, delusional and hallucinating for nearly twenty-four hours after surgery, often talking to people who weren't even there. The hallucinations didn't frighten her, but they did unnerve one of the nurses who was especially vigilant given the still-developing criminal case. Each time he heard her talking, he ran into her room to ensure no one was there, sometimes even looking under the bed. When she became lucid late the next day, he jokingly chastised her: "You gave me hell while you were out." He told her about her numerous "conversations," making her laugh. A morphine pump had been connected to her IV, enabling her to dull the pain when needed. She was pleased to see the nurses so on top of things.

The bad news was that she had more brain damage than initially believed. The good news was that the somewhat novel surgery seemed to be effective, and

Carol was once again on her way to recovery. While her doctors did not know what the lasting effects of the brain damage would be, and weren't sure if she ever would be able to return to her job, Carol was determined to do it.

The surgeries had created some new physical problems for her. Her surgeon tried to help her focus on the positive. He had taken the fat from her abdomen, using her previous incision, he told her. "I think you'll be very, very happy. I didn't have to leave any more scars on your body," he said, knowing how many operations and procedures she had endured both before and since the shooting. After the brain surgeries, she lost most of her sense of smell, which, in turn, diminished her sense of taste—the one thing she had not wanted to lose. Although disappointed, she no longer dwelled on it, realizing the brain surgeries gave her another chance at life and regaining everything she had lost. She once again was looking more toward her future.

After a week, there was no evidence of a CSF leak and the lumbar drain was removed.

Carol was moved out of ICU and into a large room in the neurosensory unit of the Jones Building. A corner room with windows on two sides overlooking the bustling Medical Center, it was a much cheerier atmosphere than ICU. Flowers from her father, colleagues and friends seemed to fill her room, giving her the wonderful sensation of being in a spring garden instead of an impersonal hospital room.

Dr. Newton Coker, a handsome neuroaudiologist, was called to evaluate Carol's hearing loss and injuries to her right ear. Checking her ear, the doctor saw that the ear canal was normal. The eardrum, though, was virtually gone—only its edges remained. Her hearing loss was severe as sound vibrations could not be conducted to the inner ear. He recommended that she undergo reconstruction of the eardrum and ossicle, the small bones that carry the sound waves from the eardrum to the inner ear.

Carol was apprehensive about returning to her mother's house and dealing with the stress of that situation. John Christ seemed to have no apprehensions about trying to manipulate the situation, regardless of the anxiety he was creating for the woman he claimed to love. He sent Margaret Edwards a letter beseeching her help in winning back his wife. First he complimented Margaret on her appearance following the face-lift and nose job he had performed and actually asked that she stop by his office the next time she was in Houston so he could photograph the results.

This time, Margaret Edwards dismissed his ploy as "so much trash." Wisely, she didn't toss his letter, turning it over to the prosecutor instead to be used as evidence against him.

On Saturday, August 1, a social worker visited Carol Christ and gave her a much-needed opportunity to vent her frustrations and feelings about the shooting, her injuries and surgeries, her estranged husband, her family problems and the pending trial. She longed to live in Houston, where she would have the support of her friends and trusted doctors, and hopes of resuming as much of her former life as possible. When the social worker left, she noted on the chart: "Very brave woman."

Before she would return to Arkansas, far from her trusted doctors, she would spend a few weeks staying with friends. First she would recuperate at the home of her former sister-in-law, Lynne O'Keiff Youngblood, and then at Betty Steinfeld's. Both women were nurses and far more nurturing than her mother; they understood what Carol most needed now. While she was no longer bedridden, she still was emotionally fragile, weeping easily and worrying heavily, and was overly sensitive to loud noises or any excessive stimuli.

On Wednesday, August 5, armed with just five prescriptions, Carol Christ was again discharged from the hospital, her anxiety as oppressive as the hot and humid summer. She hoped her future would be as bright as the tropical flowers Houston's weather nurtured. Colorful, she could finally do without.

Twenty-one

Carol Christ's stay in the Arkansas Ozarks was a short one, lasting just ten days. This time, it was not the pressure in her head but the pressures from her family.

But before she headed south to Houston, the Edwardses took Carol to Nashville for Dani's seventh birthday. An emotional reunion, it was the first time mother and daughter had seen each other since Carol had been whisked away from their home by ambulance four months earlier. Now they hugged each other tightly and cried. The pain of their separation had been excruciating and still was as they knew their visit would be just a short one. Although she still was weak and her face was bruised and disfigured, making her look much different than she had before the shooting, Carol looked better than Dani had expected and the little girl was relieved to see her. Mother and child couldn't keep their hands off one another during the weekend and hugged frequently.

Dani had been doing well with the O'Keiffs. When she first moved in, the couple had been surprised to learn their niece still wore pull-up diapers at age six. They worked with Dani, buying her fancy underwear as an incentive to overcome it, and she finally conquered that problem. They had a harder time getting her to clean up her room and understand their rules—and the disciplinary consequences for not abiding them. She seemed to enjoy the chores they gave her, such as setting the table, and she liked to be around people. Dani came to feel like a little rich girl and she loved it, other than the fact that she thought of her temporary home as a "touch-me-not-house." The O'Keiffs were collectors of various valuables, including glass, artwork, books, kimonos and mineral specimens, which they displayed. While the children were allowed to hold them, they were reminded to be careful.

The O'Keiffs had been having fun taking Dani on trips and events around town, including to the local ballet, museums and city festivities. That summer, they enrolled her in weekly ballet classes, although nothing too structured as it was more for fun. The children put on a recital at the end of the classes and Dani was the adorable star of the show, playing the lead in *The Princess and the Pea*.

Dani seemed to Gus an intelligent child who lived in her own fantasies. "It broke my heart one day when she got one of our big boiling pots, took it outside and was splashing around in it," he said. Dani told them that birds were flying down and landing on her shoulders. O'Keiff wasn't worried, believing his niece was just imaginative and creative. At first, she had seemed uninterested in making friends but eventually made some and came to enjoy her new school.

So Dani had a lot to tell her mother when she finally saw her. It was a brief visit but a badly needed one. Carol still had sutures in her head from her recent brain surgery, and Dani was more intrigued than shocked by it. When it was time for Carol and her parents to leave for the hotel, where they would be spending the night, Dani cried and begged to go with her mother, not wanting to be away from her for even a minute of what she knew would be a short visit. Carol agreed, but Gus and Helayne protested. They pointed out that Dani tired her out and they worried out loud that she would manipulate her mother.

"No, I won't, Mommy," the child, hearing the accusations, promised. Carol was angry that it had been said in front of her emotionally fragile daughter and was bothered by what she saw as their circumventing of her parental rights, something to which she was already sensitive. She felt pressured by the Edwardses and O'Keiffs, who were asking her to sign away temporary custody of Dani. They wanted to be sure they had legal guardianship in case Dani needed medical treatment or they, for whatever reason, needed to prove they could make decisions regarding her welfare. Carol feared that if she signed, they would try to take away permanent custody of her daughter later, perhaps using her injuries as an excuse to do it. The O'Keiffs had no intention of trying to do that as long as Carol could care for her.

Dani stayed with her mother that night, tucking herself in her mother's arm as they slept in the king-sized bed in the hotel room. When Carol left her daughter in Nashville, her anger at her husband intensified again. "I despise him for taking away my precious mother role, even temporarily," she wrote in her journal. By now, she expected that Dani would have to stay at her brother's for a year and that was too much for her. "I was also jealous of the beautiful room and clothes my brother has bought Dani," she wrote honestly. "I'm happy for her, but very jealous that I haven't been able to do that and worried that Dani will want to permanently stay with Gus for the material things she's acquired." The first night following her visit, Carol cried herself to sleep. She didn't have to worry about Dani's affections. The little girl missed her mother terribly and, although she grew to love her aunt, uncle and cousin, was anxious to go home to her mother. She thought she could help take care of her. Dani once told her mother that she often woke up in the middle of the night and cried a little as she was so sad to be away from her mother, who told her to write or call whenever she wanted. "I will always be there for you, no matter what," Carol promised.

Even so, she relented to family pressure and signed a temporary custody agreement making her brother and sister-in-law Dani's legal guardians with the provision that she would have her child again when she was medically able. Still, that didn't reduce her anxieties, and she knew she would never feel better about it until her daughter was living with her again. While staying at her aunt and uncle's, Dani sometimes told fantastic tales of things she had claimed to have seen while playing alone in their backyard—a skunk with green smoke coming out of its rear or an eagle flying down to sit on her shoulder and allowing her to pet it. When she relayed these tales to her mother on the phone, Carol initially thought they were funny but became more concerned when her daughter insisted these were true stories, not just her active imagination. Carol enjoyed her daughter's creative side when she admitted that it was just that but worried when she seemed determined to stick with an obvious lie.

The family pressure on Carol escalated. First her mother asked her for the $500 she had spent on plane tickets for her trip to rush her back to Houston because of the CSF leaks. Carol told her mother she could not afford that now but would pay her when she got a large sum of money from her insurance settlement as expected.

Just a week and a half later, Margaret handed her daughter a bill for nearly $3,000. She wanted Carol, who had no hope of returning to work in the near future—if ever—to reimburse her for her and her husband's expenses during their extended stays in Houston after the shooting as well as some of their other expenses related to her daughter's injuries, all of which she had itemized. Carol was amazed and distraught that she couldn't get the support she needed from her family, even now. She needed to go back to Methodist soon for surgery and she couldn't stand being at her mother's any longer. She threw all her things into her car and impulsively headed toward Houston, tormented but now driving alone, still adjusting to using just one eye. She spent the night alone in a roadside motel, crying and writing in her journal, her only outlet.

Margaret Edwards said she was angry at her daughter at the time and included everything she could recall. She had given her daughter a lot of money over the years for moving expenses, utility deposits and other things, even when Carol had been working. She and Dan said they had drawn up the bill only to show Carol how much they had spent on her. They realized she couldn't afford to pay them back, but, they admitted, had she come up with some money, they would have taken it. Carol said that she did pay them back, at least partially, after her insurance company paid her $40,000 under its dismemberment policy for the loss of her eye. The Edwardses disputed that, saying they never got any money, although they and Carol agreed that the bulk of that insurance settlement went to pay Herzog's legal fees.

When Carol Christ arrived in Houston the next afternoon, she headed for Betty Steinfeld's large, elegant town house, designed by Betty's now-deceased architect husband, where Carol could stay without charge. The drive took her through the Medical Center, a city unto itself with more than forty hospitals and scores of towering office buildings. Stopped at a traffic light, she saw

John Christ jog past her car, but he didn't notice her. She pulled into a parking lot—one she knew he would pass by on his usual route—and sobbed, pounding on her steering wheel. Soon he jogged by again, still oblivious to her presence. She only watched. Shaken, she headed to Steinfeld's, where no one else knew she was. She considered herself in hiding, but she did receive harassing phone calls, one of which asked for her husband by name.

Steinfeld was proud of Christ for achieving all that she was doing in her still-recovering state, including making such a long drive alone as she still was adjusting to having just one eye. Her first day back in Houston, Steinfeld and her boyfriend drove her to Bonney, forty-two miles to the south, to see Joe; it was a happy reunion until it was time for her to leave. Joe had had to move again with his father and stepmother, who were building a new, larger house. In the interim, the family of four lived and slept in the one-room cabinlike house their ancestors had built long ago, although an indoor bathroom had since been added. Joe was now forced to start the eighth grade at yet another new school. He hated it, had trouble making new friends and wanted to live with his mother, but she wasn't able to take him in yet.

That wasn't the only difficult encounter on Carol Christ's agenda. She met with Kelly Siegler for what the prosecutor referred to as "a come to Jesus meeting." Not only did she need to know everything that had happened the day of the shooting, she absolutely had to know about everything hidden in Carol's closet, each gory or sordid piece of dirty laundry, although not necessarily every accompanying nitty-gritty detail.

At twenty-nine, the petite prosecutor had a huge reputation, widely considered the best trial lawyer in the DA's Office by both colleagues and opponents. In a cosmopolitan town in a state still proud of its colorful countrified ways, the Mensa member could easily argue like a good ol' boy without making it look false or condescending.

From the small Texas town of Blessing, midway between Houston and Corpus Christi, Siegler saw herself as "a little hick girl" when she enrolled at the University of Texas, an institution nearly one hundred times larger than her hometown. The valedictorian of her high school class of forty-four, she felt overwhelmed at the 48,000-student campus in Austin. Dubbed "the hick" by those in her dorm, she rushed through her studies so she could graduate in three years, earning a degree in international business. Each weekend, she made the nearly three-hour drive home to work at the restaurant her mother managed, returning early each Monday morning. While many UT grads pronounce Austin as not just the state's best city but the world's greatest, Siegler couldn't wait to leave. She chose the South Texas College of Law in Houston, an even larger city but one where she could live with her aunt and enjoy the comfortable familiarity of family.

Since she was twelve or so, Siegler had her sights set on being an attorney. She thought she wanted to be a high-powered corporate attorney, thinking it was the more glamorous branch of the profession, until she worked for such a firm while in law school. She couldn't imagine hating it more, bored by the writing and research rather than the courtroom drama she had envisioned or interaction with clients. In 1986, she landed an internship at the Harris County District Attorney's Office's Family Division and loved it. Working primarily on cases dealing with battered women, doing things as routine as securing restraining orders, she felt she was making a difference. "Where I grew up, it happens all the time," she said, and she encouraged the victims who came to her in Houston to leave and make a better life for themselves. It wasn't just the optimistic naïveté of a gung ho graduate dispensing advice from afar; she had some firsthand experience. Her parents had a tumultuous relationship, separating when Siegler, the oldest of three children, was in the first grade. Her mother then ended up in an abusive relationship, she said. Even so, Siegler saw her mother as a strong woman and the biggest influence in her life. Her mother had overcome a rough childhood and successfully raised her children, preaching that they could do whatever they wanted. Siegler's father was a local justice of the peace who often held court barefoot in his Blessing barbershop.

A barroom brawl in Blessing was her introduction to her husband-to-be. Kelly was on a date with a genuine bull-riding cowboy when he got into a fight with Sam Siegler, a medical student eight years her senior in town on a hunting trip. She ended up marrying Siegler, a family practitioner who held both law and medical degrees, in 1988.

Kelly Siegler was good at getting her witnesses to open up and knowing every detail of her case, even those that would never be admissible in court. This time, Carol Christ gave a clear account of the shooting and Siegler now believed she would be an effective witness. The only part of Carol's story that the prosecutor didn't quite buy was her recollection that as she waited for paramedics to arrive, her husband dialed the phone and uttered: "Swordfish," presumably to his brother across the country. She didn't think the victim was lying but rather that she had been hallucinating because of her injuries. It was just too weird. More bizarre was the fact that the accused not only admitted it later but defended it as perfectly reasonable.

"Here's our options," the straightforward prosecutor told the victim during that crucial meeting. First they could go ahead with the trial as planned, but that would

mean both Carol Christ and her daughter would have
to face her husband in court and detail that horrific
day. Or, they could let John Christ plea-bargain, eliminating the need to go to trial at all. Carol wanted to
know what Siegler thought. The assistant DA, who
thrived in the courtroom, wanted to go to trial and get
the potentially deadly doctor put behind bars for as long
as possible. She was confident that her case was strong,
but there were no guarantees, she said. Although she
did not legally have to, she would go along with whatever the victim decided.

Still scared of her husband, Carol Christ wanted him
behind bars, punished for the extreme damage he had
wreaked upon her life. "I want to go to trial," she said.

"The trial is going to be hard—real hard," Siegler
warned again.

"I don't care if it's hard or not; I want to go through
with it," she said determinedly.

"You can't hide anything from me if I'm going to do
anything with this case," Siegler told her pointedly. The
prosecutor already had heard about some of Carol's colorful past and the assistant DA suspected there was
more. Surprises in court could irrevocably damage a
case, and Carol should not underestimate the defense's
ability to unearth anything from her past, no matter
how closely guarded a secret she might believe it was.
She would have to bare her soul for this case to go
forward, something she was only beginning to do with
her psychiatrist.

Carol wanted her husband to pay for what he did to
her, to finally be held accountable for his horrendous
actions. She was ashamed of her past but knew it had
nothing to do with why he pulled the trigger. Feeling
as though nothing could hurt her more than what already had happened, she was willing to sacrifice whatever dignity she had left to insure he was punished for

what he had done and to keep him from inflicting more injury on her, her children or anyone else.

Carol Christ laid out all her dirty laundry for the prosecutor, from her tumultuous childhood through her sixth marriage, the promiscuity and sexual adventurousness to the abuse and humiliations, the problems she had created to the ones she had endured. Later, one of the defense attorneys would call with some newly discovered dirt from Carol Christ's life, such as another marriage license, but it was news only to them. The prosecutor never was surprised and it only bolstered her respect for the victim.

Neither of John Christ's ex-wives, both of whom suffered physical abuse in his hands, were forthcoming or willing to help send him to prison. Siegler had difficulty even talking to Ruth, now reportedly remarried and living in New York. After leaving messages with her family, the prosecutor eventually heard from Ruth, but she was obviously still terribly frightened of her ex-husband, sharing little with Siegler and even refusing to give the state law-enforcement officer her phone number.

Gay's case seemed more clear cut. John Christ had pleaded no contest to the assault charge and served probation while Gay had made no secret of what he had done to her, spilling details to friends and acquaintances and filling volumes of court records with her recounting. Yet when Siegler called her, she tried to back out of it, saying it hadn't happened. "I don't believe you, Gay," the prosecutor said bluntly. "I'm holding the police report in my hand."

Gay couldn't deny it, but she was just as blunt. She didn't want to be involved, and she told Siegler that she needed the child support payments her ex was paying because her children attended private schools. It was too late; Gay already was involved. Since her ex-husband called her after the shooting, she was a witness, like it or not, and, unlike Ruth, within easy reach of a subpoena to compel her testimony.

Around the Medical Center, the Christ case seemed constantly full of news and innuendo, and the buzz that Gay now was denying what she had once widely proclaimed was stunning. To sell out her own character and morals, to stand by someone seemingly devoid of any just to keep a comfortable lifestyle, was appalling and unconscionable to most. Even the defense attorneys believed Gay was solidly in their corner because of the child support and alimony she would have to do without should her ex be locked away.

John Christ was given more than one opportunity at a plea bargain—not because the DA wanted it, but because she didn't want to put the emotionally fragile victim through more than she could handle. Years later, Siegler and Bailey had different recollections of exactly what the plea bargain would have been. Bailey said the offer was to allow John Christ to escape any jail time if he pleaded guilty to attempted murder, served probation and turned over his medical license. All the attorneys on his defense team advised him to consider it, but they didn't believe he had given it any serious thought.

Despite all of Carol's legal and medical problems, she appeared nearly as upbeat as ever as she struggled to rebuild her life. The one notable exception to her cheerful demeanor was that she lived in terror that her husband would find her and finish the job. Betty Steinfeld felt that was a possibility, too. The short-term memory problem was the most obvious deficit in her friend, who used to juggle the many responsibilities on their unit where fourteen things could happen at once. Steinfeld wondered how Carol would be able to return to her demanding job, which was hard enough even for a healthy person. Carol remained determined, however, renting an apartment for herself in a huge complex on Chimney Rock, just off the Southwest Freeway, where she could move to a larger unit when her children returned to live with her. Steinfeld and her kids sometimes drove Carol to her various doctors' appointments and were impressed that she could laugh and joke about those intense things, even when going to get fitted for an artificial eye.

Doctors' visits filled much of Carol's time, seeing her psychiatrist twice a week and visiting her other surgeons and specialists several times a week. Realizing she now had short-term memory problems, Carol carried a notebook in which she carefully recorded her many doctors' many instructions. Generally, it worked as she always kept appointments, took her medications and followed their instructions. Each doctor had a different style and approach with her and later recalled their visits with her differently. With some, she was weepy and in need of discussing her personal problems as well as her medical ones; with others, she was more straightforward and controlled, seldom discussing anything but whatever medical problem had taken her to that doctor. After a while, most of her doctors avoided discussing her husband directly, although Appling often asked about him. "Have you seen him? How's he doing?" he generally asked, irritating his patient that he would show concern for the man who had done this to her.

With her asthma and her numerous medications, some of which had problematic side effects, Carol visited Dr. Sims, the specialist in internal medicine, every week or two. Her biggest complaints continued to be the frequent, intense headaches and the persistent facial pain and numbness. Sims still worried that a serious infection could kill her. Always cheerful when she arrived, Carol generally was in tears within a few minutes, detailing her many problems, both medical and personal. She was frustrated that she could no longer do some of the things she had done before, but she was determined to go back to work. Sims attributed her survival to her will to live and the love for her children, but he worried that everything might someday overwhelm her and cause her to commit suicide.

Despite his busy, patient-filled schedule, Sims ushered her into his office to ask more personal questions after the physical exam was finished and he had inquired about her physical health. Concerned, he asked about her social life, how things were going with her children and her emotional well-being. He wasn't just being polite; he genuinely cared. He always sat down when they spoke, as if to signal he was taking time to listen, not asking questions with one hand on the doorknob, ready to exit as other hurried doctors did.

Dr. Stal, too, took an interest in Carol Christ other than just her medical problems. He was one of the few doctors who asked about her near-death experience. As she had been sitting on the floor in the kitchen listening to the 911 operator and waiting for paramedics, her fear and anxiety suddenly left. Emotionally and physically, she actually felt good. She remembered thinking, "This is it; I'm dying." She felt only a tingling over her whole body, centered at her sternum. "It was almost an orgasmic-type feeling," she recalled later. "A really fantastic feeling." She felt as if her essence, or spirit, was being sucked out of her body, like from a vacuum cleaner. Suddenly everything became bright and clear. She saw the kitchen, but not from her vantage point—it was as if she were looking down from the ceiling. She saw herself, sitting against the white cabinet, her head bloodied and hanging at her chest. Unalarmed, she still felt great. Dani was crouched down in front of her, one knee up, crying and repeating, "Mommy! Mommy!"

"I can't die; I can't die," Christ decided, and felt an

urgent need to get back into her body. Her child needed her. She felt herself reentering her body. It had lasted less than a minute but was a beautiful experience and one that convinced her that there was an afterlife and a heaven and hell.

Most doctors dismissed her experience as the result of neurotransmitters being released in her brain— something she herself had believed until she had experienced it—but Stal listened, asked questions and told her about a few other similar experiences he had heard about. He suggested a book she could read on the topic.

Dr. Hamill found her particularly sweet and interesting, but a bit unusual. Since he had not met her before, he couldn't be sure how much of her peculiarities were due to her brain injury or how much were innately her, something some of her other doctors wondered, too. After the shooting, Carol sometimes laughed or cried easily, sometimes inappropriately, but that was not unusual for people with frontal lobe injuries. She seemed especially emotional and needy, although he thought that was understandable given all she was going through. She seemed to be someone not in charge of her own life, like someone being carried away on a current, he thought. He tried to help how he could, mostly by listening. She talked a lot about what was going on in her life, medically, personally and legally, to him and to his staff, in much more detail than most patients.

Always well dressed for her appointments, Carol wanted to look normal and wondered what she would be able to do once she recovered. She worried about her future, her children and her husband's trial. "She would put this smorgasbord of problems on the table," Hamill said. She was exceptionally afraid of her husband, and the ophthalmologist wondered if she always had lived her life in fear or if the shooting had engendered it. He felt a lot of sympathy for his badly traumatized patient. He didn't know what to do other than be a sounding board and offer some occasional, unbiased feedback. He didn't mind as he had her best interests at heart. She often asked for his advice, but he believed she probably did that with most people. Although he was just five years older than Carol, he sometimes felt like a father figure to her. She seemed like a victim who didn't understand why it happened. As much as she told him, he suspected there was more going on. He had heard rumors that she had been married often but was surprised to hear she had been down the aisle six times. Her life was like a soap opera, he thought, but knew it was true because he was observing much of it firsthand. "There was a lot in her background that's not standard, suburban apple pie," he said, but he really liked her.

He had heard a lot of good things about her, too. She was well respected as a nurse and person, although he and others wondered if she would be capable of holding down a job any longer. As her recovery progressed, Hamill became more optimistic about her chances for success and thought she might be able to pull it together.

With Dr. Patrinely, Carol Christ was rather emotional, although not tearful, but he expected that. She was rational but genuinely frightened of her husband, convinced that he would go after her at some point. She spoke of the shooting in vivid detail, without breaking down. Talking about how exceptionally smart John Christ was, she worried that he would find a way out of the attempted murder charge.

Even so, she always had a positive attitude about her recovery and all she had to go through because of her husband. She was a good patient, always doing whatever was asked of her and eager to move through her recovery. "She always wanted to take the next step and go as far as she could," Patrinely said. Unlike some patients, Carol's expectations for what was surgically possible were realistic and she was openly grateful for what he and the other doctors had accomplished already. He had seen other patients get angry when the results didn't match their overexpectations of what was even possible. That was not Carol. She had a sharp, critical eye for what she wanted and an understanding and accepting nature of what he and the other surgeons told her.

She had a quick wit, good sense of humor and laughed easily. Sometimes, though, she bordered on being a bit goofy, laughing loudly and exaggeratedly when it wasn't appropriate. He sometimes wondered, too, if that was part of her personality or the effects of the brain damage she had suffered. He, too, provided a listening ear as she talked a lot about how the shooting had impacted her life.

Carol freely praised her plastic surgeons, Patrinely and Stal, for the amazing work they did rebuilding her face. Others in the field would often stop her in the elevator or the halls when she was there for an appointment, and openly admire the surgeons' work, sometimes putting a hand gently beneath her chin to turn her face for a better look. She didn't mind showing off their work and was pleased when others confirmed what she believed—they were doing an incredible job with the plastic surgery. She knew she was still a work in progress. She once quipped about her husband: "I think every time I have a surgery they should do the same procedure on him—reconstruct his head—but have the residents do it."

She also found herself wrapped up in legal matters, with the criminal trial and her divorce and injury cases. Her civil attorney, Harry Herzog, was doing his best to make John Christ answer for what he had done. When

Herzog tried to depose him in the divorce case, Christ
fought it. His attorney, Thano Dameris, filed a motion
to put off that deposition, pending the outcome of the
criminal charges as well as protecting his client from
"undue annoyance, embarrassment, oppression and
expense." Ironically, he noted as a reason for putting
off the deposition, the criminal court's order that Carol
and John were not to communicate in any manner.
Carol had never planned to attend the questioning and
the two would obviously see each other at court proceedings in the criminal case. Writing that ". . . the Motion is not well taken," the judge ordered the defendant
to appear for the questioning. On September 21, Dameris officially withdrew as Christ's attorney in the civil
cases and was replaced by Bruce C. Zivley. That same
day, Christ countersued for divorce, citing the standard
conflict of personalities. As part of his claim, John asked
that his wife be held liable for his attorney's fees and
expenses. By the end of September, John Christ had
borrowed more than $58,000 from NationsBank, the
majority for criminal attorneys' fees and, he reported,
that his medical practice was operating at a loss of nearly
$11,000.

Herzog found meetings with his client both inspiring
and difficult. Carol Christ had a great attitude but often
forgot things they discussed because of her short-term
memory problems. Once the information made the
cross to long-term memory, however, she was able to
retain it; it was just a process that took more time than
usual. She carefully took notes during their meetings
as she did at all her doctors' appointments. "I want to
remember when I get home," she explained to him.
Still, it wasn't enough. After she got home, she often
called Herzog asking for explanations of things she had
read in her notes. It was the only client he had had with
that type of brain injury and he tried to understand but

found it challenging. It had been easier for him when the Edwardses had attended all their meetings as well.

Most of the time, Carol was upbeat, happy and even making jokes about everything going on in her life, but every now and then, her anger lashed out at everyone around her. At the end of one meeting with her attorney, her temper exploded in anger over something her husband was trying to pull in the case. "That bastard's not going to get away with it!" she screamed in his reception room, alarming all of Herzog's coworkers. After a thirty-second tirade, she stormed out. Herzog was stunned. He had heard her temper a few times during phone calls, but this was the first time he had witnessed it firsthand. "There was no such thing as calming her down," he said. Her moods could vary from one extreme to another. Within an hour of making the scene in his reception room, she called to apologize: "Sometimes I just go off the handle."

She had reason to be angry at her husband for the things he was doing and it worried her attorney as well. So when she wanted some of her things that had been left in the couple's house, Herzog asked that John Christ give them to his attorney, who, in turn, sent everything to his office. When Carol Christ arrived to pick up her things, Herzog suggested she open them in front of him first, just in case. When she did, she found some of her things covered in her own dried blood—the blood she had spilled making that critical journey from her bed into the kitchen, when, as her husband would insist repeatedly, she hadn't been "actively bleeding." Taken aback, she shed a few tears at the unexpected reminders. They also found two cards hidden amongst her things. The first was a birthday card to the stepdaughter he had so tormented. Inside, he wrote in all capital letters: "HAPPY BIRTHDAY DANI! I MISS YOU. I LOVE YOU." He signed it, "Daddy John." He also had his oldest two children sign it. Carol had no intention of upsetting her daughter by showing it to her.

The second card was addressed to Carol. Its plain cover read: "The Best Part Of A Relationship Isn't Just Going Out . . ." The inside explained: "It's Going In And Out, In and Out, In and Out." The card was printed to say "Anonymously Yours." Had it not been in the box of things he had sent, there still wouldn't have been any doubt who it was from. Few people possessed the unmitigated gall and sense of bad taste he so capably displayed time after time. To Herzog, that was a good thing. Every outrageous and inappropriate thing John Christ did strengthened the case against him. Clearly, the surgeon refused to see how he came across to others, but the attorney knew few others could miss it—especially, he hoped, any judge or jurors hearing his case.

Nearly everything Christ returned to Carol was damaged in some way, some blatantly, some not, but most of them permanently. When she took her large fish tank out of the car, the bright sunlight flickered off what she thought was a scratch. Examining it closely, she saw that incisions had been made near each of the seams as if with a glass cutter. Had someone filled the forty-eight gallon tank, it would have shattered.

Carol Christ turned to her journal frequently, trying to work through her painful life, both her present and her past, so she could move forward successfully. "Getting shot by my lover/husband opened my eyes to some painful realizations about myself," she wrote one September evening. "Why didn't I leave when I discovered these things about John and when he had been abusing myself and my children? Am I destined to pick and stay with abusive men?" She and Sermas had been discussing her past and the patterns of her relationships. So now, in her journal, she turned her thoughts to her past long ago, ready to dig up painful memories she thought she had dealt with decades earlier and left behind safely.

She still had her quirky sense of humor, even about her problems. As she visited with Youngblood and some of Lynne's relatives one evening, they were asking about her acrylic eye. Carol popped out the eyeball, pretending it was by accident. Letting it drop and bounce across the kitchen floor, she yelled, "My eye! My eye!" Carol and her niece, Erin, burst out laughing while Youngblood and the two other women ran from the room screaming as if they had seen a frightful spider. Soon they all were rolling around the floor, laughing until they cried. When the Youngbloods went to New Orleans, a city indulgent of black magic, Carol asked for a souvenir—a voodoo doll. Her former sister-in-law bought her two.

On particularly emotional or physically painful days, Carol spent time with her John Christ voodoo doll, trying to inflict pain on the man who had destroyed her life. Since he enjoyed running so much, she aimed often at the knees. The doll's left eye and head got stuck where she had been shot, and just for pure vengeance, she needled its groin, twisting and turning all the needles for as much as fifteen minutes at a time while she concentrated on seeing him in pain. She had heard that the doll needed to be by a personal article of the intended target's, so she laid it on a sock of his which had been amongst her things that he had returned. She didn't think she really was causing her husband any pain, but she still hoped. She found these voodoo sessions immensely therapeutic and a harmless release of her stress and emotions. And she had so much built up inside of her, she was willing to try almost anything to release it. Sermas thought this was a good way for her to do it and also suggested she buy a cheap set of dishes to throw against the wall when she was especially angry. It worked. As each plate or cup shattered, so did some of her tension. Her walls had a few gouges, but she was proud of them; they were just more scars in her long healing process.

Dani called her mother on Thursday evening, October 8. She was happy and bubbly, telling her mom about her new friend, an upcoming Halloween party and dancing. She turned somber, though, as she talked about missing her mother. "I love you, Mommy, and I miss you," she said, and began crying. Carol fought back her own tears as she tried to reassure her daughter.

When Gus O'Keiff got on the phone, Carol asked him for what seemed like the hundredth time to take her daughter to a psychologist. As usual, O'Keiff insisted that his niece did not need one. He said that Dani might go into accelerated classes, which only upset Carol more. She absolutely did not want that. Last year, Dani had had a hard time keeping up with her classmates because she was emotionally immature. Her teacher at the time and Carol had discussed holding her back for another year or putting her in a slower-moving class. With everything going on, Carol did not think her daughter needed the added pressure of accelerated academics. O'Keiff then asked his sister when she could send him money for Dani's expenses. She could not send any at the moment because her doctors' and attorney's fees cost so much, she explained, feeling both guilty and angry. After saying good-bye to Dani one more time, Carol hung up and wept. She pulled out her journal and confided her pain to paper: "I can hardly stand this. I want to send money but I can't right now. My mother asked me today if I was getting more money! I have such tremendous anger at them. Can't they just let me heal?! Don't they realize how tremendous my bills are, and my income is decreased?"

Sermas noted that his patient was somewhat anxious and feeling the pressures of her circumstances that day. As she had when she lay in the hospital with nothing to do but think, Carol was becoming increasingly anxious and fearful again and turning to her psychiatrist more frequently for help. She struggled with issues of having been so victimized and the sense of helplessness that wrought. She had nightmares, flashbacks, panic attacks, bouts of depression and times in which she withdrew from those who cared about her. She was anxious about her husband's prosecution, but before she would see him in criminal court, she would have to face him in divorce court.

The legal process, although stressful and intrusive, became one of the most empowering aspects of the ordeal for Carol, as it often did for victims, according to her psychiatrist. "They can do something to fight back," he said. A sense of obtaining justice, of standing up for themselves, of being believed, often gives victims a needed emotional boost, he said. The problem, however, was that the criminal and civil cases both required that she discuss the shooting and its aftermath, all the surgeries and resulting problems, and look at some of the gory photos of her injury and possibly the crime scene. Doing that tended to dredge out all the feelings and fears of having gone through those things the first time, he said. What Carol dreaded most about the legal process, though, was having to be in the same room with her husband, something she had not done since she lay dying on the floor, wondering if he were coming after her again.

As Carol Christ sat in her psychiatrist's office on October 13, openly trying to examine her life, John Christ sat in her attorney's office across town defiantly responding to questions.

John Christ believed he was ready for the deposition

when he arrived at Herzog's office. Sitting opposite the attorney at a long conference table, Christ was confident to the point of being cocky. His divorce attorney must not have been pleased with his conduct, but his criminal defense attorney would be furious—astounded that such an intelligent man could not keep from further damaging his own case.

Under oath, John Christ said he did not want a divorce.

"Well, why did you sue for divorce if you don't want one?" Herzog asked.

"The divorce is not from Carol Christ; it is from her family," he said.

"Is there discord or conflict between you and Carol?"

"There was none," the doctor responded, not directly answering.

"Is there any now?" Herzog clarified.

"I don't know." She had accused him of attempted murder, filed for divorce and sued him for punitive damages; he claimed he didn't know if there was "discord" between them.

After listing the various plastic surgeries he performed on his third wife, he said: "She asked and I consented to put a labial ring that was done at the time of her surgery at the Methodist Hospital for putting in her breast implants."

A few minutes later, Herzog asked: "Are you withdrawing your previous offers to amicably resolve the divorce?"

"Yes."

"Why?"

"Because I've not been treated fairly, honestly, and I don't believe that I am dealing with Carol Christ. I am not dealing with her in this incidence at all. I am dealing with Dan and Margaret Edwards, and that's what this thing is about. It is a vindictive vendetta against something that they do not understand or comprehend. They do not know the relationship that Carol and I have. I am being condemned without having an opportunity to resolve this face to face."

During this deposition, he said that the only physical problem he had was an inguinal hernia and none that would affect his ability to practice plastic surgery. At his criminal trial four months later, he would testify that he was still recuperating from the bullet wound to his little finger.

Turning to more practical matters, Herzog asked about the big-screen television Carol had bought shortly after they were married in Massachusetts, thus making it community property. John Christ had refused to give it to his recuperating wife.

"What is your vision?" Herzog asked.

"Why?"

"Twenty-twenty? Twenty-thirty? Without glasses."

"I don't know."

"With glasses?"

"It's twenty-twenty."

"Do you know what your wife's vision is currently?"

"No."

"Would you be agreeable to allowing her to use the big-screen TV during the pendency of your divorce?"

"No."

"Why not?"

"Because it's community property and it's staying right where it is."

"Why?"

"Why does she need the TV?" John Christ asked.

"Well, what do you think your wife's vision is right now?"

"I answered that question."

"What do you think it is?"

"I have no idea."

"Do you know if she can see out of one or two eyes?" Herzog persisted.

"I heard that she can see out of one eye."

"I'll represent to you that that is correct. Assuming, if you would, that your wife can only see out of one eye and that your vision corrected with glasses is approximately twenty-twenty, would you be willing to allow your wife to use the community property, the big-screen TV, during the pendency of your divorce?"

"No," Christ snapped. "Have you ever heard of Sandy Duncan? Have you heard of Sammy Davis Jr.? They are one-eyed."

With that absurd answer demonstrating the doctor's arrogance and ignorance, Herzog let the issue drop and turned instead to the house and what items of Carol's might still be there. Christ first said none of his wife's personal things were still in the home. After listing what furniture of hers still was there, he added: "Any clothing, personal effects have been packed in boxes, and they are stored in the garage."

"Is it your desire, if a divorce is granted, for you to obtain title to the home?" Herzog asked.

"Yes."

"You want to stay in the house?"

"I'm going to get the house," he answered defiantly.

After asking if his wife had any of his possessions that he wanted returned, he said that other than what "I believe the Edwardses raped from my house," he wasn't aware of anything, so if she did, "it must be insignificant."

Then the doctor told his wife's attorney: "You didn't ask me what I wanted."

"Well, that was coming. I'll go ahead and ask it now. What do you want from the divorce?"

"I want to be reimbursed at one thousand dollars a month for eighteen months of child support. I want to be reimbursed for the surgical services that I supplied to Carol . . . I want to be assured that she will pay her 1990 income tax . . . I did want to be reassured that she is going to maintain the payments on the Ford Explorer."

Now he was claiming to have supported his stepchildren, but during written interrogations in the personal-injury case filed by Gay, John had claimed that Carol paid for the family's groceries and school lunches and "she additionally contributes to the payment of child support for my children whenever an amount is needed." His previous statements weren't discussed now; instead, with John's astonishing new requests on the record, Herzog turned to the shooting.

"I'm going to ask you some questions now, and I want to, as I promised you earlier, forewarn you based on our earlier discussion with regard to the Fifth Amendment," Herzog told him. "If you desire to invoke the Fifth Amendment, that is your legal right, and I will allow you to do so without debate. I just don't want to sneak up on you with these questions. Were you in your house on May 9, 1992, when Carol was injured?"

"Yes."

"Did you see her get injured?"

"No."

"Were you in the room when she was shot?"

"No."

"Do you know how she was injured?"

"No."

"Were you injured?"

"Yes."

"How?"

"I think that I need to invoke the—well, the statement that I gave to Officer Swaim was that I was unloading the Colt .45 and it suddenly went off in my hand. It was an accidental self-inflicted wound." After a few more questions about how he wounded his finger, the doctor invoked the Fifth Amendment when asked where he found the gun.

He said he told Swaim about his injury because "I thought it was critical to my treatment."

"Did you talk to anyone with regard to the injuries to your wife?" Herzog responded.

"No."

"Did you think that that might be critical to her treatment?" Again Christ took the Fifth.

"Do you believe that she shot herself?" The doctor again took the Fifth.

Asked how his wife looked after she was shot, he said: "She was walking upright and appeared to be conscious." At that point, Bruce Zivley said a few private words to his client. His wife was bleeding, Christ added, and again took the Fifth when asked if he treated her.

Herzog asked about Christ's stepdaughter: "Did you talk with Dani about the injuries to Carol at the time?"

"That little monster! I didn't say a word other than 'Mommy is going to be all right.' That's all I said to her. I tried to reassure that little girl from being hysterical. That is the biggest liar in the world. That is a big monster. She is a baby, borderline personality disorder."

Herzog calmly asked: "Have you talked with the daughter since May ninth?"

"No, I don't even know where she is."

Asked if his wife said anything to him before or after the shooting, Christ again pleaded the Fifth.

"Do you have any belief that an intruder injured her?"

"I'm going to take the Fifth." Then, after a couple of questions, he said he did not have any reason to believe that a stranger shot his wife.

"Would you agree with me that the decision that's going to have to be reached by some independent factfinder is whether she shot herself or you shot her? Are those the two options that we're down to?"

"No," Christ said, surprising Herzog.

"OK. What third option is there?"

"That there was an accident."

"OK. Is there any person that you believe could have had their finger on the trigger of the gun when the gun discharged sending a bullet into your wife other than you or her?"

"Dani," he responded.

"OK. How old was Dani at the time?"

"She was six and a half."

"Do you believe that she may have been the one that fired the pistol?"

"I'm going to take my Fifth Amendment right." He continued invoking the Fifth Amendment when asked: "Did you see her with the gun in her hand?" and "On any day other than May 9 of 1992, have you ever seen Dani with the gun in her hand?"

Asked if Carol ever spoke with him about inflicting injuries on herself, Christ said she had, but when asked when, he said: "I need to invoke my Fifth on that. I need to reserve those answers."

"Before May 9, 1992, did you believe that Dani had the mental desire to injure her mother?"

"I don't know. All I can tell you is that she brutalized my youngest son. She was in the habit of hitting my older two children, and she would consistently lie to her mother that it was my children's fault. She would draw pictures of death and destruction. Her mother always thought it was funny. She would draw pictures of dead people, stabbed, dismembered." He didn't have the drawings because, he said, "they've been taken from the house." Having forced Dani to witness the brutal aftermath of his attempt to kill her mother, this grown man now was attacking an innocent child. He truly did try to blame everything on her.

Herzog concluded by asking: "Have you thought of anything else that you want as a result of the divorce?"

"I want Carol from her financial status to pay for her own attorney's fees. I also do not want her to work at the Methodist Hospital ever again. I'll give her five years not working at the Methodist Hospital."

"Why is that?"

"Because my office is there and I don't intend on moving my practice," said Christ.

Zivley had no questions for his client—at least on the record and in front of opposing counsel. It was incredible that Christ didn't realize how he sounded or didn't care, even with his own future at stake.

John Christ's criminal attorney, Joe Bailey, was incredulous when he read this and felt haunted by what it could do to their case. "I read through the deposition, and I would go home at night and hope it didn't exist and it was just a nightmare," he said. "From a [defense] lawyer's standpoint, that would be like being in outer space and being told you had one tank of oxygen to get back to Earth with." From his vantage point, the most potentially damaging remarks had been the doctor's venomous and unsolicited descriptions of his stepdaughter as a "demon child," "little monster," "biggest liar in the world" and "a baby borderline personality disorder" and insinuating that the six-year-old had shot her mother. Attacking a little girl with such hostility was a suicidal defense strategy, Bailey believed.

As outraged as Bailey was, Herzog was thrilled, having his case so implausibly bolstered by the defendant. "He was pulling the pins on grenades and swallowing them and too arrogant to know it," he said. Forevermore, the civil attorney would show off prime parts of it when lecturing on topics such as "How to take the $100,000 case and turn it into a $1,000,000 case." That was how he felt professionally. From a personal standpoint, when he heard the defendant blame six-year-old Dani for trying to kill her mother, he said, "I wanted to puke and beat him up." After Christ and Zivley left his office, Herzog called his client and excitedly gave her a rundown of what her husband had said under oath. The doctor had been so extremely arrogant, his comments so outrageous, the attorney felt sure the deposition would not only win their case but could go a long way toward convicting the doctor as well, he assured her.

After their conversation, Carol Christ turned to her journal, not wanting to forget what her attorney had told her. She was learning to take copious notes whenever she needed to remember anything as her short-term memory problems still were irritatingly severe. But, still emotionally devastated that her husband had been angry enough to try to kill her, Carol found a different reason to be optimistic than in the ways her attorney intended or could have even imagined. "John's deposition was today," she wrote in her journal. "My attorney, Harry, just called me to let me know how it went. Harry said John acted like he still loved me, in body language and facial expressions." Although wanting to believe he still loved her, she enumerated the outrageous requests he had made for their divorce case, the ways in which he wanted her to support him.

"John also said that I had talked of suicide before. The only thing I ever said about suicide was how horrible it is, and I thought it was a chicken way out," she wrote.

Two days later, Carol Christ went for neuropsychological testing at the Baylor College of Medicine. The neuropsychologist, Dr. Gayle M. Rettig, thought the patient made her best effort throughout the five hours of testing, although she admitted being under great stress because of her husband's upcoming trial and their pending divorce. Carol's overall IQ was determined to be ninety-nine, about what it was when she was tested at age six. Still in the average range of intelligence for an adult, it was far below what she had displayed prior to the shooting. Immediate recall of digits and words was high average, but her practical judgment and reasoning skills now were rated on the low end of average.

That month, Joe happily moved back in with his mother, and he was happy to be reunited with many of his old friends in school. He repeatedly swore to his mother that he was fine, that he had not been affected by what had happened. Joe had had a support system with his father's family through the ordeal, and since he had not been in the house at the time of the shooting or seen his mother immediately afterward, he was convinced he did not need to go to counseling. Still, he clearly was worried that John Christ would try to hurt them. When she awoke in the middle of the night, which she often did, Carol frequently found her son standing alone in a darkened room, peering out the window and watching the street. During the day, when they were driving somewhere, he always seemed to be on the lookout and frequently told his mother: "That looks like John's car." It never was. Joe had a newfound interest in going to the upscale Galleria Mall to browse a small shop specializing in spying gadgets. He tried to talk his mother into buying him an expensive nightscope and other surveillance items that they could ill afford. Carol was touched that her son wanted to protect her but concerned that he was trading in his childhood to do it. She was scared of her husband beyond anything she had ever felt before, but she did not want her son to become unduly fearful or paranoid, especially since she knew that if her husband did come after her, her thirteen-year-old son would not be able to do anything to stop it.

Finally, Carol convinced him to give counseling a try. He went to group therapy with others, but after just a few meetings, Joe announced he had had enough. "Mom, I don't need it anymore," he told her after one meeting. She agreed to respect his decision, knowing he was not one to open up much around others. Through the months that followed, Carol would try to draw him out about his feelings, but he would have none of it, quickly cutting off any such discussion by saying: "Oh, Mom, cut it out! I'm fine." And for the most part, he seemed to be coping well. It was just his hypervigilant watching for his stepfather that concerned her.

Carol Christ called the county's Victims Assistance program to make arrangements to go into group therapy with people facing similar situations. She looked forward to going as she was having a difficult time getting through this, and she knew it would be a while before things were anywhere close to normal again. She had thought getting her own place would help her return to her old life, but she was having a hard time being alone most days. She couldn't concentrate on anything for long, although she had so much nervous energy she found herself moving around her small apartment from one task to another, never really accomplishing anything but tiring herself out. She looked at the clock often, hoping the day would pass quickly, but usually found it had just been thirty minutes since she last looked. She cried often throughout her long days, partly because of the physical pain but mostly because she still was so hurt and angry about what her husband had done. She worried incessantly about how she and her children were going to get through its seemingly endless aftermath. She later found a group she liked through her former marriage counselor's office.

She was longing for a normal life, especially a sexual relationship, and told Sermas about it in terms that the psychiatrist thought sounded more like a guy. "If you weren't my doctor, you'd be on the floor right now," she told him. They both laughed, each knowing that would never happen. Although she sometimes was flirtatious with some of her doctors, especially those she found attractive, she never was seductive or sexually aggressive with Sermas. Neither felt that the professional boundaries had been crossed by her joke. She later admitted, although not to him, to having a crush on her psychiatrist, something that happens so often in therapeutic situations that it has been labeled "transference." Sermas never even detected a hint of her attraction and didn't think it had caused any problems. In their sessions, though, she did talk about which of her other doctors she found attractive. Patrinely's name came up often, though he, too, said he had had no idea.

On November 19, Carol woke up feeling terribly depressed, lonely and unloved. The calls from concerned friends had waned as they realized she would survive and they resumed their busy lives. "I'm forgotten," she lamented. She wanted to talk to someone, anyone, just to have a human connection. But she realized, "I don't have anything to talk to people about except lawsuits." Since the court system moved at a snail's pace, she had nothing new to report anyway. Besides, most people didn't want to know every little unjuicy detail with which she had to concern herself as victim and plaintiff.

She considered going out for a walk around her sprawling apartment complex, thinking maybe the fresh air would revive her spirits, or maybe she would run across someone she could talk with, just to pass some time. But her fears won out. She was frightened of going outside, afraid her husband may be lurking out there somewhere, maybe just to keep an eye on her, maybe waiting for a chance to finish the job. And even if she did meet someone to talk with, she knew she would just be uncomfortable, no longer trusting others—or her own impressions of them. Instead, she decided to stay in, turning to her journal to release her frustrations.

"John ruined my life when he walked into it three years ago," she wrote. "Why didn't I realize the full impact, though, until he shot me? My face hurts every day; my left eye bothers me. I feel useless, bored, scared, angry. I had just bought a house, got a promotion and things were going great until he walked in and ruined it."

When Betty Steinfeld visited Carol, she was surprised to find her one afternoon lying on the couch, wrapped in a blanket, and obviously depressed. Unlike previous months, she didn't seem to be able to cope any longer and it was a way in which Steinfeld had never seen her, even when Carol had lived in her home. Joe seemed like a "little dad," older than his years, and feeling a lot of weighty responsibilities on his still developing shoulders, including watching out for his mother's safety, Steinfeld thought. As a result of the stress and worrying, Joe had trouble focusing and his grades suffered. He even failed a few classes. He also got into a few fights at school when boys, who did not realize what had happened, made derogatory remarks about his mother. Because she was still recovering, Carol slept a lot, something her son had been unprepared for when he came home. She tried to make it a point to go and do fun things with him, like seeing movies, but he spent a lot of time with his friends and worrying about her.

Those worries only intensified when they began regularly receiving harassing phone calls, although her number was unlisted. Carol notified authorities and the calls were traced to a phone booth near their Timberside house. After law authorities confronted John Christ, the calls stopped. After she had separated from John Christ, Gay also complained of getting harassing calls, which even now continued.

John Christ tried to find out his wife's and stepchildren's addresses, but she and her attorneys refused to provide them. Citing his constitutional right against self-incrimination in the pending criminal trial, Christ refused to answer many of the written questions posed by his wife's attorney in the divorce case, many of which dealt with the events of May 9, 1992, or his alleged abusive treatment of past wives and mistress. He denied shooting Carol or being in the room with her at the time, although he admitted shooting himself accidentally and giving a statement about his injury to the police because he thought it was critical to getting treatment. While he now admitted that no intruder or stranger had shot his wife, as he had said in his deposition was a possibility, he stubbornly refused to say if Dani had. Among the potentially incriminating questions he refused to answer: Had he ever insinuated poisoning Gay? Had he ever hit her? Ever broken Ruth's leg or ever hit her? Had he ever struck Novak? Had he been violent with women in the past?

He said he had requested a leave of absence from Methodist Hospital but refused to say if anyone suggested he do so or if the hospital had started proceedings against him. While Carol said she had not had sex with anyone since her marriage to John Christ, he refused to answer such questions, including one that asked if he had had sex with any of his patients during that time.

The day before a scheduled hearing in the divorce case, when she would have to face her husband for the first time since he shot her, Carol Christ met with Dr. Sermas and they discussed her terror. He told her how much inner strength she possessed. "You're a survivor. Just look at what you've done in your life. Don't let John intimidate you or take that away. You can beat him," Sermas said, knowing his patient needed a little pep talk. Hearing it helped Carol find her strength. While she was still scared, she was again convinced that she could get through the next day's ordeal.

But her husband only was getting more bizarre, apparently determined to assault her emotionally and psychologically at every opportunity. As she sat in court waiting for the hearing to start, Herzog told her that her husband wouldn't enter the courtroom, claiming to be afraid of her. Carol Christ laughed at the ridiculousness of it. The judge was not amused and ordered his attorney to get him into the courtroom. Before he arrived, Carol Christ and Cynthia Olsen, an attorney who worked with Herzog, left to use the rest room. When they returned, John Christ sat at the attorney's table across the aisle from where Carol needed to be. Sitting there thinking of all that happened and knowing her husband was sitting so close by, Carol began to cry. The anger, fear and sadness welled inside. Her husband stared intently at her. Olsen grabbed her hand and led her out of court and into a private room, where she broke down and sobbed. Olsen suggested her client call her psychiatrist. Carol did and Sermas interrupted a session with another patient to take this emergency call. She briefly told him what was happening, adding: "I don't think I can do this."

"Yes, you can," he assured her. "You have to, Carol." Sermas spoke a little more sternly than she was accustomed. "Remember, John put a gun to your head and pulled the trigger. Go out there and put that gun to his head." She knew he was right. Her psychiatrist, trying to appeal to her anger instead of her fear, added one more incitement before they hung up: "Go get that bastard!"

It was only later that Carol realized her husband had made the same claims about his former mistress, Susan Novak, claiming to Carol that he had been afraid of her because she was a black belt and had wanted to hurt him after their breakup. Once again, her psychiatrist's short pep talk was effective and helped her find the strength to get through another step in her long ordeal. These were words she would never forget and from that day on, she recalled them whenever she faced another confrontation with her husband. And there would be many. Back in the courtroom, John Christ had the gall to flash her the sign language symbol for "I love you," something he would repeat again when he had the opportunity. It angered her, but she gave a sarcastic smile, like to say he was sick, and she looked away as if unfazed.

On the witness stand, John Christ again proclaimed to love his wife. As he testified, he stared often at Carol, making her nervous; she tried not to show it. He admitted that he had paid his defense attorneys tens of thousands of dollars, his ex-wife the $3,150 in child support and alimony, but had not helped his severely injured wife since she had been shot—even though he claimed she had shot herself. He said that he had not given her medical attention after she had been shot because of his injured pinkie.

When Carol was on the witness stand, Zivley asked her why she wasn't living off her trust fund or at least the interest from it. She told him she didn't have one. He asked why she had not tried to get child support from her children's fathers but expected Christ to support them and her while she didn't work. She was getting $100 a month from Joe's father, but she didn't say this.

Instead, she told him: "I want Dr. Christ to help support me and my children because since Dr. Christ shot me, I can't work to support them."

Three and one-half weeks later, the judge ordered Christ to pay his wife temporary support of $1,500, payable in two payments, through February 28, 1993. He also was ordered to return to her, in less than two weeks, the big-screen television, the den couch, four bookcases, a VCR and all her personal property. In exchange, Carol was ordered to give her husband the nineteen-inch television and cable-converter box. When Carol got her things, nearly all of it, particularly the expensive and sentimental items, had been injured in some way. The picture tube in the big-screen television was damaged irreparably; sugar added to the lawn mower's gas tank had destroyed it. A treasured baking dish, made by a New Mexican artist from half-inch-thick stainless steel and given to her by her father, looked like a sledgehammer had beaten up on it. Some things were just inexplicably missing, including a seal-skin coat that her mother had given her, some of her jewelry and a photo that had been a gift from her brother.

Things were only getting worse for her. The administration at Methodist Hospital decided that she no longer would be able to perform the job she so loved and terminated her employment effective December 1.

When Carol saw Sermas two days later on her thirty-sixth birthday, she wasn't in much of a mood to celebrate. John Christ's criminal trial was scheduled to start on the fourteenth and she was fearing that as well. Although she had been anxious to get Dani back with her, she was nervous about being able to properly care for her when she returned at the end of the month. After their session the following week, Sermas noted that she was more depressed and feeling pressured but not suicidal. Three days later, his opinion changed. That was the day her husband's criminal trial had been scheduled to start, but the day before, she had learned it had been postponed. His patient admitted that she was having self-destructive thoughts and impulses and had been thinking seriously about suicide, though she had not made any attempts. Deeply depressed and speaking slowly, Carol Christ seemed to have lost all hope. She believed that no one would ever find her attractive again, she wouldn't be able to return to her job, and one way or another, her husband would eventually kill her anyway. Doctor and patient agreed she should be hospitalized, and Sermas made arrangements to put her in Methodist's psychiatric unit, 7 North, that afternoon. She checked in under the name "Polly Haden," the name of her paternal grandmother. Sermas prescribed lithium carbonate in addition to the antidepressant, antianxiety and numerous other medications she already was taking.

Along with meeting privately with Sermas, she attended group therapy and gradually became more outgoing and self-confident; she overcame her suicidal thoughts. None of the nurses there, who spent a lot of time talking with patients, believed that she had been suicidal prior to the shooting, nor did any of her many doctors, as far as her psychiatrist knew. She was released from the hospital six days after being admitted, with a renewed determination to go on with her life. She hadn't been suicidal until her husband tried to kill her.

Twenty-two

Dani was given two tempting options for Christmas that year. The seven-year-old desperately wanted both, but the almost cruel reality was that she had to choose which one to accept. The O'Keiffs were planning to take Dani and their son on a holiday vacation to Disney World and Universal Studios in Orlando with Dan and Margaret Edwards. Everyone, especially Dani, was looking forward to the festive getaway. The plans already had been made by the time Carol Christ called and said she was ready for Dani to return home. Carol longed to have both her children with her for the holidays. They had been through a lot but had much to be thankful for. She wanted to start the new year as a reunited family. The adults left it to the young child to decide which she most wanted to do. Carol had not been invited on the family holiday, and she simply could not afford to pay her own way. After briefly considering her choices, the lure of the "Happiest Place on Earth," where she had never been and which her life certainly didn't emulate, and a long-awaited reunion with her mother, whom she loved and missed fiercely, Dani opted to go to Houston. By the time she left, Gus had come to love her as much as his own kids. He and Helayne cried when they had to send her home, but they knew she was happy to be with her mother again. They told Carol that if things didn't work out, they would be willing to take her back.

So just after Carol Christ was released from the psych ward, an emotionally fragile Dani returned home. The child spent the Christmas break in a new home preparing to go to yet another new school. Thrilled to be back with her mother and brother, she soon realized how different Carol was. Like Joe, she soon found out her mother was much more volatile and prone to dramatic mood swings. Once energetic, her mother now slept a lot and seemed always to have doctors' appointments. Dani frequently went along, waiting patiently for the perpetual patient, often handing the surgeons and doctors who had saved her mother's life a thank-you note or colored picture. Occasionally, she even asked to hug one of them.

Carol also had to trek regularly to family court for hearings related to the divorce proceedings. Generally, she arrived and left alone, meeting with her attorney inside the downtown courthouse. Her husband frequently tried to catch her alone and talk despite the restraining order that instructed him to stay at least fifty feet away from her. To Carol, it seemed that he was lying in wait, popping out from behind a pillar or other obstruction just as she approached, catching her off guard. Soon she dreaded walking to the courthouse and constantly looked around for him, believing he would jump out at her. He often did.

John Christ did not pay her the January and February support and a contempt-of-court hearing was set for March 4, 1993, in which it also would be decided if he would have to continue paying support beyond the original order. Because she desperately needed the money, Carol accepted her husband's check for $2,000 in exchange for postponing the hearing three weeks.

But that was not a sign of better compliance in the future.

As a result of the hearing, John Christ was found guilty of contempt of court, was sentenced to three days in jail and ordered to continue to pay support to his wife through the end of May, when the divorce trial was scheduled. The judge, however, agreed to suspend the jail time only if Christ made all future support payments on time and, within two months, paid Herzog $750 in attorney's fees to cover the costs of the contempt action.

He defaulted on five of eight payments to Carol, but continued to make his $3,150 monthly alimony and child support payments to Gay.

At some point, John Christ's privileges at Methodist, suspended by Spira almost immediately after the shooting, had been reinstated. He again was seen regularly, much to the horrified dismay of his colleagues. Fearing liability problems, hospital officials told some employees that they had to allow him to continue unless he was convicted. Betty Steinfeld couldn't stand to even look at Dr. Christ and did her best to avoid him. Other employees made his professional life miserable; some nurses reportedly refused to work with him, walking out of the operating room if he had a procedure scheduled. His legal bills mounting and his business sliding, he claimed in divorce papers to have just $250.

In early January, Carol Christ again had surgery. First, Dr. Coker rebuilt her middle ear. The eardrum he had repaired four months earlier looked good, except two small cysts had formed, which he marsupialized, a surgical technique used when removal would not be the best choice. Instead, the cysts were opened and drained and their edges attached to surrounding tissue. Coker sliced a line behind her right ear, cutting it away from her head until it fell forward on her face, like a flap. He then rebuilt her middle ear using a prosthesis, which had been carried into the operating room in a tackle-type box. In it were different size prosthetic bones from which he selected the right fit for her ear. After the procedure, Carol could hear as well as she had before the shooting, but she was warned that the prosthetics would wear down over time, probably in about five years, making it hard to hear once again. Even now, she still had a constant ringing in both ears that had never stopped, but at least it was no longer the roar it once had been.

Dr. Edward H. Withers, a plastic surgeon, next put in saline implants to replace her silicone pair, one of which had remained constricted even after John Christ had tried to manually fix it nearly a year earlier. Scar tissue had grown around the left implant and had to be cut away. While she had not wanted implants initially, certainly not as large as those she ended up with, she went ahead and chose slightly larger ones. That, too, had to do with the shooting. Now that her face was disfigured, although it was getting better with each operation, she said, "I'd rather have people look at my bustline than my face. They were big, but I'd grown to be fond of them."

After all her previous surgeries, these operations were a breeze, she thought. The next big event in her life, however, wouldn't be so simple. In five weeks, her husband was going on trial for trying to kill her.

As the February trial approached, prosecutors and defense attorneys coached their witnesses. Kelly Siegler was pleased with her main witness; defense attorneys apparently were less happy with John Christ. He stubbornly refused to take their advice at times and had disobeyed court orders repeatedly.

Siegler told Carol Christ to tell her story honestly to the jurors, looking directly at them. "Talk to them; they're people," she said. They discussed the topics

Siegler would cover on direct examination. The assistant DA had never squared off against Sussman, the defense's lead attorney, but told Carol just to answer honestly, even regarding the less than noble things. Since the defense was basing its case on allegations that she had tried to commit suicide, it would be especially important for Carol Christ to appear left-handed, the prosecutor said. Everyone uses both hands to do some things, but in Carol's case, jurors and defense attorneys likely would pay particularly close attention to her actions, so she should be sure to only use her left hand while in court, Siegler cautioned. Carol had recently heard something she had not known—that most left-handers wear their watches on their right wrist and though she had never done so before, she switched now. Being left-handed, she knew that most left-handers used their right hands more than right-handers used their left because that is the way the world is designed—even can openers, scissors and corkscrews are designed to be used one way and Carol had had to adjust through the years. Sometimes, though, she made her way around it. When opening a bottle of wine, for example, she often stabbed the opener into the cork and held it still while she turned the bottle with her stronger left hand.

Joe Bailey, himself a prosecutor with the Harris County District Attorney's Office for six years, had known Siegler since her first day with that office in 1987, fresh from the bar exam. The two quickly became friends and, once Bailey crossed the aisle to the defense table later that year, respected adversaries. If Siegler or one of her friends needed a criminal attorney, the prosecutor said she herself would head to Bailey's office. He knew her well enough never to underestimate her or let his clients make that mistake.

He also tended to explain things to those he was representing ad nauseam. "I am verbose to a fault. I tell clients more than they ever want to hear. They're holding up signs saying 'please stop,' " he said. The problems with John Christ, though, were that his arrogance outshone even his education and he frequently ignored the advice of his lawyers.

The job of his defense team had been to study the case from every imaginable angle and present it in the light most positive to their client. Christ didn't make it easy, having changed his story dramatically, failing to aid his wife after her alleged "suicide attempt" and assaulting his second wife and apparently other women. Then there was the hard-to-overcome fact that the victim, severely deformed from when the bullet had pierced her skull, had consistently said that he had shot her.

But they also saw factors they thought could point to the doctor's innocence; chief among them, they thought, was the physical evidence. The victim's description of the events, specifically that she said she had been standing or sitting when she had been shot, didn't line up with the trajectory of the bullets. The one in the mattress indicated she had been lying down at the time, although the defense disagreed with the state on the exact angle. The bullet found in the floor supported John Christ's claim that he had shot himself accidentally, at least to the point that the gun had not been aimed at someone's head. In addition, the fact that homicide detectives had missed the second bullet and its spent hull, even when their suspect clearly indicated two shots had been fired, suggested to the defense attorneys that police had rushed to condemn John Christ. Cops had searched for facts that fit their theory instead of evidence that developed it, the attorneys would argue.

The way they looked at the evidence, or, more important, the way they could slant it, suggested that it was possible that Carol Christ had tried to do herself in. Viewing her as histrionic and plagued by problems, they thought a jury might believe she had tried to kill herself, or at least enough to give jurors reasonable doubt that their client had been the one who shot her. Her problematic psychiatric past, though, could work against them, arousing ever more sympathy than customarily extended to victims. Defense counselors were convinced that she was ambidextrous, as her husband insisted. Jurors, though, were amused by the weak evidence they presented—photos and videos of Carol using her right hand to pet a rabbit, light birthday candles or hold a knife, and testimony that she did her nails and loaded the dishwasher with her right hand as well.

Also bolstering its case, the defense team believed, was that the book *Final Exit,* about carrying out assisted suicide, had been lying on her nightstand the morning of the shooting. Although the book dealt specifically with euthanasia for terminally ill patients, defense attorneys thought they could make a case that it went to her state of mind. She would testify later that she had indeed started reading the much-talked-about *New York Times* best-seller by Derek Humphry. Defense attorneys apparently were unaware of two facts, however. It was John Christ who had suggested his wife read it in the first place, and being a nurse, she was naturally interested. They also seemed unaware that the book they had photographed when they met their client at the couple's house several days after the shooting was not actually the same one she had been reading. When the Edwardses had gone to the house to retrieve Carol's and Dani's things, Margaret had spotted the book and packed it with her daughter's belongings. She wasn't doing anything illegal or even inappropriate. The crime scene had been released by authorities, and they had the right to get her property. The prosecutor knew about this, however. When she asked Christ about it under oath, he insisted he had not put the book there.

Suicide attempt or not, the jury would undoubtedly have sympathy for Carol Christ, the defense attorneys knew. "There was no denying the fact that this woman had been through hell and back," Bailey added.

Then there was the issue too hot for either the prosecution or defense to touch, not knowing whose case would be hurt by it more—the Christs' sex life. After hearing some of the details, both sides agreed to keep that area closeted. Judge Joe Kegans, a feisty no-nonsense jurist in the 230th judicial district, whose name belies the fact that she came up through the ranks as a pioneer among women in criminal law, would hear the case. While most judges had risen through the prosecutorial ranks, Kegans was a former defense attorney and, Sussman believed, more understanding than some of her counterparts of what they face. Likewise, Siegler viewed her as "a champion for women," a tough-talking broad with a soft spot for females in abusive situations.

Siegler, now eight months pregnant with her first child, and Carol Christ were confident going into court, convinced the strength of the evidence, bolstered by the defendant's actions in the months since the shooting, all but guaranteed a victory.

The fact that detectives had not discovered the second bullet or its shell before clearing the crime scene was not a huge issue with the jurors, try as the defense did to make it one. Called to testify by the prosecution, Detective Swaim admitted police overlooked them and that it had been an embarrassing mistake but one that made officers change their mind about when and how John Christ got hurt, but not when or how his wife did.

The state was dealt a severe blow when Kegans ruled that the victim's past psychiatric history, dating back to when she was six years old and taken to a therapist to discuss her parents' impending breakup and her brother's troubles, would be admitted into evidence. Worse for the prosecution, the ruling came only after Siegler had rested her case, not only blindsiding the prosecutor, but allowing defense attorneys to trumpet out her past as if she had been trying to hide it from jurors. The ruling allowed the defendant to be the one to first bring up this history, even though he hadn't learned about much of it until after the shooting. He could talk about her extensive marital history, revealing how he had felt misled to learn he had been her sixth husband, not her third. Now the jury would hear all the sordid details of the victim's life, and since she already had testified and not been asked about it, it likely would appear to the jurors as if she or the state had tried to hide it. Suddenly it seemed that the roles of perpetrator and accuser had been switched. If Carol Christ was not on trial, then her problem-plagued past certainly was. Some thought that the defense strategy went so far as to suggest that her history and personality were practically justification for trying to kill her. The doctor legally was protected from having his past violent and vengeful offenses and at times irritating personality used against him.

John Christ broke down in tears twice during his testimony—once while discussing the prescription drugs his wife had been taking. The defense was trying to make it appear as though she had turned to "drugs" (seldom, if ever, referring to them as medications or prescriptions) to deal with her many personal and emotional problems. Admitting he had prescribed most of them for her at some point, John Christ said, "I feel terrible. I didn't know how sick she was. I thought I could make her better." He began crying so hard that Sussman, at Kegans's suggestion, opted for a recess. In a sidebar, out of the jury's and public's earshot, the judge cracked to the defense attorney, who was her friend outside the courtroom: "When Sir Laurence Olivier gets through crying, we can resume."

About ten minutes later, a recomposed John Christ returned to the witness stand, his testimony redirected to other issues he could explain away, mostly by pointing the finger at Carol. For example, he testified that almost from the time they were married, his wife talked about wanting a gun, specifically a 9mm Browning. "She said that she was familiar with semiautomatic and automatic weapons and had even fired an Uzi," he told the jury.

His wife wanted him to buy a gun for protection around the house, the surgeon said, but "I was afraid for the children."

"But you eventually bought a gun?" Sussman asked.

"I was eager to please."

Apparently, his attorney was not pleased with his client's answer, because he quickly corrected him, saying: "I'm sorry. Listen to my question."

After discussing how the shooting had happened and the argument that had led up to it, Sussman ventured into an area he knew was sensitive to his client, seemingly trying to clue him in as to how he should answer. "Now, let me ask you this: Comparing your injury—and I understand to a surgeon that's a serious injury—compare your injury to Carol, would you say hers is how much more serious? How do you feel about the relationship of the two injuries?"

John Christ didn't take the hint, even though it was an area his attorneys must surely have addressed with him previously. "Well, I think hers was life threatening, but how can you compare the injuries? They were both severe to each individual."

By the time Siegler squared off with the egotistical doctor on cross-exam, she knew enough about John

Christ to loathe him and didn't try to shroud her disdain in front of jurors. She couldn't wait for the chance to draw out his vehemence, planning to provoke him in both subtle and obvious ways. "All our really smart defendants are narcissistic, but he's probably off the scale," she observed later. Having argued fourteen death penalty cases, she had put thirteen people on death row and she hated John Christ more than any of them. She was able to arouse his anger and conceit somewhat during her cross, but not to the extent she had hoped.

Now that Christ had introduced his wife's psychiatric history, the defense went full bore with that strategy, calling two psychiatrists to support their contention that Carol Christ had borderline personality disorder. That, they hoped, would fortify the heart of its case: Carol was a woman so plagued by emotional and psychological problems from such a young age that her alleged downward spiral was understandable and even textbook.

Dr. Richard Coons, a psychiatrist from Austin, Texas, hired by the defense to review the victim's psychiatric records dating back to 1970 when she had been in The Brown Schools, was first. Coons's professional background was impressive, including both law and medical degrees and a two-year stint in the army, in which he achieved the rank of major and worked as a psychiatrist. Although he had never met the victim, only read what other psychiatrists and counselors had written about her, he testified that in his opinion, Carol Christ fit the criteria of having a borderline personality disorder. Her history of running away, drug use, sexual promiscuity, feelings of abandonment, mood swings, number of marriages, seductive behavior toward men, depression, irritability and poor self-image all led him to that opinion, he said. A person who has borderline personality disorder is about ten times as likely to commit suicide, he said, and that someone who also has major depression, as Carol had been diagnosed by another doctor, would be at higher risk of killing herself still.

People with the disorder can function well at times but deteriorate when under stress, he said. Jealousy could trigger impulsive acts, he said, boosting the defense's case, which argued that the victim had been jealous of John Christ's relationship with his children, particularly Stephanie, and had been set off by his plans to spend the day with his daughter.

Siegler quickly sought to discredit the witness and portray him as someone bought by the defense. He admitted he was to be paid $3,000 plus expenses to review the records and testify. He also was forced to acknowledge that the only records he had reviewed had come from the defense, that he never contacted the prosecutor or any of Carol's doctors or counselors and never met the victim before forming his opinion. He was not, however, saying that the victim had tried to kill herself, he testified, only giving an opinion on the disorder. Through her questions, Siegler was able to highlight what some of those same notes said about the suspect, although the witness seemed less familiar with those observations, such as that the defendant didn't think he had any problems, that all the problems were the fault of his wife and that he was narcissistic and easily angered.

The next witness, Dr. Jaime Ganc, the victim's former psychiatrist, could talk about his own observations with the victim. Originally from Mexico, where he attended medical school, Ganc also studied at McNee University in Montreal and the Baylor College of Medicine, where he did his residency. He stayed in Houston, going into private practice after graduating from Baylor in 1974. Defense Exhibit 34 was copies of his notes from his six sessions with Carol Christ in 1991. He testified that she had told him she had radical mood swings and crying spells, was having trouble relating to her husband, decreased motivation, a tough time with her stepchildren and poor self-esteem. She had felt that no one cared for her. She admitted to him that she was in her sixth marriage, but lied when she had told him that the first time had been at age twenty. In his notes, Ganc wrote that she had dysfunctional relationships with men, a fear of abandonment and a fear of closeness.

"Did you notice that her borderline personality comes up easily?" Sussman asked.

Yes, the psychiatrist answered. "It's a very well established pattern of behavior that is very difficult to modify and to treat. You know, it's like a lifestyle behavior in a patient and it's very hard to address it." Reviewing his notes on the witness stand, the doctor tried to recall why he thought his former patient had a borderline personality disorder. "I was really thinking mostly of the mood swings, the personal relationship, difficulty in personal relationship, deep-seeded; that is, people with borderline personality have . . . extreme response to the perception of being abandoned, of being rejected. They respond in a very intense manner."

"Let me stop you there," Sussman said. "You said when somebody . . . with borderline personality disorder feels rejected, they respond in a very—did you say violent?"

"No," Ganc corrected him. He had not said violent. "They feel very intense about that. . . . People with borderline personality will have a hard time to tolerate even sometimes minimal rejection."

"Could that trigger impulsive behavior on the part of a borderline personality disorder? One of the traits?"

"In some cases."

"And did you consider her suicidal at the time you treated her?"

"No, I wouldn't," he said. Generally, people with borderline personality disorders tend to be more impulsive and do things that could put them in danger, he said. "They can drive fast. I remember one case, who was shoplifting almost in front of the police because she wanted to be caught, almost in a dangerous way. There have been incidents of overdosing with drugs," he said.

Sussman pressed, perhaps one step too far. "Assume for a moment that a person like Carol with a borderline personality disorder didn't receive treatment, didn't have a therapist for four or five months and had added to that an amount of deep depression on top of borderline disorder, is that person more or less likely after not receiving treatment . . . to be more impulsive or self-destructive?"

The psychiatrist said he did not know, but from what he saw with Carol Christ, he testified: "She was maintaining quite a good level of functioning, and as a matter of fact, I think that if you read the notes, it seems she was coming back." People with such a diagnosis are hard to predict in terms of prognosis. "I will say with her, when she comes to me, she was working and she was very happy working and she was doing her job very well. So you see, it fits, but you know, there was a very good quality in this person. She wanted to work out her relationship with her husband, which is very strange, you know, to hear it from a person who has this interpersonality relationship. Most of them say: 'I am tired of things. I want to move on. I don't want to work with things. I am up to my ears; I want to quit.' She wanted to work out this problem. . . . That's why I referred her to a family therapist, so I can deal with the depression and he deal with the marital problems."

Sussman had undone perhaps what points he had

made with this witness, but he pressed on. Referring to when therapy stopped, he asked, "Is it a fair statement to say there is no telling what could happen with the borderline personality?"

"We don't know," Ganc agreed. With that seemingly small concession, Sussman passed the witness.

Under cross-examination, Ganc said that the statistics on whether people with borderline personality disorder are suicidal vary from 20 percent to 67 percent and are false. "If you read the literature, you go crazy," the psychiatrist said, not noticing the pun. He admitted that psychiatrists don't always agree on whether a particular person has a borderline personality disorder.

"If somebody has the best psychiatrist in the whole wide world and goes home to a spouse who's very critical and abusive, are they going to get a whole lot better real fast?" Siegler asked.

"Theoretically, not."

"Would that kind of spouse make it hard for a psychiatrist to build up his patient's self-esteem?"

"Absolutely," Ganc said. "You have somebody who is pushing you down. Yeah."

Asked about how Carol Christ felt about her job, he said, "She was very proud of her work and she was an excellent nurse. I think the people at work loved her." Siegler stressed that Carol "wanted very much for her marriage to be a success," and the doctor agreed. He said she told him that she stopped going to therapy with him because of financial problems. He said that she tried very hard to understand her husband. When he heard about her background, the psychiatrist said he was "afraid, because I got a person who has a whole history of security problems since very early age." In spite of that, she was able to graduate from college, function successfully at work and raise two children, about whom she was concerned, he pointed out.

"That's why I felt in some ways very positive and optimistic and I concentrated my work on the depression,"
he said. During the time he saw her, he never thought
she was suicidal, he said, and would have hospitalized
her had he thought so.

Scoring critical points, Siegler finished with the witness. Sussman, though, wanted to leave the jury with
the impression that people with the disorder could
seem fine for a while but suddenly turn impulsive if
they sense rejection or failure—and said so in a wordy
question to Ganc.

"Yes, some," the doctor agreed. "Yes, in a minute
they can change—in a second." He likened the severity
of the disorder to cancer, saying it is difficult to treat.
With that, Ganc and the defense's case were finished.

Because she was a witness, Carol Christ was not allowed to sit in the trial listening to testimony. Her
mother attended each day, dutifully keeping notes of
what went on for her daughter to read after it was over.
Sitting alone in a long, lonely hallway outside the courtroom, the three defense attorneys passed by Carol on
a recess. One apologized for having been rough on her
during her testimony.

"That's OK," she told them quietly. "I know you're
only doing your job." Siegler overheard and was surprised; others in the same situation probably would
have made an ugly retort or at least ignored them altogether.

Siegler could have called Dr. Sermas on redirect examination to knock down or at least counteract the defense witnesses' theories. He had seen her in therapy
much longer than had Ganc and was convinced his patient was not a borderline personality disorder. Carol
Christ did not view things through a pure black-and-
white lens, as was typical of such patients. Borderline
personalities tend to see someone in one extreme or

another, even though their opinion might change from one day to the next as to what end of the spectrum they are on, he said. For example, one day someone might think her boyfriend was perfect, as if he had hung the moon, but when she was angry at him, she might think he was absolutely terrible, with no redeeming qualities, he said. That was never the case with Carol Christ, even regarding John Christ and her mother; she saw and discussed both the good and the bad, he said. Also, her constancy with her children went against her being a borderline personality disorder.

Sermas did view her as somewhat histrionic. She could be extremely good with people and wonderful in social settings, but she had difficulty doing things she found boring or isolating.

Siegler explained to the psychiatrist that it was obvious that Carol Christ had problems, but she worried that a jury might assume if she had a shrink, that meant she were crazy. The prosecutor also worried that because of Christ's recent hospitalization for suicidal thoughts, the jury could believe she had attempted it before. Sermas knew that the suicidal feelings stemmed from all she had been through—having half her face blown away, being brain damaged and having her career in jeopardy—and thought he could make an argument for that. The prosecutor believed that, too, but didn't want to risk how a jury might view it and didn't call him.

Following a few more prosecution witnesses and a long weekend, jurors heard closing arguments the following week and retired to deliberate. After nearly twelve hours of deliberations over two days, the jury was at an impasse, 7-4 in favor of Christ's guilt (one juror had been excused earlier in the proceedings) and the judge declared a mistrial.

Carol Christ was devastated, shocked that anyone

would believe she could have shot herself. Within the hour, she and Siegler agreed they would not let the surgeon get away with his heinous crime. He would be prosecuted again. Siegler took full blame for the hung jury, openly admitting she had done a poor job of jury selection by allowing a paralegal to make the cut. Although four jurors voted not to convict Christ, the others felt that three would have come around eventually had the paralegal not been amongst them. That was the last time Siegler would allow a paralegal to make it onto one of her juries. She wouldn't be too downcast for long as a few weeks later, Siegler gave birth to a healthy girl.

The prosecution once again offered the original plea bargain. If John Christ pleaded guilty and handed over his medical license forever, he would get probation and a clean record after ten years. His attorneys again urged him to consider taking the deal, but, with what he too optimistically viewed as a win in court, he seemed uninterested. Bailey and the other members of his defense team told him not to equate a hung jury with an acquittal as it might have resulted more from sheer luck than any valid reason. Short of taking the plea bargain, they all would be back in court trying to convince twelve more people of his story, one that had been bought by only four of the previous eleven.

"Christ was even more convinced that he was invincible," Bailey said later in a sworn affidavit. "It became readily apparent that, the facts of the case aside, one of the biggest obstacles for the defense to overcome in the September trial was John Christ's attitude and demeanor."

Reeling in the aftermath, Carol Christ became angry at the female jurors who hung the jury, she believed, by refusing to believe her husband was capable of such violence. She was convinced that they had been attracted to the defendant. Sermas found that improbable but left that topic alone, knowing the real issue to his patient was that others had misinterpreted the facts of the case. It was ironic: Carol Christ thought her husband got away with things he shouldn't because women fell so easily to his charms; meanwhile, he blamed women for causing so many of his problems. He imagined himself as the figurehead of women's groups looking for a high-profile man to use as a scapegoat.

Sermas and Carol Christ believed that her psychiatric history had been too big a focus, allowing it to mire her with mud that had nothing to do with the crime. She took consolation in two facts: John Christ could and would be retried and he was being hit hard financially to pay for his defense. But she also knew that those two things inevitably made him even angrier at her, so she remained terrified he would still hurt her physically. To Sermas, the defense strategy had been clear—to use the victim's problematic past to convince the jury of one of two ugly scenarios: Either Carol Christ had been capable of killing herself and then unscrupulous enough to blame someone else when she failed, or, without directly saying it, defense attorneys implied that it was understandable why someone would want to shoot that kind of person.

Carol Christ was trying once again to focus on her future, buoyed by the chance to return to nursing.

Carol had begged her former bosses at Methodist Hospital, Marcella Louis and Mary Shephard, for a chance to prove herself at her former job. Her husband had taken away so much that she valued; she was not going to let him take her career as well. Although Christ was convinced she could make it work, both privately told her that they did not think she could do the job but were willing to let her try.

Sermas admired his patient's unrelenting desire to

return to work, but he personally doubted her post-injury abilities. A nurse has to juggle so many things simultaneously—sometimes doctors called out verbal orders as they walked by—and he expected her short-term memory difficulties would be a problem. The neuropsychological tests she had taken demonstrated that "set-shifting" was a significant problem for her. A nurse also had to be able to bounce from one task to another, which mainly is a function of the frontal lobe, where Carol suffered damage. Like other doctors, he had seen lots of people with disabilities and physical pathologies less profound than Christ's and thought they should be on disability. Almost certainly, Carol Christ could have qualified, but she steadfastly refused to go that route.

Before she returned to work, she had to get another difficult operation out of the way, so on March 5, she underwent another extensive reconstructive surgery under the scalpels of doctors Stal and Patrinely. Stal began with a facial degloving, cutting across the top of her scalp from one ear to the other. Because Dr. Narayan had used the temporalis muscle eight months earlier to patch the hole in her brain, the left side of her face now was beginning to cave in. Some bones that had been put in during the reconstructive surgery nearly ten months earlier had been absorbed by the body, and Stal and Patrinely had to again try to build up those areas. Tissues once there also were missing as a result of the gunshot wound, so the surgeons took bone from her skull and tissue from her arm and leg to build up her once prominent cheekbone, which had sunken and was no longer symmetrical with the right side. Taking more bone from her skull, they grafted pieces to the orbital area, which also had been caving in, as well as to the section over and just above the left temple, affixing them with screws up to half an inch long. They then covered those areas with tissue but knew these screws could only stay in for a limited time before they would cause problems.

Scar tissue formed after previous surgeries had pulled her eyelid away from the eyeball and that needed correcting as well. While Patrinely had fixed these before, subsequent surgeries had altered them and Carol could no longer close her eye completely. Although she endured a painful surgery, she was pleased with the results. She also was happy to be put in a room on Dunn 8 West, where she had worked. She got a kick out of the nurses there, who tried to do everything perfectly for their boss-turned-patient and made her feel special. After six days, she went home to her children.

On her way to a hearing in the divorce case, Carol Christ's soon-to-be ex-husband suddenly popped out from behind a pillar and walked alongside her, trying to engage her in casual conversation as he had so many times before when they were due in court. "Saturday is Michael's birthday," he reminded her. "He keeps asking about you. He really does love you."

"Tell him 'Happy Birthday,' " she said and walked faster, breaking free of him for now. John Christ seemed willing to drag his kids into his contentious legal battles, using his wife's alleged jealousy over his relationship with his daughter as the reason she had tried to commit suicide and now her obvious fondness for his son to try to win her back.

Inside, Carol sat in a hallway waiting for her attorney when her husband walked up and sat across from her. She was scared but figured he wouldn't try to hurt her inside the courthouse.

"How are your surgeries going?" he asked.

"They're going fine, but they're going to have to do more work," she responded, not wanting to give him the satisfaction of seeing her scared and running away.

"Well, I don't know why you're going through this, you're going to die, anyway," he told her matter-of-factly. She didn't take it as a threat that he would kill her, just that the injuries she already suffered would take their toll. "It was almost like inside he was just laughing, thinking of the most malicious thing he could say to hurt me, psychologically, because he always was so psychologically abusive. A patient has to have hope," she said. "I had the strongest hope in the world." Still, his audacity infuriated her. Now, she did walk away. "He was so smart; he could damage somebody psychologically as well as he could physically," she said.

Dani was also having a rough time readjusting to life at home. She said she was hearing voices and a couple of times a day reported bizarre stories to her mother, tales the child seemed to fear and were convinced were real. She believed that an aggressive man with a knife was after her. The first time she had seen him, he had been hiding in a bush. Carol ran and checked and didn't see anyone. When it happened again, she knew something was up. At times, she would run out of her bedroom, saying, "Mommy, I saw him in the corner of my room." If she had been outside, she would run in and claim she saw the man in a tree. Carol always checked in an effort to reassure her daughter. The man she described was not her stepfather and never changed. Carol suggested Dani draw a picture of the man. She sketched a piratelike pursuer, sporting a kerchief on his head and a large red ruby in the center of his forehead. Her mother believed her daughter probably was hallucinating but wondered also if maybe it was part of the child's desire for attention, which Carol knew she badly needed. She knew her daughter was hurting and did not have the coping skills to adjust.

She discussed her concerns with Sermas, who recommended a psychiatrist for Dani. That psychiatrist now also diagnosed Dani with post-traumatic stress disorder as a result of the shooting, and recommended that she be hospitalized. Dani was taken to a small, independent mental hospital. Her mother was not allowed to talk to her by phone while she was there and was allowed just one brief visit a week, lasting just half an hour. About a week after she had been admitted, Carol visited for the first time. As soon as she saw her mother on the floor, Dani ran and hugged her. They sat down in the recreation room; staffers were across the room but far enough away to give them a little privacy. The seven-year-old child was excited about seeing her mother and proudly gave her the pictures she had drawn. A half hour later, Carol was told that their visit was over. She left heartbroken, tears falling down her face as she rushed to her car, where she sat for another half hour sobbing. "I hurt so badly that this child had to go through this," she said, but she knew she was where she needed to be in order to get better. Already the hallucinations had stopped, although it was still too soon to know if it would be a lasting cessation or just a reprieve.

Three days later, Carol Christ had to face another trying ordeal. The Christs' divorce attorneys wanted them to do a walk-through of their house before the divorce was finalized the next month. She would see John face to face in the house where they had planned their future, the bedroom in which they spent many passionate nights making love, the kitchen in which they prepared dinner side by side, rehashing their days and discussing ideas. Yet, she knew, it was also the house that had become an anxiety-filled trap for her and her children, the bedroom in which he had shot her in the head and left her to die and the kitchen where he had tried to divert paramedics' attention from her injuries to his.

As the two attorneys made the plans, Herzog told

Zivley he didn't want John Christ there to upset his client. Zivley insisted his client would be there and promised he wouldn't do anything. Both lawyers were a little worried about what might happen, given the personalities involved.

"Your girl seems a little flaky," Zivley told him.

"True," Herzog agreed. "My client is a little flaky; she had to be to be married to your killer."

When Carol pulled up in front of the house, the three men were already there, waiting. Herzog walked confidently over to her car, hoping to reassure his frightened client, greeting her with his characteristic big smile. Now Carol Christ confided that she had a pistol with her that Dan Edwards had given her for protection after she had been shot and living in fear that her ex-husband would return. "I've got my gun with me. If he tries to shoot us, I'm going to shoot him," she told Herzog. After a lot of persuasion, he convinced his client to leave the gun in the car. When her psychiatrist heard much later that she had packed a pistol when she saw the man who had used one on her, he wasn't surprised. Dubbing it "a Valium in her handbag," he said he didn't think she would have used it offensively.

As the four walked through the house, John Christ seemed intent on getting his wife alone, but she stuck close to her attorney. In the master bathroom, Herzog noticed a calendar on the wall in which a winged Greek god was depicted swooping down on a beautiful, voluptuous woman, lying tied up and helpless on rocks. "When John Christ looks in the mirror, that's what he sees," the attorney mused to himself. As they walked through the ranch, John Christ seemed overly friendly to Carol, who tried to maintain her composure while sticking close to Herzog. When they went out back, a Dalmatian puppy was chained there. Carol immediately thought it was a bribe, her husband's subtle way of letting her know he now was willing to make concessions if she took him back. She wasn't biting.

Eventually, she relaxed, realizing that her worst fear had not materialized—John Christ had not produced a gun and shot her again. Instead, he was armed with charisma, trying to charm her and remind her of what their relationship had once been, how agreeable he could be. It was as if he thought that by acquiescing to all the small things she had wanted during their marriage would be enough to win her back now. After nearly a year apart from him, she was beginning to understand him better than she ever had. John Christ did get a few minutes with his wife out of their attorneys' earshot. After they walked through the house, Herzog and Zivley walked down the driveway to go over a few details.

"Carol," the surgeon said, smiling sheepishly, "remember that bet where whoever hit the gate first owed one hundred dollars to the other person?"

"Yes," she said, skeptically thinking he was asking her for the money.

"Come here," he said, walking toward the automatic gate across the driveway. "Look at this dent in the gate," he said, pointing to a gouge in the metal. "Hold out your hand."

Carol complied and he placed a $100 bill in her palm.

"Harry!" Carol yelled. "Harry, John's trying to bribe me!" Herzog looked over, raising his eyebrows as if to say: "What are you talking about?"

"He gave me one hundred dollars for an old bet," his client reported.

Herzog stared at her for a moment before responding: "You won—take it!" So she did, slipping it into her purse and remembering that she had had to remove her security from there earlier. The attorneys resumed their private conversation. Thinking that her husband had lowered his guard in his efforts to charm her, she realized she might have a chance, however fleeting, of getting what she most wanted out of John Christ now. An explanation.

She turned to him and asked bluntly: "John, why did you shoot me?" No one else could hear them, so she hoped that he would tell her the truth. She knew if she ever reported it to anyone he would deny it, and any confession would do nothing more than give her the answer she could get nowhere else. He didn't respond immediately; his eyes shifted back and forth as he thought. Carol nervously waited in anticipation. He had confided some wild stuff to her before, so why not this?

Looking at her almost as if in disgust, his nostrils flaring as they had every time she had angered him, he said flatly, "I didn't shoot you."

Now Carol was repulsed, but could only manage to glare at him.

After a moment, her husband made another offensive suggestion. "Carol, you know you could make a fortune off of [the pharmaceutical company]. Remember, you were taking Prozac," he said, referring to news reports at that time in which some people speculated that the popular antidepressant made some people suicidal, prompting their relatives to file lawsuits. If she took the bait and filed suit, he would be off the hook for trying to kill her.

Even Dr. Christ wasn't that charming. "You shit," Carol hissed, and walked away.

When she visited her daughter a week later, Dani seemed better yet, calmer and closer to her usual self, although not quite. This time, Dani showed her the bedroom she shared with another girl and told her about the schoolwork she was doing there. Carol told her she was doing well and that she was proud of her.

"Mommy, I want to come home," Dani said.

"You are going to come home," she reassured her,

"but this is the best place for you to be right now because you're so afraid. They're going to help you with
that."

After another week, Dani was released from the hospital. She remained hallucination-free and saw a psychiatrist a few times. Carol's insurance refused to pay
for her child's ongoing mental treatment, so the counselor recommended a social worker, who gave Carol a
cut rate. Dani loved her weekly therapy sessions with
the social worker, who used play and anger therapy with
her, and her mother noticed significant improvements
in her daughter's attitude and behavior. She seemed
more of her old, playful self and returned to activities
she had once loved but had stopped doing after the
shooting, such as putting up lemonade stands and wearing costumes around the house.

Nearly a year after being shot in the head, Carol
Christ returned to work as the assistant head nurse on
the busy plastic surgery and orthopedics floor. She was
nervous but convinced she would be an even better
nurse now that she had had so much experience as a
patient. Sermas worried that she was setting her expectations of herself too high but knew she had to try it.
While she had grown up with much of the material and
status privileges of wealth, she had lived in a chaotic
house with a lack of nurturing and consistency, he knew.
Nursing was one of the main motivators that had re-
versed the tumultuous course of her adolescence and
early adulthood. Being on staff at Methodist, Sermas
knew more about what this patient was going into than
he might have with some others. He saw a genuine affection between Carol and her supervisor, Louis; he
knew Marcella Louis as a gracious and nice person but
a tough, demanding boss. The fact that Carol had held
her position prior to the shooting spoke highly of the

abilities she had once had, but Sermas knew that some of that invariably had been lost.

Her friends, colleagues, family and doctors—those she worked with and especially those who had treated her—were rooting for her, albeit with mixed expectations. Some thought she might be well enough to pull it off; others were worried about the effects of the stressful, demanding job. Knowing Carol Christ, they knew she needed to give it her best effort. Realizing her short-term memory and speed were her biggest obstacles, she continued to carry a notebook.

Right away, Carol found the job much more difficult than before and tougher than she had anticipated, but, as usual, it would be a little while before she admitted this to anyone, even her psychiatrist or herself. She caught herself making mistakes—nothing horrific or dangerous to patients—but frustrating as she would have to redo her work several times. While she never did, she worried about mixing up medications and re-read her notes incessantly. She was much slower now as doctors barked out orders and she missed things, leaving her no other choice but to call the doctors and to ask them to repeat her instructions. No one was more frustrated by this practice than Carol, and she was overly apologetic to the doctors, who were patient and supportive. "Take your time," they said, hoping to reassure her. Embarrassed, she clutched a microcassette recorder, snapping it on whenever doctors, most of them accustomed to talking fast, rambled off their orders. She did not want to forget anything or make anyone repeat themselves. This practice, though, slowed down her hectic routine, and nearly every evening, she stayed a couple hours extra to finish up her work, never wanting to burden someone else with her responsibilities and never claiming overtime pay.

Carol could no longer calculate dosages of medications properly. No longer willing to trust herself or risk making a potentially harmful mistake, she had to get another nurse to do it for her. "That's when I got to realize how bad it was. I'd have to ask for help so much it was overwhelming me. I was embarrassed," she said. She didn't like interfering with others as they tried to do their own jobs. But, because Narayan, her neurosurgeon, had said the other side of the brain would start taking over for the injured parts, she wanted to continue trying to do her job. The stress, coupled with the need to exert five times as much energy as she had once utilized, quickly exhausted her mentally, physically and emotionally. Within a few weeks, she discussed the problems with Sermas. She became fatigued easily, had a lot of facial pain and was frustrated that she no longer found her work as easy as she once had. A short time later, blood tests revealed Carol was hypothyroid, meaning her thyroid was underactive, which only exacerbated her fatigue and emotional reactions. She was put on Synthroid, a medication she would have to take for the rest of her life.

In mid-May, John Christ made what he said would be his final offer to settle the divorce case. He offered to pay Carol a total $15,000 in alimony, to be paid in $125 monthly installments over ten years. He had agreed to pay Gay nearly five times that after breaking her nose. Having been told by Carol not to settle for less than $35,000, Herzog declined. The divorce would go to trial as well.

On May 13, 1993, John Christ filed an inventory and appraisement of community and separate properties, listing the current market value of the Timberside house at just $145,000. That was $24,000 less than what they had bought it for less than two years earlier, and $2,000 less than they still owed on it. He listed what he considered as "community liabilities," meaning both he and Carol would be responsible for paying them, as $30,000 to his criminal defense attorneys, $4,100 for his divorce attorney, $14,000 for Carol's civil attorney, $9,000 in credit card debts under his name, and $30,000 owed to his company (which he was claiming as his separate property) to cover loans to his own medical practice, which, of course, he listed as his separate property. In terms of cash, he claimed to have only $200 in a checking account in his name and $487 in checking accounts in the names of his two businesses. As part of the community property, he wanted included the $1,300 in contributions made to Carol's retirement plan during their marriage as well as her car, but not his.

By the end of May, just two months after having gone back to work, Carol Christ, with the help of her psychiatrist, was facing that she could no longer perform at her job the way she once had—and the way she demanded of herself. She began considering a change. Dejected but knowing she had to face it, Carol went to Louis, crying, and said: "I don't think I can do it. I didn't realize it was this bad. I tried." Louis agreed. "The last thing I wanted to do was hurt anybody," Carol said.

She knew it had had to be done, that it was the right thing for her and the hospital, but the loss of the position she had loved threw her deeper into depression. It was another cherished thing her husband had ripped from her life. Hospital administrators searched for another, more suitable and less stressful position for her.

Following a one-day trial at the end of May, the Christs' divorce was finalized on June 10, 1993. John Christ was ordered to pay Carol $16,000 as part of the division of community property, to be paid at $500 a month beginning on July 1, 1993. Among the property she was to get were "any and all policies of life insurance insuring the life of Carol Christ." There had been no evidence that he had taken an insurance policy out on her as they had discussed shortly before the shooting, but the provision was made in case one was discovered later.

Among the property the court ordered him to "peaceably" transfer to her was listed a "tattoo of shooting star and any other bodily parts of Carol Christ currently in John Christ's possession."

"It had been a part of me and I didn't want him to have any part of me," said Carol, who once again returned to using her maiden name. Additionally, John was to pay Herzog $20,000 for attorney fees. He never paid a penny.

On June 16, 1993, Zivley faxed Herzog a letter outlining a proposed settlement for the $16,000 Christ owed his now ex-wife. Because of his financial burdens and the imminent foreclosure of his house, he was offering to give Carol O'Keiff furniture in lieu of the money. He estimated that the items he was offering were valued at more than $25,000, including an Oriental rug, which he said was assessed at $12,000. Among the other items he offered was his china cabinet, where he had insisted the gun had been hidden, and the king-sized bed, where Carol had nearly bled to death. O'Keiff needed money, not furniture. When he had given her property in the past, it had been damaged beyond repair. She refused. "If he wanted to get the money, he could sell it," she said. She never got any money or any more possessions from him.

Financially, emotionally, physically and psychologically, in every conceivable way, Carol O'Keiff was worse off for having become Mrs. Christ.

In June, Carol O'Keiff was made a quality assurance nurse, a relatively new position at Methodist, heavy on the paperwork and devoid of direct patient care. It came with a substantial pay cut.

Throughout June and July, O'Keiff continued to see Dr. Sermas, but it would be a while before she admitted even to him that her new job still was overwhelming her. In mid-July, he noted on her records: "New job situation seems to be working out fairly well." He knew about the other difficulties and pressures in her life and thought she was holding up as good as could be expected. Generally, her mood was appropriate and stable.

Dr. Patrinely said the general feeling around the hospital was that the administration had wanted to help and protect Carol O'Keiff initially; as time passed, they seemed to view her situation as more of a nuisance and were unwilling to coddle her indefinitely. Administrators seemed to believe that she should be able to do more than she could and the initial support she once enjoyed largely evaporated, he said.

In early August, O'Keiff finally admitted to Sermas her frustrations with her new job. Her psychiatrist, who knew the inner workings of the system, could see from where the problem stemmed. Methodist, a private, elite hospital, was relatively late bowing to the demands of managed-care insurance. Being new to the game, Sermas didn't think hospital administrators, who really did want to help their aggrieved employee, were aware of just what a difficult, stress-filled job they had given her, looking at it as merely a paperwork job. Instead of giving her an easier job, she ended up in one that was even more stressful. The position made O'Keiff the go-between for insurance companies questioning or refusing to pay for treatments and doctors who weren't used to having their orders challenged and sometimes took it out on the messenger. This was a new practice at the hospital, recalled Sermas. "Physicians at Methodist took this very badly, because somebody was stepping on their authority and their egos. And the person that would catch it would be the quality assurance nurse because they're standing right there," he said. "A quality assurance nurse never has good news for a doctor."

Less than two weeks later, she told him she probably would have to return to Arkansas and hoped that she would be able to find a more low-key nursing job in the small town. Knowing what a rushed place Houston's Medical Center was, Sermas thought perhaps that could be a realistic outcome as far as her career went and didn't try to dissuade her from giving nursing another try. "One of the worst things we can do for any patient is rob them of hope," he said. O'Keiff realized what a good nurse needed to do, and her psychiatrist knew the last thing she would ever want to do would be to risk hurting someone else. He was confident that if it were too much for her, she would admit it.

O'Keiff saw Dr. Stal in his office on September 3, Dani's eighth birthday. The screws put in her face six months earlier were easily visible beneath the skin and were threatening to pop through, a common occurrence over time as bones were absorbed and tissues atrophied. The area around her eye socket was still hollow, sunken and painful and needed to be rebuilt once again. Stal emphasized that the upcoming surgery would not be her last. Her thin skin and the fact that so much bone was missing would make further augmentation of some sort likely in the future.

"When I wake up, I want to have Goldie Hawn lips," O'Keiff joked to her plastic surgeon, referring to fat injections popular at the time.

But she wasn't going under for cosmetic reasons this time. True, the reconstruction would improve her appearance, but the necessity now was to alleviate the pain and prevent further damage should the hardware in her head dislodge. On September 8, doctors Stal and

Patrinely performed another major reconstructive surgery on O'Keiff.

It meant another agonizing surgery, another facial degloving, more bones being cut from her skull and grafted to her face. The plastic surgeons removed the screws and hardware and harvested six bone pieces from her head, shaping them into smaller pieces that they used to remold her orbital structure, cheekbones, upper jaw, temple and forehead. This time, they utilized hydroxyapatite, a natural, corallike substance, to replace some missing or damaged bones. Over time, the surrounding soft tissues, blood vessels and some bones would grow into the latticelike pieces. Patrinely and Stal also used more tissue grafts to pump up those areas. The surgical alterations to her skeletal structure once again distorted her eyelids, so Patrinely readjusted those as well.

This time, she was released from the hospital after just three days, still swollen and badly bruised. She was happy to be on her way to recovery, no longer having to worry that the screws were about to rip through her skin, and excited to know that she would, eventually, be in less chronic pain.

Christ and his defense attorneys were furious when she walked into the courtroom a week and a half later looking as if she had just been beaten up.

Twenty-three

So overconfident in his case, John Christ waltzed into court for his second criminal trial for the attempted murder of his third wife, with his fourth wife-to-be on his arm.

The betrothed planned on marrying at the end of the week. Already armed with a marriage license, taken out four days earlier, and a reservation at the scenic Vargo's restaurant for the ceremony, Christ just needed to get the bothersome trial out of the way. Karen Mabray, married and divorced at least twice herself, seemed to be a poised, professional woman; those who saw her in court wondered what she could be thinking and if the lure of marrying a doctor was really worth the risk.

Bailey wasn't pleased that his client again would risk anything interfering with the strength of the defense's case, and if the prosecutor found out, which she did, this could create yet another hurdle. The defense strategy still was to hammer away at O'Keiff's emotional and psychological stability, and one of the biggest tools it had was the fact that she had been up and down the aisle so many times, she had worn a path. Now their own client, who already had given sworn testimony about how her six marriages troubled him, was about to wed for the fourth time. And there were at least two others whom he had planned on marrying but didn't. On the other hand, Bailey had to applaud his client's optimism.

The attorney felt even worse when he saw O'Keiff walk in, bruised, bandaged and surgically battered.

"Good God," Bailey said with a gasp when he saw her.

Kelly Siegler smiled.

Convinced that O'Keiff had orchestrated the surgery so its brutal aftermath would coincide with the trial date of September 13, defense attorneys didn't want her to evoke any more sympathy than she already would get naturally. "I was trying to crawl under the table for that," Bailey recalled.

Patrinely would testify it was his and Stal's schedules that dictated the timing, not the patient's, but no one could convince the rankled defense team of that. Siegler knew the truth but wasn't exactly displeased with the fortuitousness. "It didn't hurt. I remember when Carol walked in, I kind of smiled," she said.

Six of O'Keiff's doctors were called to detail her extensive injuries, painfully grueling operations, agonizing recovery and future limitations, in more graphic detail than asked at the first trial. During Patrinely's testimony, the gruesome photo he had snapped before O'Keiff's first surgery, one which made her blood-filled eye appear to have been lifted slightly from the socket with a wire speculum, the stellar exit wound flaring beneath, was projected onto a three-by-four-foot screen. The eight-by-ten-inch photos were bad enough, Bailey thought, but now this. He had no legal basis to stop it, though.

Having been forewarned by the first trial that O'Keiff's turbulent psychological history would be revisited, the prosecution was able to diffuse its impact by having her cop to it up front, instead of allowing defense attorneys to highlight it as if the state had been trying to keep it under cover. This time, Siegler also beefed up her witness list, calling a couple of the patrol officers to reinforce how much pain the badly bleeding O'Keiff had been in after the shooting and how callous her husband was as he stood by worrying about his own, barely bleeding pinkie finger.

The patrol officers had not followed the case through the judicial system, and when Hutchinson and Hackett were subpoenaed to testify, they assumed it was the first trial. When they got to the courthouse, they heard that a previous jury had been unable to reach a verdict. "We were just dumbfounded that it could go to trial without us," Hutchinson said. "No wonder they got a mistrial," Hackett added. Siegler told them she thought it had been a solid case and the officers had to agree. "To me, it was an open-and-shut case," Hutchinson said. Even so, Siegler didn't want to go over his testimony beforehand as most district attorneys did. "I'll lead, you follow," she told him. "Just answer the questions I ask you."

Hutchinson got his first good look at O'Keiff at the second trial; she had been surrounded by paramedics at the scene and he only got glimpses of her injuries. "In a way, it was shocking to see her and it was amazing," he said. "I was a little shocked when I saw her. . . . This was obviously a pretty girl and she'll never come back from this. . . . If you take a woman's looks from them, you're taking a lot." He had been surprised that she had lived. She did not look good, but she was better off than he would have ever expected. She tried to be upbeat and friendly and thanked him for taking care of Dani at the scene. Because of the rule prohibiting it, they didn't talk about anything connected to the case.

The defense once again portrayed O'Keiff as someone so knocked down by a past plagued with never-ending problems that she had tried to kill herself, its witnesses again testifying that she had a borderline personality disorder. This time, Siegler called Dr. Sermas to refute those allegations. What she suffered from, her psychiatrist testified, was post-traumatic stress disorder as a result of being shot and her unrelenting terror of her ex-husband. He explained her suicidal thoughts of the previous December to the jury, why she was feeling that way and how; when she felt unable to control them, she had admitted it to him in order to get help and overcome them. "It was the right side of the brain that absorbed the trauma of the bullet and that's where her brain damage resides. And it's fairly well established that people who sustain an injury to the right side of the brain have a greater propensity to become morbidly depressed than people who sustain an injury to the left side of the brain," Sermas explained.

Siegler ended her questioning of the psychiatrist by asking: "Dr. Sermas, if you had to pick one word to describe Carol Christ, what word would that be?"

"Survivor," he said.

Thus far, John Christ had survived, too; he remained a free man. To continue doing so, he was going to have to withstand another combative cross-examination by Siegler. Bailey's philosophy, which he explained to his client over and over, was not to coddle him, not in private meetings and not when the defendant took the stand. Believing that he would appear as "a whining at every opportunity" lawyer if he objected to every line of questioning, it would appear to the jury as if the defendant was hiding or ashamed of something. Throughout the previous sixteen months, John Christ had thrown up some lightning rods with his comments and behavior; now he was going to have to deflect a few bolts. There was no way to avoid having to answer for his often outrageous conduct. Better to let him tough it out as much as possible, his attorney believed. Specifically, Bailey believed that Christ, a highly educated professional, needed to explain away his original statement that "we shot each other." He warned the doctor that the prosecutor would try to bait him. Bailey predicted that Siegler might go so far as to try to provoke him into hitting her to illustrate his violent temper and assumed hatred of women, and the defendant should avoid being roped in by that. Handed a copy of his previous sworn testimony during trial preparations, Christ was told to know it in minute detail, as every answer he gave now could be checked against it and any discrepancies used to discredit him.

Bailey had done his best to prepare Christ for his testimony. But the veteran defense attorney was nervous as he called his client to the stand, knowing the jury expected to hear from the defendant but aware that the surgeon was overconfident, perhaps even cocky. The defense attorney knew that, ideally, the jury should like Christ, but he'd settle for them believing him. The problem was, however, that no one seemed to like Christ as much as he liked himself. Christ assured his attorney he knew what was at stake and that he had understood his legal team's detailed instructions, advice and explanations. As soon as Christ took the stand, it seemed he was ready to disregard all of it, much to his own attorney's frustration.

After stating his name simply as "John Ernest Christ," uncharacteristically not adding the cherished initials that he had earned, Bailey noted: "And we've been referring to you throughout the course of this trial as doctor. Tell us about your educational background, if you would, please. Just give us a brief summary."

"I have devoted my entire life to helping people," the defendant said arrogantly.

"Objection!" Siegler said after just the second question. "Nonresponsive."

"Sustained," Kegans ruled.

Bailey advised his client calmly but firmly: "Can you listen to the question that I ask you and just tell us briefly your educational background?"

This time, Christ did as asked, "I have two doctorates." He said he had just three children, leaving out Phillip. He said he married Carol in October 1990 after knowing her for about ten months. She had told him that she had been married twice, he testified. "I guess I'm a pretty gullible person, because I believed those were the only two marriages. There was no reason to expect otherwise."

Asked about their relationship before they married, Christ answered: "Well, the relationship was like every initial relationship, as far as I can think. I mean, there were the adjectives—wonderful, idealistic. We just seem to be made for each other. There seemed to be no limits. We were starry-eyed and in love."

Things changed about a month or so into the marriage, he said. "The marriage seemed to change everything. Close proximity brought us closer together and we just got to know each other better and you know, I guess, you know, my mother used to say you don't know anybody until you sleep with them and that doesn't necessarily mean sex. It means you learn more about their behaviors and their patterns and God knows we are not perfect. I'm not perfect and she's not perfect and we started interacting and having some problems, I guess." Her moods changed periodically, he said. "She was erratic. She became distant and a little more argumentative. And I learned very quickly when she became this way that me and the children would just have to back off and let her cool down and wait until she became herself."

He said that he considered Dani and Joe his children since they were there all the time. Carol, he testified, "didn't like my children and she resented when they came over. She would go immediately to the refrigerator and pour herself a glass of wine and go to the bedroom and virtually slam the door in front of all of us and stay in there painting her nails. And she only came out to maybe cook dinner and, you know, clean up the dishes after we were finished and then she would disappear again. I was the caretaker. I was Mr. Mom. I did everything." He didn't say specifically what he did but had just admitted his wife had cooked and cleaned up after everyone.

Carol had been home with his children only three or four times during their entire marriage, he said. She was in charge of the schedules where she worked, he added. She never expressed her feelings, but, he said, "it was quite obvious that she was depressed in her—the way she looked." Asked about her mood swings, he said she became withdrawn and noncommunicative, the same way she had described him to the jury. But Christ went further. "There were times when she became violent," he testified. "I mean, she was throwing dishes around and smashing them. It was frightening. She would—she would swear like a sailor. She used more F words than I've ever heard in my life. I didn't think women would use those words." He apparently was trying to appear prudish before the jury. "She said she was interested in family and I told her this sort of thing is not something that is good around the children."

After his wife stopped seeing a psychiatrist, she and he decided that he would continue to prescribe Prozac for her because she was feeling better while taking it, he said. "Now, it's common medical practice to include an antianxiety agent along with an antidepressant," he said, and since she was under a lot of stress at work,

Christ prescribed Xanax for her as well. For her headaches, he prescribed Fioricet, which he described as "Tylenol with a very minuscule bit of Phenobarbital." His wife went to his office and helped herself to his free samples of Vicodin, a narcotic pain reliever, he testified. In early 1992, she also took Axid for her acidic stomach, he said, but didn't say that another doctor had prescribed that.

With that, Bailey introduced eight bottles or vials of the prescriptions in Carol Christ's name. Defendant's Exhibit 45 was a printout from the Scurlock Tower Pharmacy in John Christ's office building, listing the seventeen prescriptions Carol had filled there from January through June 1, 1992, of which twelve were written by the defendant. None of those listed were filled after the May 9 shooting.

Bailey also put into evidence photos of the top of John Christ's china cabinet, where he claimed the gun had been hidden in the Timberside house. Defendant's Exhibits 46 and 27 were the receipts for the dress he had gotten out of layaway and the flowers he had ordered for his wife from her children, both Mother's Day gifts.

Christ said his wife wanted a gun. "She was always familiar with guns and she wanted one from almost the first time I met her. . . . She said she had had a previous gun. She never said how she disposed of it," he testified, implying she had done something untoward with it, "but she said she wanted another gun for protection. . . . She wanted a nine-millimeter Browning, whatever that is." He said he bought the gun in the spring of 1991 from his secretary for $500 cash, because she needed the money, and he wanted to please his wife. When he showed it to Carol, "she was absolutely thrilled beyond belief," he said. He said they kept it locked in his office file cabinet and that he and Carol had the only key. He twice spoke of the key in the singular but didn't explain how they both could have had one key. After they moved to the Timberside house in September 1991, he took the gun home. "The only instruction I ever got was how to load and unload the gun from Carol herself. . . . She showed me how to put the clip in and how to cock it and how to unload the gun."

Bailey asked Christ again about his wife's problems. He testified that she had been depressed and was having problems at work and with her children. "She was having a lot of problems at work. She couldn't handle it. She would come home and have crying spells. She was thinking of quitting her job. She hated her job."

He said the only time he heard Carol talk about suicide in terms of herself was when Kolberg, their marriage counselor, asked if she had discussed it with her other therapist and she said she had.

Bailey asked him about the state of his marriage during the two weeks prior to May 9, 1992. The witness characteristically answered with more information than he was asked. "Well, we didn't have much physical contact for the two months prior, and I was acting like Mr. Mom, and I was trying to keep the family together. I had arranged for a family outing. First time, got all the kids together, and I said, 'This is going to be great. We will take the five kids together. We will go to the Mayan Dude Ranch for a family outing and we will be all together,' " he said. That was the weekend prior to the shooting, but he neglected to say that it was an Indian Princesses outing and that he had insisted on driving separately, alone with his kids, for the long drive. He said that the kids had had a great time, but that his wife "was sort of standoffish and moody."

The ranch was, he said, "really a neat place for kids and big kids like myself."

He testified that his wife accused him of loving his

daughter more than her. "I told her, 'Hey, that's stupid. You are my wife, you know.' " Asked about the Indian Princesses, Christ said: "When there was an Indian Princesses event, I could expect to be abused a little bit, either verbally or just not having any physical contact with her. I mean, she was moody." He said that his wife asked him to get Dani involved in the Indian Princesses and he wanted to do that. "I also wanted to baptize Dani. I wanted to be her godfather, but she wouldn't let me," he said, referring to his wife.

He said he had told his wife that on May 9 he would be going to the Indian Princesses outing ahead of time and kept a flyer on his nightstand for nearly a week to remind himself.

"On May 9, 1992, did you shoot your wife?" Bailey asked.

"I love my wife, Mr. Bailey. I didn't shoot her, no."

That morning, he said, he got up about 7:00 A.M., went to the bathroom and, again saying he was "Mr. Mom," claimed to have fixed cereal for his stepdaughter and turned on the television for her, both of which the child claimed to have done for herself. Christ said he fixed coffee and took one for his wife and one for himself back to the bedroom. His wife had been lying in bed, not saying anything, he said. "After I finished packing, I turned and I was going to leave and said, 'I'm leaving for Indian Princesses,' something like that. And suddenly she jumped out of bed—she dashed across the bed. She leaned in front of me, and she had this crazed and angry look on her face. . . . I was stunned." She then pounded his shoulders with her fists, he said. "She says, 'I'm—John, I'm not going to take that anymore. I'm just not going to take it anymore. I want a divorce.' "

Bailey tried to walk his client through the crucial events in a way he believed was most beneficial to his client's case, but the doctor seemed to have other ideas, veering off course with answers not directly responsive to his own attorney's strategic questioning.

Just ten minutes after Christ had taken the stand, Bailey thought his client was on the verge of doing irreparable harm to himself, blindly ignoring the repeated warnings his attorneys had drummed home during practice sessions. Fearing a disastrous result, Bailey approached the bench and calmly asked the judge for a short recess. They had just reconvened before the defendant took the stand, she reminded him. He knew that, he told her, and asked again. About to say no, Kegans caught the unspoken plea in his eyes and gave him the break he needed. It was a huge concession from the time-conscious judge and the attorney was grateful. He pointed Christ toward the men's rest room, their makeshift conference room, where the lawyer condemned his egotistical client's performance and tried to get him back on the track they had so carefully laid out.

Back on the stand, Christ seemed to take the advice, but not for long.

Watching her courtroom adversary sitting across the aisle, Siegler noticed Bailey's face reddening and the veins in his neck swelling as he tried to maintain an unruffled facade while inconspicuously trying to lasso an out-of-control defendant in front of an attentive jury. Obviously, Christ was unable to rein in his ego even with friendly counsel; Siegler knew she had a good chance of inciting Christ's smoldering temper in a way she had failed to do during the first trial.

Christ had been slightly eager to testify in the first trial; his attitude today suggested that he thought that he, unlike his wife, was bulletproof.

Before that day, his wife had never said anything about wanting a divorce, John Christ claimed. After

Carol yelled and hit him, he didn't do anything, making her madder. She knocked the duffel bag out of his hand and kicked it across the room toward the door. His wife yelled "Ouch!" and he thought he saw a flash go off from inside the bag, he testified. He calmly told her, "Carol, don't do that," he said. He picked up the bag and went into the den, where Dani was watching cartoons; then he heard a shot, he said. "I immediately ran back into the room."

He testified that he saw Carol lying on her side of the bed, facing the dresser. She moved and he saw blood on the pillow and the gun within her reach. He picked up a blue towel at the foot of the bed. "You know, as a doctor, my first intent, hey, you have got to help out and then—" he said before his attorney cut him off.

"We will get to that," Bailey assured him. "Then tell us what you did next." Christ said he took the gun from the middle of the bed; "And I know nothing about guns other than what Carol has shown me," he said. Pushing a button, he dropped the clip to the floor. He said he knew—because his wife had told him—that there should have been another bullet in the gun, so he wanted to get it out. As he tried to do so, he said, "the gun exploded in my hand."

"So the gun goes off and what happens?"

"I feel the most amazing sensation of my life. The bullet went through my finger and I hardly felt it."

Things were chaotic, but he recalled that his wife started moving and said, "John, John, what happened? What happened?" He ran to the kitchen, called 911, threw the clip in the trash compactor and took off his wedding ring because his hand was starting to swell. Saying he was hysterical when he called 911 and spoke to a dispatcher, he again claimed that: "We've shot each other" was a grammatical error. Asked about his mental state at the time, he said, "I was trying to do everything

I possibly could to keep my head clear and to do the things that were right."

"After you called 911, what did you do?"

"Well, best place for an injured person is in bed, and I turned and I was amazed. Here was this woman that had shot herself in the head and she was walking upright without assistance to the kitchen." He said Dani was hysterical when she saw her mother and asked him if she would be all right. He told her she would be. Carol grabbed the receiver, but he said he didn't know who dialed 911. He said he held Dani while Carol talked to 911.

After she finished talking to 911, he said he took the phone from her hand and hung it up. He unlocked the door and then called Gay. He was supposed to pick his daughter up at 9:00 A.M., about ten to fifteen minutes from his house. Stuttering slightly, he said he phoned his brother in Andover. "I mean, the president of the United States, the FBI, they have code words. I know it's not so silly to have a family code word and," Christ said, excitedly launching into a defense of his family practice before he was even asked.

"Is that what you are talking about, this word, 'swordfish'?" Bailey asked.

"Right. I said, 'Swordfish.' This is an immediate—it's like national security. The Russians are bombing us and I really want the family to get together and help. We have a critical thing going on." He said he made the calls from the kitchen phone since both his brother and Gay were on the speed dial.

"OK, what did you do next as both a husband and doctor, if anything, to assess the situation and help?" Bailey asked.

"Well, first thing is *primum non nocere*," the doctor answered, not offering to explain this any further.

"I'm sorry?" Bailey asked.

"*Primum non nocere.* It means first do no harm—first rule of being a physician. I looked at her, I saw the blood on her face, looked like the bullet had come pretty close to her eye, and I don't have an operating room. I don't have bandages. You don't put a Snoopy bandage on this thing and there was nothing that I could do."

Asked what the first thing a doctor should consider after not doing the patient harm, Christ said it was to make sure she was breathing, which his wife obviously was. "She was sitting upright, and she was speaking. She was breathing."

"Well, was she having trouble breathing?"

No, the doctor said. He said he wanted to avoid injuring her eye and possibly blinding her by putting pressure on it. "Hell, she had a life-threatening injury; I didn't have to compound it by destroying her eye," he said. After acknowledging that his own injury was not as serious, Christ was asked if he spoke to his wife while trying to evaluate the situation.

He didn't answer directly, saying he was standing next to Carol trying to comfort a hysterical Dani. "I was trying to maintain consciousness. I mean, I was dizzy," he said, adding new details to how he had been injured.

"Did you at any point in time attempt to dissuade the individuals that were treating your wife from treating her and tend to your pinkie finger?" Bailey asked.

"Hell, no."

He admitted that he tried to get paramedics to take his wife to Methodist instead of Ben Taub, perhaps doing himself more damage when he chose to add: "Well, although the president of the United States goes to Ben Taub if he's ever shot in this city, God forbid, and the best trauma service is at Ben Taub, I know personal physicians that could have saved Carol, prevented all the misery that she went through," he said, apparently ignoring the obvious fact that her misery was inflicted by the bullet, not the hospital care. The best neurosurgeon in the world, the one he would go to, was at Methodist and didn't work at Ben Taub, he said.

Asked if he tried to call an attorney that morning, Christ responded by again not answering his own lawyer's question: "When the police came on the scene, they got ugly real quick. I mean, I'm a man, she's a woman; I obviously shot her in the head. I didn't do anything. She shot herself."

"All right."

"And they assumed that I did it."

Asked again if he had called an attorney that morning, he said that he had no personal memory of having done so, but that Dameris, his lawyer at the time, called him a month ago, "and said, 'Hey, do you remember there was a tape recording on my phone that day?' "

He said he very clearly recalled a conversation with Sergeant Swaim that morning. "I was in the squad car and Sergeant Swaim came there and I said, 'Well, how is my wife?' And he looks at me with a mean look, and he says, 'Isn't it a little bit late?' and slams the door in my face." He said he had not spoken to Swaim earlier, because "having been manhandled by the police, I decided to stay quiet, and I don't even remember them reading my Miranda rights." Again, these were new details to his story.

He claimed that Carol said she was ambidextrous and he saw her using both hands equally well. As the defense had in the first trial, they showed jurors video excerpts from home movies showing Carol using her right hand to light candles on a birthday cake, holding a package, gesturing, opening a door and cutting a birthday cake.

Switching to another subject, Bailey asked if he had been instructed "by one source or another not to attempt to contact her" after the shooting.

"I believe so," he said. He thought that he wasn't supposed to contact her in person or by telephone but that a letter would be OK. He loved his wife on May 9, 1992, and afterward, he said. "I felt helpless that I couldn't assist," he said of her hospitalization.

He had sent her the rose when she had been registered in the hospital as Juanita Toller and signed his name Juan, because, he said, "she had a sense of humor. I thought it would cheer her up and also to let her know that I still loved her."

Bailey asked if he had had conversations with Carol outside the courthouse during their divorce proceedings. Christ chose an inopportune time to try to be funny, asking his defense attorney: "You are not going to tell the judge, are you?"

His attorney was not amused, repeating: "My question, sir, is whether or not y'all had conversations?"

"Yes, we did."

In May 1993, he, Carol and their divorce attorneys were at the Timberside house and he spoke to his wife out of earshot of their lawyers, he said. That time, it had been Carol who initiated the conversation, asking him: "John, did you shoot me?" according to the defendant. He said he told her, "No, Carol, I didn't shoot you."

With that, Bailey nervously passed the witness to Siegler; the defense attorney was certain the DA would try to antagonize his client and make him look even worse in front of the jury. Bailey had tried to rein in his client; as usual, the doctor had done exactly what he wanted, oblivious to how he came across.

Siegler looked forward to cross-examining Christ again. She hadn't provoked him the way she had hoped during his first trial, but she and everyone else who watched him testify both times could see that the doctor was, if possible, even more arrogant and nonresponsive this time, seemingly edgier and possibly closer to an outburst. Carol O'Keiff hoped that the prosecutor could bring out the worst in her ex-husband, but she worried about the prosecutor's safety, fearing Christ actually might slug her if pushed too far. She warned the prosecutor to back off physically if she saw the defendant's nostrils flare. That was the telltale sign she had noticed each time right before he blew up with her. The hard-hitting prosecutor would look for that sign—and push him further if she saw it, not back off in any way. But before she got her chance to try, the judge decided to recess for lunch instead. That gave Bailey and the defense team yet another opportunity to calm down their client and remind him of the warnings he seemed intent on ignoring.

Despite the seemingly endless hours of preparation and the dress rehearsal seven months earlier, Siegler's cross-examination of Christ would go worse for the defense than Bailey expected. Had he known how poorly his client was going to do, he would have kept him out of the witness chair.

After lunch, the testimony got more heated. Christ already had borne cross-examination by the tough prosecutor before a different jury and so had some idea of what to expect now. From the onset, Siegler's disdain for the defendant was clear.

He was a difficult witness, often not answering her questions directly, forcing her to repeat them, only highlighting to the jury how annoying he could be. From the moment he was back on the stand, she noticed his nostrils flaring, just as she wanted.

She launched her attack on his defense by hoping to provoke him into a fit, asking him to step down from the witness stand to demonstrate how his wife had hit him on the shoulders that morning.

"Show me how she hit you," Siegler said.

"She took her fists like so and hit me on the shoulders like so," he said, demonstrating gently with the prosecutor.

"While she was hitting you on the shoulders, sir, what was she saying to you?"

"She said, 'I can't take it anymore. I want a divorce.' "

"Did she use any cuss words?"

"No."

"No cuss words at that time?"

"No."

"You be yourself and I'm going to be Carol and let me see if this is an accurate demonstration of what happened that day," she told him; his eyes glared at her. "You say to Carol, 'I'm leaving now. I'll see you later.' She gets up out of the bed and she said, 'I can't take this anymore.' Is that correct?" Siegler said while hitting him hard enough to force him to step back.

"She didn't hit me with her fists in my shoulder," the defendant said.

Continuing to hit him, Siegler said, "She's screaming at you and hitting you, 'I can't take this anymore. I want a divorce.' Is that right?"

"Yes."

After she knocked the bag from his hand and kicked it across the floor, he said, he calmly told her, "Carol, don't do that."

With the antagonistic face-off finished, Christ returned to the witness chair, and Siegler sat down at the prosecution's table many feet in front of him. Surprising as it was to observers, Bailey was pleased with this showdown, especially with the fact that Christ failed to overreact in any way. Siegler was disappointed. She had gotten to him, drawn out his animosity, arrogance and temper more than she had in the first trial, but not liked she had hoped. She believed much more was seething just below the surface and she had hoped he would erupt like an angry volcano kept dormant too long.

The defendant confirmed that he had told several people immediately after the shooting that he and Carol had shot each other and that he was locked into that explanation.

"Once you told it, you had to stick to that story, isn't that correct?" Siegler asked.

"That's not a story. That's what happened."

"That's what happened. But you never told your ex-wife, Gay, that Carol tried to kill herself. Did you, sir?"

"Everything was in chaos."

She repeated her question, adding: "Yes or no?"

"I indicated what I said."

"Yes or no?"

"Grammatically, no, I did not say that."

"Grammatically. You like that explanation for your way of talking, don't you, sir?" the prosecutor said, emphasizing his weak response.

"Your Honor, that's argumentative and sidebar and I object," Bailey said.

"Sustained," the judge ruled.

"I ask the jury be instructed to disregard," Bailey pressed.

"The jury will disregard the prosecutor's last statement," Kegans instructed.

Siegler had an even better way to make her point. What does it mean, she asked the defendant, if a man and woman say, "We love each other"?

"That means a certain relationship between two people."

"Does it mean that I love him and he loves me? Yes or no? Normal, common sense, ordinary understanding of the English language. We love each other. Does that mean I love him and he loves me? Yes or no?" Siegler insisted.

"Yes."

"It does not mean—does it, sir?—I love myself and he loves himself, does it, sir?"

"Right." He had no choice but to agree.

Referring to records of his 911 call, in which the operator had told another dispatcher: "A man said he shot someone," Siegler asked: "Because that's what you meant when you called 911 that day, wasn't it, Mr. Christ?" She referred to him as mister instead of doctor, knowing it would bother him and hoping he would let his anger over the slight show. She might have to insult him subtly a few times, all the while appearing to jurors to show him respect by using a title, but she wasn't going to give up.

This time, he didn't bite, only answered her question. "No, it was not," he said.

She asked "Mr. Christ" if it was complicated to say, "My wife tried to kill herself."

"Under those circumstances, yes," he said, after she twice asked. First he told her only that he had been hysterical, in shock and caring for a small child. "What came out of my mouth, I barely recollect."

Asked if he had been testifying earlier that the doctors who treated his wife had done any less than a miraculous job, he said he had no opinion.

"You have the nerve and the audacity to sit up there and say those doctors that testified to this jury this week did not do a wonderful job compared to what you did on May ninth when your wife lay there dying?" the prosecutor asked, clearly disgusted.

"Objection. Argumentative," Bailey said.

"Sustained," the judge ruled again

Siegler undoubtedly knew these objections would be sustained, but, nevertheless, she was making her points to the jury as she wanted as well as trying to draw the surgeon's ire and display that to the panel.

Asked again about why, as a doctor, he didn't treat his wife that morning, Siegler argued: "As a matter of fact, what you really did—isn't it correct, sir?—was that you stood there in the kitchen, probably tapping your foot, thinking, 'God, can't she die already? What's taking her so long?' Isn't that what you were really thinking and doing that day?"

"I was—I called for an ambulance to get help. I did not have an operating room in my house. I did not have bandages. I unlocked the door. I was taking care of a hysterical child. I was watching over her like a guardian angel. I was there," the defendant said, throwing out another needlessly arrogant comment for the prosecutor to pounce on.

"Watching over who like a guardian angel?"

"My wife. She was sitting upright, Indian style, right next to me."

"Since you were acting like a guardian angel, did you ever go to her and get down on that cold floor and take her hand and rub her hand? 'Baby, honey, everything is going to be OK. Hang in there. Help is on the way.' Did you ever do that?"

"I was talking to Dani. I was reassuring her mommy was going to be all right. Things were chaotic."

"I'm talking about your dying wife," the prosecutor reminded him before repeating her question, adding that Carol had been lying there, hoping to survive.

"I was holding Dani. I did not touch Carol."

Asked if he had put the clip in the trash compactor to hide it, he responded: "I was—I put it in the trash compactor to hide it from Carol so that she could not reload the gun and shoot either herself, Dani or I."

"Wouldn't it have made more sense if you found that gun in your wife's reach to take the gun and throw it to the side and run to the phone and call 911? Wouldn't that make more sense?"

"That would have left the gun in the room. The gun had to be disarmed."

"And your wife with a gunshot wound through her head was going to crawl around the room to find the gun and shoot herself again? Is that what you thought?"

"I don't know what I was thinking. I was concerned about her safety. I went for help. I called 911. I called for the ambulance. She was critically ill."

Noting that before he called for help, he first disposed of the clip and removed his wedding ring, Siegler asked: "And you took your ring off your finger because you had already had an opportunity while your wife lay there in the bed bleeding to death to look at your hand and decide, 'Oh, oh, the little finger is hit, that means the next finger might swell up, and I don't want them to do anything with the second finger, so I'm going to take the ring off to set it on the counter to avoid further possible injuries to myself'; isn't that right?"

"No," he said, then was forced to admit that he was concerned about the swelling to the finger next to his injured one.

Acknowledging that he had testified that the only time he had heard his wife talk about suicide was during a conversation in their marriage counselor's office, he admitted that he had reviewed Kolberg's sixteen pages of records and found no mention of suicide.

She asked him about "some Latin phrase" he had testified about earlier, again subtly reminding the jury of his haughtiness. He repeated the phrase, its meaning of "first do no harm."

"That's the number one thing we learn in medical school," he said.

"Thank you, Mr. Christ," Siegler said. "So in following that Latin tradition that you learned in medical school, you decided and acted on the fact that when you look down at your wife as she lay there on the floor after miraculously getting herself to the telephone, she was breathing OK, wasn't gasping for breath. 'Hey, I'm not going to do anything.' Isn't that what you decided?"

"I was chief resident of plastic surgery at Ben Taub in my training," he boasted.

"I didn't ask you that," the prosecutor said, and turned to the judge to ask that he be instructed to answer her question. Before Siegler could finish her request, however, Kegans cut her off and told Christ to answer what was being asked of him.

Asked again about deciding not to treat his wife, he said, "That's all I could do. There was nothing else I could do. I did not have an operating room there. I had no equipment, and I had only one hand to use."

"Well, are you saying that every time, if any of us come upon an emergency and we don't have an operating room with us in the car or on the sidewalk or wherever we see it, we better not do anything? Is that what you are saying?"

Still, refusing to answer directly, he said: "If someone has a broken neck and you move their neck, they can be paralyzed for life." Prompted by Siegler's questions, he said his wife's injuries had been life-threatening, but that all he could do was stand by and wait for the ambulance. He now said he didn't remember if he had said comforting words to her but had to admit that he had not brought her a blanket, pillow or helped her lie down. "Things were happening so quickly. The ambulance was there. It seemed like an instant. If there was a longer period of time, yeah, sure, I would have done a lot of other things, but this was a very short period of time. . . . The EMTs, the emergency people, were there instantly, and like I said, if it were necessary, I would have gotten those other things, but it was not necessary."

"Were the two telephones on either side of your bed

in the bedroom, were they both working that day?" Siegler asked.

"I cannot testify whether they were—they were working that day. I assume they were."

"Give me a break," the prosecutor replied, drawing an objection from Bailey and a warning from the judge.

"I'm sorry, Mr. Christ," Siegler said.

"Dr. Christ," he corrected. Finally.

"I'm not going to call you doctor," Siegler announced.

"Judge, again, may I object?" Bailey asked.

"You can object, but I'm not going to instruct her one way or another," Kegans said.

"No, Judge, I object to the argumentative nature and the sidebar comments," he corrected. Kegans said she already told the prosecutor.

Siegler began her next question by addressing him as "Mr. Christ" once again; knowing he already had lost that argument, Christ didn't comment this time.

After a series of questions about the phones in the bedroom, Siegler asked: "You testified earlier today that when you got off the phone and you turned around and you saw Carol standing in the doorway of the kitchen that you were shocked that she made it to that location by herself. Do you remember saying that this morning?"

"Yes."

"And the truth is that you were shocked because you thought you had killed her. Didn't you, sir?"

"No, she had shot herself and I thought as a nurse she would have stayed lying in bed since . . . it would be more comfortable there. I thought I said, 'I'll call 911.' I thought she understood that. And it just came as a complete shock she was coming out of the room. I thought—"

"Because she would have been more comfortable had she stayed in the bed?"

"People don't sleep on the floor in hospitals; they sleep in beds."

"Did you hear your wife calling out to you for help that morning?"

"No, I did not."

"Mr. Christ, you never heard her call for help?"

"No."

"Did you ever hear her call Dani for help?"

"No."

The prosecutor sought to stress once more that while he did nothing to help his dying wife, the surgeon had the presence of mind to remember to call his ex-wife, knowing that he wouldn't make a 9:00 A.M. appointment with his daughter.

"The memory of what I was supposed to do that day was long implanted. The events that morning were short term. The events of what I was supposed to do is long term; obviously, I would think about that. I mean, that's not something that this hysteria of the moment would dissipate from my mind."

"Thank you for that answer, Mr. Christ," she said, knowing she would use it against him later in her closing argument. "My question was: you did have the presence of mind to call your ex-wife, did you not?"

"What do you mean presence of mind?"

"You remembered to call Gay, didn't you?"

"It was a thought that I had, yes."

"Did you call her?"

"Yes, I did." The defendant apparently was unaware how much he was hurting himself by choosing to square off against the prosecutor in such a confrontational way.

Asked about calling his brother in Massachusetts and the code word, Christ said: "This is a family code word, like the president of the United States or the FBI or any enforcement agency; it was a code word, a global thing. It is not specific to me or my brother or my mother or my sister or anybody. It is a family thing. It's as if, you know, the Russians are going to bomb us. You know, it's a code word."

"So if on the way home today you heard on the radio the Russians are fixin' to attack, you would pick up your car phone or go home and call your brother and say, 'Swordfish.' Is that what you are telling me?"

"Absolutely."

"Absolutely?"

"Yes. There is nothing silly about that."

"Oh, I agree with that, Dr. Christ. It's not silly. It's kind of sick, isn't it, sir?" The prosecutor now switched to calling him doctor, subtly contrasting his intelligence with his odd or illogical actions and responses.

"Then the United States is sick, too."

Siegler charged that he was calling for help because he knew he was about to be arrested for murder or attempted murder and wanted help for himself.

"My wife had just shot herself in the head. I had shot myself in the hand. I had a hysterical child. I didn't know; I didn't have any help in that house. The ambulance was not there yet. I needed help," he said, not explaining—and this time not even asked—how his brother, nearly 1,900 miles away, could provide help sooner than an ambulance rushing to the scene, which he had testified just moments earlier had arrived "instantly."

Still justifying his actions, he said: "It just takes an instant to punch speed dialing. I am forty-seven years old. That word has been in my mind for forty years."

Repeatedly, Christ didn't answer the prosecutor's questions directly when asked—many of them just requiring a simple yes or no, forcing the judge to instruct him to do so and giving Siegler yet another chance to ask her questions, laced with details that did nothing but make him look coldhearted and even guilty.

He said he didn't remember interrupting the paramedics as they worked on his dying wife, asking that they treat his little finger.

"Are you in any way trying to tell this jury that the injury to your pinkie is in any way comparable to the injury that your wife had that day?"

"In what sense?" he asked.

"Life threatening?"

"No."

Turning to the drugs he prescribed for his wife, he admitted that he had prescribed some prior to 1992, when the list the defense presented as an exhibit began.

"Correct me if I'm wrong, Dr. Christ, but as a doctor, isn't it common medical practice and maybe even ethically correct that you don't prescribe medication for your own family members?"

"I think that that is an area that is a little gray. I think that when—who is the best plastic surgeon for your loved one, if it's not yourself?" he responded. He admitted that he should have left it to his wife's psychiatrist to prescribe Xanax, which he acknowledged was a very addictive drug, but claimed he had given it to her "in good faith."

While acknowledging that "the perception of the patients and staff around her always felt she was friendly and kind and a good nurse," he insisted that his wife hated her job and had problems dealing with patients. She also had problems dealing with her kids as well as his, he claimed.

"Would you agree with me or not, sir, she might have had a few problems being married to you?" Siegler asked bluntly.

"I beg your pardon." Christ said that he recognized Carol needed help and suggested she go to therapy.

"You didn't think you needed any help, did you?"

"I considered the possibility by agreeing to go to family therapy with her."

"Mr. Christ, will you agree with me or not that part of the problem Carol had might have come from the fact that she was married to you?" Siegler asked for the third time before finally getting an answer from the witness.

"No. I disagree with that wholeheartedly." A few questions later, he added: "During the time that I was married to Carol, I didn't see any monumental problems at all."

"You don't think there is anything wrong with a husband telling his wife all the time how ugly she is, sir?"

"I never told Carol that she needed to change. I accepted her the way she was. She was a beautiful woman."

"Before?"

"She didn't need surgery. She asked for it."

"She was beautiful, in your opinion, before or after you did all those plastic surgeries?"

"Oh, before. Before. Why do you think I would marry her? I wouldn't marry an ugly woman," Christ asserted.

"You sure wouldn't. You did plastic surgery on your first wife, Ruth, didn't you?"

"No, ma'am. I operated on her brothers."

"Did you do a nose job on your wife Ruth?"

"No."

"Did you do plastic surgery on your wife Gay?"

"Yes."

"Did you do a nose job on your second wife, Gay?"

"No, Dr. Mel Spira at Methodist did her nose."

"Did you have a chin job done on your second wife, Gay?"

"Dr. Mel Spira."

"Did you get a boob job done on your second—"

"Dr. Robert Wiemer did the first and I did the revision. They became hard."

"It's a coincidence that two women you marry have all of these plastic surgeries done?"

"Both of them are in plastic surgery; both can observe what can be done by plastic surgery. It's, you know, you can see what can be done and you know what the end result can be; certainly, they wanted to be a part of—"

"The beautiful people?"

"Of course."

"And a woman that is twenty-six or twenty-seven years old has her nose done, and her chin done, her boobs done, and then another woman who's in her thirties has seven different surgeries done, and it is your testimony that you never in any way tried to get these women to have the surgery or never criticized them or anything like that?" Siegler asked.

"I was not responsible for them. . . . It was strictly on their request. I accepted them the way they were. I did not say, 'Hey, you know, you want your nose done?' No. They ask."

"You are just real good at picking out women that like to have plastic surgery and marrying them. Is that what you are saying?"

"I think that as a doctor, the people I come in contact with most often are nurses, medical people, you know, yeah. I come in contact with those type of people. My first wife was a cytotechnologist; second, nurse; third, nurse. We are medical people."

"Have you ever had plastic surgery done to yourself?"

"No."

"You don't need it, do you?"

"I don't want it."

Switching gears, the prosecutor asked, "And you want this jury to believe that a woman . . . who in an emergency room when her left hand was injured used her left hand anyway to write, would take a forty-five-caliber loaded weapon and point it to her head with the other hand, with her weak hand and try to blow her brains out; is that what you want this jury to believe, sir?"

"She shot herself with her right hand because it's a right-handed gun. Left-handed people use right-handed instruments with their right hand."

"Mr. Christ, on the day all of this happened, you never told one person that your wife tried to kill herself, did you?"

"No, I did not."

He admitted that he had previously said under oath that it had been possible that Dani had shot her mother because she was in the house, but now admitted: "There are three people in the house. There are three possibilities. Carol, Dani, or I. I was with Dani there. It was not possible for Dani or I to shoot Carol. Carol shot herself."

Turning again to the prescriptions Carol had been taking, he acknowledged that some were samples from his office that he should not have let her have. When he started to say more than he was asked once again, the judge did not wait for an objection. "Wait a minute. Wait a minute," the judge interrupted Christ. "Maybe you didn't understand what I said. Let me make myself amply clear—answer the question you are asked and then hush. Understand me?"

"Yes, ma'am," he said.

Although he had testified earlier in the day that he did not remember calling his attorney, he now said that he called him after the police arrived.

"Did you call your lawyer because you wanted to tell him that Carol tried to kill herself?" the prosecutor asked.

"No," he said simply, but later added: "No, I called

him because the police had gotten the wrong impression."

"The police didn't let you call Thano Dameris, your lawyer, while they stood there in the kitchen, did they? Did the police let you call your lawyer as you stood there in the kitchen with your wife? Yes or no?"

"I don't remember."

"You called your lawyer before the police even got there, didn't you, sir?"

"No." He seemed to contradict himself several times as she questioned him.

Prepared by the first trial, Christ now had an explanation for why he hadn't mentioned in his letters to his hospitalized wife her alleged suicide attempt. "I think the best way around it would have been to reassure her she is OK, that she is loved. I mean, to tell somebody outright don't kill yourself, that doesn't get to the root of the problem. If she felt like she was abandoned and unloved, she had to feel loved and so she would not think about these horrible things," he said.

Siegler then introduced his letters to Carol into evidence, as well as the one he had written to Margaret Edwards, and had the defendant read them to the jury. Not one mention of suicide was made in any of them.

"When you wrote those letters, sir, and during the time your wife was in the hospital at Methodist, were you aware of the fact that she was under armed guard?" the prosecutor inquired.

"I did not know the circumstances under which she was kept."

"Were you aware of the fact that you were not allowed or not to be allowed in her hospital room?"

"My attorney at the time told me that I was to have no contact."

"You knew you weren't supposed to try and contact her, is that right?"

"That was my understanding," Christ agreed.

Claiming that had she tried to commit suicide that day, she probably would have been emotionally unstable while she was hospitalized, he said, "I tried to avoid mentioning that because that would just bring back like a flash what she had just done to herself. I was trying to reassure her that I was still there. I still loved her, you know. I cared for her."

"And the reason for that, sir—is it not?—is because you were just trying to get Carol to take you back so all of the charges against you would be dropped? Isn't that why you really wrote the letters?"

"It was my understanding at the time these letters were sent, I was not indicted." He had, however, been charged with attempted murder, which Siegler pointed out.

Christ said he hadn't seen anything in writing regarding the charge when he had written the letters to his wife and "just had a vague verbal conversation with my attorney."

"Did you think it was all a bad joke and he was making it up? There weren't really any charges out there?"

"I thought this was a nightmare," he testified.

Although Kegans sustained Bailey's objection, the jury already had heard this highly educated man claim that he was only vaguely aware that he was facing an attempted murder charge, implying he didn't know or ask the details of something so serious.

He admitted seeing at least five therapists, not all during his marriage with Carol, including one in medical school. "I went to one session and he was crazier than I and I didn't go," he said, adding: "There was nothing wrong with me."

He said once again that he thought Dani "was a baby borderline personality disorder."

After saying that Carol must have been contemplating

suicide before that morning because the gun had been moved from the china cabinet, even though she hadn't left the bedroom that morning, he said that he didn't think she knew what really happened because of the blast to her brain.

"Well, the most logical assumption—wouldn't it be, sir?—that you moved the gun because you were planning on killing your wife before that morning?" the prosecutor asked.

"Not at all."

"Would it be a better assumption for us to say that you lost it that morning and you had the gun there in your duffel bag because you were fixing to be traveling to Lake Jackson, Texas, and you figured, 'I can't take this bitch anymore' and you tried to blow her head off? Isn't that what really happened?"

"Why would I carry a gun to an Indian Princesses outing? I did not do that."

"What you are telling us, that is, want us to believe, that Carol had the presence of mind as soon as she came to and picked up the phone and called 911 and told the emergency people, 'I've been shot.' And that means in ordinary English language, somebody else had shot me. Does it not?"

"Yes. No. No. Wait. Say it again."

" 'I've been shot.' What does—what is the normal understanding in our language of what that means?"

"It could be either way."

"What does common sense tell you that it means, sir?"

"I've been shot by a gun. That doesn't indicate a person."

"Do you remember if you ever cried for your wife's possibly losing her life?"

"I don't remember."

"You don't remember crying for your wife?"

"I don't remember having any pain." Apparently, he was trying to avoid directly answering the prosecutor's question as he had done all day, but this time, his response made him appear even more coldhearted than what she had asked.

Siegler repeatedly asked the doctor questions about his failure to treat his wife after the shooting, which he continually tried to justify. Whenever she asked about the calls he had made that morning, she said that his first call had been to Gay. Sometimes he corrected her, and at other times, he didn't.

After Siegler listed more than a dozen officials Christ spoke with after the shooting, he admitted he hadn't told them—or anyone else—that his wife had tried to kill herself and had asked only one, Sergeant Swaim, about her condition. Swaim testified that the doctor never had asked about his wife. On the witness stand, Christ seemed eager to discuss his own condition before the judge cut him off, as he had not been asked.

Bailey gave him that chance on redirect. While still at the house, he had felt no pain from his injury, but, he said, "I was barely standing up. I felt dizzy." His condition worsened once he got to the hospital, he claimed. With that, Christ's annoyingly arrogant testimony was finished. Never would he seem to understand, even after years of reflection in which he apparently had reread his testimony, how much damage he had just done to himself. At the next break, he was overheard boasting about what a great job he had done on the stand. Moments later, a frustrated Bailey was overheard saying: "He blew it. He blew it."

John Christ's testimony was the defining factor in his case. And he killed his case.

Without first taking a vote, the jurors reviewed the evidence and some of the testimony, looking for a reasonable doubt. They discussed the case and when the foreman called for a vote the first time, it was unanimous: Guilty. He filled out the required forms, handed them to the bailiff, and the jurors filed back into the courtroom to hear their verdict pronounced.

O'Keiff felt positive when jurors reentered the courtroom and several made eye contact with her. Her mother's hand protectively on her leg, she felt confident. "Thank God," she whispered after the verdict was announced. Joe cheered loudly and began clapping. Kegans shot him a stern look and he quieted his outward enthusiasm. Effie Christ, John's mother, fainted in her seat. Court was recessed for lunch. When Christ turned to leave, Kegans thundered her reproach at him. He wasn't going anywhere, she told him. He was a convicted felon. She told deputies to take him away. He was handcuffed and put in a holding cell to await the sentencing hearing.

At that time, the legal waters in Texas changed with the judicial and political tides regarding what volatile evidence from a felon's past could or could not be presented, even in the penalty phase. It wasn't just the trial judge that attorneys worried about, they had to consider what would hold up on appeal. Today, nearly everything from a convict's past can be considered in the punishment phase. In 1993, however, what might float in one case, might sink another. That left cautious counselors wary of diving into the depth of such issues, choosing instead to skim across the top.

After the lunch break, Siegler called the West University Police who had arrested Christ after his attack on Gay. They said that they believed him to be a violent man, without being allowed to say why.

For fear of opening the door and allowing Christ's long history of alleged abusive behavior into the record, his three character witnesses, including his mother, weren't asked much other than their avowed beliefs that the now convicted felon would abide by the terms of probation if that were his sentence. After Christ promised to do so, jurors once again headed to deliberations.

Again, on the first vote, the jury came to a unanimous consensus—the maximum penalty allowed. They lamented that that was all they could give him. They thought he deserved a harsher sentence than twenty years.

The biggest thing that convinced juror Dr. Darren Williams, thirty-six, a veterinarian, of the defendant's guilt was the defendant himself. "He got up on the stand and that made up my mind. He sunk himself. He was very arrogant," he recalled later. "He never had a good explanation for what happened." Had Christ not testified, the jury might have reached a different conclusion since the victim had had her back to the defendant that morning and couldn't say with certainty that he had shot her, Williams said. Christ's attempt to explain why he hadn't treated his wife—because he hadn't had an operating room in his kitchen—didn't help his case, either, the juror said, adding that a surgeon should know enough basic first aid to help his wife. The fact that he was more worried about his own finger than her head injury made him look even worse. Williams saw the doctor's explanations for many things as "unreasonable" and "his lame attempts to justify not doing anything for her."

He also had been swayed when, in the jury room, Dani's testimony was reviewed. She had clearly remembered hearing a noise and then seeing her stepfather coming out of the bedroom. Her brief testimony had come first and it was only later, as jurors reviewed it, that its significance became fully apparent. Seen as "an objective third party," her testimony had verified the sequence of events for jurors, supporting the prosecution's time line.

Of the defense's attempt to paint the victim with a borderline personality disorder, he said, "Whatever that is, which to me sounds like a bullshit diagnosis" was raised to distract attention from the crime. What she had done in her teens was too long ago to be relevant, especially since she had gone to nursing school and, at the time of the shooting, was holding down a responsible job, Williams thought. "Her psychiatric history had no bearing on the case," Williams said, as no one, other than the defendant, testified that she had been suicidal. Besides, the evidence did not support that theory, especially the trajectory of the bullet, which had been shot from behind. What about the video of Carol cutting a birthday cake with her right hand and the defense photos introduced to prove their contention that she was ambidextrous? "It was a nice touch, but it didn't impress us," Williams said. "We kind of laughed about that in deliberations."

He didn't see the evidence as overwhelming of Christ's guilt, but certainly beyond any reasonable doubt. "There were not too many alternative scenarios," he said. "There was nobody else that it could have been." While some people connected to the case believed that had Carol died before ever being able to tell her story, Christ would have surely gotten away with murder, Williams didn't think so. The evidence spoke loud enough, he said, and could have been backed up by Dani's testimony.

The fact that Christ changed his story a couple of days after the shooting, the juror said, "added to his general untrustworthiness."

Christ's behavior after the shooting, his obvious lack of concern for his injured wife, his lack of remorse, were among the reasons he drew the maximum sentence, the juror said, adding: "By the time it was done, everyone pretty much agreed he was a scumbag. We would have given him more time if we could have."

Williams and the other jurors hugged Carol after the trial was concluded. They empathized with her for all she had been through, much of it described in graphic detail by her surgeons and the detectives. It was only then that jurors learned that a previous jury had been unable to reach a verdict, presumably because some had been swayed by Carol's psychiatric history when the defense hammered away at it. That explained why the prosecution brought out her problematic past in this trial, which these jurors didn't think mattered to the case, Williams said. "She came across as very credible. I wish she could have come out and said, 'My husband shot me.' She couldn't; her testimony was very truthful," he said. Christ, however, seemed to be a self-absorbed man who sought to re-create the women he married. "Everybody thought he was a bastard and gave him the maximum twenty years." Had he been remorseful, his sentence might have been less, Williams speculated. "He's proof the justice system does work sometimes." Most at Methodist Hospital felt the same way.

Kelly Siegler sent Carol O'Keiff a cheery bouquet of spring flowers to celebrate the long-awaited conviction of her ex-husband and her newfound freedom. In a not so subtle mocking of Harris County's newest prisoner, the prosecutor signed the card: "Tuna Fish."

Twenty-four

As the civil trial approached, there was some confusion as to whether John Christ was representing himself in the case or had an attorney. Months earlier, the judge had granted Bruce Zivley's request to withdraw from the case.

At a pretrial hearing on February 25, Judge Russell L. Lloyd told Harry Herzog to make every effort to insure that Christ could attend the trial if he wanted, giving authorities enough notice to make arrangements to transfer him back to Houston. Three days later, Herzog sent a letter to the Bastrop County sheriff, where Christ now was being imprisoned. He also sent a letter to Christ, informing him the trial had been set for a two-week period, March 28 through April 8, 1994. Herzog estimated that the case could be tried in just one hour, without a jury. He told the court that O'Keiff and Christ had discussed settling the $36,000 judgment against the doctor in the divorce case but had not been able to reach an agreement. "There have been no attempts to settle this case," he noted.

Once again, Carol Christ needed more reconstruction of her face; this time, it was not as severe as previous operations, limited to the left cheekbone and removal of some of the hardware put in six months earlier. A week and a half later, Dr. Stal augmented his surgical work with injections of hydroxyapatite.

Christ had only minor swelling when the personal injury case was called to trial April 6, 1994, in the 334th District Court of Harris County. By his choice, John Christ was not present, having sent a hand-printed letter to Herzog, dated March 4, 1994, saying he would not return to Houston for the trial. He claimed that Thanos Dameris had agreed to represent him on an interim basis, though his former attorney later denied that. "I have requested a motion for a continuance although it baffles me why this needs to be pursued at all," Christ wrote. The Timberside house had been foreclosed on December 7 and his loans amounting to more than $90,000 were overdue, he noted. "The only asset I had has been taken away from me. That asset was my ability to practice medicine. Any and all judgements [sic] against me will yield nothing. I no longer have anything. You are wasting your time." Still proclaiming his innocence, he wrote: "The system has destroyed my life, my practice, my family and my children's future. I hope you are all happy now." He signed his name, uncharacteristically omitting the most cherished initials after his signature—M.D. and Ph.D. As a postscript, he wrote: "Nobody can take away my real and only wealth, i.e., the things I know, the things I can do with my hands, and the truth!"

Christ also sent a letter to the court's trial coordinator, saying he did not want to attend the trial, citing the case number. "I am currently appealing my case and it is inappropriate for any other actions at this time," he wrote, referring to his criminal conviction. He was trying to seek a continuance, but made no mention of Dameris in his letter to the court. He ended this letter with the insistence: "I am innocent of all this nonsense and will be free again soon." This time, he remembered to add M.D. and Ph.D. after his signature.

Fight or no fight, Carol O'Keiff needed to have her case heard, Herzog believed. It would be cathartic and help rebuild his client's self-esteem. As he had gotten to know O'Keiff over the last twenty-three months, he saw her as an incredibly strong, determined woman but, at the same time, someone desperately searching for validation and self-esteem. She had tried to find it in the wrong men, especially Christ, and now her attorney hoped that Lloyd would use this case to try to reclaim that for her.

Lloyd agreed. The judge believed that it was part of his job to let people tell their stories, especially in particularly heinous cases like this one, hoping it would help give them closure. And with the amount of damages the victim was seeking, he certainly wanted to hear some information as well as review the stacks of paperwork Herzog presented as evidence. Along with the medical reports of the victim's numerous surgeries and injuries, Lloyd also was presented with inflammatory excerpts from John Christ's deposition in the divorce case, the defendant's letters and cards to his wife, the victim's handwritten notes scrawled shortly after the shooting, photos of O'Keiff before and after the shooting, crime scene photos and Christ's financial records. The trial lasted less than two hours.

Herzog believed the strongest evidence in the case was the 911 tapes, particularly Carol's pleas for help. "When her voice came across, it instantaneously melts your heart," he said. Very dramatically retelling his courtroom tale, the attorney, with his voice bouncing from his own even-keeled narrative to imitations of the judge's louder directives and his client's strained speech, said: "The innocence, the childlike innocence and horror of the tapes cracked the judicial veneer. It took the robe off the judge. 'Uh, I'm a hard-nose judge, and I ain't giving anybody any money for anything, and why am I listening to this, and who cares?' All those attitudes. And I'm not saying that Russell Lloyd had every single one of those attitudes but judicial hardness evaporated. You could feel it in the air; you could see it in his eyes. I was reduced to tears. My memory is that Carol was crying, hearing the tape. And the judge maintained judicial composure, but the wall was gone. Instead of 'We're gonna have a three-minute trial,' he opened his heart to hear the case. . . . Oh, he told us, 'I used to be a DA. I've heard plenty of 911 tapes. I don't need to hear your 911 tapes. I know what happens in 911 calls. Call your first witness.' See, yes, sir, my first witness is the 911 tape, and I'm ready to play it. I hit the button, despite him telling me not to.''

Although he wasn't there, Christ's own words were used against him once again, through his deposition and written answers to questions. "I did my very best to present that in a dramatic way, and it worked," Herzog said, adding: "Not Hollywood crap, real stuff." Among Christ's statements that he highlighted for the judge was Christ's description of six-year-old Dani as "a little monster," saying it was possible that she had been the one "who shot her mother in the head with a .45 semiautomatic." As he read from the deposition, Herzog showed the judge a photo of the cute child holding a teddy bear. The judge just grinned. "The more of John Christ that I put into the courtroom, the higher the damages went," Herzog said.

"It was just a malicious act by a bad person," the judge agreed. But what struck the judge most about the case was that the surgeon had not treated his wife after she had been shot. "I remember that. That really pissed me off," he said later. From what he knew, the doctor had exhibited typical sociopathic behavior patterns, including refusing to take any responsibility for his actions.

O'Keiff was awarded an incredible $170,960,000. Of that, $150 million was awarded specifically for "exemplary damages for malicious battery," known elsewhere as punitive damages. Another $10 million was assessed on the claim of breach of duty and good faith and fair dealing, because the surgeon, with more than ten years' experience, failed to give his wife medical aid after the shooting. It was the largest personal injury judgment in Texas at the time, according to Herzog.

Lloyd, who years later couldn't recall how much the judgment was for as he was not concerned about setting any new records, said that a large award was the only way to make a statement about what a truly heinous crime it had been as well as to send a message to the community. The defendant already was in prison at the time, and the judge knew Carol O'Keiff wouldn't be able to collect any money then and possibly not ever. Herzog, however, remained determined to collect something from John Christ once he got out of prison and reentered the workplace.

The remainder of the judgment was: $2 million for future pain and mental anguish, $800,000 for lost earning capacity in the future, $1 million for future disfigurement, $500,000 for future physical impairment, $2.1 million for past physical pain and mental anguish, $60,000 for past lost earnings, $4 million for past disfigurement and $500,000 for past physical impairment. Noting that O'Keiff had extensive medical treatment in the past and may need future treatment as a result of the shooting, she had not produced "evidence satisfying the minimum legal standards of proof of necessity of the medical services or reasonableness of the charges," the order said, and so was to get nothing from Christ for past or future medical care. Herzog sought that exclusion because, despite repeated attempts, he could not get the needed documentation from the various billing and insurance agencies in time and he didn't want O'Keiff to ultimately pay for their delays. Generally, if a person received damages to cover medical expenses, the insurance companies demanded to be reimbursed for what they already paid out for surgeries and hospital costs and they expected to be paid first. O'Keiff's medical costs already topped $350,000 with more in sight, Herzog said.

The attorney believed that the short trial and huge judgment were therapeutic for his client, saying: "She wouldn't be the woman she is today but for that trial."

Naturally, it was important to her attorney as well to be able to have such a significant win on his record. That afternoon, Herzog threw a victory party in the bar at the Inn at the Park, an upscale hotel. About twenty people attended, including O'Keiff and her son. She didn't stay long, feeling out of place, as if it had been more of a victory for her attorney than for her. An attorney who obviously enjoyed being involved in high-profile cases, his reception room displayed reminders of his two largest to date: a framed copy of the $171 million judgment against John Christ, complete with an unflattering photo of Carol O'Keiff taken before the shooting, alongside the framed indictment of Wanda Holloway. Dubbed the "Pom Pon Mom," Holloway grabbed international headlines after her arrest for hiring a hit man to kill the mother of her daughter's cheerleading rival so her daughter could win a coveted spot on the squad. Although primarily a civil attorney, Herzog represented her after her arrest, then handed the lead to a criminal defense lawyer.

A week later, Carol Christ unexpectedly had to go under the knife yet again. A few drops of blood fell like occasional tears from her blinded left eye. She thought that perhaps the prosthesis was aggravating the tissue around it, so she went to the ocularist who made it. The fake eye wasn't the problem; the scleral buckle that had been put in her eye shortly after the shooting to hold the retina in place was now sticking out of her real, shrunken eye, which sat under the fake one, putting her at risk of infection. The buckle was removed.

A month later, she had to undergo yet another operation to repair a problem created by a previous one. Scar tissue had adhered to the surgical implants, including the hydroxyapatite put in her cheekbone, and now was pulling her eyelid askew, distorting her appearance. Dr. Patrinely performed the delicate procedure so critical to her appearance. The ophthalmic plastic surgeon cut away the dense scar tissue and adhesions, releasing a muscle tugging at the lower lid. Using cartilage taken from a cadaver rib, he grafted it to the area. The needles used to suture kept tearing the soft cartilage replacement, so he used surrounding muscle to make a pocket to hold it in place.

O'Keiff's displeasure with her demanding job and its lack of patient contact and the administration's dissatisfaction with her performance led her to resign from Methodist Hospital. Still struggling to recover physically, emotionally and financially and with nowhere else to turn, she and her mother decided it would be best if she and her children moved in with the Edwardses in Arkansas. Everyone knew it would be difficult. O'Keiff wasn't giving up her career, however. She hoped that the atmosphere in the hospitals in the smaller, rural communities near her mother would be relaxed enough so that she could find a less stressful and demanding nursing position where she could still do the work she loved and earn enough to support her struggling family.

With the legal dramas and most major surgeries—

those that could be anticipated anyway—behind her, and her ex-husband safely locked away, O'Keiff hoped to find a way to use her adversities as an example that could help others. She lectured locally on domestic violence, telling one of her audiences: "A violent assault by someone you love and trust not only damages the victim physically and mentally, but permanently tattoos pain, fear and distrust on the person's soul. It makes us feel as though we walk a different path than others because of these feelings and places us in an isolated state of being, although physically, we are not. This state of being is a lonely place, as we want so badly to feel trust and love again, but may feel we cannot take that chance." She appeared on a few television talk shows, including *The Maury Povich Show*, which Christ watched from prison. At least two of her other ex-husbands, Tommy Olson, her first, and Les Connally, her fourth, happened to catch the show and learned of her tragic struggles for the first time. She impressed those who saw her with her outward strength, optimistic outlook and her sense of humor, finding ways to laugh at some of the bizarre things that Christ had done and that had happened throughout her ordeal, even those that had been so incredibly painful at the time.

Connally also got his first look, outside of a photograph his parents had, of his daughter, who, along with Joe and Margaret Edwards and Christ's attorney, Cullom, were on the show. Connally, now living in Florida and separated from his fifth wife with whom he had two more daughters, surprised his ex-wife and daughter with a phone call saying he wanted to come for a visit.

As O'Keiff and her children were preparing to move to Arkansas, Connally arrived in Houston and made his daughter's dream come true—she finally would meet the big, tough biker dad she had only heard stories about. He arrived after she and Joe were asleep. Dani was thrilled to meet him the next morning. The four spent several days together and Connally proudly took lots of photos of his adorable offspring and promised to stay in touch. After several days, Connally suggested they all move to Florida, but O'Keiff declined, sticking to her plan. When Connally left, O'Keiff, who had her prosthetic eye replaced, gave him her first one, telling him: "It's so I can keep an eye on you."

Epilogue

Carol O'Keiff went through nine nursing jobs in five and one-half years and several cities before finally accepting that she could no longer do the job she loved and went on disability, in a constant struggle to afford the necessities of life. The loss of her career was almost as painful to her as the physical injuries. She has had twenty surgeries since the shooting and will continue to need them throughout life. Because of tissue atrophy, muscle wasting, bone reabsorption and prosthetics wearing out, further reconstructive surgeries on her head and face are likely. Her physical and cognitive problems have worsened over time, some on account of the injuries, others because of the strong medications she must take. A gifted glass artist, her projects have helped her find peace of mind and given her an outlet for her creativity. At the Edwardses', Dani lived in the main house with her grandparents, while O'Keiff lived in the one-bedroom guest house, less than fifty feet out the back door, and Joe lived in a room behind the garage, adjacent to his mother's. The arrangement was difficult on everyone and O'Keiff and the children moved on after a year and a half. She has gotten somewhat closer to both her parents, who occasionally help out financially, especially where Dani is concerned.

She now tells any man with a chance of becoming significant in her life about all her marriages, the shooting and the gory details of her life. "I'm not as desperate to be wanted as I was," she said. Admittedly, she still likes to have a guy in her life but says she puts up with less before ending it—but she still has put up with more than she should. She has not remarried.

O'Keiff felt that through therapy she had learned a lot about herself, particularly about her relationships, and not only was determined to make better choices, but was convinced that she would. Sermas was less optimistic in that regard. Although he knew his patient had made a lot of progress, faced a lot of difficult issues about herself and her past and was committed to trying, Sermas still thought she had "a poor picker" when it came to men. Her past had shown her to be someone who attracted the same type of man "like moths to a flame," he said, and despite the painful lessons, it's exceptionally difficult to change those things. "She needs to come to the conclusion that all men are pond scum, and she needs to stay away from them. She has a very poor picker," he said. His conclusion about her is extreme, because O'Keiff's involvements with men generally begin based on physical attraction and end up with her being abused, he said. She seemed drawn to guys with the suggestion of a dangerous edge. From what he heard, he believed Christ and two other men in her past had psychopathic tendencies. Sigmund Freud talked about a "repetition compulsion," in which people tend to make the same choices, even if they know better. O'Keiff, he said, didn't deal well with boredom. "She likes things a bit exciting. Guys like this can provide a whole lot of excitement," he said, adding that when it is the man calling the shots, it could take away some of the guilt feelings. Had O'Keiff been able to put her life back together more, especially if she had been able to hold down a job in which she felt good about herself, he said she might have, after therapy, made better choices in relationships. He likened it to a recovering alcoholic falling on hard times and going back to his former ways.

People with a "poor picker" try to work through unresolved conflicts with a parent by picking someone with similar characteristics. In this case, Sermas believed that O'Keiff was trying to work out issues with her mother, not her father. Sermas believed that most people, male and female, tend to marry someone with characteristics similar to their mothers.

It was especially important for O'Keiff to feel needed, wanted and be shown affection, he said. However, he did not think her sexual behavior stemmed from those issues, but rather she was just a woman who truly enjoyed sex. Even when she talked about how awful someone had been as a boyfriend or husband, she still could discuss how good he had been in bed and seemed to compartmentalize sex as separate from emotions, like most men, the psychiatrist said. If a man was good sexually, "that was a real plus, and as far as she was concerned, John was number one on the list," Sermas said.

Fearing the day John Christ will be released from prison, O'Keiff changed her name and went into hiding.

Christ said that his ex-wife has no reason to fear him and that he intends to stay as far away from her as possible once he is released from prison. He lost all appeals of his criminal conviction, and the Texas Board of Pardons and Paroles twice denied his release. He will be eligible next in March 2002. Most recently, he has been at the Stevenson Unit in Cuero, Texas, a minimum security prison. In Texas, inmates are assigned to prisons based on their behavior while incarcerated, not on the severity of their crimes. Eventually, he was moved into a dormitory-style cell, where he had a small four-foot-high cubicle in a gymnasiumlike room of 111 inmates. From there, he was free to come and go about the prison grounds during certain hours. The plastic surgeon now worked as an unpaid clerk in the prison's factory, which made office partitions for cubicles. It's considered one of the better jobs at the unit as it's in an air-conditioned area.

His medical licenses have been revoked in three of four states; in Texas, it has only been suspended. Even behind bars, where an inmate number always must accompany or replace his name, he still practically demanded that his precious academic initials be included on all correspondence. One of his most loyal and constant friends since his incarceration, Dr. Ron Beberniss, his medical school roommate, said he never puts M.D. after his own name on anything. But for his friend, he jokingly adds an additional title: John Christ, M.D., Ph.D., A.H.

Years after the shooting, John Christ continued to defend his concerns for his injured pinkie finger and insisted that, under the circumstances, he could not have done anything to help his critically injured wife, who he still claims tried to kill herself. "I've been criticized by these people, saying, 'Well, it's just your little pinkie.' But this finger has blood vessels in it. It's connected to me. It's part of my life—a major part of my life. A piano player missing a finger probably gets more sympathy than a surgeon. A surgeon's finger is just as important if not more important, because I need these things to fit into a glove to be able to do what I do. That's my life," he said.

Christ and Mabray did not get married; she told his friends she could not wait. She helped shut down his business and helped his family pack up his house. So sure was he of an acquittal, or at least another mistrial, that he had patients scheduled for surgery the following week and had made no alternative arrangements for anything in his life.

He discussed a number of possibilities for life after prison, none of which seemed firm, other than his desire to leave Texas. While his three children live in Houston, he believed that they would choose to live with him. Calling O'Keiff the enemy, Christ said he was her victim and in prison for no reason. "Sometimes I think she's evil, but I don't wish her any bad . . . I pray that she does not prey on other men," he said.

Pegged by others who knew him as a woman hater, Christ denied that, saying he loved women. In subsequent comments, he blamed many of his problems on the fact that women were involved. He thought a book should be written on the case—he plans to write his own version—but was suspicious that a woman was writing it. Still, he asserted that a book would make him famous and that readers would remember his name but forget how or why they knew it.

Christ saw himself as a figurehead for women's rights organizations looking for a high-profile man to further their causes. "I had a woman judge; I had a woman DA; I had six women on the jury panel; there were three women judges on the appellate court and there have been women that have been blocking this from the very beginning. I have become a figurehead for some sort of protest. I am a high-profile man and they picked the wrong person to convict."

Friends and supporters conducted a fund-raising campaign to pay for his appeal, even soliciting money from his trial attorneys. His appeal, however, was based partly on the grounds that Bailey provided ineffective counsel. Bailey took that allegation seriously, realizing, though, that it was not an altogether unexpected slap from a client now serving time. That slap was followed with a fierce blow, though, when Christ accused Bailey of engaging in a conspiracy with the judge and prosecutor against his own client. The charge demanded a response from Bailey to the appeals court, eliciting observations, opinions and strategy the respected attorney employed in defending Christ that otherwise might have remained under the protective cloak of attorney-client privilege. In an affidavit responding to those allegations, Bailey said, "John Christ received a fair trial. I remain convinced that it was as much John Christ's own arrogant attitude and his testimony which contributed to his demise as it was the strength of the facts against him."

Bailey also said in the affidavit that he worried about the jury learning that Christ had previously pleaded to assaulting Gay. "Complaint was made that he had also insinuated to Gay that he intended to use poison on her as well. While we believed that Gay was 'on our side' [in view of the child support she was going to continue to collect] I knew the reported facts behind this assault. If brought to light in front of the jury in the guilt innocence stage of the trial, it could have been devastating. It was also reported that he had threatened and/or assaulted a number of other women [girlfriends and/or ex-wives]."

Bailey may never be able to forget this case even if he wanted to. To this day, whenever the judge's bailiff sees Bailey around the courthouse, he greets him with: "Hey, Swordfish!"

In the interview, John Christ also blamed one of his appeals attorneys, Mike DeGuerin, another highly respected Houston attorney, for not working as his advocate, despite taking tens of thousands of dollars for the case. The one time he came close to expressing regret, Christ said that he should not have disliked Dani so much as she had been only a child, albeit a problem one. He spoke with great animosity, however, toward Gay Christ, his second wife, and Dr. Spira and Dr. Shenaq, still unable to let go of the dispute over credit on an academic paper even as he sat behind prison walls convicted of attempted murder.

One of his friends said that part of the reason that Christ wants to get his conviction overturned is so that he can practice medicine again, something he will be unable to do with a felony on his record. The friend said that Christ believes that since he already has served so much time in prison, the state would not exert the time or expense to retry him as he likely wouldn't be punished further.

Christ shouldn't underestimate his tenacious adversary. Kelly Siegler, who once won a conviction and death sentence for a child murderer after three previous trials ended in hung juries, said she wouldn't hesitate to prosecute the doctor again if necessary. She said she hates him more than any of the murderers she has put on death row. Either way, she'll continue to regale colleagues over beer with bizarre tales of the weird *Dr. Christ*.

Dani has had a difficult life and a rough time dealing with the overwhelming emotional fallout of all that has happened in her young life. She has had some serious problems and only limited counseling. Dr. Sermas said, however, that no amount of counseling would prepare any child who had experienced such a trauma to emerge unscarred or even be able to completely cope with it in a healthy manner. She was not old enough to process all of her emotions, let alone equipped to deal with them adequately, he said. She will need therapy as an adult in order to truly move beyond this traumatic part of her life and to keep it from continuing to affect her, he said.

Joe Jackson dropped out of high school at age fifteen

and immediately took and passed the GED. He, too, had a lot of problems, saying the shooting "messed up my life a lot." His strongest memory of the years that followed was of his mother going in and out of the hospital. He spent a couple of years in the navy, now works in a factory and plans to become a firefighter. He admitted that he has repeated some of his parents' bad patterns, but he is aware of them and trying to do better.

When John Christ went to jail, Gay Christ told others she lost 60 percent of her income. She and their three children, now in public schools, did lower their standard of living, but to one most would still consider comfortable. Gay is reportedly happy and doing a good job as a single parent raising her children, who seem happy, according to those who have spent time around them.

ACKNOWLEDGMENTS

First and foremost, Carol O'Keiff. For everything.

Danielle Connally and Joe Jackson, O'Keiff's children, for bravely recounting the details of the most horrendous and confusing times of their young lives and for their invaluable insights. May they be smart enough to learn from the mistakes of others and confident enough to know they can overcome anything—but fortunate enough not to have to. May the same be true for each of John Christ's children, none of whom were in any way involved in the writing of this book, but their lives have been greatly impacted by the events that led to it. They, of course, are to blame for none of it.

Margaret Edwards, O'Keiff's mother, who generously gave her time, insights and photos, sharing the private details of her life, heartaches and thoughts, acknowledging even her shortcomings. Like her daughter, she did so courageously, honestly and with a sense of humor. Unlike her daughter, she didn't choose this project, yet she embraced it from the beginning.

Numerous people graciously shared their time, insights, recollections, observations and expertise, providing truly immeasurable assistance in piecing together this story. To each one, I am sincerely grateful. They include: Dr. Chris Sermas, Dr. W. Douglas Appling, Dr. M. Bowes Hamill, Dr. Raj K. Narayan, Dr. James R. Patrinely, Dr. Ronald Sims and Dr. Samuel Stal; Harris County Assistant District Attorney Kelly Siegler; defense attorneys Joe W. Bailey II, Bob Sussman, June Cullom, John Greenwood and Thano Dameris; attorney Harry Herzog; Judge Russell L. Lloyd; Detectives John Swaim and Glen Matthews of the Houston Police Homicide division, and Officers Charles K. Hutchinson, Jeff Hackett and Clemente Reyna; Houston paramedic Roland Hobbs, and Dr. John Christ.

In addition, thanks to those who had more personal connections to the story for their willingness to share their private stories, thoughts and feelings: Tommy Olson, Les Connally, Dan Edwards, Mason O'Keiff, Gus O'Keiff, Helayne O'Keiff, Dr. Ron Beberniss, Jerry Damé, Mildred Hall, Dr. Gerald Johnson, Dr. John Long, Dr. Jim Moore, Helen Mousoudakis van de Bruinhorst, Lynne O'Keiff Youngblood, Erin O'Keiff, Betty Steinfeld, Raven Vance and Dr. Robert Wiemer. Also, Texas Department of Criminal Justice officials, including those at the Stephenson Unit in Cuero, and the numerous Harris County clerks, particularly those in criminal courts, who put the civil back into civil servant.

Numerous people preferred not to be mentioned by name but whose insights, memories and help were graciously appreciated whether it was hours of discussions or a single comment.

Much gratitude to editor Karen Haas and editor-in-chief Paul Dinas of Kensington Books for giving a first-time author a chance as well as for their patience and advice, and to agent Janet Wilkens Manus for her persistence and belief in this project and her husband, Justin Manus, for his legal counsel and services.

Thanks to first reader A.J. Roebuck for countless hours of research, travel assistance and editing; Bernard Roebuck for research assistance, and to both my parents for supporting me in this and every dream and project in life. Appreciation to Bob Carpenter for his support and assistance at numerous times throughout this undertaking, especially under deadline pressure.

Grateful acknowledgment to attorney and friend Stephen L. Thompson for his much-appreciated legal advice and for lifting my spirits even when I'm not down.

Thanks to friends and relatives who supported and encouraged me during this time in ways large and small, often coming unexpectedly but at times when it was most needed. You all know why it was especially significant; I want you each to know I am deeply grateful.

Journalist and author Anne McDonald Maier, who long ago put me onto this story. True crime author Carlton Stowers, for his much appreciated pointers in the early stages.

Journalism instructors Tom Schwartz, Rosemary Armao and Dr. John Clarke, three extraordinarily gifted professionals who taught me so much about the craft and ethics and encouraged and inspired me.

Thank you to all those who generously provided photos, only some of which could be reprinted here.

HORRIFYING TRUE CRIME
FROM PINNACLE BOOKS